IMAGINED WORLDS

Imagined Worlds

Essays on some English Novels and Novelists in Honour of John Butt

EDITED BY

Maynard Mack and Ian Gregor

METHUEN & CO LTD · LONDON

First published 1968
by Methuen & Co Ltd
11 New Fetter Lane, London E C4
© *1968 Methuen & Co Ltd*
Printed in Great Britain by
Robert Cunningham & Sons Ltd
Alva, Scotland

Distributed in the U.S.A. by Barnes and Noble Inc.

Contents

PART THREE

Preface

With this transatlantic collection of essays we pay an affectionate personal and academic tribute to John Butt, formerly Regius Professor of Rhetoric and English Literature in the University of Edinburgh. Though it is likely he will be remembered chiefly for his work on Pope, we have taken his great interest in Dickens, as providing an opportunity for looking at the novel as a whole. As an editor of distinction and a teacher of infectious enthusiasm, he continually sought to make the great names of the past come alive. We hope these essays will have caught some of that spirit and so stimulate others to consider again a literary form which was for him a constant source of pleasure and delight.

M. M.
I. G.

In Memoriam

JOHN BUTT

M.A., B.Litt., F.B.A.

1906 - 1965

Address by Denys Hay, M.A.,
Professor of Mediaeval History

Saturday 11th December 1965

John Butt

Of one thing we may be certain this morning. Students of English literature will for a great many years ahead remember the man we are commemorating. John Butt's contribution to the scholarship of his subject is secure. It has been and will be appraised by qualified judges and I am competent to say only two things about it. He made his reputation with work on a major writer and he was an acknowledged authority on another major writer. Pope and Dickens admit success only to those of their critics who measure up to an exacting standard of sense and sensibility. Butt was of the required dimension. The second observation can be illustrated from the same material; the range of his sympathy was very great. It is the fate of historians of literature, as of historians in general, to be associated with a period, and Butt was (I suppose) an eighteenth- and early nineteenth-century man. Yet the emotional distance between Pope and Dickens is as great as can be imagined, from the majestic astringency and grand effects of an Augustan world to the warmth of lamp-lit parlours and the terror of bleak alleys; from above stairs to below stairs. His catholicity of taste was evident to those of us who were not professionally engaged in similar studies. It would be hard to imagine a quality more appropriate to the man who undertook, annually and *ex officio*, the award of the James Tait Black Memorial Prizes.

I shall not try to recapitulate the details of Butt's career. This also will be dealt with more fully on other occasions, and in the meantime we can be grateful for the fine notice which appeared in *The Times*. I shall instead try to speak briefly about the man himself.

It was in conversation that those of us who had the privilege of knowing him could readily appreciate his wit, learning and humanity. His mind was well-stocked, like his bookshelves, and he was in command of both.

He liked to talk and, unlike some gifted men, his talk was not a monologue but was provoked by the ideas and replies of his companions. Like any genuine enthusiast his current interests were reflected in what he had to say and in these last years it has been for some of us a delight to move from one chapter to another of the volume of the Oxford History of English Literature which he was writing. For me the last months were particularly stimulating for he had reached the historians. It is a personal grief that all these occasions are now at an end and that I shall not see again that eyebrow go up quizzically, herald of some mild malice about Gibbon or Boswell. Many others present will have their own particular sense of loss and emptiness on this occasion; in speaking of mine I hope you will allow it to stand for yours. And I may perhaps also be allowed to add that contact with such a man enables all of us to imagine, however imperfectly, the sorrow of Margot Butt and her children.

Yet in some ways it is wrong to regard this as an entirely sad moment for John Butt had accomplished much that we can be glad of. Quite apart from his writing and editorial work, he had been an active teacher for thirty-five years and more. Though Edinburgh had his last years of service, and this the rewards of his maturity, it is right to recall today that he will be remembered by large numbers of former students at Bedford College, London, and King's College, Newcastle, as well as by many colleagues there, in Oxford and in America. I doubt very much if John Butt knew how good a teacher he was. A school master can see in the faces of his pupils light reflected from the windows he has opened. The tutor or lecturer at a University often feels less sure that he has spoken the right word or encouraged the right train of criticism; his pupils are contra-suggestible, given to displaying disquiet at the new equality that they are encountering, resentful sometimes that they are free now to be foolish. As for the professor, his title and his age, real or supposed, add further barriers and further perplexities, for he can be (as John Butt was) something of a public figure. Here a man's colleagues are probably better judges of his effect or influence than he can possibly be himself, for they meet his students as they cannot ever meet their own. Many of us have good grounds for believing that John Butt was one of the most successful of our colleagues. The research students attracted by his expertise tell their own story: their number rose steadily over the years; he was teaching them until his death. These are, however, young men and women who are already embarked on their own voyages and I am thinking now rather of undergraduates whose notions of their destinations and sailing orders are vague. The proprietorial air of some of the young people doing honours in English with Butt could be almost provoking to those of us who are less certain that we have the respect of the new generation. On more than one occasion his compassion and understanding have, I know, transcended the rules and regulations to make a student once again feel that life could be reasonable. As for the beginners, our Scottish system let Butt loose on a large first year class. If numbers rose embarrassingly he had, in a way, only himself to blame. When a professor sings madrigals to the First Ordinary Class of English literature in the Pollock Hall he is taking his subject seriously, but he is also likely to make it seem significant to those hesitating before the claims of other disciplines.

Another matter which those of us who were not in the English department could observe was the department of English Literature itself. Chance gave Butt a set of collaborators much younger than he was. With them, it seemed to the outside world, he was tolerant and sympathetic, offering just the right degree of neutrality and caution. I guess (for I do not know) that within the department schemes came and went, hotly advocated and denied; what finally emerged from such meetings (and this I do know, for it had to survive the scrutiny of the Faculty and the Senate) was sensible and interesting and, since it had been thoroughly discussed by everyone concerned, it certainly got general support from those who had to carry it out.

Hard worked and indeed overworked they were, not least Butt himself; but they worked together, and the observer never had the feeling that Butt was driving or coercing but only that he was part of the team.

Talents like these were, happily, not restricted to English as a subject in the Faculty. He was ready to serve any group which made deserving demands on his time – the desperate cause of the theatre in Edinburgh, for instance, or the cause, almost as desperate, of the University Library; and the cause – this attended with complete success – of chamber music in Hexham when he was living in Corbridge. And, thank goodness, not just groups or causes. We took to him our own problems, whether a gap in our bibliography or an awkwardness in our dealings with other people. I think what I have said can be summarized in this way: he was a marvellous friend.

I have never known a man who conveyed more the impression of not being in a hurry. I suspect that this was in some degree due to an ingrained habit of being systematic, of pursuing purposes thoroughly. In the last months of his life, when (as I have mentioned) he was working on the chapter in his book dealing with the eighteenth-century historians, he read – carefully and appreciatively – Gibbon, Hume and the others. Often in pain, with every excuse for haste, he did his work with a dignity, an honesty and an application which I find almost overpowering. So many would have taken short cuts; so many men would have felt they had every right to take short cuts. But habitual thoroughness is, I believe, only part of the answer. The rest is humility. In John Butt's passing we salute the death of a gentle and a humble man. I cannot conceive of higher praise than that.

British Academy
Obituary

John Everett Butt
1906-1965

John Butt was born at Hoole in Cheshire on 12 April 1906, and educated at Shrewsbury School and at Merton College, Oxford. He went up to Oxford in 1924 intending to follow his father into the medical profession, but before long he transferred to the School of English Language and Literature. As an undergraduate at Merton he had the good fortune to become a pupil of David Nichol Smith. How far the Merton tutor consciously shaped the pupil in his own image, or how far the pupil consciously or unconsciously absorbed the influence of the leading eighteenth-century scholar of his day it would be impossible now to determine; but in so far as Nichol Smith founded a school of eighteenth-century scholarship Butt became one of its most notable products, and perhaps the most eminent example of its virtues. All this, however, lay in the future. Butt matured gradually (he was never in a hurry, physically or intellectually), and he took a second in Schools in 1927.

It was just about this time that the B.Litt. was being reorganized by Nichol Smith and George Gordon. With its new courses in Textual Criticism, Bibliography, Palaeography and the History of English Scholarship it became available for Butt, who was one of the first to obtain the degree under the new dispensation. Nichol Smith had an amiable way of listening to suggestions for subjects from his pupils, and then quietly but firmly directing their wandering desires to some minor eighteenth-century poet. At all events, Butt was to write his thesis on Thomas Tickell, thereby greatly increasing his own knowledge of eighteenth-century poetry and of the literary and social background of the period, but also making some interesting additions to the canon of Tickell's writings. His first appearance in print came in 1928 with "Notes for a Bibliography of Thomas Tickell" in the *Bodleian Quarterly Record*. Another interest of those early years was expressed in his more substantial "Bibliography of Izaak Walton's 'Lives' ", which was published two years later in the *Oxford Bibliographical Society Proceedings and Papers*. His interest in Walton was lifelong, and might at one time have led to a full-length book. He did, however, publish an interesting essay on "Izaak Walton's Methods in Biography" (1934), and almost twenty years later, when invited to give the Ewing Lectures at U.C.L.A., he chose to speak on English biography, and Walton (along with Johnson and Boswell) was one of the three authors discussed.

He began his career as a university teacher in 1929 at Leeds, where he held a temporary post as an assistant-lecturer. He returned to Oxford in 1930, and was for some time the all-but-honorary Sub-Librarian of the English Schools Library. Later in the same year he became Lecturer in English at Bedford College, London (with Lascelles Abercrombie and, later, F. P. Wilson as head of the department), and there he was to remain, with a long break in the war years, until 1946. He was always a good lecturer, and as his knowledge grew and his ideas matured, he became an excellent one. Like his Merton tutor, he had no patience with the more pretentious and esoteric developments of modern literary criticism, but kept to the high-road of the demonstrable; and if his knowledge ran far beyond that of his student audiences, his contact with them remained unbroken, and the deep pleasure that he took in Pope or Johnson or Wordsworth or Dickens was unaffectedly communicated to them. One of his great assets was a fine resonant voice; and a lecture by him was not only well informed and well organized, but was enlivened by passages of verse or prose beautifully timed and delivered. The voice that was heard at Butt's lectures can be heard again in his prose, which, like so much else about him, became fuller and more assured as he grew older, and took on something of the poise and finality of his favourite century.

The war years brought out new qualities in him that had only been waiting for a chance to find expression. In 1941 he became a Temporary Administrative Assistant in the Ministry of Home Security, and in 1943 he was transferred to the Home Office, where he was a temporary Principal. Here he proved so successful that at the end of the war some pressure was brought to bear upon him to remain in the Civil Service. Butt, who was a splendid administrator – systematic, thorough, equable, and friendly – was tempted to stay on in an environment that he had found so congenial. He had, too, the extraordinary notion that he wasn't really a good teacher. For some time it was touch and go, and either decision would have been the right one; but in the end he decided to return to academic work. He went back to Bedford College in 1945, but only for a short period. The following year he was appointed to the Chair of English at Newcastle, at the age of forty. In 1947 he succeeded the present writer as Editor of *The Review of English Studies*, just when the flood of post-war contributions was beginning to break its banks. I can well remember his mild exasperation at having to work off a number of dull articles I had accepted (when scholarly work was almost at a standstill), before he could publish those he had accepted himself. He proved himself to be a wise and indefatigable editor for seven years, until pressure of other work forced him to resign.

One of the two main scholarly enterprises of his life was now well under way. In 1932, at the age of twenty-six, he had been invited to become General Editor of the projected Twickenham edition of Pope. He planned the edition carefully, chose his editors judiciously, and gave them clear and unambiguous instruction. His own volume, *Imitations of Horace* (1939), an admirable model, was the first to appear; and in spite of wartime difficulties a second volume was published in 1940, and a third in 1943. The edition was completed in seven volumes, as originally planned, in 1961; but in the meantime the publishers had been persuaded to include the translations from Homer, and those (in four further volumes) will shortly appear. Owing to the death of Norman Ault, Butt became a good deal more than the general editor of Vol. VI (*Minor Poems*), and had in fact to carry out a detailed revision of Ault's manuscript and make himself ultimately responsible for determining the canon of the minor poems. Long before his death he must have had the satisfaction of knowing that the quickened interest in Pope's poetry in recent years was in large measure due to the edition to which he had given so much time and thought, and to which he had himself contributed so much. In 1963 he brought out a one-volume edition of the Twickenham text of Pope, together with select annotation: a volume running to 850 pages, and yet in the circumstances a notable work of compression. His interests, however, were far from being confined to Pope or to eighteenth-century poetry. A translation of *Candide*, for example, made in 1947 for the Penguin series, proved to be very successful, and was followed, in 1964, by translations of *Zadig* and *L'Ingénu*.

The years at Newcastle were happy ones. In 1941 he had married a former student of Bedford College, Enid Margaret Hope, and with their young family of a son and two daughters they were now living in a handsome eighteenth-century house at Corbridge, which they had tastefully modernized, much in the manner of Pope imitating Horace. It was to this house, during a railway strike, that Mr. (now Professor) Peter Butter drove one summer day from Edinburgh, carrying with him a bundle of scripts for the external examiner. When Butt, who was expecting him, opened the door himself and said: "I'm Butt", his visitor made the inevitable reply, "I'm Butter". It was during the Newcastle years, too, that he made his first visit to the United States, where he taught in 1952 at the University of California, Los Angeles. He was a visiting professor at Yale in 1962, and he also lectured from time to time in various European countries.

In 1954 he delivered the Warton lecture at the Academy on "Pope's Poetical Manuscripts". After giving a general account of the surviving manuscripts, he proceeded to pay more detailed attention to a draft of the *Epistle to Dr. Arbuthnot* in the Pierpoint Morgan Library, New York, and then showed that another manuscript fragment in the Huntington Library is not, as was then generally supposed, a second autograph manuscript of the poem, but a continuation of the Morgan draft. The various lectures delivered each year at Burlington House are normally received in a decorous and even formidable silence; but anyone who was present at Butt's Warton lecture will recall that although this particular argument held the audience spellbound, the climax of it produced a sudden release of feeling.

> If we have any remaining doubt [the lecturer said] whether two sheets now separated by 3,000 miles were once contiguous, there on the last Morgan sheet is a tell-tale blot from a correction Pope had hurriedly added to the Huntington fragment.

At that point there came a sudden burst of applause that was at

xxi

once a tribute to a beautifully conducted argument, and to the dramatic timing of the lecturer.

Over the years Butt had written a number of interesting papers on eighteenth-century literature; he had contributed a useful volume, *The Augustan Age* (1950), to Hutchinson's University Library, and a *Fielding* to the British Council's "Writers and their Work" series. The steady and thoughtful quality of his criticism is well seen in the paper on "Johnson's Practice in the Poetical Imitation", a lecture to the Johnson Society of London which was later published in a volume of studies compiled for the 250th anniversary of Johnson's birth (1959). Yet sound as his critical work on Pope, Johnson, and other eighteenth-century writers undoubtedly was, it was not, by the very highest standards, outstanding. One still thought of him primarily as an editor who was capable of turning from the establishment and annotation of Pope's text to judicious and well-informed criticism of his poetry, or as a literary historian whose judgements of literature were well weighed and always sane, but not especially original. When, in the 1940s, however, he became interested in what was to prove the second main field of his scholarly activity, the novels of Dickens, he seemed as a literary critic to take on a new dimension. True, his approach was still that of the editor, and in 1958 he was to become joint-editor with Kathleen Tillotson of the Clarendon Press Dickens. But the problems involved in editing Dickens raised critical questions of the greatest interest, and these questions were of a kind peculiarly suited to Butt's critical gifts. With Pope, none of the surviving manuscripts except that of the *Essay on Criticism* was intended for the press, and their readings were therefore, as Butt himself put it, "provisional only, liable to rejection, and frequently in fact rejected". With Dickens the situation was quite different, and a good deal more complex. It was the habit of Dickens to send to the printer the corrected first drafts of each instalment of a novel; and the manuscripts of all but the first three novels have survived complete, and of the first three, considerable portions are extant. These manuscripts frequently contain passages that had to be excised because Dickens had overrun the space available for his monthly or weekly part, and sometimes contain passages which he had been compelled to add to make up the necessary length. All this material (together with corrected proofs, revisions made by Dickens for later editions, and much else) makes the establishment of the text a delicate and complicated task, and one calling for a judgement that takes everything into account but is not overwhelmed by detail. Since the new edition of the novels was from the first a joint undertaking, it required also two minds able to work together on a plane of complete understanding and shared interests; and this was indeed an editorial partnership from which the highest quality of work could confidently be expected. In such circumstance it is difficult to separate the work of the two general editors; but it is fair to say that it was Butt's interest in the Dickens manuscripts and his perception of their significance in establishing a critical text that made clear the need for a new and authoritative edition. In Pope studies he was one of the best in a long line; in Dickens studies he was a pioneer. He did not live to see the publication of the first volume (*Oliver Twist*, edited by Kathleen Tillotson), but he had managed to read most of the proofs. He himself was editing *David Copperfield*, but his progress was impeded by the serious illness which developed in 1963, and which (although there were several periods of intermission) was ultimately the cause of his death.

The editorial work on Dickens was accompanied by, and indeed preceded by, a critical investigation of the conditions under which Dickens wrote, the effect of serial publication on his writing, the extent to which the contemporary world entered into his fiction and suggested its themes, and other related topics. It was in his inquiries into the effect of the instalment system of publication on the novels that he made his most original and important contribution to modern literary criticism. The first public sign of this new interest was an article in the *Durham University Journal* (1948), "Dickens at Work" (the title was to be used again for the volume of studies which he published jointly with Mrs. Tillotson in 1957), and further papers on Dickens's mode of composition appeared in the next few years in various learned journals. These, very substantially revised, were collected in the volume just mentioned, and additional studies were to appear on *Bleak House* and *Little Dorrit*, on "Editing a Nineteenth-century Novelist", and on "Dickens's Manuscripts". Those various critical papers showed Butt at the most mature stage of his scholarship. He always liked to work with facts rather than conjectures, and here he had not only facts in plenty, but a complex mass of evidence which had to be brought together, carefully scrutinized, and intelligently interpreted. The result was a new and illuminating commentary on Dickens, and the opening of a fresh approach to the study of nineteenth-century fiction that must always be associated with his name and that of his collaborator.

In 1959 Butt's high standing in the field of English studies was recognized by his appointment to the Regius Chair of Rhetoric and English Literature at the University of Edinburgh. He gave his inaugural lecture (very appropriately both in place and time) on James Boswell, and quickly plunged into a busy life of teaching and administration. To one of his subsidiary duties, the annual award of the James Tait Black Memorial Prizes, he gave his customary close attention; and his influence was soon to be felt, not only in his own department, where considerable developments took place and to which a growing number of post-graduate students were attracted, but on the higher levels of academic administration. But here, as always, his priorities were right, and he gave his best to his students.

> If numbers rose embarrassingly, [one of his colleagues, Professor Denys Hay, has remarked] he had, in a way, only himself to blame. When a Professor sings ballads to the First Ordinary Class of English Literature in the Pollock Hall he is taking his subject seriously, but he is also likely to make it seem significant to those hesitating before the claims of other disciplines.

The singing to which Professor Hay refers was not just the result of a momentary whim, but a long-standing interest of Butt's. He had a fine bass voice, and had sung in the Wigmore Hall with the Oriana Madrigalists, and on other occasions with the Fleet Street Choir and at Bedford College.

On one other major task he was working right up to the time of his death. As the hours ran out he was striving with unbroken fortitude to complete his volume for the Oxford History of English Literature, *The Mid-Eighteenth Century*. Shortly before his death I had a letter from him (dictated to his wife) in which he told me of the progress he had made, and what still remained to be done.

I am not writing, because Gibbon in particular requires to be read; but I have reached the position of being able to say that seven of my ten chapters are quite complete, and that substantial sections have been written for the other three.

In this same letter he told me that he was hoping to resume "a strait-jacket designed by the orthopaedic chaps to hold up my head and shoulders". A little later his wife wrote to say that he was cheerful and active, but very much immobilized and in some pain:

O.H.E.L. proceeds, Gibbon is read and being written on – some pretty garbled bits get taken down by anybody that is available, and he can't always bear in mind that we don't do shorthand. Nearly every day there is a student or colleague or predecessor on the job . . .

Only one week later I had the news of his death. His gentle endurance of increasing pain and disability in those last months had been heroic, a shining triumph of the spirit over a body that did him "grievous wrong".

The mind inevitably goes back to the tall slim figure of his youth and early manhood. Although he was never much of an athlete he always looked robust, and he was a great walker, at Corbridge, at Edinburgh, and in the Lake District, where he was a Trustee of Dove Cottage. He can hardly have known a day's illness until the first symptoms of bone disease became evident in 1963. Genial, anecdotal, and with just enough severity to give his anecdotes a flavour, he was the best of company, and he made and kept friends wherever he went. He was immersed in his work; yet, unlike that Duke of Newcastle who was said to have lost half an hour in the morning which he kept running after for the rest of the day trying to overtake, he seemed always to have time for everything and everybody. His friends and fellow scholars, all of whom held him in the greatest affection, were well aware of what he had done; they were even more conscious of what he was. In the Berkshire village where I now live, when they want to praise a man, they have a way of saying, "He's always the same". To meet John Butt after an interval of time was to experience that satisfaction to the full: the warm, friendly personality, the sense of fun, the delightful conversation, the moral and intellectual integrity – nothing had changed, he was always the same. In a troubled, acrimonious, and often petty world he radiated not only good sense, but generosity and positive goodness. To be in his company was to be with a man who had for so long been going right that it would have required some abnormal concentration of circumstances to make him go wrong. His scholarship, too, was the natural by-product of his habitual right thinking, and of the application of a serene and unbiased mind to the facts before him. If he had still much to give, he had also accomplished much:

Thus far was right, the rest belongs to Heav'n.

JAMES SUTHERLAND

For help in writing this memoir I am especially indebted to Professor Geoffrey Tillotson, Professor Kathleen Tillotson, Professor Denys Hay, and Mr. Geoffrey Carnall.

Part One

AUBREY WILLIAMS

Congreve's *Incognita*
and the Contrivances of
Providence

[i]

Critical appraisal of William Congreve's first published work, *Incognita: or Love and Duty Reconcil'd* (1692), has been decidedly mixed, and altogether vague and general. Though it had been reprinted at least four times by 1743, Samuel Johnson maintained that he would "rather praise it than read it",[1] and both Macaulay[2] and Sir Leslie Stephen[3] later thought it a work of inconsiderable esteem. Twentieth-century opinion has been more kind, especially since Mr. H. F. B. Brett-Smith described it as "probably the most important as well as the most deliberate achievement of the English novel between *The Unfortunate Traveller* in 1594 and *The Life and Strange Surprising Adventures of Robinson Crusoe* in 1719".[4] To Mr. Bonamy Dobrée the novel "certainly shows style and critical acumen",[5] Mr. D. Crane Taylor believes that no one who would understand Congreve's "development as a dramatist can pass over this novel with a glance",[6] and most recently Professor A. Norman Jeffares has stated that the book "was an impressive piece of work for a young man to produce".[7] But whether *Incognita* has been prized or misprized by individual critics, a trait common to all discussion of the novel has been a certain merely appreciative vagueness of commentary: *Incognita* is a "poor novel", or one "of no great value"; its interest to us "lies in the fact that in it Congreve reveals an important side of his nature, namely, the

3

love of graceful living, a desire to poetize the rougher sides of life, or at least to withdraw himself from crudities, and dwell in a realm where politics and Pretenders did not exist"; Congreve attempts "a formal portrait of manners, in which the decencies of polite society are touched with a gentle satire on humanity and its foibles". The "motive of the novelist is patent: he takes pleasure in contriving an ingenious plot and effective situations, and he enjoys depicting polite flirtations between young people of breeding, and letting himself appear now and then before the curtain to utter some gently cynical remark". The critics speak much about the "charm" of the work and of its surprising "maturity" as the creation of a youth who must have been somewhere between seventeen and twenty-one when he wrote it, yet nowhere does one find, to put the matter most simply and even baldly, any discussion of what *Incognita* is "about".

If *Incognita* is important in the development of the English novel, and if it does stand in some significant relationship to Congreve's plays, then some attempt at a more precise delineation of its structure and meaning seems highly desirable. In the absence of any such precise account of the nature and implications of the novel's fable or plot, it seems merely idle to state that the "plot of *Incognita* is well enough handled, but it is a formal plot, and the merit of the book lies elsewhere" – especially when that "elsewhere" is never exactly located. Just as inadequate appears the statement that *Incognita* "handles a conventional theme with a quiet success which was not lost upon its own age" – particularly when that "conventional theme" seems to have been either mistaken or misunderstood or simply left undefined.

That *Incognita* does handle a "conventional theme", and with a "quiet success", will be the argument of this essay. No attempt, as such, will be made to determine *Incognita*'s place in the history of the English novel, but several efforts will be made, both directly and by implication, to establish the exact nature of its main design and theme and to suggest the book's close connection with the themes that give to Congreve's plays their fundamental shape and meaning.

4

[ii]

In the Preface to *Incognita* Congreve emphasized his resolve "to imitate *Dramatick* Writing, namely, in the Design, Contexture and Result of the Plot". And he went on:

> The design of the Novel is obvious, after the first meeting of *Aurelian* and *Hippolito* with *Incognita* and *Leonora*, and the difficulty is in bringing it to pass, maugre all apparent obstacles, within the compass of two days. How many probable Casualties intervene in opposition to the main Design, *viz.* of marrying two Couple so oddly engaged in an intricate Amour, I leave the Reader at his leisure to consider: As also whether every Obstacle does not in the progress of the Story act as subservient to that purpose, which at first it seems to oppose. In a Comedy this would be called the Unity of Action; here it may pretend to no more than an Unity of Contrivance.

In spite of his statement that the design of *Incognita* is "obvious", it is noteworthy here that Congreve yet goes on to stress the very fact of "design" and "contrivance" in his story, and more particularly goes on to stress the notion that "Obstacles" and "Casualties" (i.e., mishaps, accidents, unforeseen events) of themselves seem in the end to "act as subservient to that purpose, which at first" they seem "to oppose". This stress, in the Preface and throughout the story itself, points us, I think, to the most important fact about the novel: the very *design*, the very *contrivance* of events, becomes in *Incognita* the supreme and implicit emblem of its meaning.

Since *Incognita* is seldom read today, full appreciation of its patterning of events requires here a rather full review of the elaborate contrivances and intricate "casualties" that form its narrative. The story opens in Siena, where Aurelian, a young Florentine, and Hippolito di Saviolina, a young Spanish nobleman, have for some time pursued their studies. The time for Hippolito's departure on further travels having arrived, Aurelian persuades him to journey first to Florence in the hope that he can there gain his father's permission to accompany him on his tour. Reaching Florence they find a grand public festival about to begin in honour of the nuptials of a young woman closely allied to the Duke of Florence. Deciding to keep their identities secret, so as to enjoy the festivities with less restraint, they provide themselves with habits and masks, Hippolito obtaining his from the valet of a Florentine gallant who has been mortally wounded in a duel. The pair proceed to the Masquing Ball at Court, and there Aurelian is smitten with the wit and charm of a young woman who, at the end of the evening, gives him the choice of knowing her name or seeing her face. Aurelian naturally chooses to see her face, which proves to be utterly beauteous. When he then entreats to know her name, she says he must be content to know her, for the present at least, by the name of "Incognita". For his part, Aurelian had already deceived the young woman as to his identity by presenting himself under the name of Hippolito di Saviolina.

While Aurelian is thus engaged, his friend Hippolito is approached by a young woman who mistakes him, because of his dress, for her cousin Lorenzo, the wounded young man. She warns Hippolito that kinsmen of the man Lorenzo had killed may set upon him after the ball. Hippolito encourages the mistake, and when Leonora, as the young woman is called, reveals her face momentarily, he is as bewitched as was Aurelian by his "Incognita". Pretending faintness from wounds, he leaves the ball with Leonora, and contrives to get her handkerchief and a means of communicating with her the next day. He then returns to his lodgings to compose a letter which will excuse his deceit and reveal his love.

Aurelian is returning to the same lodging when he sees a man in his friend's apparel beset by two unknown persons. Aurelian disarms the assailants, and finds their victim to be Claudio, Hippolito's governor, who had assumed his master's dress in order to partake of the festivities. Having seen the wounded Claudio cared for, Aurelian then enters the bedchamber he shares with Hippolito, who at this point sits totally abstracted in thoughts of his Leonora. Startled by Aurelian's entrance, Hippolito knocks over the lamp, thinks his friend an intruder, and in the darkness tries to run him through, at which point this statement is made: "But such was the extraordinary Care of Providence in directing the Sword, that it only past under his Arm giving no Wound to *Aurelian*, but a little Bruise between his Shoulder and Breast with the Hilt".

Recovered from these confusions, the pair confide their loves to one another, and Hippolito further tells his friend that Leonora had informed him that Aurelian's father, in the interest of patching up the quarrel between the families concerned in the wounded Lorenzo's duel, had agreed to a marriage between Aurelian and a certain Donna Juliana. Aurelian, his beauteous Incognita "rooted in his heart", is confounded at this news, while Hippolito is chagrined to learn that Aurelian had taken his name for his own amour. They decide to continue the deception, however, Hippolito signing his note to Leonora with Aurelian's name. The note is sent, and Leonora, after some very feminine reasoning and hesitations, concludes that she must have this "Aurelian", even though she at this time thinks him to be betrothed to her dear friend Juliana.

The next day, in spite of a sleepless night, the two lovers carry off most of the honours in a tournament, in obscure ways "identifying" themselves to their mistresses and also quite inadvertently giving Aurelian's father reason to suspect their presence in Florence. Ordering their lodgings to be sought out, Aurelian's father now presses the young men in time and place, while Juliana's father orders her to be ready to marry Aurelian on the morrow. Since Juliana (bless us!) is really the beauteous Incognita, and fancies herself in love with the Spaniard Hippolito, she is "confounded at the haste that was imposed on her", while Leonora is "ready to swoon" at the thought of losing her "Aurelian". In her dilemma Incognita seeks her lover's aid, but when her coach arrives at his lodgings, Aurelian fears it to be his father's and flees his apartment. Incognita enters and finds Hippolito, the man she thinks she seeks. Hippolito, fortunately, apprehends her mistake, and tells her he will fetch the man she wishes. But he is delayed in his search for Aurelian, and Incognita composes a note to leave to her lover. Then she hears a noise, thinks it to be her lover, and tears up her note, only to find that the noise is caused by the entrance of Aurelian's father. She leaves in disguise and confusion, Hippolito returns and manages to get rid of the old gentleman, and then goes again in search of Aurelian. Aurelian returns to the empty apartment, picks up the torn fragments of the note he can find, and also leaves again. When he pieces the note together he finds that his Incognita "earnestly desired him . . . to meet her at Twelve a Clock that Night at a Convent Gate" – but "unluckily the Bit of Paper which should have mentioned what Convent, was broken off and lost".

7

Wandering on "unwittingly", Aurelian finds himself in the ruins of an old monastery, and there he hears sounds of someone being throttled. Fancying the choked voice to be a woman's, he demands the matter, whereupon an obscure figure levels a dark lanthorn and a pistol at him. And then: "*Aurelian* seeing the irresistible advantage his Adversary had over him, would fain have retired; and, by the greatest Providence in the World, going backwards fell down over some loose Stones that lay in his Way, just in that Instant of Time when the Villain fired his Pistol, who seeing him fall, concluded he had Shot him". Aurelian recovers himself, kills his attacker, and unbinds the unknown victim, who of course turns out to be his Incognita. She, it seems, had entrusted a servant to take her to a convent in order, she tells Aurelian, to avoid a forced marriage. But the servant had betrayed his trust and carried her to the "old ruined Monastery, where it pleased Heaven, by what Accident I know not, to direct you". While each then continues to mix fiction with truth in their accounts of their actual identities and situations, Aurelian persuades Incognita to stay that night at his lodgings.

All this time Hippolito has "wandered" in search of Aurelian, only to arrive finally at the Gate of the Convent of St. Lawrence, situated immediately adjacent to the house of Leonora. The Convent is astir with friars at prayer for the wounded Lorenzo, now on the verge of death. In hope of seeing Leonora, who has come to join in the prayers, Hippolito enters her garden and there conceals himself. And Congreve then specifies: "By Computation now (which is a very remarkable Circumstance) *Hippolito* entred this Garden near upon the same Instant, when *Aurelian* wandred into the Old Monastery and found his *Incognita* in Distress". In the garden Hippolito overhears Leonora confess her love for him in a soliloquy, and persuades her to a hasty marriage with him that very night. Together they then persuade her confessor to perform the ceremony, which is barely concluded when her father enters upon the scene. He is greatly outraged, but is finally calmed when Leonora tells him that she has married the esteemed young "Aurelian".

Hippolito, Leonora, and her father now proceed to Aurelian's lodgings and there find Aurelian and his father as well as the father and a kinsman of the Donna Juliana. Aurelian begs his father's approval of his own choice for marriage, and when his father demands to see his unknown young woman, Aurelian leaves the room and returns with Incognita, now publicly revealed as the very Juliana he had sought to evade. Juliana discovers that her pseudo-Hippolito is really the Aurelian for whom she had been destined all along, and Leonora and her father are made happy with the fact that her young man comes of a distinguished Spanish house. In such a manner are their loves and duties reconciled.

[iii]

The very diction of *Incognita* is dominated by a small set of terms which are completely responsive to the novel's intricacies of event and which are also highly suggestive of its most essential meaning. The four main characters, as well as most of the minor ones, are continually involved in "designs" or "contrivances" of their own manufacture which usually defeat the very purposes for which they strive. At the same time the characters are also continually involved in "errors" or "mistakes", whose nature is best suggested by such a statement as this: "So that although *Leonora* was indeed mistaken, she could not be said to be much in the wrong". All such self-defeating contrivances and designs, along with all such happy errors and fortunate mistakes, seem in their turn to point towards certain crucial and highly emblematic situations in which characters are said to be in a "maze" or "at a loss", or (better still) are said to "grope" in the dark or to be "left in the Dark". At such moments "in the Dark", when a character has "wandred into the Dominions of Silence and of Night", there occurs, in a most critical "Instant of Time", an act of Providential design. The effect of such terms and of such situations in the novel is to suggest that amidst all human contrivances, and amidst all human "success" and all human "error", there work the contrivances of Providence, which sees that a kind of "justice" is done.

The pattern of the novel's diction, as well as its stress and tendencies, are easily illustrated. Leonora first approaches Hippolito because "she had mistaken him" for her cousin Lorenzo, and in the ensuing conversation Hippolito quite "forgot his design of informing the Lady of her mistake". Resolving later "to humour the mistake a little further", he of a sudden "found the success of his design had prevented his own endeavours". Then, "after so many Contrivances as he had formed for the discovery of himself", he decides to wait till the next day so he "might inform her gently of her mistake". His "design took", and "with a Heart full of Love, and a Head full of Stratagem", he betakes himself to his lodging. When his governor Claudio then dons his masking habit to visit the ball, he is beset in the dark by two ruffians who are frustrated in their attack by Aurelian's "timely Assistance" and who later confess "their Design to have been upon *Lorenzo*". When Aurelian goes on to Hippolito's room, the overturning of the lamp leaves them "both in the Dark, *Hippolito* groping about with his Sword". When Aurelian steps back to the doorway, hoping to "inform his Friend of his Mistake, without exposing himself to his blind Fury", Hippolito makes such a thrust at him that, had it not been for "the extraordinary Care of Providence in directing the Sword", he would surely have killed his friend.

When the pair confer about their loves, Aurelian is "Confounded at the Difficulty he conceived on his Part", for on the one hand he must inevitably disoblige his father if he continues to conceal himself, and on the other, if he now discovers himself, he must just as inevitably disoblige him by refusing to marry Donna Juliana. He also now repents bitterly "his inconsiderate Choice, in preferring the momentary Vision" of his Incognita's face "to a certain Intelligence of her Person". Hippolito is likewise distressed, for he reflects now that Leonora "had not the least knowledge of him but through mistake". He takes it as "an unlucky thought in *Aurelian*" to have usurped his name, but at last they decide to continue the "Contrivance", arguing themselves "into a Belief, that Fortune had befriended them with a better Plot, than their regular Thinking could have contriv'd". Hippolito frames "his Letter design'd for *Leonora*", and she, upon receiving it, "immediately concluded him to be Aurelian". In his letter Hippolito tells her that her "Innocent (Innocent, though perhaps to me Fatal) Error" has made him love's desperate victim, and says that in the tournament he will wear her handkerchief, that "dear, inestimable (though undesign'd) Favour which I receiv'd from you". Leonora "wondred at her own Blindness" in mistaking this "Aurelian" for Lorenzo, and she reflects upon "Aurelian's" discretion in "removing her farther from her Mistake" until he could prepare her "for a full and determinate Convincement". Having proceeded "thus far in a maze of Thought", she "no longer doubted" the letter to be from Aurelian – and here Congreve intrudes to observe that "although *Leonora* was indeed mistaken, she could not be said to be much in the wrong".

The next day, at the tournament, the two friends mistake a merely honorific challenge on behalf of the guest of honour as the real thing – while in truth it "was only designed for show and form". Here citations from one page alone suggest how heavily Congreve at times emphasizes the idea of "mistake" in human events: "our Cavaliers were under a mistake"; a gentleman "told them their mistake"; they are "much concerned for their mistake"; another gentleman demands the right "to inform those Gentlemen better of their mistake, by giving them the Foyl"; they are "informed of their Error"; they state "how sensible they were of their Error"; and they beg "pardon for not knowing" the Bride's picture.

Having distinguished themselves in the tournament, the pair steal back to their lodgings, where for some time they sit "fretting and contriving to no purpose". Although they "rack'd their Invention till it was quite disabled", they "could not make discovery of one Contrivance more for their Relief", and so "Night came upon them while they sate thus thoughtless, or rather drowned in Thought". At this point, when Hippolito asks what they must do, Aurelian replies, "We must suffer", and then goes on to utter a high-flown and exaggerated complaint which, in spite of its comic overtones, nevertheless seems to recall all the traditional outcries made by man since Adam when a seemingly insoluble predicament or dilemma causes him to question the order of justice which rules his world: "Oh ye unequal Powers", he exclaims, "why do ye urge us to desire what ye doom us to forbear; give us a Will to chuse, then curb us with a Duty to restrain that Choice! Cruel Father, Will nothing else suffice! Am I to be the Sacrifice to expiate your Offences past; past ere I was born?" The rhetoric, for a tale of this sort, is certainly grandiloquent and even bombastic, and perhaps is saved from grotesquerie only by the comedy of the situation. But however well Aurelian's complaint is adjusted to the novel's patina of gallantry, it nevertheless does question the

11

order of justice imposed on man by the "unequal Powers" above – and by implication suggests that even in the misadventures and adversities of lovers as stylized as these there is an occasion for Providence, by Its contrivances, to bring about a reconciliation of the claims of love and duty, and thus to vindicate Its ways to man.

It is soon after this we have the episode in which Aurelian returns to his empty apartment and finds the torn pieces of paper which ask him to meet Incognita "at Twelve a Clock that Night at a Convent Gate". Because the "Bit of Paper which should have mentioned what Convent, was broken off and lost", Aurelian walks about "unwittingly" till he finds himself "in that part of the Town, whither his unguided Steps had carried him". Having wandered, as Congreve says, "both into the Dominions of Silence and of Night", he "would willingly have groped his Way back again", when he hears the sounds of an assault on some unknown woman. Then, as we have seen, in this silence and darkness, he is saved from death "by the greatest Providence in the World", and rescues the unknown victim, who gives him "Prayers, Blessings and Thanks" and calls him "a Thousand Deliverers, good Genius's and Guardian Angels". Being "at a loss" what else to do, Aurelian takes the stranger to his lodging, there to find that his steps have been directed to the rescue of his beloved, who in turn is full of wonder at the "miracle" by which he had preserved her. She tells him how her villainous servant had led her "into an old ruined Monastery, where it pleased Heaven, by what Accident I know not, to direct you". And she also tells him, though in ambiguous and distorted terms, of the marriage about to be forced upon her, so that Aurelian is "confounded at the Relation she had made, and began to fear his own Estate to be more desperate than ever he had imagined". As they talk on it becomes more and more obvious (and ironically so) that the counterfeits and fictions they employ to conceal their identities become the very means by which they frustrate (in spite of the "miracle" just wrought on their behalf) their own most warm and urgent desires. The irony appears fully in such a passage as this: Aurelian "feared least her knowledge of those designs which were in agitation between him and *Juliana*, might deter her more from giving her consent" to him.

We now turn to Hippolito, who had "wandered much" when
he reached the "Gates of the Convent of St. *Lawrence*, whither
he was arrived sooner than he thought for". Here, by entirely
"unexpected Means" (the orisons for the dying Lorenzo), he
receives hope of seeing Leonora. He enters her garden "near
upon the same Instant, when *Aurelian* wandred into the Old
Monastery and found his *Incognita* in Distress", and in the
garden, in the glimmering moonlight, he finds "a Hallow" in
a myrtle tree, "as if purposely contriv'd for the Reception of one
Person, who might undiscovered perceive all about him".
Leonora enters, plays a song on her lute, and in a soliloquy
laments that her "Aurelian" must marry the "happy" Juliana.
At this moment Hippolito comes forward and tells his astonished
mistress "that Heaven conducted" him hither to hear his "bliss
pronounced by that dear Mouth alone".

In the last few pages of the story, after the marriage of
Leonora with her "Aurelian", the mistakes and contrivances
are multiplied still further. But in the final scene in Aurelian's
apartment, when Aurelian himself is "most at a loss, for he
knew not of his Happiness", there is a full *éclaircissement* for
everyone – and a good deal of mirth between Juliana and
Leonora over their "unknown and mistaken Rivalry" and over
the "several Contrivances" they had employed to evade their
own best hopes and destinies. At this point the reader has
"leisure to consider", as Congreve had said in his Preface,
"whether every Obstacle does not in the progress of the Story
act as subservient to that purpose, which at first it seems to
oppose". And as to anything more "particular" in his story,
Congreve in his Preface had also said that he would "leave it to
show it self, being very well satisfy'd how much more proper it
had been" for the reader "to have found out this himself, than
for me to prepossess him with an Opinion of something extraordinary in an Essay began and finished in the idler hours of a
fortnight's time".

[iv]

The year after *Incognita* was published, Congreve's first play,
The Old Bachelor, was staged,[8] and in the ensuing seven years,
from 1693 to 1700, there appeared the other four plays that

were to complete, by the time he was thirty, the body of his dramatic work: *The Double-Dealer* in late 1693, *Love for Love* in 1695, *The Mourning Bride* in early 1697, and *The Way of the World* in 1700. It is at least a part of the proposition of this essay that *Incognita*, early as it is, stands as a fitting prologue to the plays that were so soon to follow its composition.[9] Slight and facile and fashionable as the novel may appear, it yet reflects the theme most basic to Congreve's plays and of most concern perhaps to the men of his time: the contrivances of Providence as they operate in and through all the intricacies of human motive and act, even the most modish and polite, to bring truth and justice to light. In *The Double-Dealer*, for example, an utterly subtle interplay of human will and Divine Will is posed directly and finely in Maskwell's question, "Was it my brain or Providence", and the same interplay is posed again in his "disclosure" of his plot to Mellefont: "'Tis the only thing that Providence could have contrived to make me capable of serving you, either to my inclination or your own necessity".

In *The Old Bachelor*, the first and least assured of Congreve's plays, the mistakes and contrivances and ironies so characteristic of *Incognita* are again both emphatic and thematic. Vainlove, one of the two principal characters, is told "Thou dost not know what thou wouldst be at", for he endlessly pursues women only to turn from them at the moment of consent or return of love. By his "assurance" in his own mistakes and folly he seems in the end to have forfeited any chance of marriage with Araminta, the play's most sensible and spirited woman. Captain Bluffe and Sir Joseph Wittol attempt to outwit one another, and Vainlove as well, in a plot to get themselves married to Araminta, but they overreach themselves and discover they have married a cast mistress and her maid. Fondlewife, an aging City Banker, is so obstinate and doting as to insure his own cuckoldom; as his young wife tells him, "you will have your ends soon". Heartwell, the old bachelor of the play's title, is the supreme example of the way men sell themselves to laughter and are by themselves betrayed. Completely infatuated with Silvia, a woman already whored by his friend Bellmour, he finally resolves to marry her, in spite of all his doubts and hesitations, and to "run into the danger to lose the apprehension". At the last he is saved from all the consequences of his own lust and mistakes

14

by Bellmour, who has donned the guise of a fanatic puritan divine and who performs a fake marriage from which he is later able to release Heartwell. Throughout the play we are presented with characters who pursue their own ills and contrive their own disasters; if any are saved at all, they seem saved in spite of their own resolves and designs.

The Double-Dealer again presents us with a set of characters who seem perpetually to connive at their own destruction and loss, and who are all "confounded in a maze of thoughts, each leading into one another, and all ending in perplexity". Thus Mellefont is forced to admit to himself, "spite of all my care and foresight, I am caught, caught in my security", and thus other "pitiful contrivers" are eventually seen to "cheat nobody" but themselves. Maskwell, the most consummate contriver of all, is himself ultimately the victim of his own contrivances: as his fertile brain incessantly hatches plot after plot after plot he just as incessantly seems to forward his own exposure and defeat. He is right to question whether all his plots spring from his own "brain or Providence", for by the end of the play we may see in his "long track of dark deceit" what Pope later was to call "Th' Eternal Art educing good from ill".

If the stress in *The Old Bachelor* and in *The Double-Dealer* is on those whose "successes" are "prevented" by their very "endeavours", *Love for Love* presents a hero who in the end must lay aside his contrivance of pretended madness and be mad enough indeed (at least in the eyes of the world) to ruin himself for love of his mistress. In this play Valentine wins Angelica by playing "with a losing hand" or by playing at "Losing Loadum" – a card game in which the player who takes the most tricks is actually the loser. Thus all those characters who pursue their own most selfish purposes are in the end betrayed by themselves and by one another, "as tho'f a couple of privateers were looking for a prize, and should fall foul of one another". The manoeuvrings of all such characters as these last are given their proper context in the words spoken by Valentine, at the end of the play, to the man who would have robbed him of his love: "Tattle, I thank you, you would have interposed between me and Heaven; but Providence laid Purgatory in your way: – you have but justice".

Even more conspicuously than the comedies. *The Mourning*

15

Bride is concerned with characters who are "officious in contriving, in executing puzzled, lame and lost", and with a "hand of Heaven" and a "care of Providence" which sees that the very ill men do may yet work out to a general justice. At the very beginning of the play, Almeria asks the basic theodicean questions:

> Is there necessity I must be miserable?
> Is it of moment to the peace of Heaven
> That I should be afflicted thus? – If not,
> Why is it thus contrived? Why are things laid
> By some unseen hand so, as of sure consequence,
> They must to me bring curses, grief of heart,
> The last distress of life, and sure despair?

Yet finally both she and Osmyn (Alphonso) understand how those who have so afflicted them have worked "subservient to that end/The heavenly powers allot", and also how "The just decrees of Heaven" have turned on the villains of the play "their own most bloody purposes".[10]

In *The Way of the World* the Providential nature of Congreve's dramatic world has become almost totally tacit. Yet once again we are confronted with schemers who endlessly pursue their totally selfish contrivances and designs only to find, as Fainall expostulates, that they are sure to be "outwitted – to be out-jilted – out-matrimony'd". As Mrs. Marwood says to Fainall, "Truth and you are inconsistent", and because of this basic inconsistency it is inevitable, the play affirms in countless ways, that he will be exposed and discovered for what he is. Eventually, as all the play's imagery of time and birth so emphatically asserts, Fainall and his secret will have "grown too big for the pretence", and "all will come out". Of all the contracts made in the play, it seems in the very nature of things that those only succeed which are made by just and generous persons; only the just and generous may ultimately contrive a lasting relationship, while "each deceiver to his cost may find,/That marriage-frauds too oft are paid in kind".

In both *Incognita* and in the plays Congreve seems to explore the ways in which men and women, even those in the most elegant of drawing-rooms, may be frustrated by their own ingenuity and designs or saved by their own seeming limitations

16

or apparent folly or even by their mishaps and stumblings – as Aurelian is when "by the greatest Providence in the World" he "fell down over some loose Stones that lay in his Way, just in that Instant of Time when the Villain fired his Pistol". The elaborately contrived plot of *Incognita* (like the complications of plot in the plays) thus comes to seem an emblem of the way a contriving Providence may shape all human actions, even those most beset by obstacles and "casualties", to a fitting conclusion. And to the extent that *Incognita* and the plays do reveal God's hand in the most fashionable intrigues, and in the most fashionable settings, these works must be read as being, in their own special ways, so many justifications of the ways of God to man – as being so many drawing-room theodicies of the greatest civility, urbanity, and wit.

NOTES

1 *Lives of the English Poets*, ed. George Birkbeck Hill (Oxford, 1905), II.214.

2 In his review of Leigh Hunt's edition of *The Dramatic Works of Wycherley, Congreve, Vanbrugh, and Farquhar* ("Comic Dramatists of the Restoration"). See *The Complete Writings of Lord Macaulay* (Cambridge ed., New York, 1905), VIII.149.

3 See *Dictionary of National Biography*, IV.931.

4 *Incognita: or Love and Duty Reconcil'd*, ed. H. F. B. Brett-Smith, No. 5 of The Percy Reprints (New York and Boston, 1922), p. xii.

5 *The Mourning Bride, Poems, & Miscellanies*, ed. Bonamy Dobrée (World's Classics ed., London, 1928), p. vii.

6 *William Congreve* (New York, 1963), p. 21.

7 *Congreve: Incognita and The Way of the World*, Arnold's English Texts (London, 1966), p. 16.

8 The first draft of *The Old Bachelor* may have been written four years earlier, in 1689. See John C. Hodges, *William Congreve the Man* (New York, 1941), p. 40.

9　A full-scale critical study of the plays is designed by the present writer.

10　The epigraph to *The Mourning Bride* is relevant here: *neque enim lex aequior ulla est,/Quam necis artifices arte perire sua* (Ovid, *de Arte Amandi*, I.655-6). "For there is no juster law than that contrivers of death should perish by their own contrivances", Loeb Classical Library Edition, tr. J. H. Mozley (London, 1939).

IRÈNE SIMON

Early Theories of Prose Fiction:

Congreve and Fielding

[i]

Congreve's Preface to *Incognita* is the first important document in the criticism of fiction[1] and foreshadows Fielding's classic Preface. Both writers were indebted to French classical theory, though each turned it to different account: by imitating dramatic writing Congreve gave a more graceful form to the *nouvelle*, but he did not initiate a new genre; Fielding, on the other hand, applied the theory of prose epic to the matter of the *roman comique*, and thereby created a new species of writing.

By the time he published his little "trifle" Congreve was already conversant with dramatic theory. He may have read d'Aubignac's *La Pratique du Théâtre*,[2] in which he would have found a reference to the current theory of prose fiction in France.[3] French critics defined *le roman* as an epic poem in prose and laid down rules for it accordingly: its action was to be one, and the episodes were to be subordinated to the main design; the time of the action was not to exceed one year, but the place need not be the same throughout. Congreve resolved to imitate dramatic writing "in another beauty",[4] that is, by observing the unities more strictly: in his novel the scene is Florence, the time two days, and all the incidents are subservient to the main purpose; the unity of design thus achieved, which "in a Comedy [. . .] would be called the Unity of Action", pretends to no

19

more, Congreve tells his reader, "than an Unity of Contrivance".[5]

Incognita is indeed a pretty contrivance, in which "two Couple so oddly engaged in an intricate Amour" are finally married "maugre all apparent obstacles", each obstacle acting "as subservient to that purpose, which at first it seems to oppose".[6] The plot and the incidents are as nicely controlled as in a comedy of intrigue, and Congreve's narrative is in fact a *pièce racontée*, with the narrator commenting on the action or on the sentiments of the lovers, like a mature spectator smiling at the antics of youthful protagonists on stage, yet enjoying the very excesses which he deflates. The narrative continually leads up to dialogues, whether presented directly or reported, a method which suggests Fielding's habit of "breaking his action into scenes",[7] while the narrative manner, the asides, and occasional "impertinent digressions" also give us a foretaste of the later master.

Though its sources are unknown, the novel recalls comedies of intrigue of Spanish origin which were popular in the seventeenth century in England and France, particularly Thomas Corneille's *Le Galand Doublé*, which derives from Calderon's *Hombre Todo Ez Trazos*.[8] Whether Congreve invented this little scenario or beguiled "the idler hours of a fortnight's time"[9] in Staffordshire by turning into narrative a play he had seen in his Dublin days, the plot of it is as intricate and the "obstacles" as many as in *The Double Dealer* or *The Way of the World*. He obviously relished such intricacies and the difficulty "in bringing to pass" the design of a novel or of a comedy; the beauty of dramatic writing he imitated in *Incognita* made the difficulty all the greater by confining the story within narrower bounds than those of current novels.

The pleasure the reader derives from this compact little piece is partly due to Congreve's clever handling of the plot, but it is considerably enhanced by his "surety and lightness of touch".[10] The dialogue and the narrator's ironic comments often suggest the world of the witty comedies of the period, their urbane talk or fine raillery; on the other hand the lovers' feelings, especially when lost "in a maze of Thought" and trying to tread back "the path of deluding Fancy",[11] recall the sixteenth- or early seventeenth-century imitations of Italian novellas, though the sentiment is now and then punctured, and the inner monologue cut short, by the author's irony. *Incognita* is a sophisticated novella, in which the confusions arising from mistaken identities result in comic situations, and in which wit and feeling play alternately, very much as the heroics and the pranks alternate in Etherege's *Love in a Tub*. The writer's poise and his control of the style and narrative manner make the story a delightful trifle, and delight, Congreve tells his reader, is the proper end of novels. In taking the drama as his model he was only concerned with the contrivance of the plot; his Preface directs the reader's attention to the nice intricacy of the incidents and therefore to the skill with which he has solved the difficulties.

Congreve also attempted to define the genre by distinguishing it from the romance. In this kind of work, he says, "lofty Language, miraculous Contingencies and impossible Performances, elevate and surprize the Reader into a giddy Delight" but leave him "convinced that 'tis all a lye"; novels, on the contrary, "are of a more familiar nature; Come near us, and represent to us Intrigues in practice, delight us with Accidents and odd Events, but not such as are wholly unusual or unpresidented".[12] The distinction was not unprecedented either; by the time Congreve wrote *Incognita* it had long been a commonplace in French criticism of fiction. Early in the seventeenth century the educated public in France had turned from the "histoires fabuleuses des anciens chevaliers" to the *romans de bergerie* such as *Astrée*, which seemed to offer "quelque chose de vray-semblable".[13] This taste for *vraisemblance* was fostered by the novellas from Italy and especially from Spain, as Charles Sorel explains in the chapter of *La Bibliothèque françoise* (1664) on "Des Romans vray-semblables et des Nouvelles";[14] and it led to the development of the heroic romance, which narrated the exploits of historical heroes and had at least some foundation in truth. The fact that these romances were filled with miraculous contingencies and recounted feats of invincible courage in lofty and often extravagant language did not prevent their authors from claiming that they adhered to truth and observed probability, though they sometimes reminded their readers that probability was of two kinds, natural and supernatural. Indeed, they often expressed their contempt for the marvellous events and incredible heroes of earlier romances,

which by "adhering too much to wonders" created mere
monsters; they believed, or pretended to believe, that "the more
natural adventures are, the more satisfaction they give".[15]
Scudéry claimed to have observed in *Ibrahim* "the Manners,
Customs, Religions, and Inclinations of People" and to have
made "the foundations of (his) work historical, (his) principal
Personages such as are marked out in the true History of illustrious persons, and the wars effective"; in order to eschew the
marvellous, he said, he had "not caused so many Shipwrecks, as
there are in some ancient Romanzes". In spite of this Congreve,
like others before him, must have been convinced that Scudéry's
tale was "all a lye". The claim to probability and truth continued to be repeated in preface after preface to such extravagant romances, though the better critics soon made fun of their
monstrous heroes.[16] Meanwhile readers fond of stories of a
more familiar nature could turn to the many *nouvelles* imitated
from Spain, which, unlike the *romans*, related things "comme
elles sont", as Segrais stated in the Preface to his *Nouvelles
françoises* (1658).[17] Congreve's distinction between romances
and novels thus had a long tradition behind it. Whether he derived it from Segrais or from some other source, it is hard to
say;[18] it may have been suggested to him, for instance, by a
conversation in Scarron's *Romant Comique* (1651), a book that
he seems to have relished.[19]

When defining novels Congreve adds that they are related to
romances as comedy is to tragedy, but he does not develop the
point, nor does he consider, as Fielding was to do, what is the
specific quality or effect of comedy or of the novel, beyond
stating that it produces delight, not wonder. Although his
parody of poetic flights looks forward to Fielding's occasional
use of the mock-heroic style, and echoes the incidental mock-
heroics of Scarron and other writers of *romans comiques*, it does
not seem to serve a general purpose such as Fielding defined
in his theory of the ridiculous. In fact the wry comments and
the charming pictures (such as the portrait of Incognita, which
recalls Lyly's Campaspe and looks forward to Pope's Belinda)
stand side by side; they are not integrated into a complex
pattern, as the praise and satire were to be integrated in *The
Rape of the Lock*.

Though the *nouvelles* were indeed of a more familiar nature than the *romans*, many of them were romantic stories of star-crossed lovers; some related *aventures galantes* rather than *aventures amoureuses*; some, notably La Fontaine's, were frankly cynical. It is characteristic that Congreve chose for his novel matter of the romantic kind, of the same kind in fact as the *nouvelles* inserted in the *romans comiques*. In repudiating the impossible performances of the romances he was not trying to be realistic. He observed probability in the conduct of the plot and adhered to truth in presenting the scene,[20] but his prime concern was for the formal arrangement of his *intrigue amoureuse*. The interest of the Preface lies not so much in Congreve's preference for matter nearer to reality as in the confession of the pains he took in the composition of the story. His novel is a delightful arabesque, and the chief merit of the Preface is to have insisted on the need for form, or at least for clever contrivance, in fiction as in the other arts. Skilful conduct of a plot in fiction is probably best exemplified in *Tom Jones*, in which every obstacle is, as in *Incognita*, "subservient to that purpose, which at first it seems to oppose".[21] In *Incognita*, however, unity of contrivance is no more than a useful compositional device; in *Tom Jones* it is a structural principle supporting the thematic developments.

[ii]

If Congreve was no innovator, Fielding claimed that *Joseph Andrews* belonged to a kind of writing never before attempted in English. Though his Preface is a classic in the criticism of fiction, there still seems to be some disagreement about its real significance and even, as a critic has recently remarked,[22] about the exact meaning of the famous formula. Thus, while A. D. McKillop regards the Preface as "the most important critical document in the history of English prose fiction up to this time",[23] Ian Watt thinks that the epic theory was not very useful, and was not even taken quite seriously by Fielding himself.[24] In a recent article,[25] Homer Goldberg has submitted the theory to a close analysis by following the argument of the Preface step by step. His interpretation of the formula can be confirmed by comparing Fielding's theory with the critical doctrine with which he was familiar and to which he indirectly refers in the Preface as well as in the novel itself. The comparison will bring out the significance of Fielding's theory and his originality with regard to his forebears.

For all his scathing references to "those voluminous works, commonly called Romances" and to "the productions of romance writers",[26] it is clear that Fielding regarded his own work as a species of romance, and that for him, as Goldberg points out, the term itself carried no pejorative meaning. The fact that the practitioners of it had debased the genre by their extravagant nonsense made him reluctant to apply the term to the one epic in prose he praised, *Les Aventures de Télémaque*, because he did not wish it confounded with *Le Grand Cyrus* and other such works *commonly* called romances; but he did call his own production a "comic romance".

As Arthur L. Cooke has shown, "the theories which Fielding himself advanced" were "strikingly similar" to the theory of prose fiction expounded by the French writers of heroic romances;[27] Cooke might have added that the notion of an epic poem in prose had been current since the time of Tasso's *Discorsi del poema eroico* and that in French criticism of the seventeenth century, as we have seen, the *roman* was generally considered an *épopée en prose*. D'Aubignac had referred to this view;[28] Le Bossu considered that *une Epopée en prose* was indeed *une épopée*, though not *un Poëme Epique*;[29] for Huet the *romans réguliers* were "ceux qui sont dans les regles du poëme héroïque".[30] The writers of romance were doing no more than elaborate, for their own purposes, a theory that was taken for granted by all, and Cooke need not have wondered whether Fielding "was guilty of unacknowledged literary theft" (p. 993) since these views were common property in France. So widespread were they that Furetière said in the opening of *Le Roman bourgeois* (1666): "Mais puisqu'un roman n'est qu'une poésie en prose, je croirais mal débuter si je ne suivois l'exemple de mes maistres, et si je faisois un autre exorde".[31] Though Fielding does not mention Furetière in the first chapter of Book III, in which he further defines his aims by referring to various French novels, he may be echoing the *Advertissement du libraire au lecteur* in *Le Roman bourgeois* when he warns his readers not to seek to identify the original of his lawyer or prude since he describes "not men, but manners; not an individual, but a species".[32]

For Fielding, then, as for the French critics,[33] a romance was
an epic poem in prose, and *Les Aventures de Télémaque* appeared
to him to be a true epic since it has all the features common to
that species except verse, which all critics agreed is the least
important.[34] If he needed confirmation of this view he could
have found it in Allan Ramsay's *Discourse of Epic Poetry and of
the Excellence of the Poem of Telemachus* (1719), which he is
known to have possessed. In the section "Of the Poetry",
Ramsay praised the style of *Telemachus* because, like the true
poet, Fénelon paints the passions with art and with enthusiasm;
to the objection that *Telemachus* is written in prose he answered,
referring to the best authorities, that "verse is not essential to
the Epopaea".[35]

Ian Watt, however, contends that Fielding's distinction between *Télémaque* and the French heroic romances is a specious
one since it is "entirely based on the introduction of a new
factor, 'instruction or entertainment', which is obviously a
question of personal value judgement".[36] This would have surprised neo-classical critics, for whom the end of all poetry, and
pre-eminently of the epic poem, was to give instruction and
delight; a work that failed on both counts could not therefore
be regarded as a poem at all, least of all as an epic poem. If
Fielding was expressing a personal value judgement, it was one
that French critics had often expressed in the seventeenth century. Boileau for one condemned the romances for their *puérilité*
and their *morale vicieuse*; his *Dialogue des Héros de Roman* was
intended to expose their "peu de solidité" and the foolishness
of their heroes, who instead of entertaining Pluto send him to
sleep.[37] Far from expressing a mere personal opinion Fielding
was using as his criterion a basic assumption of the neo-classical
doctrine, which his contemporaries would have recognized, and
the logic of his argument is perfectly sound.

The absurdity of the pastoral romance had been early exposed
in *antiromans* such as Sorel's *Berger Extravagant*, which ridi-
culed the false conventions of the genre but which also sapped
the very foundations of all poetic illusion. On the other hand, it
was the purpose of another genre, the *histoires comiques ou satyriques*, to give both entertainment and instruction by presenting
material of a more familiar nature than the romances, in a style
that was close to the language of everyday life. These *romans*

comiques aimed at realism of a kind; as Sorel said in *La Bibliothèque françoise*,

> Les bons romans comiques et satyriques semblent plutost estre des images de l'Histoire que tous les autres: Les actions communes de la Vie estant leur objet, il est plus facile d'y rencontrer de la Verité. Pource qu'on voit plus d'hommes dans l'erreur et dans la sottise, qu'il n'y en a de portez à la sagesse, il se trouve parmy eux plus d'occasions de raillerie, et leurs defauts ne produisent que la Satyre.[38]

The authors of *romans comiques* sometimes compared their works with comedy.[39] This did not mean, as it did for Congreve, that they attempted to link the incidents so as to achieve unity of design or of contrivance, for these novels are built very loosely and consist merely of a series of episodes: none of them has a unified plot, and some authors rejected unity of action deliberately because they found it artificial.[40] Such rejection of all arrangement amounted to a repudiation of art for the sake of truth to reality, whether real or pretended, and obviously derived from the tradition of the *antiroman*. Not all writers of *romans comiques* went so far as Furetière, but none of them subordinated their episodes to some central action, and they usually inserted into their pictures of "reality" novellas of a romantic kind in order to diversify the material. The *romans comiques* were not *romans réguliers*, not because they were comic instead of serious, but because they had no central design; they were built like the picaresque novels, not like the epics. Yet Sorel remarked in *La Bibliothèque françoise* that "comme il y a des Romans Heroïques, on en veut de comiques"[41] and, being partial to his own work (which had appeared anonymously), he added that "Pour un Livre qui ait la vraye forme d'un Roman, on nous met en jeu l'*Histoire Comique de Francion*,"[42] thereby suggesting that the structure of the *roman comique* could also be modelled on that of the epic poem. Sorel thus seems to have assumed (or pretended to assume) that there could be *romans comiques réguliers*, and that the theory of prose epic could be applied to comic material, although no practitioners of the genre had composed their novels along these lines.

[iii]

This is just what Fielding proceeded to do, and in applying the seventeenth-century theory of prose epic to matter proper for comedy he may have borrowed some hints from the writers of *romans comiques*, which these writers had never taken seriously. He thus elaborated his conception of the comic romance; that is, of an epic in prose that is comic instead of serious; he did not intend his new species of writing to be comic epic written in prose, that is, mock-epic or burlesque in prose.[43] The hesitation about the exact meaning of his formula springs from the ambiguity of the phrase "comic epic in prose"; the confusion is all too easy to understand in view of the vogue of the mock-heroic in the eighteenth century, and in view of Fielding's own success in burlesque before he wrote *Joseph Andrews*. Yet, by comparing the serious and the comic prose epic with tragedy and comedy he made his meaning clear since his analysis of the parts of tragedy and comedy follows neo-classical criticism of the drama, which did not theorize about burlesque; and his further reference to Jonson confirms this interpretation. Moreover he pointed out that he had excluded burlesque from the sentiments and characters and only used it sometimes in his diction; *Joseph Andrews*, he stated towards the end of the Preface, is to be distinguished from "the productions of romance writers on the one hand, and burlesque writers on the other".[44] Clearly, he did not intend *Joseph Andrews* to be another *Shamela*; even there he had found the burlesque framework too narrow and had gone beyond his terms of reference to attack Methodism and other targets besides *Pamela*. He may have found it the more necessary to distinguish his own work from that of burlesque writers if he had indeed taken hints from the *romans comiques* of the seventeenth century, which mixed burlesque with satire and comedy and often resorted to the methods of the *antiromans*.[45]

Like Congreve, Fielding compared his work with comedy; but while Congreve had been primarily concerned with the unities, Fielding did not even consider this point. Instead he proceeded to define his proper province as a comic writer, the ridiculous, and the true source of it, affectation, which arises from hypocrisy or vanity. Furetière had claimed that his novel was intended both to instruct and to entertain since "quand nous voyons le vice tourné en ridicule, nous nous en corrigeons, de peur d'estre les objets de la risée publique"; but he stated that he had dealt with *bagatelles* rather than vice, for "[la comédie ou la satyre] laissant aux docteurs et aux magistrats le soin de combattre les crimes, s'arrestent à corriger les indecences et les ridiculitez, s'il est permis d'user de ce mot".[46] Though Fielding is less concerned to stress the corrective purpose of comedy, he similarly insists that vices are the proper objects of our detestation, not a source of the ridiculous.

By outlining his theory of affectation Fielding defined not only his subject but the moral paradigm that constitutes the unity of design of *Joseph Andrews*. Now, unity of design was what the seventeenth-century *roman comique* conspicuously lacked. Yet, this was the prime requirement if a comic romance was to be a comic epic poem in prose. In *Joseph Andrews* the action therefore consists, as Fielding was to say in the Preface to *David Simple*, of "a Series of Actions all tending to produce one great End",[47] though this end is not, as in *Incognita*, the progress of a plot, but the display of affectation. The adventures do fit into a general framework which, as John Butt said, may be paralleled with that of the *Odyssey*, but the guiding principle through these adventures is "the distinction between seeming and being".[48] Whatever hints for his theory Fielding may have borrowed from the *roman comique*, he transformed the genre into a true comic epic in prose, not by observing the niceties of neo-classical epic theory, but by organizing his material round a central theme, comparable to the moral or fable of the epic, and round a central hero, the modern Don Quixote, "at once lovable and ridiculous",[49] whose spirit cannot be broken in spite of his encounters with the shams of the world, and to whom Fielding quite fitly devoted the final paragraph of his Preface.

The borrowings from, or similarities with, the *roman comique* are many: the corrective purpose together with laughter as emotional purgation;[50] the incidental mock-heroics;[51] the author's asides and digressions;[52] the refusal to play the omniscient author;[53] the chapter titles;[54] the inserted stories;[55] the farcical episodes,[56] or other incidents,[57] etc. Yet the similarities only emphasize Fielding's true originality. While the digressions and asides of the *romans comiques* serve to satirize the conventions of fiction, Fielding uses them to guide the response of the reader, to establish the character of the narrator and comment on his method, and thereby to remind the reader that this is art, not reality, a formal construct, not a mere rendering of life. In the *romans comiques* the incidental mock-heroics are part of the burlesque tradition incorporated into it, but they serve no other purpose than satire of a genre; in Fielding they parody one of the many forms of affectation and serve as "wholesome physic for the mind".[58] Fielding's originality in using older devices appears best in his choice of interpolated stories. In the *romans comiques* these are mere hors d'oeuvre; in *Joseph Andrews* they are thematically linked with the main design: "The Unfortunate Jilt is a story of pretence to affection, and the story of Mr. Wilson is a tale of the pretences practised in London life",[59] while the story of Leonard and Paul anticipates the comic confusions of the night, in which the innocent Adams, like Paul, gets all the blame for the awkward situation into which his generous heart has landed him.

The artist Fielding may have known from the start how to shape his materials into such a pattern, but his study of neo-classical criticism must have sharpened his sense of the nature of epic structure. He did take his epic theory seriously and it proved useful both in *Jospeh Andrews* and in *Tom Jones*. Congreve's imitation of dramatic writing added "another beauty" to the form of his story, and *Incognita* is an artful lie contrived to give delight. Fielding's theory of comic prose epic is the foundation of his formal realism, and *Joseph Andrews* is a "just imitation of nature" which produces "a more rational and useful pleasure".[60] Congreve's characters wear masks or other men's clothes as at a masquerade; Fielding's only wear the masks of their vanities and hypocrisies, or of their simplicity, as men do in life.

NOTES

1 The prefaces to romances, such as Roger Boyle's, George Mackenzie's, and Robert Boyle's, "occupy a place in the long argument about Romance somewhat apart from the development which preceded the emergence of the novel proper in eighteenth-century England". Charles Davies, *Prefaces to Four Seventeenth-Century Romances*, Augustan Reprint Society, No. 42 (1953), Introduction, p. i. It should be noted, however, that these prefaces often echo those of French romance writers, which elaborated some aspects of the theory of prose fiction.

2 He is known to have possessed a copy of the original (1657) as well as of the English translation, *The Whole Art of the Stage* (1684). See John C. Hodges, *The Library of William Congreve* (New York, 1955), p. 83.

3 "Les Romans qui doivent estre formez sur l'exemple des Poëmes Epiques, et qu'aucuns nomment des *Epopées en prose*, quand ils sont faits par un homme intelligent et bien reglé, ne souffrent point un plus grand espace de temps [que le cours d'une année]." *La Pratique du Théâtre* (Paris, 1669), p. 152 (Book II, ch. vii).

4 Congreve, *"Incognita and The Way of the World"*, ed. A. Norman Jeffares, Arnold's English Texts (London, 1966), Preface, p. 33. References to *Incognita* are to this edition.

5 *Ibid.*, p. 34.

6 *Ibid.*

7 Maynard Mack, *"Joseph Andrews and Pamela"* in *Fielding: A Collection of Critical Essays*, ed. Ronald Paulson (New York, 1962), p. 55.

8 Congreve owned a copy of Thomas Corneille's *Poëmes Dramatiques*, 1661, 2 vols. See J. C. Hodges, *The Library of William Congreve*, No. 84; in *William Congreve, The Man* (New York, 1941), Hodges says that the names of the characters may derive from Dryden's *Assignation*.

9 *Incognita*, Preface, p. 34.

10 *Incognita*, Introduction, p. 16.

11 *Incognita*, p. 60.

12 *Ibid.*, Preface, p. 32.

13 Charles Sorel, *La Bibliothèque françoise* (Paris, 1667), pp. 174, 175.

14 "On commençoit aussi de connoistre ce que c'estoit des choses vray-semblables, par de petites Narrations dont la mode vint, qui s'appeloient des *Nouvelles*. On les pouvait comparer aux Histoires veritables de quelques accidens particuliers des Hommes. Nous avions déja veu les *Nouvelles de Boccace*, et celles de la *Reine de Navarre* [. . .]. Nous avions veu encore les *Histoires Tragiques de Bandel*, qu'on avoit traduites d'Italien, qui estoient autant de Nouvelles; mais les Espagnols nous en donnerent de plus naturelles et de plus circonstanciees, qui furent les Nouvelles de *Miguel de Cervantes*, remplies de naivetez et d'agremens." *Ibid.*, p. 178.

15 Preface to *Ibrahim* (1674), in *Prefaces to Fiction*, ed. Benjamin Boyce, Augustan Reprint Society, No. 32 (1952), pp. 4, 5, which is also the source of the following three quotations.

16 See Boileau's *Dialogue des Héros de Roman*, probably first composed in 1665, in *Dialogues, Réflexions critiques, Oeuvres diverses*, ed. Ch.-H. Boudhors, Les Textes Français (Paris, 1942).

17 Quoted in Antoine Adam, *Histoire de la Littérature française au XVIIᵉ siècle* (Paris, 1948-1956). IV.174. As Adam says, "[la nouvelle] était, par tradition, plus vraie que le roman". *Ibid.*

18 His library contained several collections of *nouvelles*, most of which were published after *Incognita*. See J. C. Hodges, *The Library of William Congreve*, *passim*.

19 He owned two copies of it (1655 and 1695) as well as Scarron's *Nouvelles Oeuvres tragi-comiques* (1665) and Tom Browne's translation, *Scarron's Comical Works* (1712). *Ibid.* For the conversation on *romans* and *nouvelles* see *Le Romant Comique* in *Romanciers du XVIIᵉ siècle*, Textes présentés et annotés par Antoine Adam (Paris, 1958), p. 645 (Part I, ch. xxi). It may be no accident that another of Congreve's statements in his Preface ("Since there is no possibility of giving that life to the Writing or Repetition of a Story which it has in the Action", *op. cit.*, p. 33) echoes another remark in the same chapter: "que l'on prenoit plus de plaisir à voir representer les choses qu'à ouyr des recits".(*op. cit.*, p. 645).

20 See E. S. de Beer, "Congreve's *Incognita*: The Sources of its Setting, with a Note on Wilson's *Belphegor*", *RES*, VIII (1932), 74-7.

21 *Incognita*, Preface, p. 34.

31

22   Homer Goldberg, "Comic Prose Epic or Comic Romance: The Argument of the Preface to *Joseph Andrews*", *PQ*, XLIII (1965), 193.

23   *The Early Masters of English Fiction* (Kansas, 1956), p. 101.

24   *The Rise of the Novel* (London, 1957), pp. 249-51.

25   See above, n. 22.

26   "Joseph Andrews" *and* "Shamela", ed. Martin C. Battestin (London, 1965), Author's Preface, pp. 7, 12. All references to *Joseph Andrews* are to this edition.

27   "Henry Fielding and the Writers of Heroic Romance", *PMLA*, LXII (1947), 984.

28   See above, n. 3.

29   *Traité du Poëme Epique* (La Haye, 1714), p. 22 (Ch. V: Du Poëme). The *Traité* (Paris, 1675), published in English (London, 1695).

30   *Lettre de Monsieur Huet à Monsieur de Segrais. De l'Origine des Romans*, prefixed to *Zayde, Histoire Espagnole*, par Monsieur de Segrais (i.e. published under Segrais's name, but the work of Mme de La Fayette), 1670. Quotation from the Amsterdam ed. (1715), p. lii. Published in English (London, 1672).

31   *Romanciers du XVIIe siècle*, *op. cit.*, p. 903.

32   *Joseph Andrews*, p. 159. Cf. Furetière: "Toute la grace que je te demande, c'est qu'après t'avoir bien adverty qu'il n'y a rien que de fabuleux dans ce livre, tu n'ailles point rechercher vainement quelle est la personne dont tu croiras reconnoistre le portrait ou l'histoire, pour l'appliquer à Monsieur un tel ou à Mademoiselle une telle, sous prétexte que tu y trouveras un nom approchant ou quelque caractere semblable. Je sçais bien que le premier soin que tu auras en lisant ce roman, ce sera d'en chercher la clef; mais elle ne te servira de rien, car la serrure est mêlée. Si tu crois voir le portrait de l'un, tu trouveras les adventures de l'autre: il n'y a point de peintre qui, en faisant un tableau avec le seul secours de son imagination, n'y fasse des visages qui auront de l'air de quelqu'un que nous connoissons, quoy qu'il n'ait eu dessein que le peindre des héros fabuleux. Ainsi, quand tu apercevrois dans ces personnages dépeints quelques caracteres de quelqu'un de ta connoissance, ne fay point un jugement temeraire pour dire que ce soit luy; prends plutost garde que, comme il y a ici les portraits de plusieurs sortes de sots, tu n'y rencontres le

tien: car il n'y a presque personne qui ait le privilege d'en estre exempt, et qui n'y puisse remarquer quelque trait de son visage, moralement parlant". *Op. cit.*, pp. 901-2. Like Fielding Furetière also compares the effect produced by the comic writer with that produced by the comic painter. His remarks imply a sense, rare enough at the time, of the difference between our response to nature and to an imitation of nature; Fielding does not mention this problem at all. Furetière's novel first appeared in English as *Scarron's City Romance* (1671), though it was not included in Tom Browne's translation of Scarron's works.

33 "As in the case of other branches of literary theory in the Augustan period, the original expression of the organized doctrine [of prose fiction] was French." See Boyce (above, n. 15), Introduction, p. i.

34 This view was still held in the nineteenth century. See the Introduction by A. Mazure to an 1881 school edition of *Télémaque*.

35 *The Adventures of Telemachus, The Son of Ulysses, by the Archbishop of Cambray: In French and English* ... (London, 1742), I, xxiii, xxvi. The Discourse was prefixed to the translation of *Télémaque*; the 1742 ed. is a revised translation; the discourse was also revised. Ramsay had been secretary to Fénelon. He seems to have been the only British critic at the time to maintain that an epic could be written in prose; the question for English critics was rather whether blank verse was as fit a medium as rhymed verse for a heroic poem.

36 *Op. cit.*, p. 250.

37 *Dialogue des Héros de Roman*. Discours sur le Dialogue suivant, *op. cit.*, p. 10. The *Dialogue* ends with these words of Pluto's: "Mais je suis si fatigué des sottises que m'ont dites tous ces impertinents usurpateurs de leurs noms, que vous trouverés bon qu'avant tout j'aille faire un somme" (p. 54). See also [Charles Sorel]: *De la Connoissance des Bons Livres* (1671), ch. ii: "Censure des Romans", particularly the section on: "Qu'il n'y a ny satisfaction ny profit à lire les Romans" (Amsterdam, 1672 ed.), pp. 137-47.

38 *Op. cit.*, p. 188. Cf. Fielding's remark: "And perhaps there is one reason why a comic writer should of all others be the least excused for deviating from nature, since it may not be always so easy for a serious poet to meet with the great and the admirable; but life everywhere furnishes an accurate observer with the ridiculous". Preface, p. 8.

39 See the opening paragraph of *Histoire Comique de Francion* in the 1633 edition, where Sorel says: "Or c'etoit ainsi que faisoient les anciens Autheurs dedans leurs Comedies, qui instruisoient le peuple en lui donnant de la recreation. Cet Ouvrage cy les imite en toutes choses, mais il y a cela de plus que l'on y voit les actions mises par ecrit, au lieu que dans les Comedies il n'y a que les paroles, a cause que les Acteurs representoient tout sur le Theatre. Puisque l'on a fait cecy principalement pour la lecture, il a fallu descrire tous les accidens, et au lieu d'une simple Comedie, il s'en est fait une Histoire Comique que vous allez maintenant voir". *Romanciers du XVIIe siècle, op. cit.*, p. 1270.

40 At the beginning of Book II, Furetière warned his readers: "Si vous vous attendez, lecteur, que ce livre soit la suite du premier, et qu'il y ait une connexité necessaire entr'eux, vous estes pris pour duppe. Détrompez-vous de bonne heure, et sçachez que cet enchainement d'intrigues les uns avec les autres est bien seant à ces poëmes héroïques et fabuleux oú l'on peut tailler et rogner à sa fantaisie. Il est aisé de les farcir d'épisodes, et de les coudre ensemble avec du fil de roman, suivant le caprice ou le genie de celuy qui les invente. Mais il n'en est pas de mesme de ce tres-veritable et tres-sincere recit, auquel je ne donne que la forme, sans alterer aucunement la matiere. Ce sont de petites histoires et adventures arrivées en divers quartiers de la ville, qui n'ont rien de commun ensemble, et que je tasche de rapprocher les unes des autres autant qu'il m'est possible. Pour le soin de la liaison, je le laisse à celuy qui reliera le livre. Prenez donc cela pour des historiettes separées, si bon vous semble, et ne demandez point que j'observe ny l'unité des temps ny des lieux, ny que je fasse voir un heros dominant dans toute la piece". *Romanciers du XVIIe siècle, op. cit.*, p. 1025.

41 *Op. cit.*, pp. 191, 194.

42 *Ibid.*

43 The opposite view is implied in John Butt's remark that "the novelty of [Fielding's] claim lay not so much in the notion of a prose epic, nor even of a comic epic *poem* [. . .] but in the conflation of the two". (My italics.) *Fielding*, Writers and Their Work: No. 57 (London, 1954), p. 8.

44 Preface, p. 12.

45 One section of Sorel's chapter on *romans* in *La Bibliothèque françoise* deals with "Des Romans Comiques ou Satyriques, ou des Romans burlesques"; he says there: "Nous avons encore à

considérer des Romans qui soient Satyriques et Comiques en
effet, mais qui soient aussi Burlesques" (*op. cit.*, p. 198); he then
mentions (scathingly) Scarron's *Romant comique.*

46 Advertissement du Libraire, *op. cit.*, p. 900.

47 *The Adventures of David Simple. Containing an Account of his
Travels through the Cities of London and Westminster, in search of a
real Friend,* by a Lady (2d ed. London, 1744), I.ix.

48 *Op. cit.*, pp. 16, 17.

49 Mark Spilka: "Comic Resolution in Fielding's *Joseph Andrews*"
in Paulson (above, n. 6), p. 61.

50 See *Histoire Comique de Francion,* Advertissement d'importance
aux lecteurs, *op. cit.*, p. 61.

51 For instance, in the opening of the *Romant Comique* (*op. cit.*, p.
531) or of the *Roman bourgeois* (*op. cit.*, p. 903).

52 E.g., in the *Romant comique, op. cit.*, pp. 552, 553.

53 E.g., *ibid.*, pp. 553, 780; *Histoire Comique de Francion, ibid.*,
p. 395.

54 E.g., in the *Romant Comique, ibid.*, pp. 540, 638, 642.

55 In the *Romant Comique,* Part I, chs. ix, xxii; Part II, chs. xiv, xix.

56 E.g., the "Combat de Nuict" in the *Romant Comique,* Part I,
ch. xii.

57 E.g., the nuns turning away when Ragotin appears naked,
Romant Comique, Part II, ch. xvi.

58 Preface, p. 9.

59 John Butt, *op. cit.*, p. 18.

60 Preface, pp. 8, 9.

JAMES SUTHERLAND

The Relation of Defoe's Fiction
to his Non-Fictional Writings

Defoe is not unique in having taken to writing fiction when he had almost reached his sixties: William de Morgan was even older when he wrote *Joseph Vance* and the other novels that succeeded it. Yet such a development so late in life is certainly unusual; and one can only suppose that the interest in human behaviour and circumstances which led to the writing of fiction was always there, but that other activities claimed the writer's attention and kept his creative gifts in suspense. In De Morgan's case those gifts were fully satisfied by the demands of a flourishing pottery business in which he was actively engaged for over thirty years. The case of Defoe is not strictly comparable (even if we remember the odd parallel of his running a brick and tile factory at Tilbury); for although he had been trading actively, he had also been writing on a wide variety of topics for more than thirty years before he published *Robinson Crusoe*. When he took leave of the readers of *The Review* in his final number (11 June, 1713), he treated them to a discourse on "the modish, tho' abominable Vice of MODERN WHORING":

> And what Whore are you for, said one that stood at my Elbow when I wrote this? – Why, I'll tell you my Case in a few words; Perhaps this Paper has been *my Whore*, at least formerly, when it pleased you; if so, then like the *Israelites*, that put away their strange Wives, I have resolved to part with her, and so I escape the lash of my own Satyr. Writing upon Trade was the Whore I really doated upon.

37

Writing on trade may indeed have been his permanant whore, but he was almost equally susceptible to the seductive charms of politics, religion, military affairs, and much else. One obvious result of all this varied literary composition was that when he turned to fiction in 1719 he was already a trained writer whose "mind and hand went together", and who uttered whatever he had to say with an easiness and readiness that have rarely been equalled in English prose.

It may still be thought odd that he had reached his sixtieth year before his first work of fiction appeared. Yet this is true only in a limited sense. A strong element of fiction is present in many of his earlier writings, and it gives to them much of their effectiveness and their lasting appeal. We may pass over *The Consolidator: Or, Memoirs of Sundry Transactions From The World in the Moon* (1705); for although this satirical piece is fiction of a sort, and has some ingenious allegorical effects, it represents in Defoe's writing something of a dead end. More important for our present purpose are those pieces in which he makes use of a persona. Like many of his contemporaries he often employed some form of indirect utterance when he engaged in the risky business of political and religious controversy. His earliest extant pamphlet, which need not detain us here, carried the title, *A Letter to a Dissenter from his Friend at the Hague, Concerning the Papal Laws and Test . . .* (1688). The fiction of "his Friend at the Hague" was no more than a conventional disguise designed to protect the real author, although it may also be said to have given the arguments used the judicious impartiality of an outsider looking on at the English scene in 1688. The first occasion on which Defoe's use of a persona was genuinely integrated with the argument and affected the presentation of it occurs in *The Poor Man's Plea* of 1698. The plea of the Poor Man is made "in relation to all the proclamations, declarations, Acts of Parliament, etc., which have been, or shall be made, or published, for a Reformation of Manners, and suppressing immorality in the nation"; and his argument is that one law for the rich and another for the poor will never lead to any effective reform of national vices. The Poor Man is an honest, steady sort of person; and in spite of what he has to say about some of the clergy and magistrates, he writes more in sorrow than in anger, knowing his place and not

offering to take too great liberties with his betters. Since Defoe
is on this occasion addressing himself primarily to "gentlemen
and others", he does not risk alienating the well-to-do or educated reader by allowing his Poor Man to write in an illiterate
fashion, or to use low and vulgar colloquialisms. Yet he does
succeed, at least intermittently, in suggesting the natural, un-
inhibited speech of the English middle class:

> The Parson preaches a thundering Sermon against Drunkenness,
> and the Justice of the Peace sets my poor Neighbour in the Stocks,
> and I am like to be much the better for either, when I know perhaps
> that this same Parson, and this same Justice, were both Drunk
> together the Night before.[1]

Here the "thundering" sermon and the ironical "I am like to
be much the better for either" have the authentic sound of
middle-class conversation. Again, the Poor Man makes his
points with some admirably homely illustrations, calculated to
come within the range of the common man's experience. In
support of the argument that the poor man's vices affect only
himself, whereas those of a rich man affect a whole neighbour-
hood, he gives us this:

> If my own Watch goes false, it deceives me and none else; but if the
> Town Clock goes false, it deceives the whole Parish.[2]

If it is objected that this is really Defoe's own personal style,
the answer cannot be a flat denial, for it is undoubtedly *one* of
the styles of writing natural to Defoe – in *The Review*, for
instance, but also elsewhere in some of his pamphlets. Yet it is
quite a different style from that of *Giving Alms no Charity*, a
pamphlet addressed to "the Parliament of England" and
accordingly written in a more elevated manner, and different
again from that of *The Shortest Way with the Dissenters*. In *The
Poor Man's Plea* Defoe may sometimes have forgotten the
persona he has assumed, but for the most part the forthright
and earnest voice we hear is that of the humble citizen who is
his spokesman.

What he had done effectively enough in this piece he went
on to do with disastrous success in *The Shortest Way with the
Dissenters*. Here the persona is a High Church clergyman of

immoderate views, prepared to go to almost any length to stamp out nonconformity. When a satirist has to deal with intolerance so extreme as to be hardly credible, the simplest way to expose it is to let it speak with its own voice. This is a sort of jiu-jitsu method by which the satirical victim is thrown by his own weight and impetuosity. Defoe caught the imperious tone of the High Church fanatics so successfully that many of them welcomed *The Shortest Way* as a powerful and unambiguous statement of their views, and, on the other side, many of the Dissenters believed that the author was really and truly calling for them to be "hang'd, banish'd, or destroy'd, and that the Gallows and the Gallies should be the Penalty of going to a Conventicle . . ."[3] To the Dissenters Defoe might well have cried, "I am Cinna the poet! I am Cinna the poet!" What, in fact, he did say, some time after the event, was a good deal more cutting:

> All the Fault I can find in my self as to these People is, that when I had drawn the Picture, I did not, like the Dutch Man, with his Man and Bear, write under them, *This is the Man*, and *This is the Bear*, lest the People should mistake me.[4]

Defoe, in fact, had identified himself so absolutely with his persona that *The Shortest Way* was almost indistinguishable from the Highflyer outburst it purported to be. If that compels us to have some reservations about his pamphlet as a piece of normal satire, it only serves to underline his ability to assume an imaginary personality and to render it convincing by the verisimilitude of the expression.

Over the years Defoe put forth his ideas under various disguises. He was at different times a Quaker, a stockjobber, a Scots gentleman, an "honest Tory", and so on. So little had he learnt from the traumatic experience of *The Shortest Way* that towards the end of Queen Anne's reign he was again in serious trouble for writing three pamphlets on the succession. Two of these, with the provocative titles of *Reasons against the Succession of the House of Hanover*, and the still more inflammatory *And What if the Pretender should Come? Or, Some Considerations of the Advantages and Real Consequences of the Pretender's Possessing the Crown of Great Britain*, were written by an apparent Jacobite who was in favour of restoring the Old Pretender to the throne of his father when Queen Anne should die. But the "reasons" and the "consequences" were so patently, and at times heavily, ironical that any Jacobite who really thought those were good reasons or desirable consequences must have been out of his mind. Still, the persona was made sufficiently plausible to effect at least a temporary deception, and to enable Defoe's Whig enemies to procure his arrest and imprisonment.

Before considering the effect on Defoe's fiction of this ingrained tendency to make-believe I shall mention another marked feature of his non-fictional writing that is relevant here: on a surprising number of occasions (and sometimes in the most unlikely contexts) he has a way of slipping into a passage of dialogue. One such passage occurs in *The Poor Man's Plea*, where, in stressing the point that the gentry not only tolerate heavy drinking, but even make it their way of "expressing their Joy for any publick Blessing", he suddenly gives us an illustration:

> *Jack*, said a Gentleman of very high Quality, when after the Debate in the House of Lords, King William was voted into the Vacant Throne; *Jack* (says he) *God damn ye, Jack, go home to your Lady, and tell her we have got a Protestant King and Queen, and go make a Bonfire as big as a House, and bid the Butler make ye all Drunk, ye Dog.*[5]

From the first Defoe had a quick ear for the varied speech of his fellow countrymen. In the pages of *The Review* there are some spirited passages of dialect conversation, as in the account of a country election (8 June 1708), or in the sarcastic comments of the mercer, the milliner, the draper, and the barber's boy while the knight and the peer, who have failed to pay the tradesmen for the clothes and wigs they are wearing, go past their shops (*Rev.* 17 Jan. 1706), or in the discussion between two west-country rustics (*Rev.* 12 April 1712) about the peace negotiations "at a great vurdern place yonder, over the zee":

> John. What, 'tis'n Youtrich, is it, William?
> Will. . . . 'tis zome zuch Name, I do think; it is *You-trik* or *We-Trik*, or zomething like that, but shure I doon't remember, vor I doon't use those Outlandish Words much.

When, in 1715, Defoe brought out the first part of *The Family*

41

Instructor he was exploiting the resources of dialogue much more fully. This highly popular work was, in effect, a series of didactic domestic plays, in which groups of middle-class characters, young, adolescent, and middle-aged, converse in language appropriate to their age, sex, and station. Dialogue enters even into the *Tour thro' the Whole Island of Great Britain* and, much more extensively, into *The Complete English Tradesman* (1725). Those passages of lively and idiomatic dialogue, which to the modern reader of *The Complete English Tradesman* are perhaps the most interesting parts of the book, were so little to the liking of the editors of the 1738 revision that they lopped most of them out, on the ground of their supposed tediousness, and because they were "on too particular a case to be generally useful". If we think of that work solely as a practical handbook, we may have to agree with the editor's decision; but by 1725, with most of his works of fiction now behind him, Defoe had become so used to the particular case that whenever an opening occurred he slid naturally into a treatment of his topic in terms of men and women, engaged here in the very human occupation of buying and selling.

If we now turn to Defoe's fiction, we find him invariably throwing his stories into the form of autobiography, in which the chief character is simply a more sustained and more fully developed persona than those he had made use of from time to time in his earlier non-fictional writing. Although critics vary in the extent to which they think they can see Defoe himself in *Robinson Crusoe* or *Moll Flanders*, Crusoe and Moll are not Daniel Defoe, but characters he has imagined, and in whose shoes he has tried (successfully for the most part) to put himself. It has been objected by Ian Watt that in *Robinson Crusoe* Defoe disregarded "the actual psychological effects of solitude", and that Crusoe's behaviour is very unlike that of those actual castaways whose stories were almost certainly known to Defoe. "What actually happened to the castaways", Professor Watt points out, "was at best uninspiring. At worst, harassed by fear and dogged by ecological degradation, they sank more and more to the level of animals, lost the use of speech, went mad, or died of inanition".[6] To this it might be answered that the ordinary reader of *Robinson Crusoe*, with no critical axe to grind, is so far from finding Crusoe's behaviour unconvincing that the whole desert-island sequence of events leaves a sharp impression on the mind of historical actuality. Much, indeed, is made by Defoe of the effect of solitude; Crusoe's fear of the savages is fully realized; and the frustrations of a solitary man trying to do work that requires many hands are expressed again and again: everything is there, except that deterioration of mind and character that Professor Watt sees as inevitable in the circumstances. What Defoe himself would have done if he had ever been cast away on a desert island it is no doubt impossible to say; but it is a fair guess that he would have behaved very much like Crusoe. This is another "particular case", but prose fiction deals in particular cases. At all events, there seems every reason to believe that in *Robinson Crusoe* (*a*) Defoe was putting himself in the place of someone else, and (*b*) the someone else behaved in the sort of way that Defoe himself would have behaved (or believed he would behave) in the same circumstances, and (*c*) this persona was therefore some sort of unconscious adjustment between an objectively realized character and Daniel Defoe's idea of Defoe. The same may be said again of the Saddler in *A Journal of the Plague Year*. Yet when this substitution process becomes more difficult, either because the personality of the imagined narrator is very different from his own (as with Moll Flanders and Colonel Jack), or even repellent (as with Roxana), he can still create a credible character.

A shipwrecked tobacco-planter, the daughter of a convicted thief who becomes a thief herself, a London saddler, a boy stolen from his family by gipsies who turns pirate, another boy boarded out as an infant with a foster mother and growing up as a thief, a French refugee who marries an eminent London brewer and becomes "the fortunate mistress": all these narrate their lives to us in Defoe's fiction. Does he make any attempt to individualize his different heroes and heroines by the way in which they tell their story? It must be admitted that there is a strong resemblance between the colloquial prose of each and every one of them, and that they all write in a reasonably educated style, not unlike one of the more habitual styles of Defoe himself.

Well, their Warrant being executed, I came readily with them.

The Officer, who presently saw himself imposed upon, and that there was not the least occasion of Violence, admitted me very frankly, being very much Indisposed, to ride on Horse-back, while they came all after on Foot, sometimes a quarter of a Mile behind; nothing had been easier than for me to have rid away from them all, if I had thought fit; but I had not Guilt enough to make me think of an Escape. The next Project was, that all this was of a Saturday, that they might Triumph over me, and keep me in their Custody two Nights in suspence, without any Release. On the Monday I tendred Bail; the scandalous Endeavours a Set of Men made use of to fright and deter Friends that were willing to Bail me, will deserve a particular Narration, and shall not want it.

Is this Moll Flanders telling us about how she was arrested for picking a pocket or stealing a parcel of lace? It could well be just that; but in fact it is Defoe himself telling the readers of *The Review* (18 April 1713) about his own arrest for writing the three ironical pamphlets already mentioned. Defoe wrote at speed, and he wrote for a public that would scarcely have appreciated a long story told in the style of, say, an eighteenth-century Augie March. In any case, his various heroes and heroines had either had a normal middle-class education or were self-educated. Crusoe had not been "bred to any trade", but was intended by his father for the law; Moll Flanders grew up in the family of the Mayor of Colchester, and had 'all the advantages for [her] education that could be imagined",[7] learning to write, to dance, to speak French, and so on; Colonel Jack was "born a gentleman"[8] and made considerable efforts when he grew up to acquire an education suited to what would have been his class if he had not been an illegitimate child farmed out on a foster parent.

Yet when he can legitimately introduce a more individualized speech idiom Defoe sometimes avails himself of the opportunity. When Moll, lying ill upstairs, hears the Colchester family talking about her,[9] he gives us the sort of authentic middle-class dialogue, nicely varied for each member of the family, that he had already written for *The Family Instructor*. A little earlier Moll has recorded an equally natural conversation between herself, aged eight, and her old nurse;[10] and in *Colonel Jack* there is again a successful attempt to reproduce the language of childhood and to enter into the mind of a child. The language of Will the Quaker in *Captain Singleton* is particularized with the appropriate "thou's" and "thee's" and the vocative "Friend". The conversation of Xury and Friday in *Robinson Crusoe* and of Mouchat in *Colonel Jack* indicates at least a rather crude attempt on Defoe's part to imitate the sort of pidgin English he may have heard spoken by negro slaves in London. (It is worth remembering that in *The Royal Slave* Mrs. Behn's Oronooko and Imoinda speak nothing but standard English.) What is perhaps odd is that Defoe makes no use in his fiction of the various English dialects with which he had shown himself to be familiar in the pages of *The Review*, nor, when Colonel Jack is in Scotland, does Defoe make any attempt to reproduce the speech of the local inhabitants, although, again, he must have known it well.

As early as 1 November 1718, a writer in *The Weekly Journal; Or, British Gazetteer* anticipated a good deal of later criticism of Defoe by referring superciliously to "the little art he is truly master of, of forging a story, and imposing it on the world for truth". For Leslie Stephen and other nineteenth-century critics this process began with *A True Relation of the Apparition of one Mrs. Veal to one Mrs. Bargrave* (1706), which was generally regarded as perhaps the earliest example of "the fictions which he succeeded in palming off for truths".[11] But the investigations of twentieth-century scholars have shown that there are very few facts in this celebrated ghost story that cannot be authenticated. Whatever Mrs. Bargrave saw, or thought she saw, when she opened the front door of her house at noon on 8 September 1705, she certainly existed; and so (until 7 September) did her friend Mrs. Veal. Mrs. Bargrave told her story to various people, and by 13 September, when the first extant report of it was written down in a letter from one E.B. of Canterbury to an unknown correspondent, it was all over the town. Other surviving letters from Canterbury, dated 9 October and 15 November, add a few facts and omit others; and by 24 December the story was in print, when *The Loyal Post* gave an account of the whole strange incident, based on "Several Letters . . . from Persons of Good Credit . . . , besides Relations we have by Word of Mouth".[12]

So fully authenticated has Mrs. Bargrave's story now become, that one hesitates to make claims for Defoe's version that may only be shown to be unjustified by the discovery of still more contemporary evidence. But the *True Relation* differs from all earlier accounts by being more circumstantial, by suppressing any evidence that would tend to discredit Mrs. Bargrave's reliability as a witness (Defoe is in fact at some pains to establish it), and by giving almost all the rather dreary conversation between the two women in *oratio recta*. *The Loyal Post* had observed that "there are abundance of Particulars of the two hour Discourse which Mr. Bargrave relates too tedious to be here inserted".[13] But to the author of the *True Relations* tediousness (or, at any rate, detailed particularization) was a guarantee of truth; and in his account of their conversation the two ladies ramble on more or less inconsequentially (but of course all the more naturally for that reason), and in its very flatness their talk seems to be utterly authentic. The narrator, too, introduces fresh matter with an "I should have told you before", and towards the end of his narrative he jumps without any logical sequence from one afterthought to another. Here, as elsewhere with Defoe, it is hard to tell whether we have to deal with the artlessness of a conscious artist, or whether the carelessness and lack of a consistently sequential narrative are due to nothing more than Defoe's haste. But on at least two occasions – both turning on the all-important fact that Mrs. Veal is not there *in the flesh* – we seem to see the hand of Defoe giving an added touch of vividness. The three earliest accounts all mention the fact that when Mrs. Bargrave opened her front door and saw her old friend standing there she offered to kiss ("salute") her. Mrs. Veal's way of evading the kiss is expressed in the three accounts as follows:

(1) But Mrs. V. clapp'd her down in a Chair, by wch she concluded her not willing, & so forbore.

(2) ... and went to salute her, but she rushed by her, and sat herself down in a great armed Chair, and fell into discourse of severall things y^t had hapned w^n they lived together at Dover.

(3) ... asked her to Come in and offerd to salute her upon which she sat herself down in a Chair Saying she was very weary.[14]

All three make the point that Mrs. Bargrave had come very near to kissing a ghost, but Defoe obviously felt that this was such a dramatic moment that it deserved to be lingered over and left uncertain till the last possible moment. His account therefore varies significantly from the others:

> Madam, says Mrs. Bargrave, I am surprized to see you, you have been so long a stranger, but told her, she was glad to see her and offer'd to Salute her, which Mrs. Veal complyed with, till their Lips almost touched, and then Mrs. Veal drew her hand cross her own Eyes, and said, *I am not very well*, and so waved it.[15]

The second occasion concerns Mrs. Bargrave's offer of a cup of tea to Mrs. Veal. The first three versions are more or less together on this episode, although the third introduces some new material:

> (1) And in their discourse Mrs. B. ask'd her to drink some Chocolate, & whether She would Eat something? Mrs. V. said if She talk'd of eating or drinking She would be gone.

> (2) Mrs. B. askt Mrs. Veal if she would drink any Coffee or Tea, she told her y^t if she talkt of eating or drinking she would be gone.

> (3) Mrs. B. then asked Mrs. V. if she would Drink any tea to which she Replied now [qy. noe(?)] but if I Would you have no fire to make it to which she replied that she wold sone have her fire nay said Mrs. Veal if you talk of drinking I am gon.[16]

Defoe's treatment of the incident comes nearest to the last of those three statements, but again there is a significant difference:

> Mrs. Bargrave asked her, whether she would not drink some Tea. Says Mrs. Veal, *I do not care if I do: But I'le Warrant this Mad Fellow* (meaning Mrs. Bargrave's Husband) *has broke all your Trinckets.* But, says Mrs. Bargrave, *I'le get something to Drink in for all that*; but Mrs. Veal wav'd it, and said, *it is no matter, let it alone*, and so it passed.[17]

Mrs. Veal's "I do not care if I do" is of course affirmative; its modern equivalent, "I don't mind if I do", is the standard reply in an English pub to the offer of a drink. Defoe's Mrs. Bargrave has again been brought to the verge of discovering that her apparently material visitor is in fact immaterial (ghosts don't drink tea), and again the discovery is avoided at the last moment because Mrs. Veal changed her mind and "wav'd it". One or two other small touches of the same kind might be noted; but for the most part Defoe seems bent on establishing the absolute truth of the story by dwelling on trivialities and recording conversations verbatim, with all their irrelevant and insignificant detail. It is (let us face it) a wasteful method of convincing a reader, but it works; and it was the method that Defoe was to employ again and again in his works of fiction. For the purpose to which he put it, the insignificant becomes significant, and the irrelevant takes on relevance because it is helping to authenticate the fictitious and make it pass for truth. It would be easy to exaggerate the influence of the *True Relation* on the development of Defoe's fiction; it was only another small piece knocked off in the course of a phenomenally busy life. Yet, as Defoe saw it, the problem presented by Mrs. Bargrave and her ghostly visitor and that presented by Robinson Crusoe on his desert island must have seemed much the same: it was the problem of how to give complete credibility to the basically incredible; how to succeed in "imposing it on the world for truth".

Defoe is a good deal more interested in human character and human behaviour than he is usually credited with being, and in short episodes he has often the power to make us enter into a situation and share the feelings of his characters. But what ultimately interests him is the individual human being coping with circumstances, adjusting himself to changes of environment or fortune, striving in one fashion or another to make a living – *gagner sa vie*. His preoccupation with the problems of earning a living is not an indication of some sordid economic bias in his mind; it is the expression of a serious concern with something which he believed to be fundamental, and which gives shape and significance to most human lives. If his characters are often criminal types, they only serve the better to let him explore the problem which seems to have interested him above all others – that of *necessity*; the will to survive that comes into collision with economic facts, that natural morality which is often in conflict with law and order. As he once put it, in one of his many pronouncements on necessity, "Men rob for Bread, Women whore for Bread: Necessity is the parent of Crime".[18] With such considerations uppermost in his mind, the autobiographical form was the one best suited to his purpose. "Who would read a novel if we were permitted to write biography – all out?"[19] The man who asked that question was not Defoe, but H. G. Wells: the two writers have much in common. Both wrote voluminously, both were teeming with new ideas, both had interests that overflowed the bounds of the conventional novel, and both wrote rapidly and at times carelessly. "Indisputably the writing is scamped in places", Wells admitted in a discussion of his novel *Marriage*. "It could have been just as light and much better done. But that would have taken more time than I could afford . . . The fastidious critic might object, but the general reader to whom I addressed myself cared no more for finish and fundamental veracity about the secondary things of behaviour than I".[20] These words, *mutatis mutandis*, might have come from the pen of Defoe. Again, when Wells says that what he was insisting upon in his novels was "the importance of individuality and individual adjustment to life",[21] he might be Defoe writing of *Robinson Crusoe* or *Moll Flanders*. When, finally, he tells us: "I was disposed to regard a novel as about as much an art form as a market place or a boulevard. It had not even necessarily to get anywhere. You went by it on your various occasions",[22] we recognize a conception of the novel that may not at present be fashionable, but that runs through much of English fiction from the time of Defoe to the present day. In such fiction what we read, and enjoy, is as much the author as the work. Those who wish to sneer at H. G. Wells may also sneer at Defoe. But should they?

NOTES

1 *A True Collection of the Writings of the Author of the True Born English-man* (2d ed., London, 1705), p. 300.

2 *Ibid.*, p. 293.

3 *A Second Volume of the Writings of the Author of the True-Born Englishman* (London, 1705), p. 27.

4 *Ibid.*, p. 28.

5 *A True Collection*, p. 292.

6 Ian Watt, *The Rise of the Novel* (London, 1957), pp. 87, 88.

7 *Moll Flanders* (Riverside ed., Boston, 1959), ed. James Sutherland, p. 18. As "editor", Defoe tells his readers that "the original of this story is put into new words, and the stile of the famous lady we here speak of is a little alter'd, particularly she is made to tell her own tale in modester words than she told it at first . . ." (*ed. cit.*, p. 3).

8 *The History and Remarkable Life of the Truly Honourable Col. Jacque* (London, 1722): title-page.

9 *Moll Flanders, ed. cit.*, p. 39.

10 *Ibid.*, pp. 12-13.

11 *Hours in a Library* (London, ed. 1899), p. 4.

12 Reprinted in *Accounts of the Apparition of Mrs. Veal*, ed. Manuel Schonhorn, Augustan Reprint Society, No. 115 (Los Angeles, 1965).

13 *Ibid.*

14 *Ibid.*

15 *Ibid.*

16 *Ibid.*

17 *Ibid.*

18 *The Review*, 15 Sept. 1711.

19 H. G. Wells, *Experiment in Autobiography* (London, 1934), II. 503.

20 *Ibid.*, p. 497.

21 *Ibid.*, p. 488.

22 *Ibid.*, p. 489.

C. J. RAWSON

Gulliver
and the Gentle Reader

" 'Tis a great Ease to my Conscience that I have writ so elaborate and useful a Discourse without one grain of Satyr intermixt":[1] this, from the Preface to *A Tale of a Tub*, outdoes even Gulliver's claims to veracity in its cheeky outrageousness. That "provocative display of indirectness"[2] which Herbert Read (in a fine though somewhat unfriendly phrase) saw in *Gulliver* governs also the mad parodic world of the *Tale*: the seven prefatory items followed by an Introduction, the sign-posted chapters of digression (one of them in praise of digressions), the pseudo-scholarly annotation (with the "commentator" sometimes at odds with the "author"), the triumphant assimilation into the notes of Wotton's hostile exegesis, the asterisks and gaps in the MS, the promise of such forthcoming publications as *A Panegyrick upon the World* and *A General History of Ears*. The "author", a creature of mad and monstrous egotism, confides his private problems, and draws garrulous attention to his literary techniques. The obvious point of this marathon of self-posturing is to mock those modern authors, "L'estrange, Dryden, *and some others*",[3] who write this sort of book straight. At the same time, the *Tale* has a vitality of sheer performance which suggests that a strong self-conscious pressure of primary self-display on Swift's own part is also at work; the almost "romantic" assertion of an immense (though edgy,

51

oblique, and aggressively self-concealing) egocentricity. Swift's descendants in the old game of parodic self-consciousness are Romantics of a special sort, like Sterne and (after him) the Byron of *Don Juan*. If the *Tale's* "Digression in Praise of Digressions" looks back to, and mocks, things like L'Estrange's "Preface upon a Preface",[4] it also looks forward to Sterne's "chapters upon chapters", and it is not for nothing that Tristram thinks his book will "swim down the gutter of Time" in the company of Swift's.[5] Whatever the ancestry of the technical devices as such, the parodic intrusions of Swift's "author" have a centrality and importance, and are made by Swift to carry a strength of personal charge, which seem to be new.[6] In Sterne and Byron, self-conscious forms of parody and self-parody openly become a solipsistic exercise, an oblique mode of self-revelation and self-display, and a reaching out to the reader on those terms. Swift has in common with Sterne, against most pre-Swiftian practitioners of "self-conscious narration", the imposition of an exceptional immediacy of involvement with the reader. The narrators are not, of course, the equivalents of Swift or even Sterne: but each is an "I" of whose existence and temperament we are kept unremittingly aware, who talks to the reader and seems to be writing the book, and through whom the real author projects a very distinctive presence of his own. Swift and Sterne also share a kind of intimate, inward-looking obliquity which sets them off, say, from their master Rabelais, who like them projects a formidable presence, but whose boozy companionable exhibitionism amounts to an altogether different (and more "open") manner. This obliquity (more or less instinctive in Swift, more coyly self-aware in Sterne) perhaps takes the place of an overt self-expression which Augustan decorum, and whatever personal inhibitions, discouraged.

There are certainly important differences. When the "author" of the *Tale* asserts, "in the Integrity of my Heart, that what I am going to say is literally true this Minute I am writing",[7] Swift is exposing the trivial ephemerality of modern writers. Similar remarks from Sterne (or, in a way, from Richardson) proudly proclaim the immediacy of their method of writing "to the *Moment*".[8] When Swift's "author", again, asserts the importance of the reader's "putting himself into the Circumstances and Postures of Life, that the Writer was in, upon every important Passage as it flow'd from his Pen", so that there may be "a Parity and strict Correspondence of Idea's between the Reader and the Author",[9] Swift is attacking modern garrulities of self-revelation which for him amount to indecent exposure. In Sterne such remarks, however fraught with all manner of Shandean indirection, are real tokens of relationship. Tristram wants to tell you everything about himself, because he and Sterne enjoy his character (including the irony injected into it by Sterne, and of which Sterne's parodic performance is a part) as a rich fact of human nature. Both want to get the reader intimately involved:

> As you proceed farther with me, the slight acquaintance, which is now beginning betwixt us, will grow into familiarity; and that, unless one of us is in fault, will terminate in friendship. – *O diem praeclarum!* – then nothing which has touched me will be thought trifling in its nature or tedious in its telling.[10]

The difference is not simply a matter of parody, for that exists in Sterne too. Swift's "author", like Sterne's, often addresses the reader and invokes "all the Friendship that hath passed between Us".[11] At the end of the *Tale*, he has no more to say but thinks of experimenting on how to go on writing *"upon Nothing"*, "to let" (in a phrase Sterne might have used) "the Pen still move on":

> By the Time that an Author has writ out a Book, he and his Readers are become old Acquaintance, and grow very loth to part: So that I have sometimes known it to be in Writing, as in Visiting, where the Ceremony of taking Leave, has employ'd more Time than the whole Conversation before.[12]

Neither this, nor Sterne's passage, is quite straight. That both are in some sense ironic need not be laboured. But Sterne's irony is of that puppyish, clinging sort which prods, cajoles, sometimes irritates the reader into a participation which may be reluctant and grudging, but which is also primary, direct and real. Swift's words assert the same intimacy, but the actual effect of the Swiftian acidity at the end of the "author's" innocent sentence would *appear* to be to sever the link, to achieve not intimacy but an alienation. Sterne's irony is one of fond permissive indulgence; the egotism, though mocked, is freely played with, and the reader offered hospitality within it. In Swift's characteristic sting, the friendly egotism freezes into a stark reminder of the fact of mockery or parody of egotism, and (more than parody though by way of it) the claim to friendship with the reader becomes a kind of insulting denial.

There is thus, in this parody, a tartly defiant presence (that "self-assertion" which Leavis diagnosed)[13] which seems to differentiate it from more normal modes of parody, whose formal business it is to mock books. It is a truism that Swiftian parody, like that of many writers who choose to make their most serious statements about life through the medium of allusions to books, is usually more than parody in that, in various directions, it transcends parody's limiting relation to the works parodied. The *Modest Proposal* is both more and other than a mockery of those economic proposals whose form it adopts. The real concern is with matters with which the parodic element as such has no necessary connection: the state of Ireland (rather than economic projectors) in the *Modest Proposal*, human pride (rather than popular travel-writing) in *Gulliver*. The problem sometimes arises of just where the dominant focus lies: a parodic energy may blur a more central intention, and there may be a hiatus between a local parodic effect and the main drift of the discourse. An aspect of this, to which I shall return briefly, is that teasing fluctuation, or bewildering uncertainty, of *genre* which critics have noted in some of Swift's works, and which gives a curious precariousness to the reader's grasp of what is going on. The *Tale* differs in a formal sense from the *Modest Proposal* and *Gulliver* in that the "modernity" which it attacks finds one of its main symptoms in the kind of book that is being parodied, so that the congruence between parody and the "real" subject is particularly close. Even so, it would be wrong to suggest that this "real" subject is merely a matter of silly or offensive stylistic habits, like garrulousness or digressiveness. The cumulative effect of the *Tale's* formidable parodic array is to convey a sense of intellectual and cultural breakdown so massive and so compelling that the parodied objects, as such, come to seem a minor detail. This in no case makes the parody expendable. The manner of the hack-author, bland proposer, or truthful boneheaded traveller are essential to the effects Swift is creating, and not merely as means of highlighting satiric intensities through disarming naïveties of style. My last example from the *Tale* shows how parody of friendly gestures from author to reader not only mocks modern garrulousness and all the intellectual slovenliness that goes with it (as well as capturing incidentally a typical social absurdity), but puts the reader himself under attack. This "Satire of the Second Person", in H. W. Sams's useful phrase,[14] is not primarily a matter of *satirizing* the reader, but of making him uncomfortable in another sense, as a person we are rude to is made uncomfortable. Swift, as much as Sterne, is reaching out to the reader, and the alienation I spoke of does not in fact eliminate intimacy, though it destroys "friendship". There is something in Swift's relations with his reader that can be described approximately in terms of the edgy intimacy of a personal quarrel that does not quite come out into the open, with gratuitous-seeming sarcasms on one side and a defensive embarrassment on the other. Such a description can only be a half-truth. And, like many of the examples I shall be discussing, the passage is much lighter than any account of it can be. It is a joke (a good one), and playful. But it is attacking play, and its peculiar aggressiveness is a quality which I believe to be not merely incidental but pervasive in Swift's major satires, whether parody is present or not. What is involved is not necessarily a "rhetoric" or thought-out strategy, so much as an atmosphere or perhaps an instinctive tone. This is not to mistake Swift for his masks, but to say that behind the screen of indirections, ironies, and putative authors a central Swiftian personality is always actively present, and makes itself felt.

[ii]

Consider a scatological passage in *Gulliver*. I do not wish to add here to the available theories about the scatology and body-disgust as such. Psychoanalysts have examined it; C. S. Lewis says, sturdily, that it is "much better understood by schoolboys than by psychoanalysts;[15] another critic says the "simplest answer is that as a conscientious priest [Swift] wished to discourage fornication";[16] others say that Swift was just advocating cleanliness, mocking the over-particularity of travel-writers, or doing no more any way than other writers in this or that literary tradition. But most people agree that there is a lot of it, and it has been a sore point from the start. Swift knew it, and knew that people knew, and early in Book I he has a characteristic way of letting us know he knows we know. Gulliver had not relieved himself for two days, and tells us how in his urgency he now did so inside his Lilliputian house. But he assures us that on future occasions he always did "that Business in open Air", and that the "offensive Matter" was disposed of "every Morning before Company came" by two Lilliputian servants. Gulliver thinks the "candid Reader" needs an explanation, so he tells us why he tells us this:

> I would not have dwelt so long upon a Circumstance, that perhaps at first Sight may appear not very momentous; if I had not thought it necessary to justify my Character in Point of Cleanliness to the World; which I am told, some of my Maligners have been pleased, upon this and other Occasions, to call in Question. (I.ii.29)[17]

It is Gulliver and not Swift who is speaking, but it is Swift and not Gulliver who (in any sense that is active at this moment) has had maligners. Gulliver does have enemies in Lilliput, notably after urinating on the palace-fire, but the reader does not know this yet, and it is difficult not to sense behind Gulliver's self-apology a small egocentric defiance from the real author. This would be true whether one knew him to be Swift or not: but it comes naturally from the Swift whose writings, and especially *A Tale of a Tub*, had been accused of "Filthiness",[18] "Lewdness", "Immodesty", and of using "the Language of the Stews"[19] (Swift called it being "battered with Dirt-Pellets" from "envenom'd . . . Mouths".)[20] Swift's trick consists of doing what he implies people accuse him of, and saying that this proves he isn't like that really: the openly implausible denial becomes a cheeky flaunting of the thing denied, a tortuously barefaced challenge. This self-conscious sniping at the reader's poise occurs more than once: a variant instance of mock-friendly rubbing-in, for the "gentle Reader's" benefit, occurs at the end of II.i, where the particularity of travel-writers is part of the joke.

A related non-scatological passage, which Thackeray praised as "the best stroke of humour, if there be a best in that abounding book",[21] is Gulliver's final farewell to his Houyhnhnm master, whose hoof he offers to kiss, as in the papal ceremony.[22] (Gulliver seems to have leanings that way: he also wanted to kiss the Queen of Brobdingnag's foot, but she just held out her little finger – II.iii.101.)

> But as I was going to prostrate myself to kiss his Hoof, he did me the Honour to raise it gently to my Mouth. I am not ignorant how much I have been censured for mentioning this last Particular. (IV.x.282)

Since the passage occurs in the first edition, Gulliver or Swift could hardly have been censured for mentioning this before. "Detractors" would be presumed by the reader to object that human dignity was being outraged, and Swift was of course right that many people would feel this about his book in general. But this is not Gulliver's meaning at all, and the typical Swiftian betrayal that follows gains its real force less from mere surprise than from its cool poker-faced fanning of a reader's hostility which Swift obviously anticipated and actually seemed on the point of trying to allay:

> Detractors are pleased to think it improbable, that so illustrious a Person should descend to give so great a Mark of Distinction to a Creature so inferior as I. Neither have I forgot, how apt some Travellers are to boast of extraordinary Favours they have received. But . . .

Thackeray's praise ("audacity", "astounding gravity", "truth topsy-turvy, entirely logical and absurd") comes just before the famous "filthy in word, filthy in thought, furious, raging, obscene" passage:[23] it is perhaps appropriate that such coarse over-reaction should be the counterpart to a cheerful complacency in the face of the subtler energies of Swift's style.

The mention of travellers in the hoof-kissing passage brings us back to parody, but emphasizes again how readily Swiftian parody serves attacking purposes which are themselves non-parodic. Edward Stone's view that this reference is proof that Swift is merely joking at the expense of boastful travellers misses most of the flavour of the passage.[24] (One might as easily say that the main or only point of the passage is to guy a papal rite. I do not, of course, deny these secondary jokes, or their piquancy.) But parody is important, almost as much in its way as in the *Tale*. Gulliver is an author, who announces forth-coming publications about Lilliput (I.iv.47-8; I.vi.57) and Houyhnhnmland (IV.ix.275) – which is a common enough device – and whose putative authorship of the work we are actually reading, as well as being the source of many of its most central ironies, enables Swift to flaunt his own self-concealment in some amusing and disconcerting ways.[25] A portrait of Gulliver was prefixed to the early editions, and in 1735 this acquired the teasing caption "Splendide Mendax".[26] The elaborate claims to veracity in "The Publisher to the Reader" and in the text itself gain an additional piquancy from this. The 1735 edition also prints for the first time Gulliver's letter to Sympson, which, as prefatory epistles go, is a notably un-balanced document, providing advance notice of Gulliver's later anti-social state and by the same token giving a disturbing or at least confusing dimension to the sober opening pages of the narrative. Gulliver's announcement in the letter that *Brobding-nag* should have been spelt *Brobdingrag* (p. 8) belongs to a familiar kind of authenticating pretence in both fiction and prose satire, but in so far as we remember it later it does make it slightly unsettling to read *Brobdingnag* with an *n* every time it occurs in the book. It is clear that these devices, though not meant to be believed, are not bids for verisimilitude in the manner, say, of Richardson's "editorial" pretence or the count-less other tricks of fiction-writers before and after Swift (the correcting footnote, the manuscript partly missing or lost, the discovered diary, the pseudo-biography). Nor are they quite a matter of pure hearty fun, as in Rabelais, meant to be enjoyed *precisely as* too outrageous to be believed. For one thing, Swift's celebrated "conciseness" is too astringent. It is also too close to the idiom of sober factuality, and some people were literally taken in.

We are hardly expected to take *Gulliver's Travels* as a straight (even if possibly mendacious) travel story. But the sea captain who claimed to be "very well acquainted with Gulliver, but that the printer had Mistaken, that he livd in Wapping, & not in Rotherhith", the old gentleman who searched for Lilliput on the map, the Irish Bishop who said the "Book was full of improbable lies, and for his part, he hardly believed a word of it"[27] (though some of these readers may have been more *ben trovati* than real) do tell a kind of truth about the work. Swift's whole ironic programme depends on our not being taken in by the travel-book element, but it does require us to be infected with a residual uncertainty about it; and these instances of an over-successful hoax fulfil, extremely, a potential in the work to which all readers must uneasily respond. This is not to accept the simpler accounts of Swiftian betrayal, which suggest that the plain traveller's, or modest proposer's, factuality lulls the reader into a false credulity, and then springs a trap. With Swift, we are always on our guard from the beginning (I believe this is true of sensitive *first* readings as well as later ones), and what surprises us is not the fact of betrayal but its particular form in each case. But if we are on our guard, we do not know what we are guarding against. The travel-book factuality, to which we return at least at the beginning and end of each book (even the end of Book IV, in its strange way, sustains and elaborates the pretence) is so insistent, and at its purest so lacking in obvious pointers to a parodic intention, that we really do not know *exactly* how to take it. What saves the ordinary reader from being totally taken in is, obviously, the surrounding context. (The very opening of the narrative, from the 1735 edition onwards, is coloured by the letter to Sympson: but even before 1735 one would have needed to be exceptionally obtuse to think, by the end of the first chapter, that one was still reading a travel-book.) But not being taken in, and knowing the plain style to be parodic, does not save us from being unsure of what is being mocked: travel-books, fictions posing as travel-books, philosophic tales (like *Gulliver* itself) posing as fictions posing as travel-books.[28] Bewilderment is increased by the uncertainty of how much weight to give, moment by moment, to the fact of parody as such and to whatever the style may be mocking, since the parody as we have seen is continuously impregnated with satiric purposes which transcend or exist outside it, but which may still feed on it in subtle ways. And we cannot be sure that some of the plainness is not meant to be taken straight, not certainly as factual truth, but (in spite of everything) transiently as realistic fictional trimmings: at least, the style helps to establish the "character" of the narrator, though this "character" in turn has more life as the basis of various ironies than as a vivid fictional personality. No accurate account can exhaust the matter, or escape an element of giddy circularity. The proper focus for Swift's precise sober narrative links is paradoxically a blurred focus, because we do not know what to make of all the precision. The accumulation of unresolved doubt that we carry into our reading of more central parts of *Gulliver's Travels* creates, then, not a credulity ripe for betrayal, but a more continuous defensive uneasiness. This undermining of our nervous poise makes us peculiarly vulnerable, in more than the obvious sense, to the more central satiric onslaughts.

The parodic element, though not primary, is never abandoned. At the end of Book IV, when any live interest in travel-writers may be thought to have totally receded in the face of more overwhelming concerns, Gulliver keeps the subject alive with some tart reminders of his truthfulness and the mendacity of other travellers. The practice is commonplace, but again there is nothing here either of Rabelais's friendly outrageous-ness as he refers to his "histoire tant veridicque", or his or Lucian's corresponding frank admission that they are telling monstrous lies, or the honest workmanlike concern with verisimilitude that we find in, say, *Erewhon*.[29] Gulliver says:

> Thus, gentle Reader, I have given thee a faithful History of my Travels for Sixteen Years, and above Seven Months; wherein I have not been so studious of Ornament as of Truth. I could perhaps like others have astonished thee with strange improbable Tales; but I rather chose to relate plain Matter of Fact in the simplest Manner and Style; because my principal Design was to inform, and not to amuse thee. (IV.xii.291)

This passage, which belongs with the well-known (and perhaps somewhat more light-hearted) remark to Pope about vexing the world rather than diverting it, emphasizes Swift's fundamental unfriendliness by a characteristic astringency (that tone is partly Swift's though Gulliver may overdo it), and by a use of the second person singular which is aggressively contemptuous. This probably parodies or inverts the common use of "thee" and "thou" in addresses to "gentle readers", where, so far as the pronoun is not merely neutral, intimacy or familiarity is the point. But one can also compare places where an author treats his reader with mild aggressiveness, as when Burton opens his long preface to *The Anatomy of Melancholy* by proclaiming his freedom to tell or withhold information which the reader wants: in fact, the passage hardly has a Swiftian tang, and Burton ends the preface by earnestly requesting "every private man . . . not to take offence" and by presuming "of thy good favour, and gracious acceptance (gentle reader)".[30] Fielding's usages range from warm friendliness (*Tom Jones*, XVIII.i), through a more ruggedly admonishing but still friendly tone (IX.vii), to a partial identification of the reader with "a little reptile of a critic" (X.i): but even here there is an initial comic relaxation (the comparison with Shakespeare and his editors), and the later concession to the reader that perhaps "thy heart may be better than thy head"; and when Fielding takes stock of his relations with the reader in XVIII.i he warmly disclaims any intention to give offence.[31]

But Swift's use of "thee" is the hostile one ("thou" and "thee" were also often addressed to inferiors),[32] where familiarity, so to speak, has bred contempt. And what we sense in Swift's attack is not the grand public voice of the Satirist, which is, for example, Pope's voice. When Pope uses the hostile "thee" in the *Essay on Man* (e.g. III.27ff., "Has God, thou fool! work'd solely for thy good, . . . Is it for thee the lark ascends and sings? . . ."), it is Man he is addressing, not the reader. Swift's refusal of the "lofty Stile" in the *Epistle to a Lady* rests on an old notion that ridicule is more effective than lambasting ("Switches better guide than Cudgels"), but he has a significant way of describing what the raillery does: it "nettles", "Sets the Spirits all a working". "Alecto's Whip" makes the victims (here specifically "the Nation's Representers") "wriggle, howl, and skip": the satirist makes clear that the whip is to be applied to "their Bums", and that he will not be deterred by the smell.[33] Nothing could make clearer the note of quarrelsome intimacy that is the hallmark of Swift's satire. It may not be very attractive, but it is not meant to be: and it has a unique disturbing effectiveness.

Gulliver's angers (whether nagging tartness, as in the passage under discussion, or ranting fury) reflect a cooler needling offensiveness from the Swift who manipulates the "switch". The chapter, and the volume, end with Gulliver's onslaught on Pride, and his petulant instruction to all English Yahoos "who have any Tincture of this absurd Vice, that they will not presume to appear in my Sight". It is Gulliver and not Swift who is speaking (here it is important not to confuse the two: saying this has almost become a nervous tic among critics), but there is really no sufficiently vivid alternative point of view that we can hang on to at this final moment. I shall return to this, and to what Gulliver actually says, later. What I want to stress here is that the final chapter begins with a needling defiance and the openly unfriendly intimacy of a petty insult, and ends with quarrelsome hysteria. The hysteria is Gulliver's and Swift seems in control. But the quarrel with the reader is one which Swift has been conducting through Gulliver, even though, when Gulliver becomes acutely unbalanced, there is an incomplete (at least a not quite literal) Swiftian commitment to what the quarrel has come to.

[iii]

Gulliver is sometimes called a gay book. Arbuthnot seems to have started this when he said "Gulliver is a happy man that at his age can write such a merry work".[34] His letter is joyful about the success of *Gulliver*, and tells of the Captain who claimed to know Gulliver, and the old man who looked up his map. Arbuthnot loved "mischief the best of any Good natured man in England",[35] and is full of happy complicity in Swift's success and the bonus of a hoax. Pope and Gay were also "diverted" by the reception of the book.[36] Part of the "merry" seems more Scriblerian in-joke than sober description. But the book really is merry, and one thinks of witty fantastications like the joke about the handwriting of ladies in England (I.vi.57),[37] or the charming comedy of the Lilliputian speculations about Gulliver's watch (I.ii.35), which Johnson praised.[38] Such things are very funny, with mild satiric overtones, but without being unduly charged with needling obliquities or any blistering intensity. This is true even in some cases where we should expect Swift to be very hostile. Much of the folly of scientists in Book III is treated thus, the flappers, the substitution of things for words, the mathematical obsession which makes the Laputians describe

> the Beauty of a Woman . . . by Rhombs, Circles, Parallelograms, Ellipses, and other Geometrical Terms. (III.ii.163)

(a joke which is not without bearing on our own habit of reducing women's shapes to "vital statistics"). *Gulliver* has a notably unbuttoned way of giving itself over to local eruptions of mood, but it may be that the very fluctuations of tone invite us (though it will not do to be too solemn) to reconsider the whole nature of the "merriment". Swift obviously enjoyed the comedy of incongruity that runs right through the work (the Lilliputian troop on Gulliver's handkerchief, various Houyhnhnm postures, the She-Yahoo embracing Gulliver): this comes through plainly in his letter to Motte discussing illustrations to the book.[39] But a good deal of this grotesque comedy, notably in Brobdingnag, is close to being rather painful. The hailstones as big as tennis-balls, the huge frog, the monkey which takes Gulliver for one of its own (II.v.116ff.) have an undeniable science-fiction humour, but Gulliver is throughout in peril of his life. This is even truer of the slapstick comedy of the bowl of cream (II.iii.108): not only is it fraught with painful possibilities for Gulliver, but it reflects a crude and bitter malevolence in the court dwarf. J. M. Bullitt speaks well of Swift's "seeming merriment" as reflecting "an almost compulsive desire to separate himself from the intensity of his own feelings",[40] and the margin between high-spirited fun and more disturbing purposes is sometimes a thin one. If notions of the jest as a breaker of tensions, a disguised means of attack, or a showy (*vive la bagatelle!*) shrugging-off of painful feeling seem too ponderous to impose on some (not all) of these passages, they are not foreign to Swift's manner as a whole, and come into his thinking about satire:

> All their Madness makes me merry:
> . . . .
> Like the ever-laughing Sage,
> In a Jest I spend my Rage:
> (Tho' it must be understood,
> I would hang them if I cou'd).[41]

And if the self-humour in these verses forbids us to take the passage at its literal intensity (as it forbids us to take at *their* literal intensity the "hate and detest" and "Drown the World" passages in the letters to Pope expressing the "misanthropy" behind the *Travels*),[42] yet the self-humour is plainly not of the kind that cancels what is said. I imagine, indeed, that the self-humour may in some ways be more disturbing than the plain uncompromising statement would have been without it. In dissociating the thing said from the full violence of the saying, the ironist both unsettles the reader and covers himself. Since we have here no firm alternative viewpoint to give us our bearings, we can only know that the ironist means part of what he says, but not exactly how large, or quite what sort of, a part; and so do not know what defenses are called for. More important, obviously half-meant self-undercutting statements of this kind ("I would hang them if I cou'd", "I hate and detest that animal called man") are more uncomfortable than if they had been wholly meant, for then we might have the luxury of dismissing them as ranting folly. In just this way, our consciousness of Gulliver's folly makes us paradoxically more, not less, vulnerable to the onslaughts on our self-esteem in Book IV. Had Gulliver been presented as sane, we should (since again there is no real alternative voice, and no firm norm is indicated) have had to identify him with the satirist behind the mask, and so have been enabled to reject both as totally outrageous. As it is, we reject what comes from Gulliver, and are left with that disturbingly uncertain proportion of it which comes from Swift. It is precisely Gulliver's distance from Swift that permits the Swiftian attack to look plausible. Much of the humour of *Gulliver's Travels* has this effect, not really of attenuating (still less of belying) the Swiftian attack, as some critics hold, but of lending it that self-defensive distancing which makes it viable. Gulliver's solemn habit of trotting and neighing, fully aware of and undeterred by people's ridicule (IV.x.279), releases the whole situation from any possibility of Swift himself seeming solemn.

The same may be said, the opposite way round, of those jokes at the expense of the Houyhnhnms, which are sometimes said to prove that *Gulliver's Travels* has an anti-Houyhnhnm message: their perplexed "Gestures, not unlike those of a Philosopher"

(IV.i.226) when they try to understand Gulliver's shoes and stockings, their language which sounds like High Dutch (IV.iii.234), their way of building houses, threading needles and milking cows (IV.ix.274). The first thing I would note is that humour about the Houyhnhnms is never of a destructive tartness: contrast some of the anti-Lilliputian jokes. It also makes the Houyhnhnms (otherwise somewhat stiffly remote, or so some readers feel) seem engagingly awkward and "human", and Swift has a note of real tenderness in some of the passages, the description of the Houyhnhnm dinner-party for example (IV.ii.231-2). Irvin Ehrenpreis, in a fine account of this humour, says that Swift is smiling at his own "whole project of bestowing concrete life upon unattainable abstractions" and "warning the sophisticated reader that [he], unlike Gulliver, appreciates the comical aspect of his own didacticism".[43] The concession conforms to the normal method of the work: one of its effects is to make it more difficult for the reader to answer back.

But the humour has other resonances too. One Houyhnhnm absurdity that some critics make much of is their complacent notion that man's physical shape is preposterous and inefficient for the purposes of life. This is a nice joke when we think of a Houyhnhnm mare threading a needle. But it turns to a cruel irony not at the Houyhnhnms', but at mankind's, expense, when Gulliver's Houyhnhnm master assumes that men are anatomically incapable (despite their impulses) of fighting the destructive wars Gulliver tells him about. Gulliver replies with an exuberant assertion to the contrary that displays a moral fatuity which also has its comic side:

> I could not forbear shaking my Head and smiling a little at his Ignorance. And, being no Stranger to the Art of War, I gave him a Description of Cannons, Culverins, Muskets, Carabines, Pistols, Bullets, Powder, Swords, Bayonets, Sieges, Retreats, Attacks, Undermines, Countermines, Bombardments, Sea-fights; Ships sunk with a Thousand Men; twenty Thousand killed on each Side; dying Groans, Limbs flying in the Air: Smoak, Noise, Confusion, trampling to Death under Horses Feet: Flight, Pursuit, Victory; Fields strewed with Carcases left for Food to Dogs, and Wolves, and Birds of Prey; Plundering, Stripping, Ravishing, Burning and Destroying. And, to set forth the Valour of my own dear Country-

men, I assured him, that I had seen them blow up a Hundred Enemies at once in a Siege, and as many in a Ship; and beheld the dead Bodies drop down in Pieces from the Clouds, to the great Diversion of all the Spectators. (IV.v.247)

This enthusiastic fit is obviously funny. It is funny partly because of the concreteness with which Gulliver generalizes, the entranced particularity with which he evokes not a real battle which happened but some sort of common denominator of war. The effect is instructively different from that of a scene in *Nineteen Eighty-Four* which seems to make some of the same points, and which (like other things in that novel) may have been distantly modelled on Swift.[44] An entry in Winston Smith's diary describes a war-film with a ship full of refugees being bombed, and a "wonderful shot of a child's arm going up up up right into the air", and a greatly diverted audience applauding and "shouting with laughter". Smith says the film is very good, and talks of "wonderful" scenes as Gulliver might. To this extent he is conditioned by the awful world of 1984, but he is struggling for his mental freedom (writing the diary is itself punishable by death), and he suddenly breaks off to think of his account as a "stream of rubbish". The scene does not become funny, because Smith is, in a deeper and partly unconscious sense, disturbed and pained by it, instead of being in Gulliver's fatuous trance of grotesque delight. Orwell drives the painfulness home by having Smith say that there was in the audience a prole woman who "suddenly started kicking up a fuss and shouting they didnt oughter of showed it not in front of kids they didnt". That there should be, within the situation itself, this glimpse of a hurt and protesting normality does not offer much reassurance: but it reaches out to the reader in a kind of complicity of despair. Neither Orwell nor the reader can stand apart from the narrator, or from the rest of the humanity described, and there can be no question of laughing anything off.

The incident in Orwell, however representative (it is in its way as representative as Swift's passage, and of similar things), is a vivid specific occurrence (though only a film), to which a pained immediacy of reaction on Smith's and on the reader's part is natural and appropriate. In Gulliver's account, even when, as at the end, he seems to turn to specific occurrences, there is a comic lack of distinction between the general and the particular, and Gulliver's all-embracing celebration has a callous yet oddly innocent absurdity. The comic note, and the fact that the horror is so diffused, ensure that no immediacy of participation by the reader in the things described is possible, or expected. For obvious reasons there is no complicity between the reader and either Gulliver or any member of the applauding crowds. Nor is the grim high-spirited comedy a congenial idiom for any complicity between the reader and Swift: the reader has, rather uncomfortably, to laugh *at* Gulliver, without having anyone very much to laugh *with*. Gulliver's folly is at this moment the moral folly of complacent acceptance, not, as later, the medical folly of unquestioning repudiation, of mankind. But there can be no question of Gulliver's folly, or Swift's comic sense, cancelling or seriously attenuating the point about war and attitudes to war which the passage makes: one of their effects, as with other examples of Swift's humour, is to remove Swift's angry attack from the plane of rant. Yet we are not, I think, very actively horrified at Gulliver's *feelings*, as we should have been if they had been Winston Smith's. In a novel, or in life, we should be revolted by his callousness. But we cannot, here or elsewhere, respond to him as a "character". He is too absurd and two-dimensional. There is a detachment of the character from what he reveals to us which is part of the whole satiric formula of *Gulliver's Travels*, and which the humour here reinforces. We think less about Gulliver than about war, and what Swift is telling us about our attitudes to it. The message is disturbing, and for all the fun, Swift is not, anymore than elsewhere, being very friendly.

[iv]

The tense hovering between laughter and something else, the structural indefiniteness of genre and the incessantly shifting status and function of the parodic element, the ironic twists and countertwists, and the endless flickering uncertainties of local effect suggest that one of Swift's most active satiric weapons is *bewilderment*. It is perhaps not surprising that this weapon should have backfired, and that there should have been so much doubt and disagreement both about the unity of the work, and

the meaning of its final section. One of the risks, but also rewards, of the attacking self-concealments of irony is that they
draw out their Irish bishops. But we are all, inevitably, Irish
bishops in some degree: and the Swift who sought to vex the
world may well be deriving a wry satisfaction from our failures
to pin him down, although he might not consent to know us in
Glubbdubdrib (III.viii.197). What one means by "unity" is
too often rather arbitrary, but there is perhaps a broad overall
coherence in the consistency and progression of *Gulliver's* onslaught on the reader's bearings and self-esteem. But it is a
tense and rugged coherence, and no neatly chartable matter,
and any more "external" unities of formal pattern or ideology
seem ultimately inseparable from, and possibly secondary to,
those satiric procedures and tones which create the commanding
impact of the Swiftian voice. An attachment to schematic patterns *per se*, of the kind for which Books I and II provide such a
brilliant model, seems to have had two results. One has been
a tendency to wish either or both the other books away. The
other has been a quest to discover in the work as a whole something of the geometrical shapeliness that exists between the first
two books. The exercise easily becomes disembodied even when
its limitations are partially recognized: it hardly seems to
matter much that Books I and III deal with bad governments,
while Books II and IV, in alternating pattern, deal with good
governments.[45]

There are of course some broad structural facts of considerable significance, such as that we are led through three books
of allegorical societies which are in principle translatable into
real life (with a mixture, as Thomas Sheridan put it, of good
and bad qualities "as they are to be found in life"),[46] and which
provide a solid background of "realistic" evidence of human
vice, into the stark world of moral absolutes of Book IV; and
that the Struldbrugs at the end of Book III are a horrifying
climax which prepares us for this. The specific fact that the
Struldbrugs give a terrifying retrospective deepening to the
Houyhnhnms' fearlessness of death is only one aspect of their
disturbing importance: their chief force, at first meeting, is to
put the concerns of the narrative once and for all on an entirely
new plane. Again, the fact, noted by Case and others,[47] that the
incidental persons in the narrative links between the four main

episodes tend to become nastier and nastier, provides an important progression, not perhaps because the reader senses it as a progression (unless it happens to be pointed out), but because the evil of sailors and others (the "real" men) in Books III and IV provides a relevantly documented and depressing background to the main preoccupations of those books. (The Portuguese Captain and his crew are an exception to which I shall come later.) The point about these patterns is not that they are neat and flawlessly progressive (they are not), and not merely that they fit in with the "themes" (though they do): it is that they have an effect *as we read*, without our necessarily being aware of them *as patterns*. After all, the real point about even the special relationship between Books I and II is not the arithmetical piquancies, but the unfolding irony about human self-importance.

[v]

This self-importance, or pride, is at the centre of the work's concerns. A principle that is sometimes overlooked in discussions not only of structural shape but of ideological themes is that these things make themselves felt, if at all, through the reader's continuous submission to *local* effects, which means in this case exposure to the Swiftian presence at close quarters. Ideologically, *Gulliver's Travels* revolves round the familiar Augustan group of concepts, Nature, Reason and Pride. Its position is basically a commonplace one, but it bears some restating because some ironies of characteristic force and stinging elusiveness proceed from it. Nature and Reason ideally coalesce. Nature is ideal order, in all spheres of life: moral, social, political, aesthetic. Deviations from this are unnatural, as murder or any gross misdeed might, in our own idiom, be called an unnatural act. If one said that the deed came naturally to one, one would be using the term in a different sense. Such other meanings were also of course available to Swift, and I shall argue that the interplay between ideal and less ideal senses provides an important irony. Reason is the faculty which makes one behave naturally (in the high sense), makes one follow Nature and frame one's judgement (and behaviour) by her just and unerring standard. So More's Utopians (in some ways ancestors of the Houyhnhnms) "define virtue to be life ordered according to nature, and that we be hereunto ordained of God. And that he doth follow the course of nature, which in desiring and refusing things is ruled by reason",[48] and the Houyhnhnms believe a somewhat secularized version of the same thing (IV.v.248). The terms Nature and Reason are often in fact interchangeable. Where this is not so, they may complete one another: Nature teaches the Houyhnhnms "to love the whole Species", Reason to distinguish between persons on merit (IV.viii.268). The Houyhnhnms, etymologically *"the Perfection of Nature"* (IV.iii.235), combine Nature and Reason in the highest sense. Their virtues are friendship, benevolence, decency, civility, but they have no ceremony or foolish fondness (IV.viii.268). This means that they have both emotions and propriety, but that neither is misdirected or excessive. They would have understood Pope's phrase in *The Temple of Fame* (l. 108) about "that useful Science, to be *good*". Their morality is pervaded by an uncompromisingly high (and instinctive) common-sense and utilitarianism, and what might be called an absolute standard of congruity or *fittingness*. Thus they cannot understand lying because speech was made to communicate (IV.iv.240), or opinion, because there is only one truth and speculation is idle (IV.viii.267). It follows that behaviour which offends against this unerring standard is readily seen as deviation or perversion. (This is a suggestion which Swift exploits very fully and painfully.) Even physically, the Houyhnhnms are rational-natural, for (thanks partly to their simple diet, Nature being, as Gulliver knows from some "insipid" meals, "easily . . . satisfied" – IV.ii.232) they are never ill, illness being a deviation from the natural state of the body. For a comic boiling-down of this mind-body ideal, one might cite Fielding's deist Square, who "held human nature to be the perfection of all virtue, and that vice was a deviation from our nature, in the same manner as deformity of body is".[49] Swift has his tongue in his cheek about some Houyhnhnm notions of the "natural" standard of mind-body integration, as when the Houyhnhnm master, in a passage of not very flattering but entirely delightful comedy, considers our physical shape unsuited for the employment of Reason in "the common Offices of Life" (IV.iv.242): but Swift *is* seriously suggesting that luxurious eating habits are a cause of human physical degeneracy, so that

70

morality and physical health are causally related and not only (as apparently for Square) by analogy. Nature ideally is one, and her laws pervasive.

In *Gulliver's Travels*, however, there is a gap between Nature and "human nature", in an actual sense, which would make Square's complacency untenable, though his *rationale* is perfectly applicable to the Houyhnhnms. The Houyhnhnms are not complacent in Square's sense because in them the ideal and the actuality are fully matched. Actually, Square's remarks also concern an ideal and, like other forms of philosophical "optimism", logically allow for an uglier reality: but, given the ugly facts, Swift (and Fielding) would see a monstrous impropriety in putting the matter that way at all. Mankind is guilty of a collective deviation from Nature and Reason at every level, and this Unreason, by the familiar buried pun, becomes in *Gulliver* (as in *A Tale of a Tub* or the *Dunciad*) a vast and wicked madness: the congruence between madness and moral turpitude is one of the most vivid and inventively resourceful themes of Augustan satire. Scientists, or those of a certain sort, are one of the traditional examples. They delve into what Nature keeps hidden, and they seek to pervert Nature (in such cases the word slides easily from an ideal sense to something approaching "things as they are") into something other than it is, "condensing Air into a dry tangible Substance", "softening Marble for Pillows and Pin-Cushions", arresting the growth of wool on sheep (III.v.182).[50] The phrase "natural philosophy" provides an exploitable pun (Fielding said natural philosophy knew "nothing of Nature, except her monsters and imperfections"),[51] and when Gulliver explained to the Houyhnhnm master

> our several Systems of *Natural Philosophy*, he would laugh that a Creature pretending to *Reason*, should value itself upon the Knowledge of other Peoples Conjectures, and in Things, where that Knowledge, if it were certain, could be of no Use. (IV.viii.267-8)

Science becomes divorced from usefulness and good sense. The Laputans are "dextrous" mathematicians on paper but have no idea of "practical Geometry" (III.ii.163). Natural philosophy is thus at least doubly unnatural, in that it variously violates Nature, and in that it is the irrational pastime of creatures who pretend to Reason. This is routine perversion, built-in to the situation. It exercised Swift, and Pope, *as* perversion. But there are further perversities. One is the encroachment of science on government. The Brobdingnagians stand out from the "Wits of *Europe*" in not having "reduced *Politicks* into a *Science*". Unlike us, they have no books on "the *Art of Government*", and despise mystery, refinement (a term which, as in many other satires of Swift and Pope, has familiar suggestions of dishonesty and other vices, as well as folly: "heads refin'd from Reason"),[52] and intrigue (II.vii.135). The Laputans, on the other hand, like our Mathematicians, have a "strong Disposition" to politics (III.ii.164), and the Academy of Lagado has a school of political projectors (though that, by some characteristic reversals, has crazed professors trying to do genuine political good, as well as schemes which hover uncertainly between outright folly and a sort of mad good sense – III.vi.187ff.). What, Gulliver asks, is the connection between mathematics and politics? Perhaps it is that "the smallest Circle hath as many Degrees as the largest", so that it might be thought that managing the world requires "no more Abilities than the handling and turning of a Globe". But he thinks the real explanation is

> a very common Infirmity of human Nature, inclining us to be more curious and conceited in Matters where we have least Concern, and for which we are least adapted either by Study or Nature. (III.ii.164)

This professional perversion or unnaturalness has connections with a whole series of ironies about perversity in the professions and occupations of men. The Yahoos are of a "perverse, restive Disposition" (IV.viii.266), and Swift seems to see human perversity as a thing of almost unending coils of self-complication. But before coming to this, the main outline may be summarized thus.

In the Nature-Reason dialectic at its simplest and purest, every vice is readily resolved into a violation of nature, and therefore into a peculiarly culpable form of unreason. The greed, quarrelsomeness, ambition, treachery, and lust of men, as we encounter them throughout the *Travels*, are in an elementary sense unnatural by definition. This unnaturalness is prone to almost infinite refinements, and therefore as we shall see open to a painful and varied series of ironic expositions. But the overriding unnaturalness, which becomes unbearable to Gulliver

72

at the end, is that the "Lump of Deformity, and Diseases both in Body and Mind" called man, should be "smitten with *Pride*": pride, in the assumption itself, in the face of so much folly, that man is a rational animal, the pride of having any self-esteem at all (as Gulliver, though perhaps not Swift, might more extremely put it), and (in the special case of scientists and their like) the pride of impiously tampering with God's creation and the normal state of things. Pride, which governs the mad scientists of Book III (and the philosopher experts in the earlier books, I.ii.37, II.ii.103-4); the puny self-importance of the Lilliputians in Book I, who play at men; and that of men, which emerges by extension in Book II, is the most deeply unnatural of all the vices because, as the other vices prove, there is nothing to be proud of.

This diagnosis of mankind is an Augustan commonplace, and many important elements of it may be found not only in an earlier humanism but also in various old traditions of classical and Christian thought. But Swift refines on it by a number of characteristic ironies which serve to undermine any comfort we might derive from having to contend with a simple categorical indictment of mankind, however damaging. Whichever way we interpret Book IV, man is placed, in it, somewhere between the rational Houyhnhnms and the bestial Yahoos. He has less reason than the former, more than the latter. The Houyhnhnms recognize this in Gulliver, though they think of him, and he eventually thinks of himself, as basically of the Yahoo kind. A Houyhnhnm state may be unattainable to man, but there are norms of acceptable, though flawed, humanity which do not seem, in the same way, beyond the realm of moral aspiration: one-time Lilliput (I.vi.57ff.), modern Brobdingnag, the "*English* Yeomen of the old Stamp" (III.viii.201), the Portuguese Captain. These positives must be taken gingerly. Ancient Lilliput and the old Yeomen are no more, Brobdingnag is hardly a European reality, there are not many like the Portuguese Captain and his crew, although some other decent people make fleeting unremarkable appearances. Still, they are there, and at worst, we reflect, we are still better than the Yahoos. But in conceding this assurance, Swift also takes it away. This is not just in the dramatic strength of the parallels between them and us, which culminate in the "objective" test of the female

Yahoo's sexual craving for Gulliver (IV.viii.266-7). There are qualities in which Gulliver is actually inferior: "Strength, Speed and Activity, the Shortness of my Claws, and some other Particulars where Nature had no Part" (IV.vii.260). Swift can be more or less playful with those "usual Topicks of *European* Moralists" (II.vii.137) about man's physical inferiority to animals, and an earlier speech of the Houyhnhnm master, already referred to, has its rich comic side (IV.iv.242-3). But it is a point meant to be taken note of, and recurs with some insistence. There is no mistaking the tartness with which we are told, in a further twist, that the Yahoos (to whom men are physically inferior!) are superior in agility to asses, though less comely and less useful in other respects (IV.ix.272-3). This is a Houyhnhnm view, but we need not suppose that Swift meant it literally in order to sense that he is having another snipe at the human form divine.

But more important is the assertion that man's portion of Reason, which theoretically raises him above Yahoos in non-physical matters, is in fact something "whereof we made no other Use than by its Assistance to aggravate our *natural* Corruptions, and to acquire new ones which Nature had not given us" (IV.vii.259). The notion that men use their reason to make themselves worse rather than better was not invented by Swift,[53] but it disturbingly weakens the contrary assurance that it is after all by virtue of our reason that we are better than the Yahoos. It is a Houyhnhnm comment, but so are the contrary ones (IV.iii.234; IV.vi.256; IV.ix.272). No one else tells us much either way. It recurs in various forms. Gulliver comes to realize that men use Reason "to improve and multiply those Vices, whereof their Brethren in this Country had only the Share that Nature allotted them" (IV.x.278). When men are under discussion, linguistic usage on the subject of Reason and Nature tends to change: Reason multiplies vices, Nature allots them. In an earlier passage there is even an unsettling doubt as to whether Reason in this case really *is* Reason. It occurs after the cruel irony in which the Houyhnhnm master supposes that, odious as men are, Nature has created their anatomy in such a way as to make them "utterly uncapable of doing much Mischief" (IV.v.247), to which Gulliver replies with the account of war which I discussed earlier. The master then says he hates Yahoos but cannot *blame* them any more than he would blame "a *Gnnayh* (a Bird of Prey) for its Cruelty",[54] but as to man,

> when a Creature pretending to Reason, could be capable of such Enormities, he dreaded lest the Corruption of that Faculty might be worse than Brutality itself. He seemed therefore confident, that instead of Reason, we were only possessed of some Quality fitted to increase our natural Vices. (IV.v.248)

This possibility, that man's Reason is not Reason, is not entertained. It goes against the run of the book's argument. But it is characteristic of Swift to place it before us, as an alternative (if only momentarily viable) affront. Either we have no Reason, or what we have is worse than not having it. The irresolution saps our defences, for we need to answer on two fronts. At the same time, neither point is true to the book, which does concede (notably through several comments of the Houyhnhnm master himself) that Gulliver is both better and more rational than the Yahoos. Swift is needling us with offensive undermining possibilities even while a moderately comforting certainty is being grudgingly established. Of the two negative, undermining streams of argument, the dominant one is that which says we do have Reason, but that it makes us worse. Its most intense manifestation occurs with Gulliver's description of the Yahoos' horrible smelly sexuality. The passage incidentally shows how germane the term Reason is, in ways we might not automatically expect, not merely to the concept "good morals" but also to the concept "virtuous passions". It drives home how the most unlikely vices tend to equal unreason (or, in the perverted human sense, not *unreason* but Reason):

> I expected every Moment, that my Master would accuse the *Yahoos* of those unnatural Appetites in both Sexes, so common among us. But Nature it seems hath not been so expert a Schoolmistress; and these politer Pleasures are entirely the Productions of Art and Reason, on our Side of the Globe. (IV.vii.264)

Though this has special resonances in the context of *Gulliver's Travels*, and a true Swiftian tang, it is also the classic language of primitivism, which is in fact a minor theme of the work. The Houyhnhnms are in some respects prelapsarian innocents, ignorant of at least some forms of evil, and with no bodily shame or any idea of why Gulliver wears clothes. They also have no literature, but a high oral tradition in poetry and knowledge (IV.iii.235; IV.ix.273-4). Utopian Lilliput and the old English Yeomen are idealized pre-degenerate societies, and Swift's concern with the idea of the degeneration of societies has often been noted. But there is the contrary example of Brobdingnag, an advanced and largely good society which, by a shaming and pointed contrast with Lilliput and England, has emerged from an earlier turpitude (II.vii.138).[55] The Yahoos prove that there is no idealization of the noble savage: and though the Houyhn-hnms do have a primitivist element, the high ideal of Nature associated with them embodies some key-values of civilized Augustan aspiration. This may partly proceed from a not fully resolved duality in the conception of Reason both as civilized achievement and as corrupting force, not to mention the sense, perhaps tending against both others, of a spontaneous rightness which "strikes . . . with immediate Conviction" (IV.viii.267).

But, if so, the confusion is not really Swift's. The fact is that both the language of ideas on these matters, and ordinary English idiom, make available these various senses. Nature and Reason were all-purpose terms, and Swift, who was not writing a logical treatise (although it has been shown that he was, in a manner, refuting logical treatises),[56] was only too ready, as we have seen, to exploit the ironic possibilities offered him by the language. His whole style in this work thrives on what from a strictly logical point of view is a defiant (and transparent) linguistic sleight of hand. The textbook definition of man as *animal rationale* simply refers to that reasoning faculty which was supposed to distinguish men from beasts – to borrow Locke's phrase in *Essay Concerning Human Understanding* (IV.xvii.1). Swift's "disproof" consists of tacitly translating a descriptive definition into a high ethical and intellectual ideal, and then saying that man's claim to Reason is fatuously and insufferably arrogant.[57] The often-quoted formulation in the sermon "On the Trinity" that "*Reason* itself is true and just, but the *Reason* of every particular Man is weak and wavering, perpetually swayed and turned by his Interests, his Passions, and his Vices"[58] shows that Swift is perfectly aware of semantic distinctions when he wants to be. It can also stand as an acceptable boiling-down of much that is said about human unreason in *Gulliver's Travels*. Swift's concern here, however, is not to boil the issue down to its commonplace propositional content, but to exploit the damaging ironies by all the verbal means which the language puts at his disposal.

The double standard by which the words Nature and Reason tend to be used in a debased sense when they refer to men, and an ideal sense when they refer to Houyhnhnms, lies at the heart of this. The dreadful thing is that man is neither natural in the high sense, nor (like the Yahoos, as the quotation about "politer Pleasures" showed) in the low. If we then grant that this double unnaturalness is itself natural to man, we find him becoming unnatural even to this nature. Suggestions of multiple self-complicating perversity exist in the accounts of all men's occupations and professional activities. One might instance the Laputan reasoners, who are "vehemently given to Opposition, unless when they happen to be of the right Opinion, which is seldom their Case" (III.ii.163); the Admiral who "for want of proper Intelligence . . . beat the Enemy to whom he intended to betray the Fleet" (III.viii.199); the kings who protested to Gulliver in Glubbdubdrib

> that in their whole Reigns they did never once prefer any Person of Merit, unless by Mistake or Treachery of some Minister in whom they confided: Neither would they do it if they were to live again; and they shewed with great Strength of Reason, that the Royal Throne could not be supported without Corruption; (III.viii.199)

the politician who "never tells a *Truth*, but with an Intent that you should take it for a *Lye*", and vice versa (IV.vi.255).[59] Most elaborate is the chain of ironies about the unnaturalness of the law. It is unnatural that laws should exist at all, since Nature and Reason should be sufficient guides for a rational creature. Other related perversities are: that while meant for men's protection, the law causes their ruin; that (for a variety of discreditably tortuous reasons) one is always at a disadvantage if one's cause is just; that lawyers use irrelevant evidence, and a jargon which no one can understand (which among other things runs against the reiterated principle that speech is only for communication); that lawyers, who are expected to be wise and learned, are in reality "the most ignorant and stupid" of men (IV.v.248-50). A major irony running through this is that man is unnatural even to his own natural unnaturalness. Assuming that moral perversion is natural to the species, it becomes, in this sense, natural for judges to accept bribes. But it is even more natural for judges to be unjust, so that

> I have known some of them to have refused a large Bribe from the Side where Justice lay, rather than injure the *Faculty*, by doing any thing unbecoming their Nature or their Office. (IV.v.249)

One becomes unnatural to one's lesser natural iniquities when a deeper iniquity competes with them. The concept of Nature is debased by an ever-declining spiral into whatever depths mankind might perversely sink to. Whatever these depths, Gulliver can follow the spiral downwards and (both in his naïve complacent phase and in his later disenchanted misanthropy) accept them as natural. The spiral has almost endless possibilities, and the reader for much of the time has not even the comfort of feeling that there is a rock-bottom. But there is, at the end, something like rock-bottom, a final insult to the nature of things which Gulliver finds completely unbearable:

> My Reconcilement to the *Yahoo*-kind in general might not be so difficult, if they would be content with those Vices and Follies only which Nature hath entitled them to. I am not in the least provoked at the Sight of a Lawyer, a Pick-pocket, a Colonel, a Fool, a Lord, a Gamester, a Politician, a Whoremunger, a Physician, an Evidence, a Suborner, an Attorney, a Traytor, or the like: This is all according to the due Course of Things: But, when I behold a Lump of Deformity, and Diseases both in Body and Mind, smitten with *Pride*, it immediately breaks all the Measures of my Patience; neither shall I be ever able to comprehend how such an Animal and such a Vice could tally together. The wise and virtuous *Houyhnhnms*, who abound in all Excellencies that can adorn a rational Creature, have no name for this Vice in their Language, which hath no Terms to express any thing that is evil, except those whereby they describe the detestable Qualities of their *Yahoos*; among which they were not able to distinguish this of Pride, for want of thoroughly understanding Human Nature, as it sheweth it self in other Countries, where that Animal presides. But I, who had more Experience, could plainly observe some Rudiments of it among the wild *Yahoos*. (IV.xii.296)

Pride, the complacency of thinking that man is a rational

animal, now becomes the "absurd Vice" which is the final aggravation of all our iniquities, the ultimate offence to Nature. Yet even Pride, the ultimate unnaturalness, is itself part of "Human Nature" ("for so they have still the Confidence to stile it",[60] says Gulliver to Sympson, p. 7), so that we may wonder whether we really have after all reached rock-bottom, or whether there is yet another opening for still deeper unnaturalness to be revealed. But things do stop here, and in this final impasse the only possible response, dramatically, is Gulliver's mixture of insane hatred and impotent petulance as he forbids any English Yahoo with "any Tincture of this absurd Vice" ever to appear in his sight.

[vi]

The book ends here, with Gulliver a monomaniac and his last outburst a defiant, and silly, petulance. We are not, I am sure, invited to share his attitudes literally, to accept as valid his fainting at the touch of his wife (IV.xi.289) and his strange nostalgic preference for his horses. He has become insane or unbalanced,[61] and I have already suggested one reason why, in the whole design of the work, this is appropriate: it makes his rant viable by dissociating Swift from the taint of excess, without really undermining the attack from Swift that the rant stands for. It is Gulliver's manner, not Swift's, which is Timon's manner, as critics are fond of noting, which means that he (like Lucian's or Plutarch's Timon)[62], and not Swift, is the raging recluse. But his are the final words, which produce the taste Swift chose to leave behind: it is no great comfort or compliment to the reader to be assaulted with a mean hysteria that he cannot shrug off because, when all is said, it tells what the whole volume has insisted to be the truth.

It is wrong, I think, to take Gulliver as a novel-character who suffers a tragic alienation, and for whom therefore we feel pity or some kind of contempt, largely because we do not, as I suggested, think of him as a "character" at all in more than a very attenuated sense: the emphasis is so preponderantly on what can be shown through him (including what he says and thinks) than on his person in its own right, that we are never allowed to accustom ourselves to him as a real personality despite all the rudimentary local colour about his early career, family life and professional doings. An aspect of this are Swift's ironic exploitations of the Gulliver-figure, which to the very end flout our most elementary expectations of character consistency: the praise of English colonialism in the last chapter, which startlingly returns to Gulliver's earlier boneheaded manner, is an example. The treatment of Gulliver is essentially *external*, as, according to Wyndham Lewis, satire ought to be.[63] Nor is Gulliver sufficiently independent from Swift: he is not identical with Swift, nor even similar to him, but Swift's presence behind him is always too close to ignore. This is not because Swift approves or disapproves of what Gulliver says at any given time, but because Swift is always saying something *through* it.

Gulliver in his unbalanced state, then, seems less a character than (in a view which has much truth but needs qualifying) a protesting gesture of impotent rage, a satirist's stance of ultimate exasperation. Through him, as through the modest proposer (who once offered sensible and decent suggestions which were ignored), Swift is pointing, in a favourite irony, to the lonely madness of trying to mend the world, a visionary absurdity which, in more than a shallow rhetorical sense, Swift saw as his own. At the time of finishing *Gulliver*, Swift told Pope, in a wry joke, that he wished there were a "Hospital" for the world's despisers.[64] (If Gulliver, incidentally, unlike the proposer, does not preach cannibalism, he does ask for clothes of Yahoo-skin – IV.iii.236 – and uses this material for his boat and sails – IV.x.281.) But Gulliver does not quite project the noble rage or righteous pride of the outraged satirist. The exasperated petulance of the last speech keeps the quarrel on an altogether less majestic and more intimate footing, where it has, in my view, been all along. Common sense tells us that Swift would not talk like that in his own voice, but we know disturbingly (and there has been no strong competing voice) that this is the voice he chose to leave in our ears.

Still, Gulliver's view is out of touch with a daily reality about which Swift also knew, and which includes the good Portuguese Captain. Gulliver's response to the Captain is plainly unworthy, and we should note that he has not learnt such bad manners (or his later hysterical tone) from the Houyhnhnms' example. But we should also remember that the Captain is a rarity,[65] who appears only briefly; that just before Gulliver meets him the horrible mutiny with which Book IV began is twice remembered (IV.x.281; IV.xi.283); that the first men Gulliver meets after leaving Houyhnhnmland are hostile savages (IV.xi.284); and that just after the excellent Portuguese sailors there is a hint of the Portuguese Inquisition (IV.xi.288). The Captain does have a function. As John Traugott says, he emphasizes Gulliver's alienation and "allows Gulliver to make Swift's point that even good Yahoos are Yahoos".[66] But above all perhaps he serves as a reasonable concession to reality (as if Swift were saying there *are* some good men, but the case is unaltered), without which the onslaughts on mankind might be open to a too easy repudiation from the reader. In this respect, he complements the other disarming concessions, the humour and self-irony, the physical comicality of the Houyhnhnms, Gulliver's folly, and the rest.

Even if Swift is making a more moderate attack on mankind than Gulliver, Gulliver's view hovers damagingly over it all; in the same way that, though the book says we are better than the Yahoos, it does not allow us to be too sure of the fact. (The bad smell of the Portuguese Captain, or of Gulliver's wife, are presumably "objective" tokens of physical identity, like the She-Yahoo's sexual desire for Gulliver.) This indirection unsettles the reader, by denying him the solace of definite categories. It forbids the luxury of a well-defined stand, whether of resistance or of assent, and offers none of the comforts of that author-reader complicity on which much satiric rhetoric depends. It is an ironic procedure, mocking, elusive, immensely resourceful and agile, which talks at the reader with a unique quarrelsome intimacy, but which is so hedged with aggressive defenses that it is impossible for him to answer back.

[vii]

Finally, a word about the Houyhnhnms. It is sometimes said that Swift is satirizing them as absurd or nasty embodiments of extreme rationalism. Apart from the element of humour, discussed earlier, with which they are presented, they are, it is said, conceited and obtuse in disbelieving the existence or the physical viability of the human creature. But, within the logic of the fiction, this disbelief seems natural enough. The Lilliputians also doubted the existence of men of Gulliver's size (I.iv.49), and Gulliver also needed explaining in Brobdingnag (II.iii.103-4). In both these cases the philosophers are characteristically silly, but everybody is intrigued, and we could hardly expect otherwise. Moreover, Gulliver tells Sympson that some human beings have doubted the existence of Houyhnhnms (p. 8), which, within the terms of the story (if one is really going to take this sort of evidence solemnly), is just as arrogant. More important, the related Houyhnhnm doubt as to the anatomical viability or efficiency of the human shape (apart from being no more smug than some of Gulliver's complacencies *in favour* of mankind) turns to a biting sarcasm at man's, not at the Houyhnhnms', expense when, as we have seen, the Houyhnhnm master supposes that man is not capable of making war (IV.v.247).

The Houyhnhnms' proposal to castrate some younger Yahoos (IV.ix.272-3) has also shocked critics. But again this follows the simple narrative logic: it is no more than humans do to horses. Our shock should be no more than the "noble Resentment" of the Houyhnhnm master when he hears of the custom among us (IV.iv.242). To the extent that we *are* shocked, Swift seems to me to be meaning mildly to outrage our "healthy" sensibilities, as he does in the hoof-kissing episode. But in any event, the Houyhnhnms get the idea *from* Gulliver's account of what men do to horses, so that either way the force of the fable is not on man's side. The fiction throughout reverses the man-horse relationship: horses are degenerate in England (p. 8 and IV.xii.295), as men are in Houyhnhnmland. Again, I think man comes out of it badly both ways: the Yahoos of Houyhnhnmland make their obvious point, but the suggestion in reverse seems to be that English horses are poor specimens (though to Gulliver better than men) because they live in a bad human world. At least, a kind of irrational sense of guilt by association is generated. We need not suppose that Swift is endorsing Gulliver's preference of his horses to his family in order to feel offended about it. At many (sometimes indefinable) points on a complex scale of effects, Swift is getting at us.

The Houyhnhnms' expulsion of Gulliver belongs to the same

group of objections. It seems to me that some of the sympathy showered on Gulliver by critics comes from a misfocussed response to him as a full character in whom we are very involved as a person. The Houyhnhnm master and the sorrel nag are in fact very sorry to lose Gulliver, but the logic of the fable is inexorable: Gulliver is of the Yahoo kind, and his privileged position in Houyhnhnmland was offensive to some, while his rudiments of Reason threaten (not without plausibility, from all we learn of man's use of that faculty) to make him a danger to the state as leader of the wild Yahoos (IV.x.279). The expulsion of Gulliver is like Gulliver's treatment of Don Pedro: both episodes have been sentimentalized, but they are a harsh reminder that even good Yahoos are Yahoos.

The main charge is that the Houyhnhnms are cold, passionless, inhuman, unattractive to us and therefore an inappropriate positive model. The fact that we may not like them does not mean that Swift is disowning them: it is consistent with his whole style to nettle us with a positive we might find insulting and rebarbative. The older critics who disliked the Houyhnhnms but felt that Swift meant them as a positive were surely nearer the mark than some recent ones who translate their own dislikes into the meaning of the book. But one must agree that the Houyhnhnms, though they are a positive, are not a *model*, there being no question of our being able to imitate them. So far as it has not been grossly exaggerated, their "inhumanity" may well, like their literal *non*-humanity (which tells us that the only really rational animal is not man), be part of the satiric point: this is a matter of "passions".

They are, of course, not totally passionless.[67] They treat Gulliver, in all personal contacts, with mildness, tenderness and friendly dignity (IV.i.224ff.). Gulliver receives special gentleness and affection from his master, and still warmer tenderness from the sorrel nag (IV.xi.283). Their language, which has no term for lying or opinion, "expressed the Passions very well", which may mean no more than "emotions" but does mean that they have them (IV.i.226). In contrast to the Laputans, who have no "Imagination, Fancy and Invention" (III.ii.163), but like the Brobdingnagians (II.vii.136), they excel in poetry (IV.ix.273-4), though their poems sound as if they might be rather unreadable and are certainly not enraptured effusions.

But their personal lives differ from ours in a kind of lofty tranquillity, and an absence of personal intimacy and emotional entanglement. In some aspects of this, they parallel Utopian Lilliput (I.vi.60ff.), and when Gulliver is describing such things as their conversational habits ("Where there was no Interruption, Tediousness, Heat, or Difference of Sentiments"), a note of undisguised wishfulness comes into the writing (see the whole passage, IV.x.277). W. B. Carnochan has shown, in a well-taken point, that such freedom from the "tyrant-passions" corresponds to a genuine longing of Swift himself.[68] I do not wish, and have no ability, to be psychoanalytical. But in a work which, in addition to much routine and sometimes rather self-conscious scatology (however "traditional"), contains the disturbing anatomy of Brobdingnagian ladies, the account of the Struldbrugs, the reeking sexuality of the Yahoos and the She-Yahoo's attempt on Gulliver, the horrible three-year-old Yahoo brat (IV.viii.265-6), the smell of Don Pedro and of Gulliver's family and Gulliver's strange relations with his wife, one might well expect to find aspirations for a society which practised eugenics and had an educational system in which personal and family intimacies were reduced to a minimum. Gulliver may be mocked, but the cumulative effect of these things is inescapable, and within the atmosphere of the work itself the longing for a world uncontaminated as far as possible by the vagaries of emotion might seem to us an unattractive, but is surely not a surprising, phenomenon.

But it is more important still to say that the Houyhnhnms are not a statement of what man ought to be so much as a statement of what he is not. Man thinks he is *animal rationale*, and the Houyhnhnms are a demonstration (which might, as we saw, be logically unacceptable, but is imaginatively powerful), for man to compare himself with, of what an *animal rationale* really is. R. S. Crane has shown that in the logic textbooks which commonly purveyed the old definition of man as a rational animal, the beast traditionally and most frequently named as a specific example of the opposite, the non-rational, was the horse.[69] Thus Hudibras, who "was in logic a great critic", would

> undertake to prove by force
> Of argument, a man's no horse.[70]

The choice of horses thus becomes an insulting exercise in "logical" refutation. The Yahoos are certainly an opposite extreme, and real man lies somewhere between them. But it is no simple comforting matter of a golden mean. Man is dramatically closer to the Yahoos in many ways, and with all manner of insistence. While the Houyhnhnms are an insulting impossibility, the Yahoos, though not a reality, are an equally insulting *possibility*. Swift's strategy of the undermining doubt is nowhere more evident than here, for though we are made to fear the worst, we are not given the comfort of knowing the worst. "The chief end I propose to my self in all my labors is to vex the world rather than divert it": and whatever grains of salt we may choose for our comfort to see in these words, "the world", gentle reader, includes *thee*.

NOTES

1 *A Tale of a Tub*, ed. Herbert Davis (Oxford, 1957: rept.), p. 29. See also p. 32. References are to this edition unless otherwise noted.

2 Herbert Read, *Selected Writings* (London, 1963), p. 127.

3 *Tale*, p. 42n.

4 See Edward W. Rosenheim, Jr., *Swift and the Satirist's Art*, (Chicago, 1963), p. 62.

5 *Tristram Shandy*, IV.x, IX.viii.

6 For a most useful survey of this "self-conscious" mode of writing, see Wayne C. Booth, "The Self-Conscious Narrator in Comic Fiction before *Tristram Shandy*", *PMLA*, LXVII (1952), 163-85. There is a good deal of this kind of writing shortly before Sterne, not necessarily derived from Swift, and my point does not *primarily* concern an "influence". See also Booth, *The Rhetoric of Fiction* (Chicago, 1961), p. 229.

7 *Tale*, p. 22.

8 Richardson, Preface to *Sir Charles Grandison*.

9 *Tale*, p. 27.

10 *Tristram Shandy*, I.vi.

11 *Tale*, p. 131.

12 *Tale*, p. 133.

13 "The Irony of Swift", *The Common Pursuit*, Penguin Books (1962), p. 80.

14 "Swift's Satire of the Second Person", *ELH*, xxvi (1959), 36-44.

15 "Addison", *Essays on the Eighteenth Century Presented to David Nichol Smith* (Oxford, 1945), p. 1.

16 Irvin Ehrenpreis, *The Personality of Jonathan Swift* (London, 1958), p. 39, on "A Beautiful Young Nymph Going to Bed". Ehrenpreis also lists parallels from other writers. See also Roland M. Frye, "Swift's Yahoo and the Christian Symbols for Sin", *JHI*, xv (1954), 201-17, and Deane Swift's *Essay* (1755), pp. 221ff.

17 All references to *Gulliver's Travels* give book, chapter, and page in the 1959 revised edition of Herbert Davis.

18 William King, *Some Remarks on The Tale of a Tub* (1704) cited by Ricardo Quintana, *The Mind and Art of Jonathan Swift* (New York and London, 1936), p. 75.

19 William Wotton, *A Defense of the Reflections upon Ancient and Modern Learning . . . With Observations upon The Tale of a Tub* (1705), in *A Tale of a Tub*, ed. A. C. Guthkelch and D. Nichol Smith (2d ed., Oxford, 1958), pp. 322, 323, 326.

20 *Tale*, ed. Davis, p. 5. Swift was not at first known to be the author.

21 *English Humourists*, etc., Everyman's Library (1949), p. 32.

22 See also *Tale*, p. 71, and Rabelais I.ii; I.xxxiii; II.xxx.

23 *English Humourists*, pp. 34-5.

24 "Swift and the Horses: Misanthropy or Comedy?", *MLQ*, X (1949), 374n.

25 Real concealment seemed a necessity, with such a subversive book, though Pope told Swift on 16 November 1726 that people were not worried by "particular reflections", so that he "needed not to have been so secret upon this head" (*Correspondence*, ed. Harold Williams iii (Oxford, 1963), 181). In any case, *simple* anonymity or pseudonymity would have served the practical purpose. Swift's authorship soon became fairly well known anyway.

26 Horace, *Odes*, III.xi.35.

27 *Correspondence*, III.180, 189. See also Mario M. Rossi and Joseph M. Hone, *Swift or the Egotist* (London, 1934), pp. 330, 411.

28 See Ricardo Quintana, *Swift. An Introduction*, Oxford Paperbacks (1962), pp. 53ff., 158f.

29 Rabelais, II.xxviii, *et passim*; Lucian, *True Story*, I.2ff.; Butler, *Erewhon*, ch. ix, *ad fin.*

30 "Democritus Junior to the Reader", *Anatomy of Melancholy*, Everyman's Library (1932), I.15, 123.

31 Contrast Gulliver's use of this convention: "I never suffer a Word to pass that may look like Reflection, or possibly give the least Offence even to those who are most ready to take it. So that, I hope, I may with Justice pronounce myself an Author perfectly blameless; against whom the Tribes of Answerers, Considerers, Observers, Reflecters, Detecters, Remarkers, will never be able to find Matter for exercising their Talents" (IV.xii.293). This hardly pretends to be a friendly, or even a plausible, gesture from Swift, though it is, of course, amusing.

32 For both these uses, see *O.E.D.*, "Thou", *pers. pron.*, 1b, and "Thou", *verb*.

33 *Epistle to a Lady*, ll.139ff., *Poems*, ed. Harold Williams (Oxford, 2d ed., 1958), II.634-7.

34 *Correspondence*, III.179.

35 *Correspondence*, III.120.

36 *Correspondence*, III.181, 182.

37 The clinching joke, though not the passage as a whole, is Swift's. See R. W. Frantz, "Gulliver's 'Cousin Sympson'", *HLQ*, I (1938), 331-3.

38 Boswell, *Life of Johnson*, ed. G. B. Hill and L. F. Powell (Oxford, 1934), II.319.

39 *Correspondence*, III.257-8.

40 *Jonathan Swift and the Anatomy of Satire* (Cambridge, Mass., 1961: rept.), p. 7.

41 *Epistle to a Lady*, ll.164-70, *Poems*, II.635.

42 *Correspondence*, III.103, 117.

43 "The Meaning of Gulliver's Last Voyage", *REL.*, III (1962), 35.

44 *Nineteen Eighty-Four*, I.i. Penguin Books (1954), pp. 10-11.

45 A. E. Case, *Four Essays on Gulliver's Travels* (Gloucester, Mass., 1958: rept.), p. 110.

46 *The Life of the Rev. Dr. Jonathan Swift* (2d ed. 1787), p. 433.

47 Joseph Horrell, "What Gulliver Knew", *SR*, LI (1943), 492-3; Case, *Four Essays*, p. 121; Samuel H. Monk, "The Pride of Lemuel Gulliver", *SR*, LXIII (1955), 56.

48 *Utopia*, tr. Ralph Robinson, Everyman's Library, 1951, p. 85. For an excellent discussion of More and Swift, see John Traugott, "A Voyage to Nowhere with Thomas More and Jonathan Swift: *Utopia* and *The Voyage to the Houyhnhnms*", *SR*, LXIX (1961), 534-65.

49 *Tom Jones*, III.iii. I hasten to say that I do not believe that the Houyhnhnms are therefore a satirical skit on the deists (or that Square, as one might just as easily "prove", was a skit on the Houyhnhnms), though the rationalisms have points in common. A. O. Lovejoy's "The Parallel of Deism and Classicism", *Essays in the History of Ideas*, Capricorn Books, 1960, pp. 78-98, makes abundantly clear that many basic assumptions about Nature and Reason were the common property of deists and non-deists alike. (My discussion here is indebted to this and other essays in Lovejoy's book.) This may be the place to say categorically that in my view Swift treats the Houyhnhnms mainly seriously and not mockingly, and that the recent arguments to this effect by Sherburn, Crane, Rosenheim, W. B. Carnochan, and others have put criticism of *Gulliver's Travels* back on the right lines.

50 These wonderfully apt examples are adapted from Rabelais, V.xxii, as is noted in W. A. Eddy, *Gulliver's Travels. A Critical Study* (New York, 1963: rept.), pp. 161-2. Jean Plattard's notes to the *Cinquiesme Livre* (Paris, 1948), pp. 324-5, show that Rabelais was literalizing a series of adages of Erasmus. See also the account of Lucian's *True Story* in Eddy, p. 16.

51 *Tom Jones*, XIII.v.

52 *Dunciad*, III.6.

53 See for example Roland M. Frye (above, n. 16), pp. 208-9.

54 This is an illuminating parallel to Swift's remark to Pope on 26 November 1725 about the kite (*Correspondence*, III.118). I have briefly discussed interpretations of this controversial letter in a review in *N. & Q.*, CCIX (1964), 316-17.

55 The passage runs pointedly against the Lilliputian (I.vi.60) and English (III.vii.201-2) examples. All rather strikingly have grandfather-grandchildren references. The contrast may reflect Swift's interest, noted by some critics, in a cyclical theory of history (e.g. III.x.210), but such force as it has on the reader *as a contrast* is simply to the discredit of England.

56 R. S. Crane, "The Houyhnhnms, the Yahoos, and the History of Ideas", *Reason and the Imagination*, ed. J. A. Mazzeo (New York and London, 1962), pp. 231-53.

57 See Ehrenpreis, *op. cit.*, *REL*, III (1962), 34. In some ways, *animal rationis capax* is not really very different from *animal rationale* in the low-pitched textbook sense. Bolingbroke may have this partly in mind when he says the distinction "will not bear examination" (*Correspondence*, III.121.)

58 *Irish Tracts 1720-1723 and Sermons*, ed. Herbert Davis and Louis Landa (Oxford, 1963: rept.), p. 166.

59 Physicians provide a monstrously concrete example of Nature turned upside down. The basis of the reversal is the perfectly fair notion, discussed earlier, that health is the "natural" state of the body: "these Artists ingeniously considering that in all Diseases Nature is forced out of her Seat; therefore to replace her in it, the Body must be treated in a Manner directly contrary, by interchanging the Use of each Orifice; forcing Solids and Liquids in at the *Anus*, and making Evacuations at the Mouth" (IV.vi.254).

60 But this parenthesis may refer to the word "degrading", and not to the phrase "human Nature".

61 Conrad Suits does not think so: "The Role of the Horses in 'A Voyage to the Houyhnhnms' ", *UTQ*, xxxiv (1965), 118-32.

62 Lucian, *Timon, or the Misanthrope*; Plutarch, *Life of Antony*, LXX.

63 Robert C. Elliott, *The Power of Satire* (Princeton, 1960), pp. 225-6.

64 *Correspondence*, III.117. See W. B. Carnochan, "The Complexity of Swift: Gulliver's Fourth Voyage", *SP*, LX (1963), 32ff.

65 "O, if the World had but a dozen Arbuthnetts in it I would burn my Travells" (*Correspondence*, III 104). Don Pedro may, in this sense, be an Arbuthnot.

66 *Op. cit.*, *SR*, LXIX (1961), 562. For another useful perspective, see R. S. Crane, "The Rationale of the Fourth Voyage", *Gulliver's Travels. An Annotated Text with Critical Essays*, ed. Robert A. Greenberg (New York, 1961), pp. 305-6.

67   See also George Sherburn, "Errors Concerning the Houyhnhnms", *MP*, LVI (1958), 94-5, and Carnochan, *op. cit.*, pp. 25-6.

68   Carnochan, *op. cit.*, p. 27.

69   *Reason and the Imagination*, pp. 247ff.

70   *Hudibras*, I.i.65, 71-2. See Ehrenpreis *op. cit.*, *REL*, III (1962), 23ff., for further illustration of the relevance of logic books. (The lines from *Hudibras* were pointed out to me by Mr. J. C. Maxwell before Ehrenpreis's article appeared). Another specified example of the non-rational animal was the ape. That Gulliver should have been taken by a Brobdingnagian monkey for one of its kind (II.v.122) gains an additional piquancy from this. Swift uses the horse, unlike the monkey, as an opposite, not as a parallel, but man is the loser both ways.

FREDERICK W. HILLES

Art and Artifice in
Tom Jones

Standing before Fielding's tomb in Lisbon, a character in Kingsley Amis's *I Like It Here* thinks to himself:

> Perhaps it was worth dying in your forties if two hundred years later you were the only non-contemporary novelist who could be read with unaffected interest, the only one who never had to be apologised for or excused on the grounds of changing taste.[1]

So positive a vote of confidence is heart-warming, but the vote is by no means unanimous, the statement by no means un-challenged. The fact is that many twentieth-century readers have found even the best of Fielding's work disappointing, if not at times embarrassing. And surely Mr. Empson cannot be taken seriously when he suggests that the moderns who have belittled Fielding have done so because they have found him intimidating.[2] Intellectuals like Dr. Leavis are not easily in-timidated. A different type of reader will be found among those students at a large state university in America who a few years ago voted that *Tom Jones* is the most overrated of English classics. Possibly like the "alert young people" for whom Ortega is spokesman[3] they were merely expressing their hos-tility to traditional art. Or their opinions might be more simply accounted for by the assumption that they had read the book with post-Jamesian spectacles. As John Butt remarked in his commentary on Fielding,[4] there are those who are inclined to

impose certain demands upon earlier novelists without reflecting whether such demands can be justified.

An aspect of *Tom Jones* that seems to disturb some moderns
is a matter that Fielding took pride in and for which he received
high praise from his contemporaries. Arnold Kettle, noting the
"carefully contrived but entirely non-symbolic plot", believes
Fielding "is constantly finding that the contrivance of his plot
does violence to the characters he has created".[5] Edwin Muir,
who asserts that a "plot should not appear to be a plot", admires
Fielding's brilliance but complains that the "plot of *Tom Jones*
is an adroitly constructed framework for a picture of life, rather
than an unfolding action".[6] Ian Watt, admitting that the book
has "a very neat and entertaining formal structure", feels that
this neatness suggests "the manipulated sequences of literature
rather than the ordinary processes of life".[7] Even Digeon, one
of the most devoted of latter-day Fieldingites, finds in this
famous plot "a perfection which is almost too severe".[8]

Educated readers of the eighteenth century were well aware
that the story had been "carefully contrived", "adroitly constructed". Note that two of the early commentators quoted at
the beginning of Professor Crane's thoughtful essay make use
of the word *artful* when expressing their admiration of the plot:[9]
"No fable whatever", wrote Arthur Murphy, "affords, in its
solution such artful states of suspense". "Since the days of
Homer", wrote James Beattie, "the world has not seen a more
artful epick fable". Such remarks are forerunners of Coleridge's
too frequently quoted praise of the plot. And Coleridge, it may
be remembered, is one of the chief English authorities invoked
by E. E. Stoll to support his thesis in *Art and Artifice in Shakespeare*. Neither Murphy nor Beattie nor Coleridge seem to have
been dismayed because the neatness of this artful plot suggested
"the manipulated sequences of literature". On the contrary this
delighted them. What they admired was Fielding's superb control
over the materials of his book.

To strengthen his argument Stoll brought in as collateral
evidence "the placid and ample pages" of the early novel, with
its "'heavy' fathers, tyrannical guardians, or amorous and barbarous aunts and duennas". What he particularly stressed when
discussing *Tom Jones* was the unlikely behaviour of Squire Allworthy, who casts Tom out into the cold world and then, some

five or six weeks later, welcomes him back while expelling Blifil.

> So lightly one cannot pass from belief and affection to disbelief and hatred, and back again. The human mind is not so immediately receptive and responsive. . . . And this no one knows better than Fielding himself, when the plot or a situation is not at stake.[10]

Stoll, then, agrees that the plot at times "does violence to the characters", but the point he makes is that *Tom Jones* is not a factual account of the life of a young man; it is a work of literature. And Fielding's fame, he says, is at least partly owing to his skill in handling those arbitrary and artificial devices that one finds in most literary masterpieces. How Fielding handled such devices is a complex subject that has been discussed, sometimes in great detail, by a number of writers. What follows is an attempt not to develop Stoll's thesis but to re-examine and hopefully to reappraise some of these frankly artificial elements. And, in the light of what is said above, the carefully worked out formal structure is an obvious point of departure.

"The form of a novel", wrote Percy Lubbock long ago, "is something that none of us, perhaps, has ever really contemplated". We cannot, he regrets, "keep a book steady and motionless before us, so that we may have time to examine its shape and design". "Nobody", he continues, "would venture to criticize a building, a statue, a picture, with nothing before him but the memory of a single glimpse caught in passing".[11] Precisely what Lubbock had in mind by form he nowhere makes clear. But if for *Tom Jones* we are willing to accept, in Mark Schorer's words, "some external neoclassic notion of form",[12] most of the difficulties that bother Lubbock will vanish. The architectural critic, when examining the shape and design of a building, cannot limit himself to the façade as, in a sense, the critic of a painting may do. He must consider its appearance from all points of the compass and must bear in mind the arrangement of the interior as well as exterior. Presumably he will study carefully a set of blueprints. Somewhat analogous is the task of the critic of the novel. Necessarily he must take into consideration its shape and design, and to do so he must schematize it as best he can.

What I have in mind when speaking of shape and design is

what E. M. Forster has called pattern – something different from the story or plot. In his words, "whereas the story appeals to our curiosity and the plot to our intelligence, the pattern appeals to our aesthetic sense, it causes us to see the book as a whole".[13] He discovers in *The Ambassadors* the shape of an hourglass, the same figure that some have seen in *Tom Jones*. More useful, it has seemed to me, when trying to see that book "as a whole", is an architectural figure. With Mrs. Van Ghent I conceive of *Tom Jones* as shaped like a Palladian mansion. Admitting with her that there is "a certain distortion involved in the attempt to represent a book by a visual figure",[14] I here rashly present a ground plan of *Tom Jones* because such a plan, however crude, does enable us to keep the book "steady and motionless before us". My plan is based on what John Wood originally designed for Prior Park, the stately home of Fielding's patron Ralph Allen. According to Wood, the extent of the whole, from the extreme left (the stables) to the extreme right (a picture gallery and bedrooms), "was proposed to answer that of three Sides of a Duodecagon, inscribed within a Circle of a Quarter of a Mile Diameter".[15]

The pattern of *Tom Jones* reflects the same mathematical exactitude. The novel is divided into eighteen books. As has often been pointed out, the first six of these deal with events in Somerset, at the homes of Allworthy and Western, and the last six with events in London. Tom and Sophia are separated in Book VI and do not see one another again until Book XIII. The central six books deal with events on the road while hero and heroine make their way from what had been home to London. Professor Crane's treatment of the plot, which as might be expected is along Aristotelian lines, results in valuable analysis but completely disguises this basic pattern, thus making it difficult for the reader to see the book as a whole. Fielding had done what he could to make his pattern obvious. As originally published the novel appeared in six volumes, three books to a volume. Nor can the reader pass from one book to another unawares. The much discussed opening chapters to each book, in which the narrator talks about his craft, emphasize the formal structure. Where the symmetry is most obvious is in the middle. Books IX and X, at the very center, contain the hilarious episodes that occur in the inn at Upton. Just before them Tom

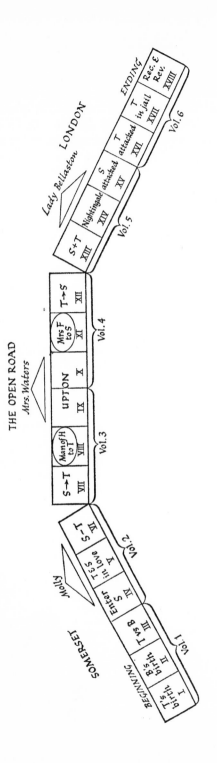

learns something about the great world as he listens to the life history of the Man of the Hill; just after them Sophia learns something about life when Mrs. Fitzpatrick talks about her unhappy experiences as a married woman. The central section begins (Book VII) with Tom on his travels and Sophia preparing to leave home. She catches up with him at Upton, hears how he is occupying himself, and departs for London without seeing him. When Tom learns what she has done he forgets his military commitments and at once sets out in an attempt to overtake her. The pursuer has become the pursued.

Just how to sum up in shorthand a particular book, or just where to end "the beginning" or begin "the ending", can easily provoke argument, and such argument is fruitless. I am happy to agree with Professor Crane in considering Books XVII and XVIII as comprising the ending. In the opening chapter of XVII the narrator talks about bringing his work "to a period", promises Sophia a good husband (Lord Fellamar or Blifil or someone else), and drops dark hints about what will happen to poor Tom. All of the chief characters are now in London ready to play their parts in that final book which in good Aristotelian fashion provides us with Recognition and a Reversal of the Situation. Crane's "beginning" takes us through Allworthy's illness and Bridget's death (midway in Book V). To me it is more logical to consider the first two books the beginning, "after which", according to Aristotle, "something naturally is or comes to be".[16] Those books give us the setting and the origins of Tom and Blifil – at least as much of that "as is necessary or proper to acquaint the reader with in the beginning of this history". The story gets under way in III where Tom and Blifil are compared. Sophia makes her debut in IV, she and Tom realize in V that they are in love, and they are separated in VI when he is expelled from home. They meet once more in XIII, but are then kept apart until the finale. Tom is involved in young Nightingale's affairs, after which both heroine and hero are plotted against and under attack, XV beginning with Sophia's near rape and XVI ending with the duel between Tom and Fitzpatrick.

When Honour unexpectedly arrives in Tom's room (XIV.ii), thus forcing Lady Bellaston to hide, the embarrassed young man begs her to whisper, "for that there was a lady dying in the next room. 'A lady!' cries [Honour]; 'ay, I suppose one of your ladies. Oh, Mr. Jones, there are too many of them in the world' ''. That seems to be the popular idea, that Tom is constantly surrounded by luscious damsels. Capitalizing upon the deserved success of the John Osborne–Tony Richardson adaptation, a new film has recently appeared that introduces "a 20th Century Tom Jones" and that, according to the advertisements, "gives a lesson in the art of pursuing the opposite sex". Presumably both producer and audience would be surprised to learn that Fielding's Tom is no gay Lothario. With the exception of Sophia there are only three women in his life, and in each case it is the lady who does the pursuing. "To confess the truth, he had rather too much diffidence in himself, and was not forward enough in seeing the advances of a young lady" (V.ii). Just how carefully Fielding has spaced these three affairs the diagram makes obvious. Molly, the young country trollop, is introduced in IV. Tom's relations with her are at their blackest in V when he once more succumbs to her although he now knows that he is in love with Sophia. In VI one of the charges leading to his expulsion is that he "yet converses" with "that wench". Thereafter she takes no part in his life. Now note that exactly balancing Tom's carryings-on with Molly is the last of his infidelities. He meets Lady Bellaston in XIII, the liaison is most offensive in XIV (he has now discovered Sophia), and it is forever ended near the conclusion of XV. The only other "lady" in his life (we readers see her as Jenny in the first and last books of the novel) is Mrs. Waters, who in regard to sophistication is somewhere between Molly and Lady Bellaston. Tom rescues her at the beginning of IX, is (with shame I write it, and with sorrow will it be read) actually in bed with her at the half-way point (the end of that book), and concludes the affair once and for all in X.

So symmetrical an arrangement calls attention to itself. Life is just not like this. Such neatness does in truth suggest the manipulated sequences of literature; the plot is indeed carefully contrived. As used by modern critics words like *manipulate* and *contrive* are pejoratives. They have not always been so and would not, I think, have been used in that way by Fielding and his contemporaries. Among definitions still authorized by the *Oxford English Dictionary* are for *manipulate*: to handle something with dexterity, to operate upon something with the mind and intelligence, to treat artistic matter, etc., with skill; and for *contrive*: to invent, devise, excogitate with ingenuity and cleverness a plan, to devise, invent, design a literary composition, etc. One meaning of *contrivance* is "the action of inventing or making with thought and skill". Now one of the silliest of Richardson's ill-tempered remarks about his rival was that he had "little or no invention".[17] Amusingly enough in the publisher's contract *Tom Jones* is said to have been invented as well as written by Henry Fielding. Certainly Fielding went out of his way to call attention, again and again, to his ingenuity. One of the best of the many commentators on *Tom Jones* momentarily slipped when, describing what happens in Book IX, he wrote: "Tom Jones and his servant Partridge arrive at the Upton inn escorting a certain Mrs. Waters . . ."[18] Of course Partridge did not escort Mrs. Waters to the inn. Near the end of the novel (XVIII.ii) Fielding asks us to

> admire the many strange accidents which unfortunately prevented any interview between Partridge and Mrs. Waters, when she spent a whole day [at Upton] with Mr. Jones. Instances of this kind we may frequently observe in life, where the greatest events are produced by a nice train of little circumstances; and more than one example of this may be discovered by the accurate eye, in this our history.

Fielding the narrator is constantly talking to us in this fashion. He is anything but "invisible, refined out of existence, indifferent, paring his fingernails". It may seem odd, then, to suggest that he was an eighteenth-century Joyce, that *Tom Jones* is an eighteenth-century *Ulysses*.[19] Fielding, of course, had Homer in mind as he wrote his epic and even refers directly to Ulysses in the epigraph on the title-page. But his relationship to Joyce is, I believe, something far more fundamental. Both were innovators; both superb literary craftsmen who enjoyed playing with words. Making allowances for the difference in idiom between the eighteenth and twentieth centuries, examine the following passage (XI.viii) where Sophia and her cousin hear

> a noise, not unlike, in loudness, to that of a pack of hounds just let out from their kennel; nor, in shrillness, to cats, when caterwauling;

or, to screech-owls; or, indeed, more like (for what animal can resemble a human voice) to those sounds, which, in the pleasant man-
sions of that gate, which seems to derive its name from a duplicity of
tongues, issue from the mouths, and sometimes from the nostrils of
those fair river nymphs, ycleped of old the Napæa, or the Naïades;
in the vulgar tongue translated oyster-wenches: for when, instead of
the antient libations of milk and honey and oil, the rich distillation
from the juniper-berry, or perhaps, from malt, hath, by the early
devotion of their votaries, been poured forth in great abundance,
should any daring tongue with unhallowed license prophane; i.e.
depreciate the delicate fat Milton oyster, the plaice sound and firm,
the flounder as much alive as when in the water, the shrimp as big
as a prawn, the fine cod alive but a few hours ago, or any other of
the various treasures, which those water-deities, who fish the sea
and rivers, have committed to the care of the nymphs, the angry
Naïades lift up their immortal voices, and the prophane wretch is struck
deaf for his impiety.

Overlooking what is immediately obvious in this excerpt, we
can see that Fielding is here greatly widening his horizon, is
enriching and deepening his narrative. Sophia and Harriet may
be cooped up in a country inn on the Watling Street, some
ninety miles from London; we the readers are not only there
but in London itself as well as near the groves and by the
streams of ancient Greece. Somewhat Joycean, I think, are the
street-cries of the fishwives; Joycean too is the far-fetched pun
on Billingsgate.

In the opening chapter of Book IV our attention is called to
"sundry similes, descriptions, and other kind of poetical embellishments" that have been interspersed throughout the story.
Presumably Henry Fielding the author here agrees with the
narrator of *Tom Jones* in asserting that these "ornamental parts"
are inserted merely to hold the reader's attention, that they have
no other function. In fact, however, these embellishments are
an integral part of the novel, and this, thanks to Joyce (among
others), the modern reader can appreciate as, perhaps, the
original reader did not. Here is the highly functional opening of
a section of *Ulysses*:

The summer evening had begun to fold the world in its mysterious
embrace. Far away in the west the sun was setting and the last glow
of all too fleeting day lingered lovingly on sea and strand, on the

proud promontory of dear old Howth guarding as ever the waters of
the bay, on the weedgrown rocks along Sandymount shore and, last
but not least, on the quiet church whence there streamed forth at
times upon the stillness the voice of prayer to her who is in her pure
radiance a beacon ever to the stormtossed heart of man, Mary, star
of the sea.[20]

With that compare the following, (V.x) less subtle to our ears,
no doubt, but performing much the same function:

> It was now a pleasant evening in the latter end of June, when our
> hero was walking in a most delicious grove, where the gentle breezes
> fanning the leaves, together with the sweet trilling of a murmuring
> stream, and the melodious notes of nightingales, formed altogether
> the most enchanting harmony. In this scene, so sweetly accomodated to
> love, he meditated on his dear Sophia. While his wanton fancy roved
> unbounded over all her beauties, and his lively imagination painted
> the charming maid in various ravishing forms, his warm heart melted
> with tenderness; and at length, throwing himself on the ground, by
> the side of a gently murmuring brook, he broke forth into the following
> ejaculation . . .

Fielding erred in dating this event in June, as an early reader
noticed.[21] Tom had only recently broken his arm while hunting and
within a month of this time was walking with shivering Partridge
on a cold winter's night. I suggest that the author was so intent
on his parody that he momentarily forgot his time-scheme.
What one expects when reading a romance is that such an
evening as this should occur in the merry month of June.

Our hero, speaking as a romantic hero should, declares that
if only Sophia were his he would envy no one.

> How contemptible would the brightest Circassian beauty, dressed
> in all the jewels of the Indies, appear to my eyes! But why do I men-
> tion another woman? Could I think my eyes capable of looking at
> any other with tenderness, these hands should tear them from my
> head.

One thinks of young Romeo, who – madly in love, he thinks,
with the fair Rosaline – when told that others are more beautiful
bursts out:

100

> When the devout religion of mine eye
> Maintains such falsehood, then turn tears to fires,
> And those who, often drown'd, could never die,
> Transparent heretics, be burnt for liars.

And then, knowing that the brightest beauties could no longer have charms for him, nor would a hermit be colder in their embraces,

> he started up, and beheld – not his Sophia – no, nor a Circassian maid richly and elegantly attired for the grand Signior's seraglio. No; without a gown, in a shift that was somewhat of the coarsest, and none of the cleanest, bedewed likewise with some odoriferous effluvia, the produce of the day's labour, with a pitchfork in her hand, Molly Seagrim approached.

Here the echo is not of "vulgar" romances nor of Shakespeare, but (compare self-parody in Joyce) of this particular novel. The exaggerated periodic sentence recalls to us our first glimpse of the fair heroine:

> for lo! adorned with all the charms in which nature can array her; bedecked with beauty, youth, sprightliness, innocence, modesty, and tenderness, breathing sweetness from her rosy lips, and darting brightness from her sparkling eyes, the lovely Sophia comes!

Molly and Tom converse awhile and then – the sequel is not elevating. Funny it is – and this because Fielding's rhetoric has prepared us for it, but the simple fact is that our hero is drunk and behaving in a fashion unbecoming to heroes – at least to pre-twentieth-century heroes. Fielding looks facts in the face, as he makes plain at this very point in the novel. But a description of what was now going on in the thickest part of the grove would obviously be out of place in this particular story. *Tom Jones* differs in tone from, say, *Sanctuary* or *Lie Down in Darkness*. It is important for Fielding to soft-pedal the entire affair, and this he does skilfully. Tom's sexual misdemeanor is, we are reminded, the result of too much drinking, and the idea of drunkenness is made to seem less reprehensible by two classical allusions, the witty remark of "one Cleostratus", and the charitable opinion of Aristotle. Instead of being shocked at

Tom's animalistic behaviour we can still look upon him with affection. Immediately after this the hiding place occupied by Tom and Molly is equated with a cave that was described by a goddess as the shelter for a famous queen and a great epic hero. Of course it is the essence of the mock heroic to juxtapose the great and the little, and Molly's masquerading here as Dido prepares us for the tone of what immediately follows.

The battle is introduced by "a simile in Mr. Pope's period of a mile" – that is, by a rhetorical passage extended, as John Nichols put it, "to a disagreeable length".[22] It may be worth noting that the magnificent simile contains another pun, this one on the New Forest, and neatly links together the purely animalistic and what the author terms sacred. The bloody battle follows, at the end of which we are given this tableau:

> In one place lay on the ground, all pale, and almost breathless, the vanquished Blifil. Near him stood the conqueror Jones, almost covered with blood, part of which was naturally his own, and part had been lately the property of the Reverend Mr. Thwackum. In a third place stood the said Thwackum, like King Porus, sullenly submitting to the conqueror. The last figure in the piece was Western the Great, most gloriously forbearing the vanquished foe.

Sophia swoons, and the author then introduces a paragraph that has irritated some critics:

> The reader may remember, that in our description of this grove we mentioned a murmuring brook, which brook did not come there, as such gentle streams flow through vulgar romances, with no other purpose than to murmur. No! Fortune had decreed to ennoble this little brook with a higher honour than any of those which wash the plains of Arcadia ever deserved.

Our hero, oblivious to what he had undergone that afternoon, flies to Sophia, picks her up and runs with her to the brook, and there revives her by besprinkling her face, head, and neck very plentifully. Moments later the author puts an end to the incident and to the book.

This whole episode, from the time Tom throws himself down by the brook until he has revived Sophia, nicely illustrates the function performed by those "poetical embellishments" that are

102

especially prominent in this part of the novel. What would the book be without them? Somerset Maugham has supplied the answer. In his deplorable abridgement of *Tom Jones* the whole character of the book has been altered. It has become (I quote from the blurb) a "lively and romantic adventure story of a young man . . . handsome, high-spirited, and gallant with the ladies, [though] somewhat of a rogue".

There have been many readers who have thought the book would be improved if altered along the lines Maugham followed. Some two hundred years ago Lord Monboddo, who admired *Tom Jones* extravagantly, thought the work perfect except for two blemishes, the author's bringing himself into the book so frequently and the introduction of the mock-heroic, that "destroys the probability of the narrative, which ought to be carefully studied in all works, that, like Mr. Fielding's, are imitations of real life and manners".[23] The same criticism is heard today. A highly gifted modern author in an introduction to a school-text of *Tom Jones* praises the book for its lifelike hero but objects to the author's intrusions that "decompose a state of mind which has been adjusted to accepting as true and inevitable all that occurred from the day when Squire Allworthy" etc. etc. etc.[24] We are back to where we started. If characters and actions are really lifelike the author blunders when, for example, he talks about his murmuring brook.

But Fielding was writing a *comic* epic. He revelled in the exaggerations that one expects to find in comedy. The years he had spent as a dramatist, a writer of farce, influenced all his later writing.[25] There are sensitive readers of today who have declared that for them Sophia never recovers from the highly artificial way she is introduced to us. Fielding, it should be pointed out, compounded that artificiality. His introduction of Sophia is in turn introduced by the anecdote of the actor who enjoys his shoulder of mutton by having disposed of the carpenters who had to precede him on to the stage. The unnamed actor, it happens, was Barton Booth; the play Ambrose Philips' *Distrest Mother*, which Fielding had burlesqued in *The Covent Garden Tragedy*. One of the most popular plays of the day, it owed its success in large part to the impressive bearing of this actor. "Whoever has seen Booth in the Character of *Pyrrhus* march to his Throne to receive *Orestes*", wrote Steele in

Spectator 334, "is convinced that majestick and great Conceptions are expressed in the very Step". In the following paper (Fielding's model for Partridge's seeing Garrick play *Hamlet*) Sir Roger tells Mr. Spectator as he watches Pyrrhus make his grand entry "that he did not believe the King of France himself had a better Strut". Steele had also written the prologue to the play, and in it declared that Pyrrhus did not need attendants to prove himself royal. Fielding gives that statement another twist. Pyrrhus is fully and happily aware of the fact that he cannot make his grand entry unless preceded by his attendants. And we notice that the tragic hero is in reality a hungry actor, his courtiers mere stage hands. Ostensibly Fielding is gravely saying that people deserving of respect are naturally surrounded by attendants, but he is saying this in such a way as to make us aware of the world of make-believe. There is a considerable difference between that world and the one in which we live.

A king with a similar name may just possibly be playing a similar part at the end of that bloody battle we have just observed. One of the four figures in the quoted tableau was Thwackum looking like King Porus. No doubt the reader is expected to call up a mental picture of the historical Porus, a warrior almost seven feet tall, whose defeat was one of Alexander's proudest victories. Perhaps the original reader would think of LeBrun's heroic painting of Porus, familiar through engravings or the tapestry brought to England while Fielding was a boy. But Porus was a name with operatic connotations. Addison and Steele have fun with him in Spectators 31 and 36, and after the middle twenties his was a famous part in a great number of operas based on Metastasio's libretto, *Alessandro nelle Indie*. In 1746, just when Fielding is thought to have begun writing *Tom Jones*, "a new opera" was put on in London, *Alexander in India*, with music by Lampugnani. The part of Porus was taken by the famous castrato Monticelli. Operatic conventions being what they were, the audience would not be surprised to see the part of the gigantic fighter taken by a slightly built Italian who had often taken female parts. Burney remembered Monticelli as "having a beautiful face and figure".[26] The finale of the opera shows the defeated Porus making his heroic reply to Alexander. In a high clear voice Monticelli sang, presumably in the original Italian:

> E la mia pena attendo.
> Sia qual tu vuoi, ma sia
> Sempre degna d'un Re la sorte mia.

– words that were translated (by Samuel Humphries?):

> Death I expect,
> And wait, thus, undismay'd. – My only boon
> Is, let my fall be worthy of the monarch.

Whether Fielding here had in mind the intrinsic artificiality of an operatic finale or not, he definitely alludes to *The Rehearsal* a few paragraphs later. Saying what he obviously meant to be serious ("surely", he remarked elsewhere [XI.i], "a man may speak truth with a smiling countenance"), he wishes that all quarrels could be decided by fisticuffs.

> Then would war, the pastime of monarchs, be almost inoffensive, and battles between great armies might be fought at the particular desire of several ladies of quality . . . Then might the field be this moment well strewed with human carcasses, and the next, the dead men, or infinitely the greatest part of them, might get up, like Mr. Bayes's troops, and march off.

A page or two later brings this particular book to an end.

With the idea of artificiality in mind an examination of Book V as a whole may prove fruitful. The opening chapter contains its share of theatrical allusions: the validity of the unities is questioned, the hoots and hisses of a hostile audience are indirectly mentioned, and a good deal of fun is made of the English Pantomime. Then in order to illustrate what he solemnly calls his "new vein of knowledge" ("no other than that of contrast, which runs through all the works of creation, and may probably have a large share in constituting in us the idea of all beauty, as well natural as artificial") he refers to the powers of cosmetics which "at Bath particularly" enable ladies that are "as ugly as possible in the morning" to appear as beauties in the evening.

Not counting this introduction the book consists of eleven chapters, the central pivotal one describing Allworthy on his "death-bed". This chapter, perfectly comic in that throughout it contrasts what is true with what seems to be true, has been misread by some critics. The chapter heading seems innocent enough: "In which Mr. Allworthy appears on a sick-bed". The man in the bed and all who surround it assume he is dying. If one is tempted to read death-bed for sick-bed all is still well. Conditioned as we are by our author's choice of words, we note the verb. One meaning of "to appear" is "to seem, as distinguished from *to be*". Even on the first reading one should not be deceived by Allworthy's illness. It is introduced in a paragraph that talks about the medical profession, ending with what "the great" Dr. Misaubin is said to have said: "Bygar, me believe my pation take me for de undertaker, for dey never send for me till de physician have kill dem". We do not need to know that Fielding had dedicated his *Mock Doctor* (out of Molière) to Misaubin in one of his most delightful ironic pieces. We do not need to know that Fielding's friend Hogarth more than once went out of his way to introduce Misaubin into his satirical pictures. The tone of this particular passage speaks for itself, and we have already witnessed a number of mock doctors, beginning with young Blifil's uncle, who "had in his youth been obliged to study physic, or rather to say he studied it". By the time Allworthy takes to his bed we have learned what to think of "that learned Faculty, for whom we have so profound a respect". If we were still tempted to take Allworthy's illness seriously, we should be shocked at the way our author phrases the reactions of some of the company: "even the philosopher Square wiped his eyes, albeit unused to the melting mood. As to Mrs. Wilkins, she dropped her pearls as fast as the Arabian trees their medicinal gums". For those who know the story (and no one has read *Tom Jones* who has not read it more than once) there is grim humour in the knowledge that although Allworthy thinks he is dying, his sister has actually died; and the humour is grimmer when we contrast Blifil's behaviour just before and just after he learns of his mother's death – and of his actual relationship to Tom.

That chapter I have called pivotal. The five chapters preceding it perfectly exemplify that new vein of knowledge we have just read about. In the first two we move from sour to sweet, from sweet to sour. Though Tom is attracted to Sophia he is honour-bound to be faithful to Molly. Then the "little incident of the muff" drives away all defences as the God of Love marches in. The problem of how to break with Molly is pleasantly solved when "the wicked rug" falls, revealing Square among other female utensils. (The wicked rug echoes the Shakespearean wicked wall of I.viii, and prepares for the reverse twist given by the bed curtains in XV.vii.) Tom is thus free to tell Sophia of his love, just before hearing that Allworthy is dying. His great happiness when with Sophia is balanced in the second half of the book by his great joy at Allworthy's recovery. This leads him to drink too much, and we have already traced what happened to him after that. Suffice it to say that the book as a whole is, like the novel as a whole, symmetrically constructed, the action in the first half occurring for the most part at Squire Western's, in the second half in or near Squire Allworthy's. Square's humiliation in the first half of the book is balanced by Thwackum's in the second. At the beginning of the book Tom is an injured hero, having saved Sophia when her horse threw her; at the end of the book Tom is an injured hero, having brought Sophia back to life after her death-resembling swoon. And central to the whole book, as it is central to the whole novel, is the basic contrast between Tom and Blifil.

Dante's Inferno is divided into an upper and a lower Hell, the one reserved for those whose sins are of the flesh, the other for those whose sins are of the spirit. In Book V Tom shows himself to be lustful and gluttonous; there is a hint too of the prodigal in him. But Blifil perfectly qualifies himself for a permanent home in the City of Dis – in the Malebolge, that eighth circle of lower Hell where the deceitful are forever punished. This, the most basic of the many contrasts in *Tom Jones*, underlies almost everything Fielding produced. Before he became a novelist he angrily wrote in the person of Job Vinegar about a Swiftian people, the Ptfghsiumgski:

All great Vices as Drinking, Gaming, injuring their Neighbour by walking over his Land, or taking away a Cock or Hen from him, &c. are very severely punished, but for little Foibles, and which may rather be called Weaknesses than Crimes, such as Avarice, Ingratitude, Cruelty, Envy, Malice, Falsehood, and the rest of this kind, they are entirely overlooked.[27]

Beneath Fielding's fine control in *Tom Jones* is a passionate hatred of deceit, a burning desire to make men open their eyes to the way of the world. *Tom Jones* is spoken of as an optimistic novel. This, I suppose, is because it has a happy ending. But the author of a tragedy is not necessarily a pessimist, and a comic epic demands a gay conclusion. The author of *Tom Jones* is certainly aware of man's weaknesses and can hardly be called naive. That "virtue is the certain road to happiness, and vice to misery, in this world", he writes (XI.i), is a "very wholesome and comfortable doctrine, to which we have but one objection, namely, that it is not true". Like other eminent writers of his time Fielding is in his own fashion bidding us to clear our minds of cant.

In his own fashion. That ever present narrator who tells us about his own likes and dislikes is forcing us to read the book the way the author wishes it read. We may want to identify with the healthy, handsome, fundamentally decent hero and believe that what he is doing is really happening, but if so we are refusing to follow the direction posts erected by the author. He is not jesting when he says (I.ii) of his hostile critics: "Till they produce the authority by which they are constituted judges, I shall not plead to their jurisdiction". In a comic epic in prose the narrator is a creator who sits above the world he has created and tells his readers what to look at and how to look at it. Allan Ramsay, one more of Fielding's contemporaries who applied the word *artful* to this story, said the reader believes it to be true "and is with difficulty recall'd from that belief by the author's confession from time to time of its being all a fiction".[28] This is not a complaint but a statement of fact. We are not allowed to identify with characters, as we are, for example, in *Clarissa*. The author insists upon our remaining detached so that we can see clearly. If we were to become involved we should no longer have that balanced view of mankind which the highly symmetrical, and in this sense symbolic, plot presents to us. The world of *Tom Jones* is not the real world; it is a reflection of a reflection of real life and thus has a form and structure denied to real life. The narrator speaks (XVII.i) of the surprise and delight the credulous reader found in the fictions of early writers. He assumes that we are more mature. He too wishes to surprise and delight, but his appeal is to the literate who will enjoy his artistry and while enjoying the story will be aware of the seriousness that underlies his comic creations.

Eliot is on record as having read *Ulysses* with surprise, delight, and terror.[29] Fielding's sagacious reader will be surprised and delighted but hardly terrified. Shocked as Dr. Johnson would be at the very idea, Fielding is that laughing philosopher who is called upon in *The Vanity of Human Wishes* to look at motley life with philosophic eye. Johnson's poem was published only a few weeks before *Tom Jones* made its bow, and it is to *Tom Jones* that we turn when seeking cheerful wisdom and instructive mirth.

NOTES

1 Kingsley Amis, *I Like It Here* (New York, 1958), p. 185.

2 Fielding ("Twentieth Century Views"), ed. R. Paulson (New York, 1962), p. 145.

3 As quoted by W. C. Booth in *The Rhetoric of Fiction* (Chicago, 1961), p. 120. My indebtedness to this fine book will be obvious.

4 *Fielding* ("Writers and their Works") (London, 1959), p. 27.

5 *An Introduction to the English Novel* (London, 1951), p. 77.

6 *The Structure of the Novel* (London, 1954), pp. 39, 31.

7 *The Rise of the Novel* (London, 1957), p. 253.

8 Aurelien Digeon, *The Novels of Fielding* (London, 1953), p. 233.

9 "The Concept of Plot and the Plot of *Tom Jones*" in *Critics and Criticism*, ed. R. S. Crane (abridged ed., Chicago, 1957), p. 62.

10 *Art and Artifice in Shakespeare* (Cambridge, 1938), pp. 65, 67f.

11 *The Craft of Fiction* (New York, 1921), pp. 3, 1.

12 *Forms of Modern Fiction*, ed. W. V. O'Connor (Minneapolis, 1948), p. 26.

13 *Aspects of the Novel* (New York, 1927), p. 215.

14 Dorothy Van Ghent, *The English Novel* (New York, 1953), p. 80.

15 John Wood, *A Description of Bath* (2d ed., London, 1769), p. 96.

16 *Poetics* (tr. S. H. Butcher) VII, 3.

17 *Selected Letters of Samuel Richardson*, ed. J. Carroll (Oxford, 1964), p. 197.

18 Digeon, *op. cit.*, p. 173.

19 In his introduction to the Mod. Lib. ed. of *Joseph Andrews* (1939), Howard Mumford Jones suggests that when writing *Ulysses* Joyce may have had Fielding's Preface to *Joseph Andrews* in mind. Bernard Benstock (*Joyce-again's Wake*, Seattle, 1965, p. 164) believes that Fielding's formula "was probably close to Joyce's interests during the construction of *Finnegan's Wake*".

20 P. 340 in Mod. Lib. ed.

21 W. L. Cross, *History of Henry Fielding* (New Haven, 1918), II.193.

22 Pope's *Imitations of Horace*, ed. J. Butt (Vol. IV of Twickenham ed., London, 1939), p. 31n.

23 F. T. Blanchard, *Fielding the Novelist* (New Haven, 1927), p. 227.

24 Collins Classics ed. (London, 1955), p. 29.

25 In his admirable *Fielding: Tom Jones* (Studies in Eng. Lit. 23, Arnold (London, 1964), pp. 40ff.), Irvin Ehrenpreis discusses at some length the theatrical elements in the novel.

26 Charles Burney, *A General History of Music*, ed. F. Mercer (New York, 1957), II.839. Burney is wrong and has led others astray in thinking that Lampugnani's *Allessandro nell'Indie* (1746) is the same opera as Lampugnani's *Roxana* (1743). In the Yale Library in Italian and English is a new edition of Metastasio's *Alessandro nelle Indie*, published in London in 1746 with the cast that took part in Lampugnani's version that year.

27 *The Voyages of Mr. Job Vinegar from the Champion*, ed. S. J. Sacket, Augustan Reprint Society, No. 67, (1958), as quoted by Andrew Wright in *Henry Fielding Mask and Feast* (California, 1965), p. 196.

28 F. T. Blanchard, *op. cit.*, p. 107.

29 *Forms of Modern Fiction*, ed. W. V. O'Connor (Minneapolis, 1948), p. 120.

In praise of Rasselas:
Four Notes (Converging)

[i]

Afterthoughts in Rasselas

Johnson most likely began to write *Rasselas* not long after Saturday, 13 January, 1759, when he seems first to have heard of his mother's serious illness. A week later, on Saturday, 20 January, he wrote to the publisher William Strahan that he would deliver the book to him on Monday night, and that the title would be "The Choice of Life/ or/ The History of . . . . . Prince of Abisinnia". The several learned editors of *Rasselas* have, accordingly, not been inclined to take literally Johnson's later statement to Reynolds, as reported by Boswell, that he not only wrote *Rasselas* "in the evenings of one week", but "sent it to the press in portions as it was written".[1] In portions, as it was corrected during days subsequent to Monday, 22 January, perhaps.[2] It is not difficult to imagine revisions and afterthoughts even during the original week of rapid composition. One of the most obvious internal suggestions of such afterthought, or at least of a certain absent-mindedness during the course of writing, appears in the development of the character of the lady Pekuah. We hear of her first, momentarily, in the escape from the happy valley (chapter XV). "The princess was followed only by a single favourite, who did not know whither she was going . . . The princess and her maid turned their eyes toward every part, and, seeing nothing to bound their prospect, considered themselves as in danger of being lost in a dreary vacuity. They stopped and trembled". A second very brief allusion occurs in the next chapter (XVI), as they arrive at Cairo. "The princess . . . for some days, continued in her chamber, where she was served by her favourite as in the palace of the valley". Thereafter, for fourteen chapters (XVII-XXX), or during the whole first period at Cairo, including the trip to the cataract of the Nile to visit the hermit, we miss this personage altogether, until in chapter XXXI, at the great Pyramid, she reappears abruptly: ". . . the favourite of the princess, looking into the cavity, stepped back and trembled. 'Pekuah, said the princess, of what art thou afraid?' " In the first edition, this was the first introduction of the lady's name. For the second edition, Johnson went back and inserted this name after the word "favourite" in the sentence quoted above from chapter XVI. We remember that Pekuah, through her terror of the gloomy inside of the pyramid, remains outside and in chapter XXXIII is kidnapped by a band of Arab horsemen and becomes the central object of attention during six succeeding chapters (to XXXIX). She reappears thereafter, to the end of the story, in every family conversation (chapters XLIV, XLV, XLVII, XLIX); and in chapter XLVI, her interest in the stars, acquired while she was a prisoner of the Arab chief, is exploited when the ladies invade and civilize the mad astronomer. Once he had conferred a few colours upon this lady, Johnson found her a convenient enough addition to his *dramatis personae*. It is possible that, having in chapters XV and XVI, provided for her presence, he then forgot her, or even deliberately left her out of sight, for seventeen chapters. But it seems at least possible – to me it seems more likely – that he first conceived of the lady Pekuah as his travellers stood at the entrance of the Pyramid, and he bethought himself of Arab horsemen on the horizon and the opportunity to give his story an impetus towards action which at that juncture it badly needed. In that case, he went back (nothing could be simpler) and inserted the allusions to a "favourite" in chapters XV and XVI, and in the second edition the name Pekuah in chapter XVI.[3]

As Geoffrey Tillotson has already observed, Johnson throughout *Rasselas* is preoccupied with the passage of time and pays close attention to the number of days, months, and years which measure out his story. At the age of twenty-six,[4] for example, when he first becomes restless in his confinement, Rasselas lets twenty months slip away in day-dreaming, then awakes and estimates with chagrin that, since the active life of man, between infancy and senility, amounts to no more than forty years, he has just allowed a twenty-fourth part of his life to run to waste ($12 \times 40 = 480 \div 20 = 24$). In contrast to such numerical nicety, the following curious sequence occurs in chapters XIX, XX, and XXI. Rasselas and his friends hear of a hermit, famous for sanctity, who lives near the "lowest cataract of the Nile". They set out to visit him but stop during the "heat" of the [first] day at the tents of some shepherds, whose barbarous conversation proves disgusting to the princess (chapter XIX). Presumably they do not linger for the afternoon or spend the night with these shepherds. But: "On the *next day* [the italics are mine] they continued their journey", says the first sentence of chapter XX. Again they stop during the "heat" of the day, but this time at the "stately palace" of a very prosperous gentleman. He entreats them to stay. They do. And the "next day" he entreats them again. They "continued", in fact, "a few days longer, and then went forward to find the hermit". Then the next chapter (XXI) begins: "They came on the third day, by the direction of the peasants, to the hermit's cell". By the direction of the peasants? Some might argue that this means simply "*the* peasants" of that region. But this kind of slipshod phrasing is not like Johnson. It appears to me all but certain that "peasants" is one of Johnson's occasional quiet or pronominal "elegant variations". He means the "shepherds" with whom they stopped at midday during chapter XIX. After that, and "on the third day" after setting out,[5] they came to the hermit's cell. It seems to me very likely that the episode of the prosperous country gentleman is something which occurred to Johnson at some time after he had written the sequence about the shepherds and the hermit (chapters XIX, XXI), and that, wishing to get it in, he wrote it in where he could, but without noticing a slight derangement of the details of the itinerary. The stop with the shepherds is a brief episode which does not sidetrack the journey to the hermit. Chapter XX, on the downfall of a prosperous country gentleman, is an extended intrusion into that journey. *Rasselas* is in a sense a travel story, but it is not on the whole a picaresque story.

The third example of narrative absent-mindedness which I wish to notice does, however, give us another exception to that rule. Chapter XL (immediately after the narrative of Pekuah's captivity with the Arab), begins: "They returned to Cairo . . . none of them went much abroad. The prince . . . one day declared to Imlac, that he intended to devote himself to science, and pass the rest of his days in literary solitude. 'Before you make your final choice, answered Imlac, you ought to examine its hazards . . . I have just left the observatory of one of the most learned astronomers in the world.' " For the space of five chapters (XL, XLI, XLII, XLIII, XLIV) Imlac continues a non-stop lecture upon the mad delusion by which the astronomer believes himself possessed of the power to control the seasons, bringing rain or sunshine to any part of the world as his conscience dictates. We discover that not only Rasselas but Nekayah and Pekuah are present during the whole conversation (chapters XLIII and XLIV). Then chapter XLV breaks into this sequence as follows: "The evening was now far past, and they rose to return home. As they walked along the bank of the Nile, delighted with the beams of the moon quivering on the water, they saw at a small distance an old man." But this does not really make sense. If we look back through the involvements of Imlac's long discourse on the mad astronomer, to the beginning of chapter XL, we remember that they are already at home and have been during the whole episode. (Looking back yet farther, a long way back, to chapter XXV, one might recall that during the first period at Cairo the prince and princess "commonly met in the evening in a private summer-house on the bank of the Nile". But this summer-house either was on the grounds of the main house rented and magnificently furnished in chapter XVI, or it was not. If not, if it was away from home, nothing in chapters XL-XLIV intimates that they have now gone there.) The episode of the mad astronomer has not been concluded. After chapter XLV, "They discourse with an old man", the long and dramatically important chapter XLVI immediately resumes the story of the astronomer, telling how he is visited by the ladies, Nekayah and Pekuah, and under the softening influence of feminine conversation is gradually cured of his delirious fantasy. Chapter XLV, devoted to the old man, a characteristically and passionately Johnsonian projection of the bitterness of old age, is a stark intrusion into the sequence about the astronomer. In its absent-minded opening, it seems to me another of Johnson's afterthoughts, so important that it had to go somewhere. Where else would seem better when the other episodes were already in sequence?

[ii]

"Structure"

I have been urging genetic inferences and have not meant to imply that the actual inconsistencies which I observe (with the possible exception of Pekuah's long absence from the stage) are in any sense aesthetic deficiencies. They do, however, appear to me as complements of and accents upon a much larger and more clearly observable character of the whole story – what I would describe as its highly episodic, and hence very lumpy or bumpy, structure. One recent critic of *Rasselas*, Professor Kolb, has said that it is arranged in two main parts, one in the happy valley, one after the escape.[6] Another critic, Professor Hilles, has discerned three main parts: 1. in the valley, chapters I-XIV; 2. the escape and a period of relatively detached and orderly *observation* at and near Cairo, chapters XV-XXX; 3. beginning with the abduction of Pekuah and the grief of Nekayah, a period of greater personal *involvement* and, at the end, of more somber experience, chapters XXXIII-XLIX.[7] In the chapters following the episode of Pekuah's abduction (if I may expand this theme a little), the mad astronomer is not merely observed, but converted from his delirium and received into the family; even the bitter old man comes home with them for a brief conversation. A climax of experience and reflection is reached in the antepenultimate chapters, with the visit to the Catacombs, Imlac's argument for the immortality of the soul, and Nekayah's conclusion: "To me . . . the choice of life is become less important; I hope hereafter to think only on the choice of eternity".

Nevertheless, I believe that the forty-nine chapters of the tale fall even more readily into another and more piecemeal pattern – more readily because with more aesthetic immediacy, more clearly segmented colouring. Thus: 1. chapters I-VI, the *unrest* of Rasselas in the valley, climaxed by the attempt at flying; 2. chapters VII-XV, the *story* of Imlac (surely too long in proportion to the whole book) and the implausible *escape* by tunnelling through the mountain; 3. chapters XVI-XXII, the first period at Cairo, *exploratory*, varicoloured, embracing the visit to the hermit; 4. chapters XXIII-XXIX, an extended *conversation*, on public and private life, on marriage and celibacy, between Rasselas and Nekayah; 5. chapters XXX-XXXIX, *adventures*: the Pyramids, abduction and recovery of Pekuah; 6. chapters XL-XLIX, return to Cairo and more *somber* experiences: the mad astronomer, the bitter old man, the Catacombs, the end. In each of these six segments, certain subdivisions can of course be seen. The first period in Cairo is notable for the rapid succession of separately sought-out episodes. The relentlessly continued conversation between the prince and his sister (chapters XXIII-XXIX) occupies the middle of the whole story as a prolonged central stasis or dead center. The sequence in which Pekuah is the focus of attention (chapters XXXI-XXXIX) is notable for the relative continuity of the adventure story. The visit to the Pyramids which begins this part, or ends the preceding, seems like a heavy punctuation mark (the accent of antiquity and the tomb), and this indeed is echoed in a second and similar punctuation, the visit to the Catacombs, which signals the end of the whole. The second period at Cairo, though it has fewer incidents than the first, is a sort of counterpart to the first, echoing its structure across the interval of the long conversation and the long adventure. Inside one episode in each Cairo period, a shorter and abruptly introduced intercalary episode, as we have seen, stands out like a special bump or knob in the grain of the story. The embittered and malignant old man looks out from his knot-hole or niche back across the chapters to the fearful and ruined country gentleman. But it is difficult to say just what is accomplished for the whole pattern by features of this sort. It is difficult, on the whole, to speak of the "structure" of *Rasselas* in a sense anything like that in which one speaks of the structure of a play by Shakespeare or of a novel by Fielding or Jane Austen. *Rasselas* has the kind of structure which satisfies, more or less, its modest requirements as a quasi-dramatic narrative – not the causal progression, the beginning, middle, and end of the Aristotelian "whole", but a

116

structure of accumulation, something like that of a series of laboratory reports, or a series of chapters on animals sighted or taken, on a hunt across the veldt with gun or camera. "Eye Nature's walks, shoot Folly as it flies, And catch the Manners living as they rise."

Both Professor Kolb and, with less emphasis, Professor Hilles point out that the story, and especially the section dealing with the first period at Cairo, organizes a series of parallels and oppositions of human states and moral ideas: "prince and princess, male and female", "wise Imlac . . . naïve prince", "normal life . . . the happy valley", "urban life . . . rural", "epicurean . . . stoic", "shepherd, landlord, and hermit", "great and . . . humble", "youth and age, celibacy and matrimony . . . past and present".[8] There is nothing wrong with this kind of analysis. This kind of order, in some degree, may well be one of the requisites for the successful telling of such a tale. On the other hand, some such order is needed too in a moral essay or treatise, and maybe there it is needed even more. (It fits the conversation of the prince and his sister even better than their explorations.) We do not contrive a story for the sake of getting this kind of order, but perhaps the contrary, for the sake of relieving the threat of its rigors.

[iii]

The Streaks of the Tulip

To put the matter conventionally and moderately, it is a paradox that a man who had Johnson's preference for both the homely and the abstract should undertake an oriental tale at all. Or better, it is a strangely fit incongruity that this tale, which both tries and refuses to be oriental, should contain as one of its most memorable exhibits a discourse on the art of poetry in which occurs the following sequence of assertions: 1. "I could never describe what I had not seen . . . I ranged mountains and deserts for images and resemblances, and pictured upon my mind every tree of the forest and flower of the valley". 2. "The business of a poet . . . is to examine, not the individual, but the species; to remark general properties and large appearances: he does not number the streaks of the tulip". 3. "He must be acquainted likewise with all the modes of life . . . and trace the changes of the human mind as they are modified by various institutions and accidental influences of climate and custom".

The local colour of *Rasselas*, the "oriental imagery" to the "charms" of which Boswell alludes, is not luxuriant. It is even very thin, and we may at moments wish it were thicker. It has a curiously deductive and even conjectural character – like the effort of a man who has read long ago a book of eastern travels for the purpose of translation, perhaps too has dipped into another book or two in the more recent past.[9]

The most conspicuous colour consists simply in the proper names of places, persons, and offices. We are "oriented" at the outset (chapter I) by the names "Abissinia", "Egypt", and "Amhara". Soon we follow Imlac (chapters VIII-XII) from "Goiama", near the "fountain of the Nile", by way of "the shore of the red sea", to "Surat", and to "Agra, the capital of Indostan", city of the "great Mogul", and thence to "Persia", "Arabia", "Syria", "Palestine", "many regions of Asia", "Egypt", "Cairo", and "Suez" – the latter names pre-establishing for us the route which will be followed by the fugitives from the valley a few chapters hence. Later, the sequence of adventure chapters (XXX-XXXIX) gives us "old Egyptians", the "Pyramids" (over and over), a "troop of Arabs", "Turkish horsemen", the "Bassa"[10] at Cairo, the "borders of Nubia", "the monastery of St. Anthony", "the deserts of Upper-Egypt", the "Arab's fortress" on an "island of the Nile . . . under the tropick".

"How easily shall we then trace the Nile through all his passage", says the aeronautical artist back in chapter VI. This is the first of altogether fifteen allusions by name to that great geographical feature and symbol. The escapees from the happy valley behold "the Nile, yet a narrow current, wandering beneath them". The hermit of chapter XXI lives "near the lowest cataract of the Nile". The "annual overflow" or "inundation" of the Nile is a leitmotif of chapters XLI-XLV, dealing with both the mad weather-maker and the sad old man. ("I rest against a tree, and consider, that in the same shade I once disputed upon the annual overflow of the Nile with a friend who is now silent in the grave.") In chapter XLIX, the Conclusion, a final "inundation of the Nile" confines the prince and his friends to reflection at home (as, long since, in the happy valley,

Rasselas and Imlac had been brought together in "domestick amusements" forced upon them by an "inundation" from the lake). "No man", says the wise and aphoristic Nekayah, concluding an earlier chapter of conversation (XXIX), "can, at the same time, fill his cup from the source and from the mouth of the Nile". But Johnson has come close to doing just this.

Another vehicle of exoticism may be identified here and there in a certain courtly, ceremonious, and archaic flourish of words – what Professor Hilles has called "the Grand Style", an aspect of the sublime.[11] This occurs a few times in the author's own voice, as in the opening of the first chapter: "Ye who listen with credulity to the whispers of fancy . . . attend". More often it is from the mouths of the characters – no doubt what the country gentleman of chapter XX detected as the "eloquence of Imlac . . . and the lofty courtesy of the princess". (It is Miltonic – like "Daughter of God and Man, immortal Eve".) As Rasselas saw the animals by moonlight, " 'Ye', said he, 'are happy . . . nor do I, ye gentle beings, envy your felicity'." (chapter II). " 'Dear princess', said Rasselas, 'you fall into the common error of exaggeratory declamation'."(chapter XXVIII). " 'My dear Pekuah', said the princess . . . 'Remember that you are companion of the princess of Abissinia'."(chapter XXXI). "Whoever thou art, that . . . imaginest happiness in royal magnificence, and dreamest . . . perpetual gratifications, survey the pyramids, and confess thy folly!"(chapter XXXII). Here Imlac echoes the rhythm of the narrator in the first sentence of the book. "Illustrious lady", said even the Arab outlaw, "my fortune is better than I had presumed to hope". "Lady", said he, "you are to consider yourself as sovereign".(chapter XXXVIII, XXXIX). Probably the most full-blown instance in the book returns us, characteristically, to geography and to the mighty river. In chapter XXV, "The princess and her brother commonly met in the evening in a private summerhouse on the bank of the Nile . . . As they were sitting together, the princess cast her eyes upon the river that flowed before her". And:

"Answer", said she, "great father of waters, thou that rollest thy floods through eighty nations, to the invocations of the daughter of thy native king. Tell me if thou waterest, through all thy course, a single habitation from which thou dost not hear the murmurs of complaint?"

Certain other details of local colour are much less distinctive. At the start (chapter I) we are treated to "mountains", "rivulets", a "lake", "fish of every species", water falling "from precipice to precipice", "the banks of the brooks . . . diversified with flowers", "beasts of prey", "flocks and herds", "beasts of chase frisking in the lawns". We hear also of a "palace" with "squares or courts", "arches of massy stone", "upper stories", "private galleries", "subterranean passages", "columns", and "unsuspected cavities" closed with "marble". Such terms, so frequent throughout the work, whenever the argument seems to call for some evocation of physical decor, work as local colour mainly or only in conjunction with the proper names of places and persons which we have seen. It seems scarcely extreme to say that these combinations make the kind of local colour a schoolboy might supply. When I was in the eighth grade, we studied geography (which that year was Africa), and we had to write an imaginary journey through Egypt. I can still remember, approximately, one sentence of my composition — because it struck me at the time as so neatly yet richly executed. "Turning a bend in the Nile, we came in sight of the giant Assouan Dam."[12]

Certain other descriptive details are indeed more specially exotic. These, however, are scarce. I attempt the following approximately exhaustive list. In the "torrid zone"[13] of chapter I, we find the "monkey" and the "elephant". At the start of Imlac's travels in chapter VIII, we have "camels" and "bales" of goods. In chapter IX and again in XII, we have a "caravan", and in chapter X the "mosque of Mecca". In chapter XVIII, at Cairo, a "spacious building", with "open doors", housing a "school of declamation, in which professors read lectures", seems, in spite of its vagueness, much like a part of the ancient Alexandrian world. The shepherds in chapter XIX live in "tents". At the estate of the prosperous country gentleman in chapter XX, "youths and virgins" are "dancing in the grove" near a "stately palace".[14] In XXI, the hermit's "cell" is a "cavern" beneath "palm-trees". In XXX, as we begin to think of the Pyramids, we hear of "fragments of temples" and

"choaked aqueducts". In XXXII appear "galleries" and "vaults
of marble"; in XXXIII, "dark labyrinths". The travel in the
desert (chapters XXXI-XXXIX) gives us "tents"[15] (nine
times), "camels" (three), "ounces of gold" (three),[16] "deserts"
and "the desert", a "monastery", a "refectory", and a "prior";
in XXXVIII appear "carpets", "finer carpets", Pekuah's
"upper vest" (with "embroidery"), "the lance", "the sword",
"palaces", "temples", "granite", "porphyry"; in XXXIX, "the
tropick", a "couch", "turrets", two special plums: "crocodiles"
and "river-horses", "needlework", "silken flowers", and
another plum: the "seraglio". In the final expedition, to the
catacombs (XLVII-XLVIII), we have a "guard of horsemen",
"sepulchral caves", a "labyrinth of subterraneous passages",
"embalming" and "embalmed" bodies, "caverns".

A few ingenious manipulations of this slender exotic store,
cunning jointures of it with the Johnsonian philosophic and plastic
staple, stand out. In chapter I, just as I become mildly annoyed
at "beasts of chase frisking in the lawns" and "the sprightly
kid . . . bounding on the rocks", I am moderately diverted by
"the subtle monkey frolicking in the trees, and the solemn
elephant reposing in the shade". (No matter whether elephants
would really be found in that mountain fastness.) By a somewhat
different sort of conjunction, it seems to me, Johnson creates a
moment of interesting local colour in chapter XXXIX, as
Pekuah looks out on the "winding" river from her island
prison: "The crocodiles and river-horses are common in this
unpeopled region . . . For some time I expected to see mermaids
and tritons, which, as Imlac has told me, the European travellers
have stationed in the Nile".[17] And here let us quote too that
moment of pregnant phrasing from chapter XXX: "The most
pompous monument of Egyptian greatness, and one of the most
bulky works of manual industry . . . are the pyramids". And
from chapter XXXVIII, the Arab's observation to the lady
Pekuah that

buildings are always best preserved in places little frequented, and
difficult of access: for, when once a country declines from its primitive
splendour, the more inhabitants are left, the quicker ruin will be
made. Walls supply stones more easily than quarries, and palaces
and temples will be demolished to make stables of granite, and
cottages of porphyry.[18]

By a slight extension of the idea of the exotic, perhaps we can bring in such learned words from the realm of *Mathematical Magick* as Johnson borrowed from his archaic dictionary source of that title,[19] or from other "philosophic" sources, and worked into chapter VI, the story of an attempt at the art of flying: "the tardy conveyance of ships and chariots", "the swifter migration of wings", "the pendent spectator", "volant animals", "the folding continuity of the bat's wings". And with these we come close to yet a wider category of somewhat notable descriptive phrases – all those, I should say, which, without including any word in any way exotic or bizarre, yet by some special energy of compression are likely to strike our attention or force on us the feeling that the description has "texture". In chapter I, the lake is "frequented by every fowl whom nature has taught to dip the wing in water . . . every blast shook spices from the rocks,[20] and every month dropped fruits upon the ground. All animals that bite the grass, or brouse the shrub . . . wandered in this extensive circuit". Such phrases as these may be looked on as Johnsonian substitutes for local colour.

A recent observer from the vantage point of Saudi-Arabia has expounded the extreme unrealism of the journey made by the princely party of fugitives, by ups and downs, through the nearly impassable tropical forests of the Abyssinian plateau, and then down the steep seven or eight thousand feet from the eastern escarpment to the narrow coastal plain and the port where they stayed several months. (This was probably Massawa, a typical Red Sea port, a "horrible place", lying under relentless sun, in saturation humidity.) No less dimly realized seem their "quick and prosperous" coastal voyage [of twenty or thirty days] in a primitive sailing dhow, their slow trip by camel caravan under the desert stars to Cairo, and finally what must have been the astonished arrival of this party of Coptic Christians amid the teeming contrasts of a vast Islamic city.[21]

Johnson, we know, had long enjoyed some awareness of the Abyssinian locale, for as a young man he had written and published (1735) a translation from a French version of the seventeenth-century Portuguese Jesuit Father Jerome Lobo's *Voyage to Abyssinia*.[22] Of recent years, the scholarship of sources has been urging Johnson's debt to other writers on Abyssinia.[23] Lobo, it is clear, could not have been his only source, for Lobo said the prison of the princes was a rocky and "barren summit". But the paradise on the Abyssinian hill was a commonplace – "where Abassin kings their issue guard, Mount Amara – by some supposed True Paradise, under the Ethiop line". One of the reasons why Johnson was interested in Lobo's *Voyage* was that the Jesuit missionary and diplomat himself was more interested in human character and mores, the hardships and vicissitudes of the human adventure, than in exotic or fantastic colourations.[24] Thus, Lobo reports of the crocodiles (which Pekuah saw from the Arab's island fortress): "Neither I nor any with whom I have convers'd about the *Crocodile*, have ever seen him Weep, and therefore I take the Liberty of ranking all that hath been told us of his Tears, amongst the Fables which are only proper to amuse Children".[25] And Johnson, in a Preface to Lobo which Boswell by quoting has made the best-known part of the book:

> THE *Portugese* Traveller, contrary to the general Vein of his Countrymen, has amused his Reader with no Romantick Absurdities or Incredible Fictions ... HE appears by his modest and unaffected Narration to have described Things as he saw them, to have copied Nature from the Life, and to have consulted his Senses not his Imagination; He meets with no *Basilisks* that destroy with their Eyes, his *Crocodiles* devour their Prey without Tears, and his *Cataracts* fall from the Rock without Deafening the Neighbouring Inhabitants.[26]

Samuel Johnson – both Johnson the man and Johnson the translator of Lobo and the narrator of *Rasselas* – no doubt believes that even the local colours, the geography, the flora, the fauna, the architecture, and the costumes, of exotic places are far less exotic than is commonly reported. Beyond doubt, he believes that human living and human nature in Amhara or in Cairo are far less exotic than is commonly supposed, are indeed essentially the same as in London.

> THE Reader ... will discover, what will always be discover'd by a diligent and impartial Enquirer, that wherever Human Nature is to be found, there is a mixture of Vice and Virtue, a contest of Passion and Reason.

General human nature is of course Johnson's theme – vice and virtue, passion and reason. Why not then generalized local colour? The deliberate simplification, even complacent ignorance about the actual colours of life in the supposed locale of Johnson's story, is a kind of counterpart and symbol of the general human truth he would be getting at.

[iv]

A Chorus of Sages

Various critical questions might be asked about *Rasselas*, but surely the main question must always be: What are we to make of the fact that the obvious element of morality is cast in the shape of an oriental tale? Or, what are we to make of the fact that the equally obvious oriental tale is invested with so much morality? The problem, or the task, of a writer who would tell a moral tale is, of course, to get the story and the morality together. He will have to do better than give us a close juxtaposition or rapid alternation of plot and sermon (programme and commercial plug), or a set of essays in a curiously wrought frame, a series of *Ramblers* inserted in a version of the *Arabian Nights*.[27] "We do not read *Rasselas* for the story", says Professor Hilles. "We read it for a view of life that is presented majestically in long sweeping phrases." But he immediately adds: "Diction, rhythms, character and plot are all of a piece".[28] So that he really has a warmer affection for the story (character and plot) than, for instance, Professor Kolb, who, while implying some distress at those critics who "have been content to praise the wisdom and ignore the narrative", at the same time (and on the same page) concludes "that the tale is not the principle which best explains . . . the book . . . the problem of happiness rather than the element of 'story' emerges . . . as the determinant by reference to which questions about the book's structure may be most adequately answered".[29] The structure is "didactic". And this seems to imply somehow that we can call it a "narrative", but not a "tale" or a "story".

In the second section of this essay, I have already given up the "structure" of *Rasselas* so far as that idea pretends to any Aristotelian or organistic and dramatic implications. But then a story does not have to have *much* structure in order to be a

124

story. It is a story if it has any characters and places at all, and if the characters do any talking at all and move about a little, from one place (or one state) to another. The story of *Rasselas* as such, a certain movement of certain persons in certain places – loosely constructed, vaguely characterized, largely undramatic or half-heartedly dramatic as it may be, unfictional fabric of a fiction that it is – has, nevertheless, some kind of imaginative bearing on the moral ideas. This is not an original thesis. "The eastern background", says Professor Kolb, "provides . . . the aura of strange and distant lands where human happiness is commonly thought to be complete and lasting; . . . reminding us of the superficial likenesses and essential differences between *Rasselas* and ordinary oriental tales with their happy-ever-after conclusions."[30] "The judgement of human life", says Professor Leyburn, "would leave a very different impression if it were presented stripped of such aesthetic distance as the regions of the Nile provide."[31] Oriental decor had been used in Augustan England for stories of adventure and fantasy (*Arabian Nights* and *Persian Tales*). It had well-established didactic uses too – as in *Spectator* and *Rambler* visions and apologues. An oriental spokesman could be used to throw a strange and skeptical perspective on Western mores (Montesquieu's *Persian Letters*, Goldsmith's *Chinese Letters* – just after *Rasselas*). The peculiar twist of Johnson's *Rasselas* is that he uses a sort of nominally or minimally exotic tale for the purpose of displaying the most homely human materials and of asserting a workaday perspective upon them.[32] The philosophy of *Rasselas* (Johnson's resistance to eighteenth-century "optimism") might readily enough become our theme now, but I am pushing, not the philosophy but the literary actualization of it, trying to improve the view that it is important for Johnson's anti-rationalist and conservative purpose that he *should* have a story, of sorts, and a foreign scene.

The Johnsonian substitutes for local colour, we have said, are abstractive, at moments "philosophic", and all but invisible. They may, for that very reason, have a broader spread than we have so far mentioned. It was Johnson himself who observed of Sir Thomas Browne that he "poured a multitude of exotick words", and Johnson's friends Boswell and Arthur Murphy who thought that Browne was a main source for Johnson's own

"Anglo-Latian" peculiarities. "How he differed so widely from such elegant models [the Augustans] is a problem not to be solved, unless it be true that he took an early tincture from the writers of the last century, particularly Sir Thomas Browne." Twenty-five years ago I ventured the opinion that Browne "deserves the name 'exotick' which Johnson applies to him", but that this name would sit "curiously on Johnson himself". "Where Browne uses remote terms to make us think of remote things" – Pharaoh, mummy, golden calf, scorpion, and sala- mander – "Johnson 'familiarizes' ".[33] That much is still true. But, on the other hand, I will now undertake to argue that Johnson's whole way of moral writing, what we may call the *Rambler* style, is a form of moderate exoticism which did not find its ideal setting until he wrote *Rasselas*. During the course of producing his 208 *Ramblers*, Johnson tried out a number of domestic settings of voices for the Rambler mood: the country housewife and her kitchen (no. 51), Mr. Frolick the Londoner in the country (no. 61), Quisquilius the curio-collector (nos. 82-83), Nugaculus the gossip (no. 103), Mrs. Busy (no. 138), Captator the legacy-hunter (nos. 197-198). But in all such in- stances, the more dramatic he makes the treatment, the more the peculiar Rambleresque pomp of phrasing thins out. This hap- pens even in the exotic setting of the Greenland idyll of Annin- gait and Ajut (nos. 186-187). Perhaps it happens too with the several oriental tales, including that of the Emperor Seged of Ethiopia (nos. 204-205). Yet with the Emperor Seged, Johnson was verging on the discovery of a curiously heightened affinity between story and philosophic idiom. Perhaps the *Rambler* had been all along a series of oriental apologues without the plot and local colour? – the Rambler himself a kind of Abyssinian sage without the name and the overt ethnic colouration? It was a strange language, that language of the Rambler in his own persona. Who really talked that way? Not Dryden or Addison, or Lord Chesterfield. Not really Johnson himself, except per- haps in the moments of his conversation when he was being the consciously pompous self-parodist or when Mrs. Thrale and Burney had come into the library at Streatham to "make" him "speak" a *Rambler*.[34]

The part of *Rasselas* which we remember best and carry away with us for allusion and quotation – the portable part – is beyond

question the aphoristic moralism, the lugubrious orotundity.
"We do not read *Rasselas* for the story." "Human life is everywhere a state in which much is to be endured, and little to be
enjoyed." Who says this? Imlac, Rasselas, Nekayah, the Stoic
philosopher, the hermit, the Arab, the mad astronomer, the old
man? Any one of these, at the right moment, might say it. Actually, of course, we remember it is Imlac, near the end of his
narrative of his own life (chapter XI) – the same Imlac who
later, seated in one of the "most spacious chambers" of the
great Pyramid, discourses so eloquently, in a vein of inverse
romantic vision: "It seems to have been erected only in com-
pliance with that hunger of imagination which preys incessantly
upon life, and must be always appeased by some employment
. . . I consider this mighty structure as a monument of the in-
sufficiency of human enjoyments".(chapter XXXII). The same
Imlac, who when the prince looks on a fissure in the rocks as a
"good omen" of escape from the valley, replies – almost like a
wound-up automaton, a speaking toy-philosopher: "If you are
pleased with prognosticks of good, you will be terrified likewise
with tokens of evil . . . Whatever facilitates our work is more
than an omen, it is a cause of success . . . Many things difficult
to design prove easy to performance".

"Marriage has many pains, but celibacy has no pleasures."
Who says this? Any one of several characters might say it.
Actually the speaker is the maiden princess Nekayah, in the
course (chapter XXVI) of that lengthy and soon quarrelsome
conversation with her brother about such profound issues: public and private life, youth and age, celibacy or marriage. The
same princess who a few pages later, in the accents of a proto-
Screwtape, "reckons" for us "the various forms of connubial
infelicity . . . the rude collisions of contrary desire . . . the
obstinate contests of disagreeable virtues, where both are supported by consciousness of good intention . . ."(chapter
XXVIII).[35] The same princess whom we have already heard,
seated in the summer-house by the bank of the Nile, utter her
apostrophe to that mighty "father of waters" who rolls his
"floods through eighty nations".[36]

The courtly and ceremonious discourse which we have already
noticed as a kind of local colour is only the most obvious instance
of a lofty and reflective idiom which plausibly pervades nearly

the whole of this oriental tale. (The notion of an oriental sage, philosopher, poet, emperor, prince, is an easy one for us to entertain. Who ever heard of an oriental buffoon or ninny?) The *Rambler* idiom, Johnson's own idiom, if we like, an expansion of homely human wisdom into the large perspective of Latinate philosophic diction, is projected across time and space, straight from London and Fleet Street, to cover appropriately, with a veil of the delicately exotic,[37] scenes which we know, by a more than willing suspension of disbelief are enacted at places along the Nile from Amhara to Cairo.

The notion of *Rasselas* as a "comedy" (Johnson's "greatest comic work") has been urged by two recent writers.[38] A third, Professor Hilles again, thinks that they "overstress" the "comic element". Probably they do overstress it. Professor Tracy sees a "comic" (perhaps, rather, a "satirical") reduction of man's fatuousness, shrewd laughter at the prince's chronic failure of common sense, demolition of the poet Imlac's "grandiloquent . . . rapture". Professor Whitley finds "pure comedy of ideas" in the episodes of the first period at Cairo, "comedy of emotion and behaviour", and "deflated oriental romance", in Pekuah's abduction, "dark comedy" in the later chapters about the mad astronomer and the catacombs. Probably we are on safer ground if we are content to say, with Professor Hilles, simply that the attitude prevailing in the story is not, as so often said, "pessimistic", not morose, not cynical, not even satirical; it is rather, gently "ironic" and "realistic". The "smile of the author is a sad smile".[39] Yes – though one may need to insist that it *is* a smile. With Professor Hilles, we must differ from certain critics who have supposed that a "tragic sense of life . . . informs it". It appears to me next to impossible that anyone should be moved either to tears or to shudders at any part of *Rasselas*. "In a short time the second Bassa was deposed. The Sultan [at Constantinople], that had advanced him, was murdered by the Janisaries." But that was, if not a long time ago, yet very far in another country. (The chapter, XVIII, where the Stoic philosopher mourning the death of his daughter is put in a position of nearly laughable contrast to his declamation of the preceding day is perhaps the only part of the whole book that verges on the uncomfortable.) "In a year the wings were finished and, on a morning appointed, the maker appeared furnished for flight on a little promontory: he waved his pinions a while to gather air, then leaped from his stand, and in an instant dropped into the lake."[40] There we have the characteristic motion of the story as action – the immediate and inevitable plunge, so inevitable and so confidently foreseen as to warrant not the smallest flourish or comment.[41] " 'I . . . resolve to return into the world tomorrow' . . . He dug up a considerable treasure which he had hid among the rocks, and accompanied them to the city, on which, as he approached it, he gazed with rapture."(chapter XXI). At many moments the comic smile of the narrator is turned directly on one or another of his characters. " 'But surely, interposed the prince . . . Whenever I shall seek a wife, it shall be my first question, whether she be willing to be led by reason?' "(chapter XXIX). More often, however, or in general, the smile of this narrator envelops in a less direct way, in a more reticent parodic spirit, the whole of his own Abyssinian tale. He is very close to the endlessly meditative and controversial nature of each of his personae. What does the narrator think of his own "Tale" when he gives his chapters titles such as these: "The prince continues to grieve and muse", "A dissertation on the art of flying", "Imlac's history continued. A dissertation upon poetry", "Disquisition upon greatness", "Rasselas and Nekayah continue their conversation", "The dangerous prevalence of imagination", "The conclusion, in which nothing is concluded"?

In real life, Johnson sometimes indulged in a complacent self-consciousness and amusement at his own inflations. His moments of self-parody are celebrated. In his essays too, *Ramblers* and *Idlers*, a sort of shackled playfulness often parodies the solemn parade. A shadow of grimace accents some restrained contrast between gravity of diction and homeliness or meanness of sentiment.[42] In *Rasselas*, the Johnsonian speaker has translated himself into a realm of sober fantasy where the grim smile, the sad smile, the wan smile, can be more or less constant. Probably it was some feeling like this about the tale that prompted Voltaire to say that its philosophy was *aimable*.[43] Indeed there are profoundly reflective and even solemn moments – and they occur increasingly in the later chapters – at the Pyramids, in the conversation about the astronomer's madness, in the confrontation with the savagely embittered old man, and finally at the Catacombs, in the contemplation of death and immortality. But the last seems to me the only place where it may be impossible to find a smile. Here the initially dominant tone is metaphysical sobriety ("as thought is, such is the power that thinks; a power impassive and indiscerptible"), and this deepens at the end to theological solemnity ("The whole assembly stood a while silent and collected . . . 'To me', said the princess, 'the choice of life is become less important: I hope hereafter to think only on the choice of eternity' "). But this is an exceptional moment, not the ground tone of the book and not its conclusion. The conclusion, in which nothing is concluded, reverts to the basic plan.

It is not possible to smile sympathetically at nothingness without a degree of participation. Johnson's way of laughter is not the high-comedy way of the wit and his butts, but a quieter way of partly encumbered rehearsal and laboured formulation. Martin Price has deftly alluded to the "gently preposterous oriental setting" of Johnson's tale, "the self-mocking formality of its dialogue, the balance and antithesis of characters as well as dialogue, and the circularity of its total structure".[44] All this is the *imagination* of Johnson's quasi-oriental and ceremonious no-tale – "the wine of absurdity", or absurdity mitigated only in its own rich self-contemplation. In our day, Albert Camus has explained absurdity in Kantian terms as "the division between the mind that desires and the world that disappoints".[45] Johnson's *Rasselas* has much in common with modern versions of the absurd – with a *Godot* or a *Watt*. One main difference, which may disguise the parallel for us, is that the modern versions of the descent take place at a level which is, to start with, subterranean, the very sub-cellar or zero level of modern man's three-century decline from the pinnacles of theology and metaphysics. Johnson's descendental exercise, with its saving theological clause in the Catacombs, takes place at a level still near the top of the metaphysical structure. It is of course all the richer for this. In the "endgame" played at the modern level, a nearly complete numbness and boredom is roused only as occasional stabs and jolts of obscenity reach a buried nerve. In the more spacious and better lighted areas available to Johnson, there was still eloquence – an eloquence profound and moving as it verges continually on a smiling absurdity.

NOTES

1 *Rasselas*, ed. G. B. Hill (Oxford, 1887, 1954), pp. 22-5; ed. O. F. Emerson (New York, 1895), pp. xii-xv; ed. R. W. Chapman (Oxford, 1927), pp. ix-xv. A third part of the statement to Reynolds, that he "had never since read it over" has to be stretched to accommodate the fact that the second edition oɪ *Rasselas*, following in June the first edition of April 1759, has about sixty emendations which bear the auctorial stamp (O. F. Emerson, "The Text of Johnson's *Rasselas*", *Anglia*, XXII (1899), 497-509); ed. R. W. Chapman (Oxford, 1927), pp. xx-xxi; D. N. Smith, *Johnson & Boswell Revised* (Oxford, 1928), p. 13.

2 Chapman, p. xv.

3 The second sentence referring to the favourite quoted from chapter XV would have required the addition of only three short words, "and her maid", and the change of three pronouns from singular to plural, to be transformed from a sentence originally referring only to Nekayah. At the end of the chapter we are told that Imlac "with great difficulty prevailed on the princess to enter the vessel". It is difficult to believe that Johnson wrote this sentence at a time when he had the fearful lady Pekuah well in mind.

In chapter VII, "The prince finds a man of learning", the first reference to Imlac is curiously abrupt, sounding as if he had already been introduced in some sentence or paragraph either earlier or later deleted. "This inundation confined all the princes to domestic amusements, and the attention of Rasselas was particularly seized by a poem, which Imlac rehearsed upon the various conditions of humanity. He commanded the poet to attend him in his apartment." Contrast chapter XIV, the first reference to Nekayah: "The prince, coming down to refresh himself with air, found his sister Nekayah standing before the mouth of the cavity". Another minor instance of absent-mindedness appears in the difference between chapter IX: "From Persia I passed into Arabia", and chapter XI: "From Persia . . . I travelled through Syria".

4 Geoffrey Tillotson, "Time in *Rasselas*", *Bicentenary Essays on "Rasselas"*, ed. Magdi Wahba (Cairo, 1959), pp. 97-104. G. B. Hill, ed., *Rasselas* (1887), p. 181, estimates, from the

indications in chapters XX-XXIII, that Rasselas is thirty-two years old at the time of his early inquiries at Cairo.

5 The lowest cataract of the Nile, just below Assouan, is (or was before it was altered by the Dam) about 600 miles upstream from Cairo – a fact which, on any interpretation of these chapters, does not help their realism.

5a O. F. Emerson (*op. cit.*, n. 1) notices that this chapter is sufficiently self-contained to have been a late addition.

6 Gwin J. Kolb, "The Structure of *Rasselas*", *PMLA*, LXVI (1951), 702.

7 F. W. Hilles, "*Rasselas*, an 'Uninstructive Tale' ", in *Johnson, Boswell, and Their Circle*, Essays Presented to Lawrence Fitzroy Powell (Oxford, 1965), pp. 111-3.

8 Kolb, pp. 707-8; Hilles, p. 112. These two essays are among the very few determined *critical* discussions of *Rasselas* I am familiar with. I have learned and have borrowed from both.

9 See below, p. 122, notes 22 and 23.

10 A third Bassa. Two have been disposed of, along with a Sultan at Constantinople, murdered by Janisaries, in chapter XXIV.

11 Hilles, p. 113.

12 Little did I realize that in turning that imaginary bend I must be very close to a spot once visited by Rasselas and Imlac. See p. 113, note 5, and p. 123, note 26.

13 This phrase occurs again in chapter VII.

14 The opening paragraph of chapter XX, on the prosperous country gentleman, is a miniature projection in highly Johnsonian terms of an English landscaped park: "Shrubs diligently cut away to open walks", "boughs . . . artificially interwoven", "seats of flowery turf . . . raised in vacant spaces", "a rivulet . . . along the side of a winding path", "its banks . . . opened into small basins", "its stream obstructed by little mounds of stone". G. B. Hill, ed. *Rasselas* (1887), p. 179, has pointed out a parallel in Johnson's description in his *Life of Shenstone* of Shenstone's farm the Leasowes.

15 "Women . . . weeping in the tents" (XXXII) may be said to have a specially oriental flavour.

16 Chapters XXXVII, XXXVIII, and XXXIX.

17 Donald M. Lockhart (*PMLA*, LXXVIII (1963), 524; see below p. 122, note 23) shows the collocation of these four creatures on the upper Nile in Balthazar Telles, *Historia geral da Ethiopia a alta* (Coimbra, 1660), and in earlier atlases.

18 Cf. Johnson in the *Western Islands* at St. Andrew's.

19 See Gwin J. Kolb, "Johnson's 'Dissertation on Flying', and John Wilkins's *Mathematical Magick*", *MP*, XLVII (1949), 24-31; revised in *New Light on Dr. Johnson*, ed. F. W. Hilles (New Haven, 1959), pp. 91-106. Somewhere just to one side of this place in our scheme, perhaps we put such terms as "solstitial rains" and "equinoctial hurricanes" in chapter I, "celestial observations" in XXXIX, and the cluster of semi-technical terms that occurs in the chapters on the mad astronomer (XL-XLII): "constellations", "emersion of a satellite of Jupiter", "tropick to tropick", "dog-star", "crab", "equinoctial tempest", "equator", "axis of earth", "ecliptick of the sun", "solar system".

20 It seems to me at least possible that this remarkable phrase involves a typographical error. Why are spices shaken from the *rocks*? From plants, shrubs, and trees that grow among the rocks? One early traveller, Castanhoso, spoke of "honey from the rifts in the rocks". See J. R. Moore (p. 122, note 23), p. 40.

21 Louis E. Goodyear, "Rasselas' Journey from Amhara to Cairo Viewed from Arabia", *Bicentenary Essays on "Rasselas"*, ed. Magdi Wahba (Supplement to *Cairo Studies in English*, Cairo, 1959), pp. 21-30.

22 See Ellen Douglas Leyburn, " 'No Romantick Absurdities or Incredible Fictions', The Relation of Johnson's *Rasselas* to Lobo's *Voyage to Abyssinia*", *PMLA*, LXX (1955), 1059-67.

23 John Robert Moore, "*Rasselas* and the Early Travellers to Abyssinia", *MLQ*, XV (1954), 36-41; Gwin J. Kolb, "The 'Paradise' in *Abyssinia* and the 'Happy Valley' in *Rasselas*", *MP*, LVI (1958), 10-6. (Kolb "rediscovers" possible sources known to O. F. Emerson in his edition of Rasselas (1895), pp. xxiv-xxviii); and Donald M. Lockhart, " 'The Fourth Son of the Mighty Emperor': The Ethiopian Background of Johnson's *Rasselas*", *PMLA*, LXXVIII (1963), 516-28. Lockhart's very learned and very clearly expounded article argues that Johnson, after an early interest in Ethiopia represented by his *Lobo*, returned to the subject during his *Rambler* period and undertook a heavy "project of documentation", a consultation of "major sources for Ethiopian features". This programme "must have been in pro-

gress and may even have been completed before 29 February 1752", when he published the first of the two *Ramblers* on Seged, Emperor of Ethiopia – essays which have a "nearly identical bibliography" with *Rasselas*. He read not only Job Ludolph's *History of Ethiopia* (Latin, Frankfurt, 1681; English, London, 1682, 1684; "Ludolph's history of Ethiopia" in the sale catalogue after Johnson's death), but other impressive texts, including substantial passages in the Spanish of Luis de Urreta's *Historia ecclesiastica . . . de la Etiopia*, Valencia, 1610. Whatever we may think of this *PMLA*-ization of Johnson's working habits (which in effect supposes deliberate heavy research not for *Rasselas* but for two *Rambler* essays), Professor Lockhart makes it at least difficult to think that by 1752 Johnson had not consulted some solid work on Ethiopia other than Lobo – (Ludolph, at least, I should think).

24 Leyburn makes this point very convincingly (p. 1067).

25 Lobo's *Voyage* (London, 1735), p. 104; Leyburn, p. 1066.

26 Lobo's *Voyage*, p. vii; Leyburn, pp. 1059-60; Boswell, *Life*, ed. Hill-Powell, I. 88. Cf. *Rasselas*, chapter XXI: "The hermit's cell . . . was a cavern . . . at such a distance from the cataract, that nothing more was heard than a gentle uniform murmur, such as composed the mind to pensive meditation".

27 Any verbal or literary integration, if viewed from the outside, is a species of metaphoric (or symbolic) compression and projection.
William Kenney, in a useful survey, "Johnson's *Rasselas* After Two Centuries", *Boston University Studies in English*, III (1957), 88-96, expounds objections often urged against three features of *Rasselas*: the unnatural *style*, the *pessimism*, the dubious or mixed *genre*. Kenney gives a good account of the nineteenth-century optimism which worked against *Rasselas*, and the more realistic attitude of our own age, which again favours it. My own reservations about *Rasselas*, difficulties, even objections, all relate to dramatic and organistic issues, and so embrace *style* and *genre*, as will be readily seen, but they do not reduce to these heads. By education, by long habit, and no doubt by inborn temperament, I enjoy a view of life antithetic to nineteenth-century optimism, and so I may claim to be a fundamentally receptive reader of *Rasselas*.

28 Hilles, pp. 114-5.

29 Kolb, pp. 699-700.

30 Kolb, p. 703. Kolb quotes Robert M. Lovett and Helen S. Hughes, *The History of the Novel in England* (Boston, 1932), p. 125, in the opinion that the setting of the story in a "non-Christian part of the world" helps Johnson to "deal with man on a purely naturalistic level". But the main characters (taken historically) are Coptic Christians. (See above Mr. Goodyear and Professor Lockhart.) And they talk and think like Christians all through the story and especially in the Catacombs (chapter XLVIII).

31 Leyburn, p. 1067.

32 See, of course, Martha Pike Conant, *The Oriental Tale in England in the Eighteenth Century* (New York, 1908); Kolb, pp. 713ff.; Geoffrey Tillotson, *"Rasselas* and the *Persian Tales"*, *TLS*, 16 November 1935, p. 534, and in his *Essays in Criticism and Research* (Cambridge, 1942), pp. 111-6. Tillotson and Kolb explore interesting parallels between *Rasselas* and certain adventuresome stories of unhappiness in *Persian Tales* Englished from the French by Ambrose Philips, *c.* 1714.

33 *The Prose Style of Samuel Johnson* (New Haven, 1941), pp. 117-9.

34 In my *Prose Style of Samuel Johnson*, pp. 74-8, I assemble the main evidence both for and against the view that Johnson wrote as he talked. I am much more doubtful now than I was then that written prose is ever very close to conversation.

35 R. W. Chapman's text (1927), following the second edition, 1759, has "disagreeing virtues". But "disagreeable" appears at least as early as the collected *Works* of 1787 (xi.78) and is so much more interesting that I admit it.

36 "The character of the Princess is wanting in dramatic power. She is sometimes Rasselas, sometimes Imlac, sometimes undisguised Johnson. What she says is often very well said, but it might just as well, and often even better, have been said by a man" (*Rasselas*, ed. Hill, 1887, 1954), p. 31).

37 "The language they speak is language that no human being has ever been heard to use". The opening sentence of the book is "incantation, applied at the outset to a never-never land" (Hilles, pp. 113-4).

38 Clarence F. Tracy, " 'Democritus, Arise!' a Study of Dr. Johnson's Humor", *Yale Review*, xxxix (1949), pp. 305-10; Alvin Whitley, "The Comedy of *Rasselas*", *ELH*, xxiii (1956), 63-5. Sheridan Baker, in an essay which appeared after I had written my own (*"Rasselas*: Psychological Irony and Romance",

PQ, xlv (1966), 249-61) stresses the humanly internal or "psychological" aspects of the ironic contrasts to romance idiom.

39 Hilles, pp. 115-9.

40 G. B. Hill's remark in 1887 that "Johnson is content with giving the artist a ducking. Voltaire would have crippled him for life at the very least; most likely would have killed him on the spot" remains as valid as ever (*Rasselas*, ed. Hill (1887, 1954), p. 165).

41 "The end . . . is immediate, flat and final" (Tillotson, *Essays in Criticism and Research*, 1942, p. 116).

42 See my *Philosophic Words* (New Haven, 1948), pp. 115-21; *The Prose Style of Samuel Johnson*, pp. 61, 76.

43 Hilles, p. 115; Boswell, *Life*, ii.500, quoting Voltaire's letter of 16 May 1760 to a French translator of *Rasselas*.

44 Martin Price, *To the Palace of Wisdom* (New York, 1964), pp. 316-7.

45 Paul West, *The Wine of Absurdity* (State College, Penna., 1966), pp. [ix], xii, 57. See the same author's "Rasselas: The Humanist as Stoic", *English*, xiii (1961), 182-5.

Part Two

Scott

and the Art of Revision

[i]

There are many possible motives for an author's hesitancy or negligence in polishing his work, or refusal to reconsider and revise, and a prudent reader will be prepared to distinguish all or any of these from such reasons as the author himself may choose to give. Fulke Greville offers this account of his own dealings with the tragedies he had formerly laid aside: "self-love . . . moved me to take this Bear-whelp up againe and licke it"; but, even while he was about this task, he reflected that whatever care he might spend on these writings would but draw attention to their short-comings. He resolved therefore to "take away all opinion of seriousnesse" from them and the handling they had undergone, "and to this end carelessly cast them into the hypocriticall figure *Ironia*, wherein men commonly (to keep above their workes) seeme to make toies of the utmost they can doe".[1] This enigmatic passage advances two considerations: how the author will stand in the opinion of his fellows; how, in his own regard. *They* will judge an artifact the more severely in so far as it is seen to be carefully wrought; *he* is resolved, as a man, to "keep above his work". In order therefore to deprecate censorious judgement and satisfy the critic within, he will "seem to make toies of the utmost he can do".

If ever great novelist followed this practice in both its branches, that novelist was Scott. His disavowal of care and pains, particularly in revision, is notorious: that is, too well known and too little understood. He was already writing in this strain some six years before he published a novel: in the Ashestiel Fragment, and the Introductions to the third, fifth, and sixth cantos of *Marmion*. Here he affects to expostulate with friends who urge him to respect orthodox literary method; but underneath the good humour and the obstinacy, the patient ear for advice and the determination to go his own way notwithstanding, there runs, from 1800 to the last pages of the *Journal*, a continuous argument with himself. The best known, and the most easily misread, of Scott's expostulations with his critics is the *Introductory Epistle* to *The Fortunes of Nigel* – ostensibly an answer to adverse reviews of his recent novels and censure of himself as a too prolific and careless novelist. It has often been quoted piecemeal, never examined whole as a piece of forensic argument. For this neglect there is some excuse: unlike the *Marmion* Introductions, the *Epistle* wants candour. Scott is playing hide-and-seek. Whereas he could have met much of this censure by showing the novels to be a mere part of his literary output, the value he still set on his fancied anonymity forbade him to associate the author of *Waverley* with the editor and biographer of Dryden. Therefore the altercation between Captain Clutter-buck, fictitious counsel for the prosecution, and the semi-fictitious defendant who, as novelist and nothing besides, is no more than a simulacrum of Scott, follows a devious course: the defence alleges the importance of the popular book trade to the prosperity of Edinburgh, the importance of entertainment to the well-being of the common reader, the importance to the author of freedom to obey the promptings of his own genius, and to enjoy such rewards as the world offers for success in any profession. This is merely the main engagement; there are so many skirmishes on the flanks, and the marshalling of the forces is so erratic, that we may fairly wish for an opportunity to ask Scott himself: "What would you think of a client who, challenged to produce an alibi, undertook to show that he had been in ten different places on the occasion in question?" "Qui prouve trop, ne prouve rien." Surely Scott's practice as a novelist, in this matter of revision, is more revealing, and far worthier scrutiny, than his defence of it.

Revision I understand in this broad sense: the whole process by which a writer returns, and reconsiders, and makes his second thoughts effectual. I have said that this process may be hindered in a variety of ways, and for reasons other than those the author alleges. Negligent revision, insufficient or ill judged, can result from two quite different habits of work – indeed, these habits arise from contrary states of mind. There is the self-concerned, calculating resolve to take no further trouble with a piece of writing that will already pass muster. Scott has been accused of this kind of negligence, and sometimes with reason, but he was the killer of his own reputation: his disavowals made negligence appear his constant practice, whereas it alternated with another, its very opposite. For his carelessness is often the result of unconcern with himself, concern with the story he has to tell. When this engrosses his attention, he leaves too much to his transcriber, or to his proof-reader, while he himself presses on, as though speed alone could capture the visionary impression. Thus he would, in a single passage, revise to an extent far beyond what is commonly supposed, yet allow errors to slip through the uneven mesh of his scrutiny. Indeed, they might well be particularly numerous in such passages because, intent on his main purpose, he had overtaxed the powers of his willing slaves: his own imagination at white heat, he was able to recapture and even recreate that vision; but he left too much to theirs.

There are other questions to be reckoned with. An artist, or craftsman, must ask himself how much reworking the fabric will tolerate. Jane Austen's recognition that hers was tough shows uncommon boldness and insight. Scott seems to have been often in doubt as to the resilience of his. Fortunately, we are sometimes able to observe him in the very act of revision, both manuscript and author's proofs having survived. Their existence for *Redgauntlet* has long been known, but investigators have been hindered from taking full advantage of this. David MacRitchie wrote on the proofs but had not seen the manuscript; George Gordon, when he described the alterations in the manuscript, did not know the whereabouts of the proofs, and to the reprint of his article he could add only a footnote. Here, to clear the record, is the order of events:- in 1890 David MacRitchie came into possession of those proof-sheets of *Redgauntlet* which bore Scott's corrections, and in 1891 lent them to Andrew Lang, who included some slight remarks on them in his introduction.[2] In March 1900 MacRitchie gave a full and useful account of them in *Longman's Magazine*. A leading article in the *TLS* for 4 September 1924 [by George Gordon] recounted a number of changes in the manuscript, which had been given to the Faculty of Advocates the year before.[3] The *TLS* for 11 September contained a letter by MacRitchie, mentioning the proof-sheets, Lang's use of them, and his own article. In 1931 Greville Worthington published his *Bibliography of the Waverley Novels*,[4] noting four cancels in the 1824 text of *Redgauntlet*,[5] and in 1932 W. C. van Antwerp reproduced two of the cancelled pages in their original state;[6] he became in 1937 owner of the proof-sheets which, with the rest of his collection, were presently acquired by the Pierpont Morgan Library. Gillian Dyson's valuable article, *The Manuscripts and Proof Sheets of Scott's Waverley Novels*,[7] relating *Redgauntlet* to the rest, and all to circumstances in the printing-house, noted the recent disappearance of another set of proof-sheets, those corrected in James Ballantyne's hand. From this tale it will appear that everyone writing on *Redgauntlet* has been concerned with manuscript, proof, or printed text, or with two of these, but none with all three. Comparison between them must be my starting-point.

Despite the pace at which the later novels went through the press, Scott enjoyed peculiar opportunities for bringing his second thoughts to bear on what he had written. By his own account,[8] this was his practice, at least until 1827: in order to preserve his supposed anonymity regarding the novels, he insisted that his hand should never be visible in the printing-house; proofs were set up, not from his manuscript but from a copy,[9] made under James Ballantyne's supervision; one set of these he corrected himself, and it then became Ballantyne's task to transfer the corrections to the other set. On this showing, there were four distinct states of *copy* in existence for any novel, before the printed text was set up; three stages at which it was possible for Scott to intervene, whether on his own initiative or at Ballantyne's request, after the completion of his original manuscript. Two more will need to be taken into the reckoning: further proofs, and cancels.

In order to test these possibilities, I have chosen those pages well known to have been revised – i.225-61, Wandering Willie's

But lackey and lass, and page and groom, all denied stoutly that they had ever seen such a bag of money as my gudesire described. Nay, he had unluckily not mentioned to any living soul of them his purpose of paying his rent. Ae quean had noticed something under his arm, but she took it for the pipes.

Sir John Redgauntlet ordered the servants out of the room, and then said to my gudesire, " Now Steenie, ye see you have fair play ; and, as I have little doubt ye ken better where to find the siller than ony other body, I beg, in fair terms, and for your own sake, that you will end this fasherie ; for, Stephen, ye maun pay or flitt."

" The Lord forgie your opinion," said Stephen, driven almost to his wits end—" I am an honest man."

" So am I, Stephen," said his Honour; " and so are all the folks in the house, I hope. But if there be a knave amongst us, it must be he that tells the story he cannot prove." He paused, and then added, more sternly. " If I understand your trick, sir, you want to take advan-

VOL. I. Q

But lackey and lass, and page and groom, all denied stoutly that they had ever seen such a bag of money as my ~~father~~ described. Nay, he had unluckily not mentioned to any living soul of them his purpose of paying his rent.

Sir John Redgauntlet ordered the servants out of the room, and then said to my gudesire. "Now Steenie, ye see you have fair play; and, as I have little doubt ye ken better where to find the siller than ony other body, I beg, in fair terms, and for your own sake, that you will end this fasherie; for, Stephen, ye maun pay or flitt."

"The Lord forgie your opinion," said Stephen, driven almost to his wits end—"I am an honest man."

"So am I, Stephen," said his Honour; "and so are all the folks in the house, I hope. But if there be a knave amongst us, it must be he that tells the story he cannot prove." He paused, and then added, more sternly. "If I understand your trick, sir, you want to take advantage of some malicious reports concerning things in this family, and particularly my father's sud-

Tale – for close examination in all three extant states,[10] and surveyed the rest of the MS cursorily, finding that the difference, as to amount of revision, has been a little exaggerated: some other passages in the novel show almost as much. The *Tale*, however, has been revised to better purpose than these, and so more is to be learned from the revision.

Although its excellence is generally acknowledged, and the story should be well known, yet it is so necessary to have its exact outline under the reader's eye that I must attempt a summary: Sir Robert Redgauntlet, though he had been a notorious persecutor of the south-western Whigs in the *killing times*, could, even after the Revolution, still command loyalty in his own household and among his tenants. One of these, Steenie Steenson, grandfather[11] of the narrator, was in some favour with the Laird, and with his butler Dougal MacCallum, on account of his piping. Being doubly behindhand with his rent at a certain Martinmas term-day, he was obliged to borrow from his neighbours, notably one Tod Lapraik. He carried the money to Redgauntlet Castle and was brought by Dougal into the presence of Sir Robert and his jackanape (monkey), nicknamed Major Weir; but Sir Robert, even as he was preparing to count the money, was taken with the pangs of death; and, in the tumult, Steenie left the Castle without a recept for it. *While the body was lying in state, Dougal confided to another old serving-man, Hutcheon, that he still heard his master's whistle at nights, and entreated his fellow-servant's company. As these two sat together in the adjoining room, the whistle sounded and, answering the summons, Dougal fell dead and Hutcheon lost consciousness.*[12] When the new Laird, Sir John, demanded the two terms' arrears of rent, Steenie could produce no witness to his transaction with Sir Robert. From a stormy encounter at the Castle he returned to Tod Lapraik, with whom he fared no better. Before entering the wood which lay across his homeward road he called at a change-house and, swallowing a pint of brandy, uttered two wishes: that Sir Robert might never lie quiet in his grave until he had done justice to his tenant, and that the devil would enable him to trace the lost money-bag. Riding through the wood, he was joined by a stranger who offered help and conducted him (seemingly) back to Redgauntlet Castle, where he found Sir Robert holding revel with his fellow persecutors. Dougal admitted him and warned him to accept nothing but the receipt due for his rent, which he succeeded in obtaining; and, when Sir Robert bade him return and do homage for this favour, he found himself able to utter the name of God. The phantom rout vanished, and he lay as though dead until morning, when he came to himself in Redgauntlet churchyard. Back he returned to Sir John, produced the receipt and delivered Sir Robert's direction to look for the money in a place which Hutcheon was able to identify. There the bag with much else was found, guarded by the jackanape, which attacked Sir John and was killed by him. He demanded that the whole affair should be dismissed as a trick of the thieving monkey; but he was induced to let Steenie tell his tale to the Minister, through whose wife it eventually got about – and then Steenie made known *his* version.

The manuscript of *Redgauntlet* (Adv. MS. 19.2.29, in the National Library of Scotland, formerly the Advocates' Library) is written on one side of quarto leaves, the *Tale* occupying ff.53 (1.19) to 60 (1.33) of the first volume.[13] His close script forbidding any substantial alteration in the text, Scott used the blank pages on the left hand for purposes ranging from corrections, made *currente calamo*, to considerable afterthoughts. Although it is not usually possible to differentiate, a few can be cited to illustrate this diversity of purpose and character.[14]

Those proofs which include the *Tale*, numbered pp. 224-61, consist of two complete gatherings and parts of two others: O8 (1 leaf), P-Q⁸, R (1-3) (3 leaves). Discontinuity between P and Q, Q and R, seems to reflect difficulties in the printing-house: the contents of P had been so much amplified that Q had to be set up afresh, with p. 240 renumbered 241; Scott's corrections were now incorporated in the text – but he added others. The overlap between Q and R is only half as great, and has not entailed fresh pagination.

The sheets had been ruthlessly trimmed, and much of the manuscript correction effaced, before they reached MacRitchie's hands; but comparison with the manuscript and the printed text allows all but a few of these marginalia to be made out. Ballantyne's "Please to read this", which appears on the first page of each gathering, must be distinguished from the results of his own proof-reading: that is, from specific queries.

Scott's manuscript of *Redgauntlet*, in the possession of the National Library of Scotland: Vol. I, fol. 58, with the corresponding left-hand page. Reproduced by kind permission of the Library.

x he looked for the stranger but he was gaen for the time — At last he justly

x gloomily

2 and whilst Bonshaw shot till blessed MeCargills under till the [...] blood sprang
and Dumbarton Douglas the trenchward under both to country and king
And there was Clavers house or beautiful

x his eyes stretched out before him, and swathed up with flannel, to the his

2 for he heard them saying as he came furious "Is not Major Weir come yet "/
another answered "the Jack an ape will be here between the moon" And when
my Grandsire came forward the Ghost Sir Roberts g [...] his ghaist in the darkling
his cheeks said "Wulf

It is, I think, clear that these were not the final proofs. The leaves of every gathering except O (a mere fifteen lines) vary occasionally from the printed page. Some of these variants are manifestly authorial, and one is of very curious interest.[15]

The two cancels in the *Tale* consist, as van Antwerp showed, of the addition of *Dougal* on p. 231 (P4^r), and the substitution of Sir *John* for Sir *Robert* on p. 239 (P8^r), after printing. Only the first is significant.[16]

[ii]

A comparative view of these several states of Wandering Willie's Tale should throw some light on the transmission of the text, and the evolution of the *Tale* as a triumph of narrative art. The two processes cannot be presented separately, the first being ancillary to the second. Moreover, the sum of the alterations falls little short of a hundred and forty – two-thirds of these, on my reckoning, significant. A choice must be made and, seeking to condense rather than limit illustration, I shall prefer examples in which both can be seen at work.

The pattern of transmission seems to run: Scott – the transcriber – Ballantyne (and his printers) – and Scott again. Despite numerous small differences between his manuscript and the proofs, I am convinced that Scott did not intervene to correct the work of the transcriber in these eight leaves. The alterations appear to me all of a piece, and such as might arise from the efforts of a faithful, and trusted, amanuensis working on this part of the manuscript, with its peculiar difficulties. I am inclined, moreover, to believe that these were the first proofs Scott saw, and that none of the differences between manuscript and proof need signify authorial intervention. The transcriber was expected to know his habits as well as his handwriting, to divine his intentions and take responsibility; and he was allowed a proportionate share of freedom. Where a sentence was manifestly incomplete, he might insert the obvious word; he might dovetail successive afterthoughts into one another, and the whole passage into the text, by means of small omissions and additions.[17] Ballantyne may have overseen the work at this stage.[18] He must have taken charge when proof was set up from transcript – and this indeed is where his hand appears. He noted sentences which required more to complete them than the transcriber had been able to supply, readings which betrayed conjecture, and invoked Scott's help: "Is this the word? The copy is with the Author".

It seems probable that Ballantyne was charged with such tasks as the silent removal of Willie's references to his *father*, which Scott had failed to carry through. Between them, they missed five – of which one survives into present-day reprints. His brief for dealing summarily with inconsistencies may have extended to the cancels. One (P8) was a necessary correction: Steenie was speaking to Sir *John*, but Scott had inadvertently written Sir *Robert*, and the mistake had eluded both his proof-reading and Ballantyne's. The other is not an improvement: when Steenie brought his rent to the Castle, he was dismayed to find himself alone with Sir Robert. Scott recaptured that moment, and saw its horror heightened by the presence of the uncanny jackanape. He added, in proof, "and the Major". Surely it was Ballantyne who, in the P4 cancel, supplied Dougal MacCallum?[19] True, Dougal was there – or near by, but that would lower the tension, for Steenie; and this addition makes nonsense of the parenthesis: "a thing that hadna chanced to him before". I suspect that Ballantyne mistook Scott's purpose, supposed him to be attending to circumstantial detail, and tried to follow suit.

Greville Worthington reports that "the leaves P4 and P8 in Vol. I are found in two states after cancellation", and that in the (presumed) later state of p. 232 *would* has been changed to *wad*.[20] Ballantyne may have been responsible for observing the convention as to Scottish spellings for certain common words. Scott undoubtedly *heard* the words in his own tongue, but he seldom troubled to mark the distinction in the first draft. His revision tends in this direction, but fitfully.

Spelling apart, the transcriber, whether of the manuscript or of the corrections in these proofs, was stiffly tested. He must use initiative, but could not always hope to supply deficiencies by casting about for the obvious word. When Scott wrote: "The like o' Steenie wasna the wood that they made Whigs o' ", someone stumbled, and the proof ran: "wasna the *worst* that". An appeal to the author brought a marginal correction: "wasna the *sort* that . . .". Either he had not returned to his own manuscript, or the blunder had warned him that his metaphor was too bold.

A similar misreading seems to have yielded a happier result. Scott's *a* and *u* are often indistinguishable. In the 1824 text, the wood through which Steenie rides at night is called, on that occasion, Pitmarkie, but Sir John presently calls it Pitmurkie. In 1827, the first occurrence is altered to agree with the second – no mere mechanical correction. In the manuscript, Sir John, anxious to discredit Steenie's tale, had proposed that they should "lay the hail dirdum on that ill-deedie creature, Major Weir, and say naething about your dream in the wood at a' —". This "a' —", in the proofs, became a blank, such as Scott's forgetfulness of names often entailed. A hand which I believe to be Ballantyne's inserted the name of the wood – in a margin so mutilated that the spelling can only be inferred from the printed text. And so one of Scott's finest place-names was rescued from oblivion by Ballantyne's blunder.

Ballantyne has become a figure of fun for anyone writing on Scott's revision, but he surely deserved some of the confidence which Scott expressed in a letter written just after delivery of the last sheets of the transcript,[21] asking him to read the proofs carefully because his corrections are valued – and a little of the credit allowed him in the *Waverley* preface.[22] Much was required of him.

There was besides a bias in Scott which might make his afterthoughts hard to follow: he would not discard. It is impossible to imagine him sacrificing that tenth chapter of *Persuasion*. Thus, if he discovered an inconsistency or repetition, he would, as it were, darn or patch, even though it might have been better to go back and begin afresh. He confesses to this habitual practice in many of his retrospective introductions, alike to poems and novels, and the *Tale* affords a small instance of it. Sir Robert's horse-shoe frown, devised to link Redgauntlets past and present, tale with novel, is not in the manuscript; it was added in proof: "Ye maun ken he had a way of bending his brows that men saw the visible mark of a horse-shoe in his forehead deep-dinted as if it had been stamped there". When the same grimace is attributed to Sir John, in the body of the manuscript text, it is described as though for the first time. Scott then notices the discrepancy, and adds in proof: "that self-same fearsome shape".

These are trifles, and although "we must confess the faults

147

of our favourite, to gain credit to our praise of his excellencies",[23] I am glad to have done with cavilling. Again and again, in these thirty-seven pages, Scott's revision bears witness to his imaginative insight. Thus, Dougal MacCallum is much more than a serviceable piece of the story's mechanism; he carries a share of its meaning, which is in accord with that of the novel. "Though death breaks service", says MacCallum, "it shall never break my service to Sir Robert". It is his master's death he has in mind, but his own which will renew his servitude: he answers the familiar summons, and is found "lying dead within twa steps of the bed where his master's coffin was placed". It is well known that those who support a tyranny have no choice but to perish in its fall. This platitude does not tell us, however, what happens when they meet their fellow reprobates in Hell, as Dougal meets Steenie – and warns him how he must act to escape. Loyalty, being an instinctive principle of association, was something Scott understood – and he did not insist that its object, whether man or cause, should be beyond reproach. (This theme runs through *Redgauntlet*.) So intrinsic does Dougal's significance prove, in the story as we know it, that to surprise Scott himself in the act of discovering it is a strange experience. He had written: "Weel Dougal died and as weel he did before the Revolution for its like it would have broke the auld carles heart". He struck this out and substituted (on the left-hand page): "Weel – round came the Revolution and it had like to have broken the hearts baith of Dougald and his master. But the change was not altogether sae great as they feard and other folk thought for".

Laurie Lapraik, the time-server, is another afterthought, woven into the story gradually – with less certainty than Dougal. He first appears on the left-hand page of the manuscript, when Steenie borrows the money to pay his rent: "The maist of it was from a neighbour they caad Laurie Lapraik – a sly tod Laurie had wealth o' gear – could hunt wi the hound & rin wi the hare & be Whig or Tory saint or sinner as the wind stood. He was a professor at this time but he liked an orra sound and a tune on the pipes weel eneugh at a byetime And abune a' he thought he had good security for the siller he lent my father over the stocking at Primrose Know". When Steenie retreats worsted from Sir John, the manuscript merely carries him to

148

"his chief creditor", and while these two are at odds a blank is left for the name, which seems to have registered faintly. But the character was indispensable, and Scott assiduously worked Laurie into the proofs in preparation for the moment when he was to provoke Steenie into abusing his doctrine. Here Ballantyne, having lost the thread, inquired in the margin: "What doctrine?" – and Scott wrote, below the question: "Laurie was a professor and had just used the cant of his sect". Ballantyne, in his capacity of common reader, should not have overlooked those two words: *professor* and *doctrine*. Laurie was not indeed one of the "puir hill-folk" whose blood was on Sir Robert's hands when he went to his "appointed place"; it was not for him to read the great roll-call of those dead persecutors by whom Sir Robert is there surrounded. Yet, as one sort of Whig, he serves not only to reduce Steenie to brandy, blasphemy, and despair by recalling his part in the persecution, but also to make us understand that the revellers in the ghostly castle are not the idle phantoms of fashionable fiction but historical figures – in a country where history reverberates a long while.

[iii]

At its best, Scott's revision furthers his artistic purpose at more levels than one: grappling us to his story and giving that story significance. On such occasions it is itself an art.

How is purpose to be divined, in an author who chose to give so misleading an account of himself? A full answer demands the scope of a book; but something may be provisionally attempted, by close attention to this closely revised *Tale*. Scott has to master certain problems, here as elsewhere; but here they are seen with peculiar clarity, and his success is beyond question. These problems can be summarily indicated in one word: equilibrium. He has to maintain a balance between conflicting claims: rights and wrongs in the historical conflict of interests; formal symmetry and naturalism in the pattern of events; supernatural and natural interpretation of what happened.

Our vantage-point for a survey of the first two will be a simple anecdote which Scott read in Joseph Train's notes to his *Strains of the Mountain Muse*.[24] His response to this little volume was the beginning of a lifelong friendship and literary association between the two men. Train's anecdote gives: the persecutor, Sir Robert Grierson of Lagg; the tenant who was deprived of the receipt for his rent by Sir Robert's sudden death; the encounter with a stranger in a wood on his homeward road; the castle and the *long dead* porter;[25] and with a legendary fiddler tuning up to play for the revellers; the strange receipt obtained, presented – and accepted by the hitherto incredulous new Laird. We cannot, however, be sure what it gave Scott; for it was never his way to reply, when offered information: "I know that – tell me something else". Only after cordial thanks and a request for further particulars would he admit, quietly, that he already had some knowledge of the matter. He had, indeed accumulated a great deal of information about the suppression of the south-western Whigs, so far back as 1803, when he was preparing to amplify the *Minstrelsy*: it furnished introductions and notes to those additional ballads, from *Lesley's March* to *The Battle of Bothwell-bridge*, which compose a consecutive passage of Scottish history. Moreover, his correspondence with Charles Kirkpatrick Sharpe of the year before shows his familiarity with the legends that had gathered round this conflict, and attached themselves indifferently to one and another of the persecutors, from famous names down to those remembered only in Galloway, or in Cameronian literature. Thus, he was doing no violence to tradition when he mounted Sir Robert Redgauntlet on the horse which the devil had given to Claverhouse, and (in *Old Mortality*) made Claverhouse himself tell Morton that he was popularly supposed to drink blood – as Sir Robert Grierson, among others, was said to have done. These and other superstitions – such as the devil's failure to protect his own against a silver bullet – had been known to him ever since he first looked into John Howie's *Scots Worthies*;[26] and he was at his best when his knowledge had undergone the process which H. J. C. Grierson happily calls *incubation*. In October 1802 he had written to Sharpe: "I have Lagg's elegy & am acquainted with the traditions of the period respecting most of the persecutors and persecuted saints".[27] He repeated this claim when he wrote to Lady Louisa Stuart after the completion of *Old Mortality*.[28] He read the tale with his usual compassionate insight: "The Covenanters deny to their governors that toleration, which was iniquitously refused to themselves".[29]

This is a characteristic observation – which offended both sides.

Scott's recognition of the irresistible hold upon his imagination which this knowledge retained, and its consequent value to himself, is evident from the risks he accepted for its sake. The time of *Redgauntlet* is fixed by Darsie's age at some twenty years afte the '45 – which raises historical difficulties of its own, but that is another story. Willie, now a man of sixty-two, had a father – presently changed to grandfather – who had been active before the Revolution. He himself was brought up in the household of Sir Redwald Redgauntlet – presumably Darsie's grandfather – who, he says, perished in the '45; but Maxwell of Summertrees testifies to Willie's fidelity at Harry Redgauntlet's end, in the aftermath of Culloden – and Sir Henry was Darsie's father. The fall of the Grierson fortunes in the '15 – not the '45 – would give an easier time-scheme for the *Tale* – and one impossible for the novel. But this game is not worth playing, unless it serves to show with what bold – surely deliberate and certainly successful – imprecision of reference Scott can set the *Tale* where he pleases, in the past, adjusting the generations in the Steenson family – and overlooking those of the Redgauntlets – while he realizes the asset he has thus created by introducing Laurie and developing the character of the new Laird, with his assured command of all the lawful means of oppression. Sir John allows Steenie to consult their own minister, because "he is a douce man, regards the honour of our family, and *the mair that* he may look for some patronage from me". The words I have italicized were added in proof, and, like much other revision, drive the nail home.

Of the reconciliation of formal symmetry with naturalism much might be said, but this must serve. Scott had, in the tale of the tenant, his landlords, and the phantom company,[30] a single train of events, the visits to the old and new Laird alternating as in a simple rhymed quatrain. By his elaboration of circumstantial detail and development of character he built, as it were, a more intricate stanza, whose virtue is that it can at once surprise and satisfy. Here are some of the afterthoughts by which this elaboration and development were accomplished: the rental-book, on which Steenie kept his eye "as if it were a mastiff-dog that he was afraid would spring up and bite him", links his two interviews, with father and son; the cryptic message, to look for the money in the Cat's Cradle, has to be interpreted by Hutcheon, because, as Steenie says, such matters are known only to him and "another serving-man that is now gane and that I wad not like to name". Such echoes are fewer and less resonant in the first draft.

The equilibrium between natural and supernatural interpretations of the *Tale* lies at the heart of the impression it leaves. Some readers have been content with a facile resolution of their conflicting claims. A. W. Verrall saw nothing but a trick, turning on a trivial discrepancy between the two accounts of Sir Robert's death, which would allow us to suppose that Steenie had got his receipt in the ordinary course, and dreamed up the rest. "Scott's own view of the facts, the rationalistic view, is implied clearly enough in the final paragraph of the story, and indeed throughout."[31] To this there are two objections. The first relates to that final paragraph: its second sentence was added after the correction of the extant proofs. It runs: "Indeed ye'll no hinder some to threap, that it was nane o' the Auld Enemy that Dougal and my gudesire saw in the Laird's room, but only that wanchancy creature, the Major, capering on the coffin; and that, as to the blawing on the Laird's whistle that was heard after he was dead, the filthy brute could do that as weel as the Laird himself, if no better". Hearsay set against hearsay does not disturb the equilibrium of doubt. The conclusion – "But Heaven kens the truth" – is no mere pious formula. Nor can the further emphasis thus given to it be fortuitous.

That inserted sentence must be part of Scott's final revision, in his last proofs. Yet it contains a very curious error. It was not "my gudesire", but Hutcheon, who ventured into the Laird's room with Dougal that night. How did Scott come to admit this discrepancy? Did he take the bold, Shakespearian, and apparently successful[32] way of sacrificing some lesser good – probability, consistency – to imaginative coherence? (This is not the moment for reminding us that Steenie, eye-witness to the rest of the *Tale*, was not there.) Was he simply careless? This, the time-honoured explanation, would be plausible, if it were not for the delicate tissue of revision by which he has enhanced the imaginative effect of Steenie's "dream". That is my second objection to the merely naturalistic interpretation of the *Tale*.

It is well known that he added "the Bluidy Advocate Mac-Kenyie" to the ghostly company in proof, but not that he had re-worked the whole passage in manuscript, adding not only cir-cumstantial detail but also this development of one circum-stance – the monkey's absence: "for he heard them say as he came forward, 'Is not Major Weir come yet' & another answered 'The Jackanape will be here betimes the morn' ". What is more, one further alteration seems to have been made in the final proofs, for the version of the printed text – " 'Is not the Major come yet?' " – differs from manuscript and extant proofs by that uncanny touch of familiarity. So it is after all the jackanape which holds the key to both interpretations. True, he was a thieving brute – but he too had his hour, and his appointed place.[33] The very waking, whether from dream or vision, has been revised with the same mastery: Steenie had originally found himself lying "in the middle of the forest the birds were singing the sun was shining and his horse was feeding quietly beside him". But after revision of the proofs he lay in the "auld kirkyard of Redgauntlet parishine just at the door of the family aisle & the scutcheon of the auld knight Sir Robert hanging over his head – There was a deep morning fog on grass & grave-stone around him and his horse was quietly feeding beside the minister's twa cows".

How are we to understand the expense of such care as this on a story of supernatural happenings?[34] *Not* for the sake of con-doning "that horrid belief in witchcraft, which cost many inno-cent persons, and crazy impostors, their lives, for the supposed commission of impossible crimes".[35] Scott's gentleness of heart made the history of that belief abhorrent to him. It is not to credulity that he speaks. We are sometimes assailed by a more pervasive fear, an enfolding darkness different from those several shadows projected by doubts of our own sufficiency, or the all too sufficient power of particular adversaries. I cannot associate this visitation with belief, for it is at variance with religion; and it enjoys too little acquaintance with either in-tellect or will to be called voluntary suspension of disbelief. Scott understood this experience: the fear of unknown powers, and of the force inherent in the spoken word for invoking them – as Steenie invokes the dead and the devil. He understood also the countervailing hope, that means may be found of revoking this too potent word, even that an ally within the enemy's stronghold may direct us to those means – as Dougal directs Steenie. Such fear and hope may be conveniently assigned to the persons of a tale; and this will be easier if one of them is telling it. Scott shows elsewhere that he can dispense with this latter condition, relying on dialogue alone to convey Meg Merrilies' faith in the effect of her curse and in her power to call it home and take the evil to herself. (Kipling, in *The Wish House*, chose the safer way.) These differences of method do not signify. Whatever the means by which a writer attributes such fear and hope to imaginary persons, he does not thereby disencumber himself of every burden which possession of the imaginative faculty has laid upon us.

These are unsounded waters – but no deeper than we must expect to reach if we bring to a great novelist our whole attention. Has Scott ever been read with the care which he himself deprecated – but which his art invites?[36]

NOTES

1   *Life of Sir Philip Sidney*, ed. Nowell Smith (Oxford, 1907), pp. 153-4.

2   Border Edition of the novels. This volume is dated 1894.

3   This leader was reprinted in *Scott Centenary Articles* (Oxford, 1932).

4   In *Bibliographia: Studies in Book History and Book Structure, 1750-1900*, ed. Michael Sadleir (London).

5   My copy contains traces of a fifth: in Volume III, S5 (pp. 281-2) pasted to a stub.

6   *A Collector's Comment on his first editions of the Works of Sir Walter Scott*, San Francisco (Gelber, Lilienthal, Inc.).

7   *Edinburgh Bibliographical Society Transactions*, IV.i (1960), 15-42.

8   General Preface to the 1829 edition of *Waverley*, pp. xx-xxi.

9   Miss Dyson cites a letter to *The Times*, 15 July 1868, by George Huntly Gordon, claiming to have transcribed thirty-seven volumes.

10 I owe the favour of photographs of these proof-sheets to the authorities of the Pierpont Morgan Library, and the opportunity of examining the manuscript to the National Library of Scotland.

11 *Father* in the first draft. See pp. 146 and 151 below.

12 This episode [* ... *] is the only part of the story not witnessed by Steenie. See p. 152 below.

13 Although the three volumes are bound in one, the divisions between them are marked, and pagination is discontinuous.

14 See pp. 148-9 below: Dougal MacCallum and Laurie Lapraik.

15 See p. 152 below.

16 See p. 146 below.

17 Some two or three variants appear to be slips, for which the manuscript affords excuse.

18 It was transcribed "under Mr. Ballantyne's eye", according to the *Waverley* Preface (above, n. 8), p. xxi.

19 Misspelled, but that signifies nothing. The spelling of this and other names is erratic throughout.

20 *Op. cit.*, p. 132.

21 Dated 3 June 1824 by Grierson, who quotes from a letter of Cadell's: "The printer got the last portion of MS on the 2d", *Letters* (London, 1935), viii.290, 310.

22 P. xx. If Scott is, as usual, too generous, the balance may have been too roughly redressed.

23 Johnson writing to Charles Burney about Shakespeare. *Letters*, ed. R. W. Chapman (Oxford, 1952), no. 177, Vol. I. p. 178, w. 16 Oct. '65.

24 Printed in Edinburgh for the Author (1814), pp. 191-5.

25 Hence (I conjecture) Scott's first draft, in which Dougal dies before the Revolution.

26 *Biographia Scoticana ... Scots Worthies* (2d ed., Glasgow, 1781) with Appendix, *The Judgement and Justice of God*, 1782.

27 *Letters*, i.161.

28 *Ibid.*, iv.292.

29 *Minstrelsy of the Scottish Border* (Edinburgh, 1803), iii.210.

30 Alexander Fergusson says that this story was "current in
    Nithsdale", and that it had been given to Joseph Train by James
    Dennistoun. (*The Laird of Lag: a Life Sketch* (Edinburgh, 1886),
    pp. 216, 217). Scott confused the issue by his note on the *Tale* in
    1832. The strain of negligence, caprice, even mischief in those
    retrospective notes requires investigation, but not here.

31 *The Prose of Walter Scott* (*Quarterly Review*, 1910), reprinted in
    Collected Literary Essays, ed. Bayfield and Duff (Cambridge,
    1913), p. 268.

32 It seems to have escaped notice.

33 In *My Aunt Margaret's Mirror*, Scott characterizes a super-
    natural tale as one in which the narrator, having professed
    general disbelief in its assumptions, confesses to "something . . .
    which he has been always obliged to give up as inexplicable".
    Chronicles of the Canongate, First Series, in the collected (1829-33)
    edition (Edinburgh, 1832), p. 306.

34 I find myself unable to accept Dr. C. O. Parsons's conclusions,
    or even, within the space available, to canvass our differences
    regarding Scott's attitude to the supernatural. See *Witchcraft and
    Demonology in Scott's Fiction* (Edinburgh and London, 1964),
    also earlier studies.

35 *Letters on Demonology and Witchcraft* (London, 1830), p. 172.

36 I acknowledge gratefully the help of Dr. Ian Jack and Dr. J. D.
    Fleeman in revising this essay. Any remaining errors are of
    course my own.

Robert Smith Surtees

Surtees belongs to the generation of Dickens and Thackeray, and supplied the novel readers of the period – though his was a smaller band – with much the same nourishment. The thirties of the last century wanted to move away from the romance of Scott, and, on a different level, of Mrs. Radcliffe; some had tasted the delights of Peacock; a few had appreciated the Brontës. What most had come to ask for was a picture of society in general, wider than that provided by Jane Austen, even of those parts of society unknown to them, except incidentally, such as Dickens showed them. Dickens, moreover, gave them characters – or at least "figures", as Henry James somewhat unsympathetically described them. Thackeray confined himself in the main to picturing the middle class to which he belonged, with special stress on their moral dilemmas, as Mrs. Gaskell did a little later. Surtees was one of this type, portraying people engaged in an activity he knew something about, bringing into being characters possibly more recognizable to readers than those of Dickens, and living in a characteristic milieu which he did something to create. It would be absurd to claim for him a rank equal to that of Dickens and Thackeray; but it is fair to say that he established a realm of his own, made up of figures perhaps unfamiliar to many – they would be much more so today than they were a century ago – who, though each was stamped with individual character, could be greeted as acquaint-

ances by any at all familiar with Surtees's world. It cannot
be said that he added much, if anything, to the development
of the novel, but it can be argued that he accompanies those
that did.

One may get a certain impression of his world by following
Kipling's Midmore as he first encounters Surtees:

> It was a foul world into which he peeped for the first time – a heavy-
> eating, hard-drinking hell of horse-copers, swindlers, matchmaking
> mothers, economically dependent virgins selling themselves un-
> blushingly for cash and lands: Jews, tradesmen, and an ill-considered
> spawn of Dickens-and-horsedung characters.[1]

This, of course, as Kipling tells us, is Midmore's own criticism,
as might be expected of a sensitive soul of "the immoderate
left"; but he felt compelled to read on, and found in the books
people very like those whom he met, and with whom he now
shared certain traits, such as objecting to hoof-marks on gravel.
"Outrageous as thought and conception were, the stuff seemed
to have the rudiments of observation." So he read more. Then
when Midmore took to hunting, he met a different group of
people, and "would go home and identify them, one by one,
out of the natural-history books by Mr. Surtees".

The world is there then, its people exist, as Mr. Siegried
Sassoon also found, as he relates in *Memoirs of a Fox-Hunting
Man* (1928), where "Sherston" and his friend Colwood:

> adopted and matured a specialized jargon drawn almost exclusively
> from characters in the novels of Surtees; since we knew these almost
> by heart they provided us with something like a dialect of our own,
> and in our care-free moments we exchanged remarks in the mid-
> Victorian language of such character parts as Mr. Romford, Major
> Yammerton, and Sir Moses Mainchance, while Mr. Jorrocks was
> an all-pervading influence. Sherston was "the richest commoner in
> England", while Colwood would often declare that he would be "the
> death of a fi' pun note – dash my vig if I won't".

It is, then, in the creation of characters that Surtees makes his
distinctive impact.

It would be as well to see how Surtees came to write, why he
continued, and what purpose he may have had. Born in 1805, the
second son of a considerable landowner, he lived at one of his
houses, Hamsterley Hall, in Co. Durham. In 1825 he was sent

to London to complete his training as a lawyer but does not appear to have devoted himself to this calling with any enthusiasm, which is not surprising if his account of the Inns in *Handley Cross* (1843) is at all accurate. Nevertheless in 1828 he was admitted a solicitor in Chancery. He seems to have spent most of his time in getting to know London life, and the many people from whom some of his characters are drawn, and hunting with the local packs, of which there were still a number near London, notably the Surrey. In 1829 he hunted at Brighton and across the channel at Boulogne and Samer, at which places he was for a short time M.F.H.

He had always read *The Sporting Magazine*, to which his friendly enemy "Nimrod" (C. J. Apperley) was the most distinguished contributor; and in 1830 (having written most of a novel that friends advised him to destroy) began himself to write for it, and it was there that first appeared in serial form *Jorrocks' Jaunts and Jollities*, which was immediately popular, and is supposed to have given Dickens the idea for *The Pickwick Papers*. In 1831 *The New Sporting Magazine* was published under his editorship. In that year his elder brother died, and he thus became heir to Hamsterley, and from then his chief interest lay in Co. Durham. In 1837 he contested, somewhat half-heartedly, the parliamentary seat of Gateshead and was not disappointed at his failure. He was often asked to stand, but he had no desire to be among those "condemned to hard labour, day and night on committees, and in the House of Commons running like waiters at the sound of the Speaker's bell" (*Plain or Ringlets?* 1860, XX). After 1838, when he succeeded to the family estate, his interests were given over to his farms and their tenants, their improvement, and the general bettering of agriculture. He continued to keep one of his father's packs of foxhounds for a couple of years; in 1842 he became a J.P. and Deputy Lieutenant for Durham; in 1844 he was commissioned as a major in the Durham Militia, but resigned when he was asked if he would be willing to serve abroad should his regiment be ordered there. His mind, it would seem, was wholly devoted to his own bit of country.

Writing, however, was an immense attraction for him, though he pretended to see no value in the sort of thing he wrote, as he explained at the beginning of Chapter XV of *Hawbuck Grange*

Writing, we imagine, is something like snuffing or smoking – men get into the way of it, and can't well leave it off. Like smoking, it serves to beguile an idle hour. Individually speaking, writing makes us tolerably independent, both of the world and the weather. We are never regularly high and dry for want of a companion so long as we can get pen, ink, and paper; and though we should not like to back ourself against such a winter as the last [1846-7], yet writing enables us to contend with a tolerable amount of bad weather. An author has pretty much the same pleasure in seeing his ugly cramped hand turned into neat print that a traveller has in receiving five-and-twenty francs for a sovereign on landing in France. Revising is something like returning to the realities of English money again. But we are getting into the mysteries of authorship.

(1847), and rejoiced in "the privilege of writing and printing *incognito*". But he goes on:

It is not surprising, then, that he did not give much attention to form: his books are all in their nature episodic, as was to some extent dictated by their often being serial, as was *Handley Cross* itself, as well as the *Jaunts and Jollities*. "It is difficult in novel-writing, to drive the two parts of the story (into which all orthodox three-volume ones should be divided like phaeton horses, and prevent one part outstepping the other)", he wrote in *Hillingdon Hall* (1848) (chapter XXX) which, incidentally, is his best constructed book. In the Preface to *Ask Mamma* (1858) he throws the blame for any deficiency in this respect on the reader: "It may be a recommendation to the lover of light literature to be told that the following story does not involve the complication of a plot". So it is not in this direction that we shall find in Surtees any development of the novel.

What he did contribute, however, was an enlargement of the field of the novel, bringing in a whole new section of society, not only the followers of hounds – numerous and varied enough – but the small country dweller, the farmer, people whose interests were entirely local, as his mainly were. It was the manner of life of such people, their idiosyncrasies, that he enjoyed depicting, delighting to dwell upon characters until they assumed the proportions of caricature. Many of his better born figures are traceable to actual individuals: Pomponius Ego is, of course, Apperley; Miserrimus Doleful, M.C. can be identified as the Master of Ceremonies at Brighton, Captain Eld; Prince

Pirouetezza in *Plain or Ringlets?* is a certain Baron Gablenz;
and the lovable Jogglebury Crowdey in *Mr. Sponge's Sporting
Tour* (1853) is the Rev. James Birkett, headmaster of the school
he went to at Ovingham.

Before going on to consider what gives Surtees his special
quality as a novelist, it may be well to glance at the didactic and
satirical elements in his work and his few comments on changing
social conditions. As to this last, he welcomed the coming of the
railway – though it brought town riff-raff into the country,
especially to race-meetings – as being the means of civilizing
the country hawbuck, enabling him to go to London, where he
can belong to a club which has a good library. He can sometimes
use a sharp note as when, in *Plain or Ringlets?* he refers to
"tender-hearted beauties, who would rush to the rescue of a
fly in a cream-jug kept poor milliner girls sewing all night, in
order that they may be gay and smart on the morrow". Usually,
however, he is in more laughing mood, as when at the beginning of *Hillingdon Hall* he speaks of two gossiping ladies Mrs.
Flather and Mrs. Trotter. The former

> by assuming her late husband's undisguised detestation of gossip
> and twaddle . . . rather inveigled people into communicativeness.
> "Oh, don't tell me any secrets, pray!" she would exclaim – or,
> "Don't tell me anything that doesn't concern myself. I never meddle
> with other people's affairs", and so on; by which means she often got
> possession of secrets that would otherwise never have been intrusted
> to her.

Mrs. Trotter, by contrast, had "a strong, unturnable resolution", "a busy, bustling woman with such a strong sense of
'duty' as frequently caused her to say and do things that most
people would have been glad to leave alone". Each, of course,
had that "essential requisite" a daughter, these competing for
marriage with the Marquis of Bray. It is all conducted amusingly
enough, in Surtees's usual manner, combined with his sense of
the absurdity of large social functions where everybody is
extravagantly dressed.

This is his most didactic novel, inscribed to The Royal Agricultural Society, and here we find an aging Jorrocks, still full of
vigour, though not quite with the old brio, devoting himself to
the improvement of agriculture, of which, to begin with, he was

"superlatively ignorant", going round lecturing about "Nitrate o' sober! guano! sub-soilin'! Smith o' Deanston! [the promotor of land-drainage]! top dressin' wi' soot, and all that sort o' thing!" We also get Surtees's strong views on the Corn Laws; and finally, when Jorrocks becomes a J.P., some shrewd, sensible illustrations of how the law should be administered by Justices. Luckily, perhaps, we are not told how Jorrocks behaved at Westminster when he became an M.P.

Surtees disliked all forms of snobbery, particularly of birth. Dukes, such as the Duke of Tergiversation, get small shrift from him; but an earl, as for example the Earl of Scamperdale, could be redeemed by a love of hounds. He scoffed, as we have seen, at husband- or wife-hunting, at garden parties, elaborate picnics, balls, but he hated racing, a well-spring, he thought, of dishonesty. He welcomed fox-hunting, indeed all forms of that sport, except where the carted stag was pursued. Hunting was "the sport of Kings, the image of war without its guilt", as Somerville had remarked in his long and now little read poem *The Chace*, to which the prudent grocer of Great Coram Street added "and only five-and-twenty per cent of its danger". Its chief virtue, however, was that it brought all the countryside together: "The 'get away' from a fox cover is a real leveller of rank, far more efficacious than any Reform Bill". Also; "In that word "unting', what a ramification of knowledge is compressed", as Mr. Jorrocks declared in his first Sporting Lector: "The choice of an 'oss – the treatment of him when got . . . the 'ounds, the 'untsman, the feeder, the Fox!" It took men out into the country, taught them about nature and wild life, self-control at the cover side, courtesy at gates. It is in *Analysis of the Hunting Field* (1846) that Surtees delivers himself of his well-known apophthegm: "More people are flattered into virtue than bullied out of vice".

He was the first novelist really to tell his readers about hunting. Lever, who is not read now, tells us very little; Whyte-Melville, who came a little later, had hard riding as his chief concern, whereas Surtees found that "real lovers of hunting are anything but a hard-riding set. Fond of seeing hounds work, they use their horses as a sort of auxiliary to their legs". Trollope has some enthusiastic passages, especially in *Orley Farm*; but too near-sighted to see much of hounds, he was more interested in the social aspects of the field, and probably would not have known whether it was the dog or the bitch-pack that was out. Surtees tells us in what the skill of a huntsman consists, how hounds must be looked after, and so on, incidentally on many occasions, more specifically through the mouth of Mr. Jorrocks in his "lectors", based as they are on a thorough knowledge of Peter Beckford's classic *Letters on Hunting* (1781).

What Surtees chiefly did was to immortalize, and partly create, a whole set of figures belonging to this hunting world; though recognizable, as Midmore and Mr. Sassoon found, they are of the nature of humours rather than characters. There are several in each book. *Plain or Ringlets?* yields us the Duke of Tergiversation; "sivin and four's ilivin" – namely old Goldspink the banker; Admiration Jack, so called "from his extreme satisfaction with himself"; Jovey Jessop, who found that his great love of hospitality involved him in having too many drinks, and so appointed Mr. Boyston as his Jug, to do his drinking for him. In *Ask Mamma* we get Major Yammerton, Sir Moses Mainchance, and Mr. Pringle, "the richest commoner in England"; and that good M.F.H. the Earl of Ladythorne, against whom Miss de Clancey is to be fitted out under the Limited Liability Act. There are literally dozens in every book, all presented in a lively atmosphere of action.

At least four of his most notable "humours" are to be found in *Mr. Sponge's Sporting Tour*, apart from Sponge himself, "a good, pushing, free-and-easy sort of man, wishing to be a gentleman without knowing how", readily accepting invitations to stay at houses that provided good hunting facilities, and dislodged only with the greatest difficulty. There is Benjamin Buckram, whose right hand trouser-pocket always contained a lot of silver, which he would gather up and let fall down in a tremendous avalanche, or half-crown by half-crown, according to the emphasis he wished to give his discourse. There is Mr. Jogglebury Crowdey, wheezing where the verbs ought to be, or to emphasize an adjective. It need hardly surprise us that he should have this "bellows-to-mend" characteristic when we read that he was a

> long-headed, short-necked, large-girthed, dumpling-legged little fellow, who, like most fat men, made himself dangerous by compressing a most unreasonable stomach into a circumscribed coat, each

particular button of which looked as if it were ready to burst off, and knock out the eye of any one who might have the temerity to walk alongside of him.

Mrs. Crowdey was intent to provide for their children by a careful selection of godparents; but Jog is laying up riches for them in the form of "gibbey-sticks", that is, young branches cut from trees, or even uprooted saplings, which he would fashion into curious-handled walking sticks, their heads carved into portraits of monarchs or great men, series after series of King Williams, of Byrons, Napoleons, Disraelis – or of beasts, birds, and fishes.

> He had accumulated a vast quantity – thousands; the garret at the top of his house was quite full, so were most of the closets, while the rafters in the kitchen, and cellars, and out-houses, were crowded with others in a state of *déshabille*. He calculated his stock at immense worth, we don't know how many thousands of pounds; and as he cut, and puffed, and wheezed, and modelled, he chuckled, and thought how well he was providing for his family.

Many figures make up the varied world that Mr. Sponge encountered, for this was a *Sporting Tour* in which there were many to be met – from the nobleman, through the gentry, to the groom and the scamp. There are, for instance, the patronizing Jawleyford, Facey Romford, whom we hear more about in *Mr. Romford's Hounds* (1865); Sir Harry Scattercash, with untidy strings to his clothes, and Lady Scattercash who "could ride – indeed she used to do scenes in the circle (two horses and a flag), and she could drive, and smoke, and sing, and was possessed of many other accomplishments". Especially are there Lord Scamperdale and his double, Jack Spraggon, both wearing horned spectacles which were interchangeable. Jack had special functions to perform as a kind of *alter-ego*, much as the Jug is to Jovey Jessop (as, for instance, going to tiresome dinners instead of his lordship). We first meet them on an occasion when Sponge, unable to control his horse, barges into people and hounds and spoils the hunt. Scamperdale as Master of the Flat Hat Hounds, rounds on him:

> you perpendicular-looking Puseyite pig-jobber! By Jove! you think because I'm a lord and can't swear or use coarse language, that you may do what you like.

So, since he's a lord and can't swear, Jack Spraggon is turned on to do the job for him. On another occasion he gets as far as calling Sponge (it's always poor Soapey!) "you pestilential son of a pantry-maid!" and then hands over – to some extent:

> "Sing out, Jack! sing out!" gasped his lordship again.
> "Oh, you scandalous, hypocritical, rusty-booted, numb-handed son of a puffing corn-cutter, why don't you turn your attention to feeding hens, cultivating cabbages, or making pantaloons for small folk, instead of killing hounds in this wholesale way?"
> "Oh, you unsightly, sanctified, idolatrous, Bagnigge-Wells coppersmith, you think because I can't swear or use coarse language that you may do what you like."

On a later occasion, with the same preface, he calls him a "sanctified, putrefied, pestilential, perpendicular, ginger-bread booted counter-skippin' snob".

Sponge himself is no mean practitioner in the art of invective but he is generalizing when, though in process of enormously enjoying taking over the job of an inefficient huntsman with Lucy Glitters as whipper-in, he breaks out:

> "Who the deuce would be a huntsman that could be anything else? Dash it! I'd rayther be a hosier, I'd rayther be a hatter, I'd rayther be an undertaker – I'd rayther be a Pusseyite parson – I'd rayther be a pig-jobber – I'd rayther be a besom-maker – I'd rayther be a dog's meat man – I'd rayther be a cat's meat man – I'd rayther go about a sellin' of chick-weed and sparrow-grass!" added he, as his horse nearly slipped up on his haunches.

Those outbursts are part of the flavouring of *Mr. Sponge's Sporting Tour*, a book you can amble through with pleasure, enjoying the fresh air of the country, seeing hounds work in the setting of woods and fields, and the picture of various societies Sponge encounters in his tour. Perhaps, however, it is the characters that remain in the memories of most readers unless they are fox-hunters, and Thackeray's letter of thanks for the book comes to mind:

> This is not to thank you for the grouse, but for the last two numbers of Soapey Sponge, they are capital, the Flat Hats delightful, & those

fellows in spectacles divine; & Scamperdale's character perfectly odious and admirable.

For Surtees, of course, Scamperdale's character was redeemed by his being so good an M.F.H. We ourselves, perhaps, can like Sponge, in spite of his sponging character; after all his great pleasure was in a blameless and healthy activity, and we are glad when he finally marries Lucy Glitters, and they set up a betting and cigar shop in Jermyn Street. We are sorry when we learn in *Mr. Romfords' Hounds* that when betting shops were forbidden by law, the business collapsed, Soapey went to the bad, and Lucy was engaged to run Facey's house for him as his sister, Mrs. Somerville. Finally Sponge and Romford foregather in Australia, where Lucy joins them, and they set up "The Romford and Sponge Bank". There is, however, a sad note in the book, Jack Spraggon being killed in a steeplechase, a form of amusement Surtees detested.

Surtees, we have seen, rejoiced in the inventive idiom, and not only in the matter of swearing, as we find again and again. When, for instance, in *Mr. Romford's Hounds* we hear of the snobbish Atkinses going the round of countryside calling, we are told how day after day they "paced the weary turnpike roads, the pompous grey horses propounding their magnanimous legs with the true airing action". He abounds in felicitous phrases. Independent Jimmy calls Romford "a man of much blandishment"; Strider in *Handley Cross* was "an immensely tall, telescopic kind of man"; Scamperdale had "a tremendous determination of words to the mouth"; Major Yammerton's after-dinner speech in *Ask Mamma* is greeted, not with mere applause, but with "a tremendous discharge of popularity"; and Yammerton later "palavers" the Earl of Ladythorne. Sir Moses Mainchance gives as a toast "the Major and his 'harriers' in a speech of great gammonosity".

Needless to say, his great achievement was *Handley Cross*. It is a real novel, since besides its great hunting scenes, it depicts the whole of the society of a newly born fashionable watering-place (possibly founded on Leamington) growing from a village to a town. It is a little world of its own. Thus it is not only to those that have "the bump of Fox-un-ta-tiveness werry strongly deweloped" that the book appeals, as is strongly evidenced by the entry in Sir Sydney Cockerell's Diary, 1 Sep: 1895: "In evening W[illiam] M[orris] read some of his favourite bits out of Handley Cross". One only wishes one knew what the "bits" were.

It is a densely populated region that Surtees asks us to live in for a while, with Miserrimus Doleful, the mournful, ambitious Master of the Ceremonies; with the A.D.C. who was showered with invitations till it was discovered that the initials stood for Assistant Drains Commissioner; there are the rival doctors, Roger Swizzle who recommends hearty meals, and whose looks suggest that he adopted the same recipe for health (as did, no doubt fat old Mr. Guzzle, who "looks the picture of health and apoplexy"): and Sebastian Mello, pale, withdrawn, studying his prescriptions as he drives along, no doubt advocating an ascetic régime. We have ladies too – the preposterously snobbish Mrs. Barnington, self-elected Queen of Handley Cross, whose nose was somewhat put out of joint by the superior claims of the wife of the M.F.H.; mothers with daughters to sell to rich husbands; Mrs. Marmaduke Muleygrubs and "the Crusher" together with "the Bloomer". Pomponius Ego, "Nimrod" pays a visit to report on a hunt. Then there are the horse-copers, the people outside, the good farmers, the bad farmers, and the little old man with the thundering good library, who, being put out when Charley Stobbs breakfasts with him, throws his cup out of the window and claps the saucer on his head (a George Borrow touch, that). But in the centre of all, naturally, is John Jorrocks, the successful grocer from Great Coram Street in London – his abrupt, and worse, wife, who occasionally in his hunting dreams Jorrocks kicks out of bed, his charming niece Belinda, Betsey the pretty maid, and Gabriel Junks the peacock who foretells the weather.

Jorrocks is without doubt an imaginative creation; he is of the race of immortal and divine fat men. In a sense he is the Falstaff of the chase, for he is something of a fairy, with a superb gift for variegated invective, of a lighter kind than Spraggon's, and unanswerable repartee. Like Dr. Johnson, he was called a bear, and like him scorned your clarety wines. He may be uncouth and greedy, but he redeems all by his wholehearted passion for hunting and is a man of integrity. One feels there is a good deal of Surtees himself in Jorrocks, the same hatred of pretension, though he knew "when to butter a booby and when to snub a snob". One cannot help loving Jorrocks, who has something about him of the heavenly simpleton which is the mark of the great comic character. How wise he was you can tell from the aphorisms he scatters. "Take not out your 'ounds on a werry windy day" does not apply only to hunting, nor was it meant to any more than "What a huntsman I'd be if it weren't for the leaps", which most of us have said with reference to one thing or another. Most delicious of all, perhaps, is Jorrocks's sigh as he pounds along all elbows and legs, rib-roasting Arterxerxes on the great Cat and Custard Pot day; "How I wish I was a heagle!" That is as profound, if not as touching as " 'I wish, Trim', said my uncle Toby, 'that I was in bed' ".

In the main, the figures – at all events the chief ones – in *Handley Cross* are more characters and less humours than in the other novels. Take, for instance, James Pigg, whom not to know is like not knowing Sam Weller: no doubt they wander together about the Elysian Fields, "hand in hand, like the sign of the Mutual Insurance Hoffice", as the M.F.H. would say, the one being witty and wise in cockney, the other retorting in the dialect of the Cannynewcassel he came from. Long, lanky, spindle-shanked, with flowing grey-streaked locks, a weather-beaten face lighted up by hazel eyes, and tobacco juice always leaking down the deep furrows of his chin, he is the admirable simpleton, devoted only to hounds and hunting, though he can't refuse a drop of brandy. Then there is Binjimin, "a stunted, pasty-faced, white-headed ginnified boy, that might be any age from eight to eighteen, and as idle and mischievous a brat as it was possible to conceive, sharp as a needle, and quick as lightning" – addicted to marmalade and to overmatching his master. He was not of much help in the field, being "no more use wi' 'ounds than a lady's maid". We meet too Charley Stobbs, Surtees's only decent and likeable young man, who pursued the fox, and Jorrocks' niece Belinda at the same time. She also is the only lovable woman in Surtees's gallery of the gentler sex. She is in marked contrast to the abominable Mrs. Jorrocks (why he ever married her Surtees asks in the *Jaunts and Jollities*). True, she might have resented his kicking her out of bed in the ecstasy of his hunting dreams, but she need not have tried to get him certified insane, or worked so hard to get Belinda married to Doleful. She did not succeed.

As might be guessed from the above, one of Surtees's great claims to popularity is his joyful use of words, for after all it is for their words that we read authors as much as for what they have to tell us. Idiom is the salt which keeps fresh meat which might otherwise lose its savour. Surtees is full of phrases, not necessarily unforgettable, but that we remember with a smile when we meet them again. The vigour, the brio of the tumbling flow of words carries us on, giving vivid life to whatever he is describing, a meet or a meal, a dance or a journey; all the clash and clatter is there. He is careless in his writing, no doubt, repeating phrases such as "third time is killing time"; every comfortable house he describes is "replete" with luxury; the horse "like Gil Blas' mule – all faults", is his veritable King Charles's head. But what does that matter when Scamperdale and Spraggon enlarge the scope of the language in a way that our armies in Flanders would have delighted in; and when Mr. Jorrocks says: "Jest put 'em on to me Charley, whilst I make one o' Mr. Craven Smith's all-round-my 'at casts, for that beggar Binjimin's of no more use with a pack of 'ounds than a hopera box would be to a cow or a frilled shirt to a pig"? And what could be more revealing, if ludicrous, than the Master's concluding a panegyric on himself as a huntsman with a quotation from *Cato*: "It's not for mortals to command success"?

And even if the words do not linger in the "mind's memory" – a Jorrocks phrase again – it is they that give added vividness to the people described. In the general atmosphere of bustle and movement the figures stand out by their words as much as by their appearance; they live in their speech as distinctively as they do in their acts. Yet one would recognize them by their looks alone (for who would fail to greet Sir Harry Scattercash with his strings all flying?) or by their gestures (cannot you hear Mr. Benjamin Buckram letting the coins slide down his pocket, one by one or in an avalanche?); and one would recognize their horses, for who would not be ashamed to see Arterxerxes or Multum-in-Parvo go by without knowing them by name? But in letting the mind wander over the novels it is detached scenes of gestures that we see, phrases that we hear: Mr. Jorrocks dashes his vig and dances with glee about the fox's corpse; or he is floundering through Pinch me near Forest, that "incorrigible mountain", that "unpardonable wilderness"; or drowning in the swimming bath at Ongar Park: Soapey Sponge cannons into Lord Scamperdale, who screams out "Just because I'm a lord and can't swear or use coarse words . . ." before, with Jack Spraggon's help, launching out into one of his most lurid torrents; Facey Romford gets his hounds round him with the help of his pretended sister, the sometime Lucy Glitters; Mr. Jogglebury Crowdey wheezes where the verbs ought to be, and Sir Harry replaces his nouns with a hiccup; that good sportsman Mr. Jovey Jessop gives the office of Jug to his friend Boyston, who is thereby empowered to drink all that his patron cannot hold; Binjimin sticks his fingers into the marmeylad; old Sivin-and-four's-Ilivin, the banker, counts his bills; Gabriel Junks the peacock prophesies the weather; and over all the hunting characters of *Handley Cross* hovers the airy spirit of James Pigg, that racy *lusus naturae*, or loose 'un by nature, invoking Cannynewcassel and his cousin Deavilboger, and keeping the tambourine a-rowling while he offers you a gob of tobacco.

Surtees, one feels it at every point, had more than the mere novelist's eye that suffices the second-rate novelist; he had the knowledge that comes from an active interest in the doings of men. His range, no doubt, was limited; his apprehensions were not profound; he had no peculiar sensibility and was, perhaps, a little too complacent: but the whiff of good strong country air is with him wherever he goes, except naturally, in London. He took a vast delight in life, its ins and outs, its queer characters, its shifts, and changes, its unexpectedness. Thus his contribution to the novel is by no means despicable, since he enables the reader to dwell in a world probably today unfamiliar to him and to understand the people that inhabit it. He makes a contribution to our knowledge of society, or at least of one of the societies that make up a nation, and to some of the problems of the countryside.

NOTE

1 "My Son's Wife", Scribner's Magazine, July 1914. Collected in *A Diversity of Creatures*, Macmillan (London, 1917), p. 333.

New Readings in
Dombey and Son

The new readings to be considered here are all in the fourth
number (January 1847) published on 31 December 1846, consisting of chapters XI-XIII. The opening chapter is "Paul's
Introduction to a new Scene", Doctor Blimber's establishment
at Brighton. Dickens had been writing it probably as recently
as the second week of December, in Paris, where he was staying
after several months at Lausanne; he had begun the novel there
in June, but since September, he had lost the advantage of his
early start, owing to the demands of his Christmas book, *The
Battle of Life*. On Sunday, 6 December, he wrote to Forster that
he had "just begun; five printed pages finished, I should say;
and hope I shall be blessed with a better condition this next
week, or I shall be behindhand". Still, he was keeping his
"spirits up . . . even under Dombey pressure . . . his school
ought to be pretty good, but I haven't been able to dash at it
freely, yet. However, I have avoided unnecessary dialogue so
far, to avoid over-writing".[1] By "over-writing" he meant
exceeding the limit of thirty-two printed pages and consequent
last-minute cutting, which had had to be done with the third
number, by post, and partly delegated to Forster. In spite of his
care, it happened again; but this was not the only casualty that
was to befall the text of the fourth number.

His intention had been "to run over to London as soon as I
have done the number"; on 15 December he was there, and

presumably had his manuscript ready to hand over to the printers. "Phiz" had received his "subjects" in advance, and had his illustrations ready to show Dickens on 19 December. So the proofs should have been ready for him to read before he left again for Paris on 23 December – or if not, they would be given to him to take back with him. (They are not marked "Send", like the proofs for the third number, which were posted.)[2] In neither case can he have had much time for them. If he took them, he would need to post them back from Paris on Christmas Eve; in London, he was beset with other concerns: the *Battle of Life*, published on 19 December, was more urgent than *Dombey and Son*, for he had also to superintend rehearsals of an authorized dramatic version, performed on 21 December; and his brief visit had two other main objects – to settle the form of the Cheap edition of his novels,[3] and the sad necessity of distressing family affairs, his sister Fanny being now "in a consumption". His letters show that he was "bothered to death" over the rehearsals, and had "a dreadful cold"; and boats and tides compelled him to leave a day earlier than he had intended.

At some stage in this "hurry and turmoil", the *Dombey* proofs reached him. They posed a major problem; he had over-written the equivalent of three printed pages,[4] and had to make a number of cuts[5] and some adjustments. Also, the manuscript, even more congested with deletions and interlineations than most parts of this novel, had sometimes puzzled even his skilful and practised printers,[6] and the proofs showed several mis-readings. Dickens caught some of them – "hero" for "Nero", "fanciful" for "principal", and "carcase" for "cavern" – but not all.

One paragraph that he had just written on the day of the letter to Forster from Paris was part of the initial description of Doctor Blimber's, designed to lead up to the Dombey family's arrival on the doorstep and to show the nature of the trap set for the hapless victim:

> The Doctor's was a mighty fine house, fronting the sea. Not a joyful style of house within, but quite the contrary. Sad-coloured curtains, whose proportions were spare and lean, hid themselves despondently behind the windows. The tables and chairs were put away in rows,

like figures in a sum; fires were so rarely lighted in the rooms of
ceremony, that they felt like wells, and a visitor represented the
bucket; the dining-room seemed the last place in the world where
any eating or drinking was likely to occur; there was no sound
through all the house but the ticking of a great clock in the hall,
which made itself audible in the very garrets; and sometimes a dull
cooing of young gentlemen at their lessons, like the murmurings of
an assemblage of melancholy pigeons.

I quote the last two lines as he wrote them; but one crucial
word was misprinted. And for over a century, readers have
been needlessly deprived of the brilliantly chosen word "cooing";
all editions read "crying". Up to a point, this is merely a
typical instance of the needs, and the rewards, of editing
Dickens's text with reference to the manuscript.[7] As often, the
printers misread a word – and "cooing" is in a cramped line
close to the foot of a page, with the two o's meeting the
ascenders of "assemblage" – and also as often, they produced a
reading superficially plausible enough to be accepted. What is
less typical is that the necessary correction *was* made, and the
evidence has been accessible in print ever since February 1847.
For on a further reading of the text of the fourth number,
Dickens did discover this and several other errors; just possibly
in a second proof which was sent to him in Paris[8] and returned
too late for press, or, more probably, when he came to read
through the published number at the beginning of January – as
he would naturally do when he decided to begin the February
number with a final scene at Doctor Blimber's ("Paul grows
more and more old-fashioned, and goes home for the holi-
days").

"Page 101, line 9 from bottom – for 'dull crying', *read* 'dull
cooing' " is the third of eleven errata, on a slip included in that
number, published on 31 January 1847. In three copies that I
have seen of No. V, it is inserted between the "Advertiser" and
the first plate.[9] But unlike some lists of errata, it seems never to
have got any further. I have seen no copy of the first volume
edition that contains the slip or corrects the errors in the text.
Copies of later issues incorporating the corrections may turn
up; but subsequent editions were based on the uncorrected text.
There was no occasion for resetting and revision until the novel

was added to the Cheap edition in 1858, and by then no doubt the whole matter had been forgotten. The two errors in the fourth number that do get corrected later are in a different category.

Though few of the other items in the forgotten errata slip are as interesting as "cooing" for "crying", all are worth re-suscitating as evidence of Dickens's care for his text, belated and in this case ineffective though it was. I shall deal with them briefly, not in order of their occurrence, but grouping them, taking first those in which, as in "crying", a misreading of the manuscript resulted in a reading that is possible but manifestly inferior. To make this clear they must be seen in their contexts.

"Page 105, line 3 from bottom – for 'auspiciously', *read* 'suspiciously' " (chapter XI, paragraph beginning "While they were gone"). Paul is watching Doctor Blimber reading.

> There was something very awful in this manner of reading. It was such a determined, unimpassioned, inflexible, cold-blooded way of going to work. It left the Doctor's countenance exposed to view; and when the Doctor smiled auspiciously at his author, or knit his brows, or shook his head and made wry faces at him, as much as to say, "Don't tell me, Sir. I know better," it was terrific.

There is obviously nothing "auspicious" about the Doctor's manner; challenged to emend, one might have suggested "inauspiciously". The manuscript has "suspiciously", but with a blot partly disguising the initial "s". In proof, Dickens's attention was perhaps distracted by finding an error of order to correct in the previous sentence, and by his decision to substitute "terrific" for "beyond measure alarming".

"Page 117, lines 3 and 4 from top – for 'when you know I want them', *read* 'when you know why I want them' " (chapter XII, in the dialogue between Florence and Susan Nipper about the books). Here the error distorts the sense of the whole passage. Florence has produced a list of the books prescribed for Paul, and says "I want you to buy them for me, Susan, if you will, to-morrow morning". But Susan Nipper objects to books on principle. Florence gently insists:

> "But you can buy me the books, Susan; and you will, when you know

[why] I want them." "Well, Miss, and why do you want 'em?"
[i.e. why *do* you?]

and is told that it is so that Florence can help Paul with his lessons.

The manuscript has "why I want them" with no obscurity; the word was presumably missed by the printer simply because it would have fallen at the beginning of a new line. Dickens missed it in proof, perhaps for the same reason; his attention might also be diverted by finding a passage he could cut, for in the original Florence and Susan each have three further speeches at this point. But he inserted the comma after "will".

"Page 121, line 12 from top – for 'doing', *read* 'being' " (chapter XIII, fourth paragraph).

> Then Perch took the newspaper, and gave it a turn or two in his hands before the fire, and laid it, deferentially, at Mr. Dombey's elbow. And so little objection had Perch to doing deferential in the last degree . . .

"Doing deferential" is not English, though "doing the deferential" might be possible. The manuscript has "being"; Dickens's way of writing an initial "be" is odd, but characteristic, and not at all like "do".

"Page 125, line 23 from top – insert a period after the words 'have reason' " (chapter XIII, in the dialogue between the brothers Carker). The Manager has just broken off with:

> "Is it not enough for you, John Carker, that I am your near relation and can't detach myself from that – "

His brother completes the sentence.

> "Say disgrace, James," interposed the other in a low voice, finding that he stammered for a word. "You mean it, and have reason, say disgrace."

In the manuscript Dickens's intentions are clear: "and have reason" is inserted above the line, with no discernible stop, but "Say" has an obvious capital. Emotional emphasis as well as grammar are improved by the correction.

"Page 126, line 17 from bottom – for 'voice', *read* 'voices' " (chapter XIII, paragraph beginning "Walter passed out").

> Walter . . . hearing the voice of the brothers again . . .

Walter of course hears two voices, not one; in the manuscript "voices" is unmistakable.

"Page 97, line 23 from top – for 'the register', *read* 'that register' " (chapter XI, third paragraph).

> For example, there was an honest grocer and general dealer in the retail line of business, between whom and Mrs. Pipchin there was a small memorandum book, with a greasy red cover, perpetually in question, and concerning which divers secret councils and conferences were continually being held between the parties to the register, on the mat in the passage, and with closed doors in the parlour.

The identity of the register with the small memorandum book is clearer with the correct reading. The manuscript, at this point particularly involved and much interlined, reads "that"; but it would take a very careful reading to discover that "the" was an error.

In the next two cases there had been no misreading of the manuscript; Dickens is having second thoughts, and the fact is important as indicating his responsibility for the corrections.

"Page 100, line 23 from bottom – for 'probably', *read* 'possibly' " (chapter XI, at end of paragraph beginning "Mrs Pipchin's system").

> This would wean him by degrees, Mr. Dombey said: probably with a recollection of his not having been weaned by degrees on a former occasion.

This involves a slight modification of tone; "possibly" makes the observation ironical – the point now being that Mr. Dombey did not consciously recollect the earlier weaning at all, but that Dickens invites the reader to do so, and even to note that Mr Dombey is using a dead metaphor which hints that "Paul's second deprivation" – the dismissal of Polly Toodle, the wet-nurse – is on his conscience.

"Page 120, line 12 from top – for 'Saturday', *read* 'Saturdays' " (chapter XII, last but one paragraph).
He rarely joined them on the Saturday now.

So the manuscript; this is a minute improvement.

This completes the nine corrections that were never incorporated in the text. The remaining two on the errata slip are of a different type; they are mistakes of fact, which Dickens or some advisor better versed in the classics and the scriptures evidently recognized later.

"Page 102, line 20 from top – strike out 'Quintius' before 'Curtius' " (chapter XI, paragraph beginning "As Mr Feeder").
After six months at Doctor Blimber's, any young gentleman at Doctor Blimber's

envied Quintius Curtius that blessed refuge in the earth.

What Dickens wrote was "Quintus Curtius"; he had confused the Curtius who leapt into the chasm with the Roman historian of Alexander, and the printer added his own confusion.

"Page 112, line 6 from bottom – for 'the first epistle', *read* 'the first chapter of the epistle' " (chapter XII, Doctor Blimber's final words to the coughing boy Johnson).

"Johnson will repeat to me to-morrow morning before breakfast, without book, and from the Greek Testament, the first epistle of Saint Paul to the Ephesians."

One's first hope is that the printer had omitted the words "chapter of the" in error; but the mistake was Dickens's, perhaps through inadvertence rather than ignorance. Even Doctor Blimber would hardly exact the learning overnight of over 150 verses in Greek.

These last two, and these alone, were corrected in the Library edition of 1859, and the correct readings appear in subsequent editions. But these are corrections that might be made independently at any stage; they do not invalidate the conclusion that the errata slip as a whole was simply overlooked and forgotten, leaving an inferior and apparently unsuspected reading in six or seven places, and a disregard of Dickens's considered second thoughts in two more.

This misfortune is not shared by the page of errata which appeared in the final double number of April 1848 (with the preliminaries), correcting six errors in earlier numbers, four in No. XIII and two in No. XVI; this page is found in some copies of the first volume edition, and the errors were probably all corrected in later issues,[10] and certainly in subsequent editions. But this was a safer position for a list of errata, and it is a pity that the eleven in No. IV were not repeated there.[11] The later list is duly recorded in Hatton and Cleaver's *Bibliography of the Periodical Writings of Charles Dickens* (1933), p. 250, in its two forms, a two-line and eight-line "Errata", the former being "given preference" as being of an earlier issue.[12] The slip in No. V is not so recorded; and one of the minor morals of the present account is that the descriptions in "Hatton and Cleaver" must not be taken as exhaustive, and the editor of any novel in "monthly numbers" will need to see as many copies as possible of the separate parts. No doubt some Dickens collectors have known of the 12-line errata slip in No. V as a "point" to be looked for in a "perfect set of the parts";[13] but co-ordination between collectors and students of the text has not hitherto been a notable feature of Dickens studies.

Most of the errors I have been considering are of a kind which incidentally exposes the carelessness of modern readers. They are, as I have said, superficially plausible; they had to be that, to satisfy the press-reader, and to escape the author's own first reading. But they should not all have survived an age of textual criticism and "close reading". Even without the evidence of manuscript, proof, and errata slip – and for some Dickens texts or parts of texts, none of these are available – the old readings might have been suspected. The keen eye that Dr. Chapman brought to the text of Jane Austen and Trollope would surely have discerned something wrong at least in "auspiciously", "when you know I want them", "doing deferential", and "dull crying".

NOTES

1 John Forster, *Life of Charles Dickens*, V.7, and VI.2 (the same letter). My other quotations, dates, and facts are mostly from letters to Forster and other letters in the Nonesuch edition (1938), Vol. I, and *Mr. and Mrs. Charles Dickens*, ed. W. Dexter (1935), which has a fuller text for a letter of 19 December. I have had the further advantage of seeing unpublished letters, but these do no more than fill out the picture of Dickens's various other activities in December 1846.

2 The manuscript and proofs are in the Forster collection, Victoria and Albert Museum. Corrections on the single proof of No. IV are almost all in Dickens's hand; the one instance of Forster's hand is a short insertion, clearly authorial in origin, in chapter XIII – perhaps a later afterthought sent in a letter.

3 This began to appear on 27 March 1847; a prospectus is included in No. VI of *Dombey and Son* (March 1847).

4 The number of "slips" or MS pages was 30, and as the "over-written" No. III had had 34, Dickens might well be taken aback. But he was not yet used to calculating the amount on pages written much more closely than for his earlier novels, and more heavily revised. He was writing with equal ease of "invention", but more slowly and with greater pains, as he explained in a letter of 30 August 1846 to Forster, who rightly lays much emphasis on it (Forster, V.5).

5 All were short passages, ranging from two lines to a third of a page, spread through the three chapters; the careful selection of what could be sacrificed must have been his chief preoccupation in reading proof.

6 The haste over setting up is indicated by the names of nine different compositors on the first 19 slips of the MS.

7 Professor E. A. Horsman is preparing an edition of *Dombey and Son* for the Clarendon edition.

8 Bradbury and Evans's accounts (MS Forster collection) show a charge under No. IV of £1.3.6 for "Postages", as against £2.18.4 for No. III. But this is not necessarily evidence for the posting of proofs, as it would include the cost of posting presentation copies of the published number.

9 Two copies in Dickens House, and one in my own possession, given to me by Wyndham Ketton-Cremer of Felbrigg Hall, Norfolk, where it had remained since 1847. This kind gift was the starting-point of my investigation.

10 I have not seen a copy in which all are corrected, but some in which one or more corrections are made.

11 A cursory survey of other novels suggests that a more usual place for a list of errata was at the end of the preliminary "List of plates", where it was almost certain to survive.

12 They also note one misprint in the earlier issue of No. XI and two in No. XIV, not included in the errata.

13 The Accounts (see note 8 above) show that it was inserted in 30,000 copies of No. V, the cost being £5. Letters in the *Dickensian*, XV, 162-3 and 219-20 (1919), from R. T. Jupp and Morris Cock, note the presence of this slip in their copies of No. V; neither shows any interest in the content of the errata, but Jupp wonders "how so many errors were made in this one number".

Addendum

Since this article went to press, I have seen the corrected readings in a single later edition, kindly brought to my attention by Mr. Frank Gibbon of the University of Western Australia, who was independently investigating the errata slip. This edition is part of the so-called "Charles Dickens Library Series", published by the Educational Book Company in 1910, with brief popular introductions by (Sir) John A. Hammerton. As we should expect, neither publisher nor "editor" mentions the source of the text; in the British Museum Catalogue the whole edition is called "a reissue of the Soho edition of 1903, 04", but this is not true of the *Dombey* volume.

Hard Times

and Common Things

[i]

Since the day when Dr. Leavis cheerfully wrote of *Hard Times*
that if there "exists . . . even an acclaiming reference, I have
missed it" (*The Great Tradition*, 1948, p. 227) the novel has
steadily been building up a bibliography of its own. One reason
for this is that it has a certain fascination for the commentator,
in that it can be so precisely documented. Dr. Leavis was no
doubt right that Dickens wrote it "possessed by a comprehensive vision" of Victorian civilization, but it also certainly
includes (as we would expect) frequent references to the
contemporary scene. Many of these have been established.[1] One
which has not, but which has particular relevance to Dickens's
vision of society, is the way in which much that he wrote on
education was linked with his own work with the Victorian
philanthropist, Miss Burdett Coutts. They both exerted themselves, particularly, to encourage better ways of teacher
training and greater common sense in the choice of subjects to
be taught. They were both impelled to do this because they
realized that much that was wrong with the schools was with
what went on in the classroom rather than with their remoter
management; and Dickens, at least, saw that the way in which
the children were taught in school was closely related with the
world outside it. It can be shown that, although the ideas on
education presented in the novel were not new to Dickens, the

183

choice of subject – and in part the way in which it was developed – seem likely to have arisen at least partly from his work and discussion with Miss Coutts.

It happens that to establish the topicality of this one aspect of the novel, in the first place, is largely an exercise in "scholarship". Yet, there is something curiously unsatisfactory as well as fascinating, in studying, teaching, and writing about *Hard Times*. For the study of it tends to show that a story that exalts fancy above fact is hardly a success if it needs to be supported with an elaborate critical apparatus; that in the main (and rather depending on the reader) it *is* what it appears to be; and that we can trust both the teller and the tale.

An instance of how further inquiry sometimes tends to return us to the starting point appears in a recent authoritative and often perceptive essay by John Holloway, for here one finds conclusions drawn from statements about the novel's topicality which are (to say the least) uncertain once one has checked the facts.[2] The author, for example, ascribes two articles by anonymous contributors to *Household Works* to Dickens himself: yet one of them is known to have been by a Mr. J. Capper and the other by a Mr. Dodd.[3] Yet we are assured in the essay, on the strength of quotations from these pieces which were not by Dickens, that the creator of Bounderby must really have admired both the "mighty . . . cotton monarchs" (or factory-owners), at this time, and the "grand-machine" of their factories. The second article, we are told, concludes with a eulogy of Titus Salt (founder of Saltaire) as a "captain of industry", and we are duly reminded that this phrase is Carlyle's, and that the novel is dedicated to Carlyle whom Dickens once assured that "there was nothing in" it "with which he would disagree".[4]

Now, it is true that Dickens probably did admire such men as Salt. Yet it is unlikely that such praise for factory-life and organization can be found in his works at this or any other time. Dickens's speech in praise of the men of Birmingham (6 January 1853) which is also quoted in reference to *Hard Times* can hardly be set against the smoke-serpents and steam-engines of Coketown of the novel; for it was not particularly extraordinary of him to say in his speech that he would rather write for "the great compact phalanx of the people" in Birmingham, than he would for an aristocratic patron. These references, therefore, can scarcely be said to prove that Dickens did not have a "balanced view of the whole situation as between manufacturer, labour, and capital", that he was naïve, or that he shared "the brusque middle-class hostilities and presumptions of those whom he thought he was criticising". They certainly come somewhat unfortunately in a section of an essay which sets out to demonstrate that the fabler who prefers fact to fancy has (unlike the critic) only "an amiable and casual grasp of the realities".[5]

There are other sections in this same essay, which is evidently intended to "trace the *exact contour* of significance which ran for Dickens himself, as he wrote the book, through the material he handled".[6] One of them is on Dickens and the Department of Practical Art, which takes up a question I first raised in an article that set out to show how part of the second chapter of the novel is directly related to the activities of Henry Cole and the Department set up by the British Board of Trade in 1852.[7] The author draws different conclusions from my own, which were then rather tentatively set down, since it seemed the first necessity to make clear exactly what had happened. It is not now the time to take up the question of interpretation as a matter for controversy except to say that perceptive and sensible as Cole and his associates were it does not necessarily follow that Dickens was no more than a "Philistine" because he disagreed with them. Dickens's joke remains that a Government institution for industrial design should have set out to teach that carpets should not have flowers on them, that we are wrong to have chintz-covered furniture, and that representational designs on crockery are in bad taste. If Dickens was a Philistine, he remains in fairly good company. There is no answer to be reached now in a dispute about who was correct. Yet one might well say that, in the world of industrial design immediately following the Great Exhibition, Cole & Co. were in the right, while in the context of the novel it by no means follows that Dickens was wrong.

Again, the same essay takes up a link between the novel and Charles Knight, first set down in an article by J. T. Boulton.[8] This took as its starting point the fact that, in 1854, Knight (who was Secretary of the Society for the Diffusion of Useful Knowledge) evidently sent Dickens a copy of his book *Know-*

ledge is Power, remarking that he was afraid from the tone of *Hard Times* that Dickens would set him down as "a cold-hearted political economist". Dickens thereupon replied denying that there was anything in common between his friend Knight and those who were satirized in the novel "who see figures and averages, and nothing else – the representatives of the wickedest and most enormous vice of this time – . . . Bah! What have you to do with these?"[9] In spite of Dickens's disclaimer (which may be compared with a cheerful admission that he wrote to Cole), some correspondences were drawn between the two books, though they seem to be no more than a comparison of two men writing about the same world at the same time. Yet Dr. Holloway goes even further, by linking the novel with another book by Charles Knight, which we do not know that Dickens read, called *The Store of Knowledge* (1841). He finds in this comprehensive *Store*, one article on the Horse and another on Education. Passing simply from these entries to reference to the novel in general and to Bitzer's "definition of a horse" in particular, we are pushed to the conclusion that "it seems certain that *"The Store of Knowledge"* directly influenced Dickens", and that the educational situation was more complicated than it might seem from the first two chapters of the novel. One is bound to say that no reason is given to show that Dickens might have read the book. The one offered argues that it is almost certain because Bitzer talks about a Horse's teeth when "defining it", and that so does the entry in *The Store of Knowledge*. This overlooks the fact that there are plenty of more direct parallels to be found with genuine school textbooks; for *The Store* was an erudite, if popular, work of the encyclopaedic kind. It is not clear what point it is supposed Dickens had in mind if there is a recognizable relationship with Bitzer's definition. Surely no one can believe that even the under-educated Dickens felt that there were grounds for complaint when an encyclopaedia gave mere facrs?[10] This might not seem to matter very much, except that it is apparently put forward as another "exact" contour-line showing the critical significance of the material Dickens used in his usual "casual" way.

If this essay about the novel is taken as an example, the critical situation is thus rather ludicrous. It is to be hoped that no one would wish to suggest that Dickens is above criticism, or that even his after-dinner speeches were never foolish. Yet it is often implied that Dickens was more remote from his own times than we are. It is sometimes suggested that he did not know as much about the industrial north of England in the eighteen-fifties as we do; or we are assured that he chose to satirize officials without understanding what was involved. His grasp of the issues of his own day has been said to be "partial and even casual"; he was a Philistine who took it upon himself to write about education; and it is implied that when he dramatized in a simplified way what he thought the issues were, he only showed that he could not appreciate their complexity. From time to time such implications are made as part of a critical seesaw, which first puts forward an elevated impression of what Dickens's pretensions were, and then tips them up to show that he failed to carry them out. Yet many of the questions he actually raised are far from being so easily decided. It is no less arguable that Dickens was a thoughtful if not an intellectual man, with the widest experience of the issues he raises in his books. Education was only one of these issues; the movement to improve teaching in schools was only part of his interest in education. But if we aim at drawing exact contour lines before dismissing him as superficial, it does happen to be possible to trace what his experience and opinions probably were on this single matter about the period when he was writing *Hard Times*.

[ii]

In 1849, Dickens's friend Miss Burdett Coutts had started a Church school in Westminster, which probably led to the interest she took in methods of education and training suitable teachers, which further resulted in her association with an important new educational movement which started towards the end of 1853.

This was a time when the sectarian controversy was at its height, and no one could agree who was to control the schools. The Education question was as topical as the Strike problem: the newspapers were full of letters, speeches, and resolutions. As a *Times* leader (28 January 1854) said:

Perhaps no subject so trite and familiar as that of education excites an equal amount of interest in the present day. We can scarcely take up a newspaper without finding remarks upon it, pamphlets are rapidly issued in the press, and public educational meetings are held in all parts of the country.

Yet only the slightest public interest was taken at this time in what should be taught and what methods of teaching should be used. The sudden appearance, therefore, of a completely new demand for better ways of teaching and a more useful selection of subjects cut right across the disputes of educational power politics, and drew the attention of a widespread public. It was to this that the *Times* leader referred, on the publication of a pamphlet on the *Ashburton Prizes for the Teaching of "Common Things". An Account of the Proceedings at a Meeting Between Lord Ashburton and the Elementary Schoolmasters Assembled at Winchester. On Friday, December 16, 1853.* This was the movement which Miss Burdett Coutts joined. And, although it has not been recognized before, it is clear that Dickens was also actively involved and strongly in agreement with most of its principles. It is not suggested that Dickens simply took ideas from this movement; for, in fact, most of the documented references we have come after the novel was finished. It is suggested that it is likely that he and Miss Coutts influenced each other, and that from the part we know they played together it is reasonable to infer that they had discussed such matters rather earlier, before the novel was begun.

The movement was led by Lord Ashburton[11] with the support of the Rev. W. H. Brookfield – now remembered for his friendship with Tennyson, Thackeray, and Carlyle, but then one of Her Majesty's most energetic Inspectors. Its intentions were first explained at the meeting at Winchester, where Lord Ashburton emphasized that it was more important that a master should be able to teach well than that he should be particularly learned.

He began by insisting that the usual way of making a child learn lists of names "which convey no ideas, present no images", was totally wrong: "You just load his memory to no purpose with unconnected and therefore barren facts". He went on to say that it was no excuse that "in teaching this multitude of facts we only scatter seeds over the boy's mind", for such a way of instructing probably resulted in permanent injury:

We do more, we force our facts upon the child's memory; we do that which the poulterer does to the fowls he fattens, he takes them and crams them with the food he has prepared himself.[12] So these poor children are crammed with nauseating facts, to the extinction of their natural appetite for knowledge. . . . Not only is their mind weakened by this process, but I doubt if it be not also to some extent demoralised; for this, like every other kind of what is called smattering, has a tendency to inflate the mind with false notions of superiority, without imparting at the same time the cultivating influences and characteristic diffidence of real knowledge.

Children, he held, should be encouraged to think for themselves, and in order to do this their lessons should be about "common things" they were familiar with. They could, for example, be taught the elementary principles of science from objects of everyday use, from gardening, domestic science, and through simple rules of health, not just because such things would be more use to them than learning long lists of places, dates, or persons, but because they could understand them for themselves and use their own powers of reasoning and observation.

So far, we might well be reminded of Mr. Gradgrind and his "facts", Bitzer and his demoralization, and Mr. M'Choakumchild and his "watersheds of all the world . . . and all the names of all the rivers and mountains", all according to his college training: "If he had only learnt a little less, how infinitely better he might have taught much more!"

As Lord Ashburton explained, the movement had been tried out for several years in the village of King's Somborne near Winchester. He disclaimed "all pretensions to novelty or originality"; the credit was the local vicar's, the Rev. Richard Dawes. Dawes had already published a number of pamphlets about the methods he had adopted, and his remarkable success had been noticed by visiting Inspectors.[13]

Since the scheme was in essence a practical one, immediate steps had been taken to put it into effect. Yet it had received only the passive encouragement of the Committee of Council on Education, and it was left to private benefactors to push the ideas of the new movement unaided. Lord Ashburton had tried to promote them by giving prizes for teachers and pupil teachers for essays on "The Knowledge of 'Common Things' "; and, at the original meeting at Winchester, it was announced that other well-known educators and philanthropists had undertaken to give similar prizes in their own districts. Among the names given were those of Lord Lansdowne, Lord Granville, Kay Shuttleworth, and Miss Burdett Coutts.

Miss Coutts must have discussed the new movement with Lord Ashburton and probably with Kay Shuttleworth (an old acquaintance); and, early in 1854, she began to organize her own contribution to it. Her work was carried out through the women's training college of Whitelands, and throughout 1854-7 and probably in later years, she worked to promote the scheme. It went so well that it was suggested that she should publish a short account of what she had done, and she did this in *A Summary Account of Prizes for Common Things Offered and Awarded by Miss Burdett Coutts at the Whitelands Training Institution.*[14]

Even without reference to Dickens's letters to Miss Coutts it is clear that he was interested in the new movement and well informed about it from the first. It was noticed almost immediately in *Household Words* (21 January 1854) in an article on "School-Keeping" by Henry Morley. Morley was himself an ex-schoolmaster, and explained:

> Prizes are now being offered to the pupils in training schools in several English counties for the purpose of promoting a knowledge of the art of conveying sound instruction in common things to the children of the working classes. In the movement that has thus been set on foot by Lord Ashburton, the whole English public claims to participate; . . . Lord Ashburton's suggestion has gone off like a gun in a rookery and has set every quill flying.

In the summer of 1854 Dickens was busy writing *Hard Times* in Boulogne; and, although he no doubt remained informed of what Miss Burdett Coutts was doing, there are no direct references to her work in his letters. We know only that her interest in the scheme must have come partly from him, and then when the novel was finished he was ready to take an active part in helping her himself. In 1855 he told her that in writing to Harriet Martineau he had mentioned "the pains you had taken at Whitelands".[15] He had also looked over some of her "Examination notes", and sent "little suggestions" for making them plainer and "not proclaiming them quite so stiffly" (12 April 1855). The examinations were set only after Dickens had checked the proofs of the papers – there were to be "no volumes of head-breaking questions", for the Whitelands students as for M'Choakumchild.

When she prepared the first edition of her *Summary Account*, in 1856, she turned to Dickens for help in writing the introduction. He replied from Paris, on 30 March, and not only do his letters show that he went over it, as he said, "very carefully", but that he entirely rewrote the introduction presumably from Miss Coutts's first draft or notes. It was chiefly a straightforward report on the examination results and what she had noticed of the manner in which lessons were given. It follows orthodox Ashburton doctrine, particularly objecting to the way in which student teachers unnecessarily used difficult words:

> The absurd result, is, that valuable time is lost in explaining the meaning or derivation of some word thus used, instead of impressing upon the children the use and history of the thing.

A prize-giving was held on 23 June when Miss Coutts gave a short address.[16] Early next month the first edition of *A Summary Account* was published, and Dickens deputed Henry Morley and W. H. Wills to notice it in *Household Words* (26 July 1856). Under the title of "Not Very Common Things" they began:

> Lord Ashburton gave to the chief rarities of his country the name of Common Things, and Miss Burdett Coutts offers prizes for a right knowledge of good housekeeping among the poor, under the names of Prizes for Common Things.

It bears the stamp of being mainly by Henry Morley, who had carefully considered opinions of his own about teaching. Whereas Dickens in his letters characteristically stressed the need for more imagination and Miss Coutts for practical utility, Morley was disconcerted to find how little evidence the published answers showed of independent thinking on the part of the schoolmistresses themselves. "Miss Coutts", the article concludes, "renews her offer, and intends apparently, to work on without flagging".

Almost at once she began to prepare the enlarged edition of her booklet, with a new introduction.

It has been possible to show elsewhere how this new introduction by Miss Coutts was also entirely rewritten by Dickens.[17] Parts of her manuscript that he heavily corrected have been found, and a section as it was first written by Miss Coutts, which can be compared with the text as Dickens rewrote it. The manuscript of the latter (a fragment of about six hundred words) had for a long time been thought to be part of an unidentified article by Dickens himself, possibly even one that he was asked to write for the *Edinburgh Review*.[18] But merely from the text it was clear that the assumption was false; and it was not difficult to show that it referred to the Ashburton movement and was part of the preface to the second edition of the *Summary Account*.

These inferences have now also been confirmed by the Dickens–Burdett Coutts correspondence, then mostly unpublished and inaccessible. It is unnecessary to quote from the letters at length; they leave no doubt that he took the greatest care in revising her manuscript – rephrasing what she had written, copying parts out afresh and then going over the proofs with his usual precision.[19] As he said, himself, when he went over the first edition, his principal object was to express everything in a clear straightforward manner "not often changing" her "words", and "never changing" her "ideas" (30 March 1856).

Although Miss Burdett Coutts was entirely responsible for everything she included, and nothing original was added by Dickens, it is probable that she actually introduced one of Dickens's letters into the preface:

The following quotation, taken from the letter of a much valued friend, whose sympathy for the working classes is very sincere, appears so apposite, expresses so clearly and forcibly the results that would attend the exercise of early prudence in life, that it is given in lieu of a feebler expression of the same sentiments: "Not only a man's own happiness, but the happiness of many others, would be much advanced by his reflecting, while yet young, that an income which is quite sufficient, or something more than sufficient for the expenses of one person, can be with difficulty eked out to cover the expenses of a large family; and by his considering that a few years of saving and forethought at that period of his life would lay the foundations of a comfortable home".[20]

The passage is given at greater length, but goes on in much the same manner: and, in spite of its Smilesian and unMicawberish sentiments (though not by any means uncharacteristic of Dickens in certain moods), it is very likely that he was her unnamed correspondent. Stylistic evidence alone is never satisfactory and always largely a matter of opinion; but there are also the circumstances of Dickens's special friendship with Miss Burdett Coutts, and the impossibility of suggesting any other such friend who could express himself so "clearly and forcibly".[21]

In general, they were in close agreement, although Miss Coutts was capable of maintaining an independent opinion. They were especially strongly united in opposition to the official desire to impart "education" to children in as concentrated a form as possible whenever they could be got into school. Miss Coutts wanted both girls' and boys' schooling to be practical rather than academic. On this, and other points, they were opposed to Kay Shuttleworth as ex-Secretary of the Committee of Council on Education, although he was also nominally one of the supporters of the Ashburton scheme. On publication of the first edition Dickens wrote to her (11 July 1856):

> I thoroughly agree with you in that interesting part of your note which refers to the immense uses, direct and indirect, of needlework. Also to the great difficulty of getting many men to understand them. And I think Shuttleworth and the like would have gone on to the crack of doom, melting down all the thimbles in Great Britain and Ireland, and making medals of them to be given for a knowledge of Watersheds and Pre Adamite vegetation (both immensely comfortable to a laboring man with a large family and small income), if it hadn't been for you.[22]

And, as they were preparing the second edition (9 December 1856) he also said:

> I send you the last addition enclosed. I omitted to say the other day that I thoroughly agree with you on that point of sending girls to school. There is a vast deal of Kayshuttleworthian nonsense written, sung, and said, on that subject; and I turn into a Man-Trap on it very often, and seize unsuspicious holders-forth by the leg, when they suppose themselves to be promenading among flower beds.

> Beauty and the Beast are therefore united, amidst the cheers of
> thousands, as they were in the story.

It is difficult to be sure exactly what this meant, which was the
"last addition", and where it was inserted; but there are reasons
for thinking it may have been a part Miss Coutts wrote which
argued that even when older girls had to stay at home (like
Lizzie Hexam in *Our Mutual Friend*) to look after the younger
children, it could not "be said . . . that they were wholly un-
educated".

[iii]

It is even more difficult to be positive whether Dickens's earliest
interest in the Ashburton movement was directly related to his
treatment of the Education theme in *Hard Times*. Yet it is
likely that it had some effect on the earlier chapters (combined
with much else) and even that without it they might have taken
a different form.

Of course, Dickens's ideas about teaching were not directly
derived from Lord Ashburton. He had always held strong
opinions about education which developed rather than altered,
and they are obvious in *David Copperfield* and the Blimber scenes
in *Dombey and Son* long before the Ashburton scheme was
started. At the same time, Dickens's own chief interests were
not always those he chose to write about first. Always seeking
for a particularly close relationship with his public, he found
his chance in movements for reform. Yet, particularly when he
published serially, he had to catch an audience ready-made and
could not afford to wait and gather one around him: in a single
number he had no time to develop entirely fresh ideas. It was
not that he was ever insincere, but that his method of publication
forced him to be an opportunist: as public opinion began to
form on anything, he would seize his chance, attract its attention, and then begin to develop the subject in his own way.
Necessarily such a practice was bound to affect his choice of
subject as well as his manner of expression: and, for a time his
style tended to become increasingly pointed, and his ideas more
and more "critical" rather than "constructive".

He and Miss Coutts had already discussed the importance of

giving children imaginative books to read, as early as 1850, when he had sent her the names of some publishers and said: "It would be a great thing for all of us, if more who were powerfully concerned with Education, thought as you do, of the imaginative faculty" (6 September 1850). It was, of course, a strong feature of the Gradgrindian system that fairy tales were strictly forbidden. Lord Ashburton's speech at Winchester was given on 16 December 1853, when Miss Burdett Coutt's name was given as one of his supporters, and there can be no reasonable doubt (although it is not directly mentioned in any of their letters) that she must have already discussed such an important new project with Dickens. The revised text of Ashburton's speech was again published, in a separate form, at the end of January, and it was just at this time that Dickens began writing *Hard Times*. According to his own account he had been considering the twin subjects of Education and Industrial Relations, off and on, throughout the whole of 1853; he decided to write the new novel early in the new year; and at once set about formulating his impressions more clearly. He then announced his latest intentions to Miss Coutts on 23 January:

I have fallen to work again. My purpose is among the mighty secrets of the world at present: but there is such a fixed idea on the part of my printers and copartners in Household Words, that a story by me, continued from week to week, would make some unheard of effect with it, that I am going to write one. It will be as long as five Nos. of Bleak House, and will be five months in progress. The first written page now stares at me from under this sheet of notepaper. The main idea of it, is one of which you and I and Mrs. Brown have often spoken; and I know it will interest you as a purpose.

Exactly what the "main idea" of the novel is, is a matter for discussion. But the first few chapters of the novel are entirely concerned with Education; and it was not until after he had visited Preston, a week later, that Dickens had even clearly considered how he should develop his story of the threatening contest between "Masters and Men". He was probably thinking of the "main idea" of the first four weekly instalments, therefore, and how he was to show the consequences of a system of education, which sacrificed Fancy to Fact, on a group of children as they grew up.

195

Another reason for thinking that the ideas in the earlier chapters may have owed something to the Ashburton scheme is that it was one of the few movements to concern itself, in any way, with methods of education. Further similarities between them are only suggestive rather than conclusive. At the same time Dickens may well have been impressed by the most prominent feature in Ashburton's attack on the usual teaching given in schools, that it forced "facts" upon the child, loaded his memory "with unconnected and . . . barren facts", and "crammed" children with "nauseating facts" to such a degree that they were "to some extent demoralised". That attack on Facts was repeated even more eloquently in the novel, and the idea that such a system of education might morally warp a child's nature is much the same as Dickens's. Although, therefore, this was not a new principle of his, he may have recognized that now it was a topic of public interest the time had come when it would make a suitable theme for a novel.

It is by no means a coincidence that Dickens should have taken to writing about Education and Industrial Relations in fiction just when they were being so widely discussed. Certainly his readers took up *Hard Times, For These Times* expecting it to refer to current affairs. The contemporary reviewers were even surprised that it was not more directly concerned with them. The *Westminster Review* said:

> When it was announced, amid the strikes and consequent derangements of commerce, that Mr. Dickens was about to write a tale in "Household Words" called "Hard Times", the general attention was instantly arrested. It was imagined that the main topic of the story would be drawn from the fearful struggle then being enacted in the north.[23]

Blackwood's reviewer wrote in the same way:

> The name of the book and the period of its publication alike deluded the public. We anticipated a story, certainly sad – perhaps tragical – but true, of the unfortunate relationship between masters and men which produced the strike at Preston.[24]

Disappointed by the absence of any adequate treatment of the disputes between labour and capital, the reviewer went on to complain that in its place Dickens had provided no more than the "petulant theory of a man in a world of his own making, where he has no fear of being contradicted, and is absolutely certain of having his own way". The *Westminster* likewise held that, in spite of the author's obvious intention, the book had no true relation to reality:

> We suppose it is in anticipation of some change in the present educational system for one that shall attempt to kill "outright the robber Fancy", that Mr. Dickens launches forth his protest, for we are not aware of such a system being in operation anywhere in England.[25]

Blackwood's even condemned the whole argument of the educational part of the story:

> The real object of the book is, to prove that the teaching of universal knowledge . . . the education which arbitrarily imposes fact and puts down fancy, is a system which makes very poor villains of our sons, and very wretched wives of our daughters, and that the perfectly opposite system of no education at all . . . produces angels, not only of goodness, but of wisdom and judicious courage almost unparalleled.

The two reviews were designedly unfair. *Blackwood's* was noted for its unbending Toryism and the *Westminster Review* for the uncompromising advocacy of the sternest principles of political economy; and after 1850 Dickens had begun to come under an increasingly heavy fire from both. Nevertheless, both reviewers also show that Dickens's general purpose of directly commenting on the contemporary scene was fully appreciated.

They were completely unjustified, however, in stating that Dickens's sketch of the methods of teaching in Mr. Gradgrind's school was exaggerated. It would be possible to substantiate almost every line of the first two chapters with the complaints of Inspectors, and other writers, who were well aware how badly the children were taught. After all, almost the only incident in the schoolroom chapters is the difficulty Mr. Gradgrind finds in getting a "definition of a horse" from Sissy Jupe, who belongs to a circus, which is relieved by the copybook answer from Bitzer:

"Bitzer", said Thomas Gradgrind. "Your definition of a horse."

"Quadruped. Graminivorous. Forty teeth, namely twenty-four grinders, four eye-teeth, and twelve incisive. Sheds coat in the spring; in marshy countries sheds hoofs, too. Hoofs hard, but requiring to be shod with iron. Age known by marks in mouth." Thus (and much more) Bitzer.

"Now girl number twenty", said Mr. Gradgrind. "You know what a horse is."

There is not the least exaggeration in this. Lessons were given to be learnt by heart; and Natural History as taught according to the *Manual* of the British and Foreign School Society, was even rather worse:

Ruminating animals. Cud-chewing or ruminating animals form the *eighth* order. These, with the exception of the camel, have no cutting teeth in the upper jaw, but their place is supplied with a hard pad. In the lower jaw there are eight cutters; the tearers, in general, are absent, so that there is a vacant space between the cutters and grinders. The latter are very broad, and are kept rough and fit for grinding the vegetable food on which these animals live, by the enamel being disposed in crescent-shaped ridges.[26]

The "cow" or "horse" example was a common one in the Ashburton movement. The original exponent of its principles, the Rev. Richard Dawes, had shown how such a subject might be introduced to the class: the teacher should first interest the children and then elicit a definition from them by inquiry:

Again, if a cow or a horse is mentioned – drawing them into a description of it – a child will perhaps say, a cow is a four-footed animal. Teacher: yes, but so is a horse; and he will point out something in which they differ. The child will try again – a cow has got horns, but a horse has not: then the teacher will point out that some cows have no horns, and will lead them on to things in which the cow and horse really do differ – such as the hoof etc.[27]

It may be a coincidence that Dickens should have chosen as an example of this kind one which is also to be found in the National School *Manuals*, and in Dawes's pamphlet, but he was certainly not exaggerating. In countless schools throughout the country – like "the little Gradgrind" – the pupil had never:

associated a cow in a field with that famous cow with the crumpled horn who tossed the dog who worried the cat who killed the rat who ate the malt, or with that yet more famous cow who swallowed Tom Thumb: it had never heard of those celebrities, and had only been introduced to a cow as a graminivorous ruminating quadruped with several stomachs.

Without attempting to do more than suggest what may have been an important influence on the novel, we may be morally certain that Dickens's choice of theme was partly dictated by widespread public interest in Education at the time, and it may well have been particularly affected by the even more up-to-date Ashburton movement. It may even follow that this ought to suggest that we should see Dickens as so concerned with issues of contemporary significance that he was far from being simply topical. For, although the first few chapters of the novel evidently include a variety of references that were of contemporary significance to Dickens, it is only recently that this has been recognized, and it is almost certain that his first readers did not, generally speaking, perceive their direct topicality in his own day. That is to say, then, that Sissy Jupe was as intimately connected with Miss Coutts and the Whitelands Training Institution as Stephen Blackpool with the Preston Strike, or the "third gentlemen" of the second chapter with Henry Cole of the Department of Practical Art.

Yet even here the relationships are ambiguous for even when the references are most certain they are completely involved in the context of the novel. The power of *Hard Times* still lies in its serious and comprehensive vision of "certain key characteristics of Victorian civilization",[28] and the most definite allusions to be detected tend to bring us back to much larger general questions, rather than settle anything.

It is impossible to leave the subjects of Dickens's apparent topicality or exaggeration without reference to his style, since this is largely responsible for the divisions of opinion about the novel. For unless it is accepted as written in the vein of dramatic comedy, it is often bound to appear over-simplified and over-drawn. Yet even Ruskin, who wished that Dickens would use a "severer and more accurate analysis", recognized in writing about *Hard Times* that "allowing for his manner of telling them, the things he tells us are always true".

Like *Bleak House* immediately before it, and *Little Dorrit* directly after it, the novel can be seen in the context of its times; and it may be thought that *Hard Times*, like *Bleak House*, "began as a tract for the times, and the more fully this is recognized, the more fully we shall appreciate the 'esemplastic power' which imposed upon a mass of seemingly heterogeneous material a significant and acceptable form".[29]

NOTES

1   See especially, Geoffrey Carnall, "Dickens, Mrs. Gaskell and the Preston Strike", *Victorian Studies*, VIII (1964), 31ff.

2   John Holloway, *"Hard Times*: A History and Criticism", in *Dickens and The Twentieth Century*, ed. J. Gross and G. Pearson (London, 1962).

3   The *Household Words* Contributors' Book is now in the Princeton University Library, but copies at the Dickens House, Doughty Street, and elsewhere were used long ago to settle the canon of this part of Dickens's work and to decide the authorship of other contributions. To anticipate a reply (although this is another matter), no doubt it is often said that as editor Dickens held himself responsible for all the views expressed in his journal: at the same time, it would not be difficult to show that he disagreed with a good deal that slipped by.

4   J. Holloway, pp. 166-7, where the assurance is set down as from a letter from Dickens to Carlyle of 29 March 1870. This is evidently an oversight for 13 July 1854; but it could be misleading to an unwary reader who supposed that Dickens could still be assuring Carlyle as late as 1870 that they were in entire agreement. Even for 1854 the remark was hardly decisive about the extent of their agreement.

5   J. Holloway, pp. 165-6.

6   *Ibid.*, p. 159; my italics.

7   "Charles Dickens and the Department of Practical Art", *MLR*, XLVIII (1953), 270-7. It is only rarely that one can establish a contemporary reference so definitely or exactly, but odd words

in the manuscript plan of the novel, the MS itself, direct parallels between the text and in publications by the Department, and a letter to Cole for once put the matter beyond doubt. An extraordinary feature is not that this had gone unrecognized for so long, but that possibly only Dickens, Cole, and a few of their associates could get the references at the time.

8 *Dickensian*, L (1954), 57ff.

9 Charles Knight, *Passages of a Working Life*, 1873, III.187-8.

10 *The Store* devotes over 400 pages of double column to only eighteen articles, on such subjects as Parliament by Erskine May, Asia by the eminent geographer Karl Ritter, and The Horse by an extremely well-known veterinary surgeon. It is true that the idea of "knowledge" as something to be "stored" is strongly associated with Gradgrind, as with Headstone the schoolmaster of *Our Mutual Friend*; but actual schoolbooks that demanded rote-learning of definitions were common: see p. 198 below, and also (for example) comments throughout Matthew Arnold's *Reports on Elementary Schools* (1852-1882), 1889, among which his instance, from a school book "lately" (1863) "much in vogue", of "the crocodile is vivaparous", is really rather like Bitzer's "graminivorous" horse.

11 William Bingham Baring (1799-1864), 2d Baron Ashburton.

12 A copy of the pamphlet in the Bodleian Library has the marginal note at this point: "This is done by the Govt. Inspectors". It is one which had been annotated by a Mr. Thomas Vaughan, a local educationist, then living somewhere near Oxford.

13 Rev. Richard Dawes, A.M., *Suggestive Hints for Secular Instruction. Making it Bear Upon Common Life* (3d ed., London, 1849); *An Account of King's Somborne School, Extracted from the Minutes of the Committee of Council on Education, 1847-8,* [1849?].

14 1856, first edition, 89 pp. There were two further editions: 1857, 213 pp., and a "new edition", 1860.

15 Letters from Dickens to Miss Coutts are from MS in the Pierpont Morgan Library, by kind permission. Some of them are given in Edgar Johnson's selection, *Letters from Charles Dickens to Angela Burdett-Coutts*, 1953. I have chiefly used those not published before, but make no distinction. Hereafter, reference by date only.

16 *Times*, 24 June 1856.

17 K. J. Fielding, "Women in the Home: An Article Which Dickens Did Not Write", *Dickensian*, XLVIII (1951), 140-2.

18 Forster's *Life of Charles Dickens*, ed. J. W. T. Ley (London, 1928), p. 301, note 259.

19 See Dickens to Miss Burdett Coutts, 3 December 1856; also the 6th, 9th, and 13th; also 24 February 1857, when the revised edition was still not quite ready for the press. It was probably published some time in the summer.

20 *A Summary Account* (B), pp. vii-viii; also quoted in "Women in The Home: An Article Which Dickens Did Not Write", *op. cit.*

21 A further reason for thinking that this passage was by Dickens is that a copy of it (in a slightly altered form) exists in his autograph. This was also once hopefully printed as a "ghost" article, by Cumberland Clark, *Dickens and Democracy and Other Studies* (London, 1930), pp. 40-2, under the title of "Charles Dickens on 'The Condition of the Working Classes': Original Autograph Manuscript". It can now only be said that the MS could either be part of a letter, a draft by Dickens, or a fair copy; but it is not what Clark said. It is likely enough that Miss Coutts had drafted what she wanted to say, that Dickens rewrote it, and that for publication she altered this once again.

22 On 5 September 1857 he also warned her, "So much Boredom, and Red Tape, and what I may call Kayshuttleworry, are associated with the word 'Education', that I fear it may repel readers". M'Choakumchild, himself, had been particularly well qualified on "all the Water Sheds of all the world (whatever they are)".

23 *Westminster Review*, VI new series (1854), 604-8.

24 *Blackwood's Edinburgh Magazine*, LXXVII (1855), pp. 451-66.

25 *Op. cit.* There is a point at which documentation begins to be nearly as involved as composition, but it is remarkable how many contemporary references there are in the first two or three short chapters – to the aesthetic teaching of Henry Cole and his colleagues, to the Ashburton scheme, and even to other educational movements. For Mr. Robin Gilmour has recently written on "The Gradgrind School: Political Economy in the Classroom", for *Victorian Studies*, refuting the *Westminster Review* and showing that men did give lessons on political economy precisely in M'Choakumchild's manner. Exactness in identification is again possible, because Dickens's references drew a public reply, and both he and the friend (Dr. William Ballantyne Hodgson),

whose doctrines he had in mind, recognized the intention to bring them within Dickens's "comprehensive vision" of the times. W. B. Hodgson (1815-80) had been secretary of the Mechanics' Institute, Liverpool, 1839; lectured in political economics at the Royal Institution, London, 1854; and was the first Professor of Political and Commercial Economy at the University of Edinburgh, 1871. Mr. Gilmour's article speaks for itself, but it can be said that it shows how little Dickens simply "exaggerated" and how much his satire was deserved. Of course, the educationalists had a case, even an innocently good one, in intention; but once again, it does not follow that because Dickens sharpened his satire of the spirit of the times with a degree of unfairness, he had only a superficial understanding.

26   British and Foreign School Society *Manual* (London, 1843 ed.), as quoted by J. L. and Barbara Hammond, *The Age of The Chartists* (1930), p. 175.

27   Rev. Richard Dawes, *Suggestive Hints for Secular Instruction Making it Bear Upon Common Life* (3d ed., London, 1849).

28   F. R. Leavis, *The Great Tradition* (London, 1948), p. 20.

29   John Butt, " 'Bleak House' in the Context of 1851", *NCF* (1955), 21.

George Eliot's Klesmer

The formidable musician Julius Klesmer stands out in the reader's memory among the two or three finest creations in *Daniel Deronda*. Though only a secondary character, he performs several important functions in the novel. Like Daniel he acts as mentor to both Gwendolen and Mirah, his opinions of their singing placing them in a strong contrast maintained throughout the story. His brutal dismissal of Gwendolen's dream of earning her living as a singer or actress marks the beginning of her painful effort to face reality, and provides an eloquent statement of the artist's proper place in society. Finally, in Klesmer's marriage love and mutual interests overcome the same obstacle that confronted Gwendolen in hers – disparity of wealth and social position – a happy note too often forgotten by the critics who insist on seeing *Daniel Deronda* as a melancholy book.

On his first appearance Klesmer is introduced as "a felicitous combination of the German, the Sclave, and the Semite". David Kaufmann sees "a fine touch of humour" in his name. "He is unmistakably a Jew, but he never betrays himself, although the unfortunate name Julius Klesmer is enough for the initiated." The Teutonic element shows itself in his matter-of-fact reply to Gwendolen's remark that he cannot like to hear poor amateur singing: "No, truly; but that makes nothing". When he is brought to the archery meeting by the Arrowpoints (though "so far out of our own set"), his foreign look makes him conspicuous among the well-bred, well-tailored Englishmen.

> His mane of hair floating backward in massive inconsistency with the chimney-pot hat, which had the look of having been put on for a joke above his pronounced but well-modelled features and powerful clean-shaven mouth and chin; his tall, thin figure clad in a way which, not being strictly English, was all the worse for its apparent emphasis of intention. Draped in a loose garment with a Florentine *berretta* on his head, he would have been fit to stand by the side of Leonardo da Vinci; but how when he presented himself in trousers which were not what English feeling demanded about the knees? – and when the fire that showed itself in his glances and the movements of his head as he looked round him with curiosity was turned into comedy by a hat which ruled that mankind should have well-cropped hair and a staid demeanour, such, for example, as Mr Arrowpoint's, whose nullity of face and perfect tailoring might pass everywhere without ridicule? One sees why it is often better for greatness to be dead, and to have got rid of the outward man (chapter 10).

Klesmer looks plainly like "one of your damned musicians", a "comic fellow", and most people at the gathering would agree with the fashionable son of the Archdeacon, young Clintock, who says "What extreme guys these artistic fellows usually are!"

Physically, however, Klesmer is quite impressive. He towers high over Mrs. Arrowpoint, even when bowing to her. He has a "massive face", "grand features", a "splendid profile", brown hair "floating in artistic fashion", "wide-glancing" brown eyes that look out through intimidating gold spectacles. Seated at the piano he would toss back the mane of hair while his hands hovered over the keys, fingers pointed down. In London drawing-rooms many knew him or knew about him, though he had not yet attained "that supreme, world-wide celebrity which makes an artist great to the most ordinary people by their knowledge of his great expensiveness". On the Continent, however, he was known everywhere from Paris to St. Petersburg, both as a pianist and a composer.

Klesmer's playing is described several times in *Daniel Deronda*: He is first heard with Catherine Arrowpoint in "a four-handed piece on two pianos, which convinced the company in general that it was too long". Next, after Gwendolen had sung, he

> played a composition of his own, a fantasia called *Freudvoll, Leidvoll, Gedankenvoll* – an extensive commentary on some melodic ideas not too grossly evident; and he certainly fetched as much variety and depth of passion out of the piano as that moderately responsive instrument lends itself to, having an imperious magic in his fingers that seemed to send a nerve-thrill through ivory key and wooden hammer and compel the strings to make a quivering lingering speech for him (chapter 5).

In spite of her wounded egotism Gwendolen is moved by the music. The common impression, however, is probably closer to that of young Clintock, who confesses to her: "I never can make anything of this tip-top playing. It is like a jar of leeches, where you can never tell either beginnings or endings. I could listen to your singing all day." The third time, when Klesmer plays at Lady Mallinger's party in Park Lane, "the torrent-like con-fluences of bass and treble seemed, like a convulsion of nature, to cast the conduct of petty mortals into insignificance" (chapter 45). There is no comment on this performance beyond the out-burst of talk that had been interrupted by it.

Polite indifference to music constitutes part of the criticism of English philistinism for which *Daniel Deronda* is notable. Popular taste favoured the simple melodies of Rossini and Meyerbeer or the aria of Bellini's that Gwendolen sang with gratifying success. But when she had finished, Klesmer told her frankly that such music "is beneath you. It is a form of melody which expresses a puerile state of culture – a dandling, canting, see-saw kind of stuff – the passion and thought of people without any breadth of horizon. There is a sort of self-satisfied folly about every phrase of such melody: no cries of deep, mysterious passion – no conflict – no sense of the universal. It makes men small as they listen to it." Henry James in reviewing Book I praised Klesmer's speech:

> There could not be a better phrase than this latter one to express the secret of that deep interest with which the reader settles down to George Eliot's widening narrative. The "sense of the universal" is constant, omnipresent. It strikes us sometimes perhaps as rather

conscious and over-cultivated; but it gives us the feeling that the threads of the narrative, as we gather them into our hands, are not of the usual commercial measurement, but long electric wires capable of transmitting messages from mysterious regions (*Nation*, 24 February 1876, p. 131).

These regions were to include not only the aesthetic, but the more sensitive fields of politics, morals, social rank, and racial prejudice.

Some of them are explored in the great scene in chapter 22 between Klesmer and "the expectant peer, Mr Bult", a man whom the world considered a suitable match for the heiress Catherine Arrowpoint. Bult, who was not only insensible to counterpoint, but could not even regard a musician "in the light of a serious human being who ought to have a vote", was amazed to hear Klesmer's vehement after-dinner outburst on the lack of idealism in English politics, "which left all mutuality between distant races to be determined simply by the need of a market . . . 'Buy cheap, sell dear' ".

Mr Bult was not surprised that Klesmer's opinions should be flighty, but was astonished at his command of English idiom and his ability to put a point in a way that would have told at a constituents' dinner – to be accounted for probably by his being a Pole, or a Czech, or something of that fermenting sort, in a state of political refugeeism which had obliged him to make a profession of his music; and that evening in the drawing-room he for the first time went up to Klesmer at the piano, Miss Arrowpoint being near, and said –

"I had no idea before that you were a political man". Klesmer's only answer was to fold his arms, put out his nether lip, and stare at Mr Bult.

"You must have been used to public speaking. You speak uncommonly well, though I don't agree with you. From what you said about sentiment, I fancy you are a Panslavist."

"No; my name is Elijah. I am the Wandering Jew", said Klesmer, flashing a smile at Miss Arrowpoint, and suddenly making a mysterious wind-like rush backwards and forwards on the piano. Mr Bult felt this buffoonery rather offensive and Polish, but – Miss Arrowpoint being there – did not like to move away.

"Herr Klesmer has cosmopolitan ideas", said Miss Arrowpoint, trying to make the best of the situation. "He looks forward to a fusion of races."

"With all my heart", said Mr Bult, willing to be gracious. "I was sure he had too much talent to be a mere musician."

"Ah, sir, you are under some mistake there", said Klesmer, firing up. "No man has too much talent to be a musician. Most men have too little. A creative artist is no more a mere musician than a great statesman is a mere politician. We are not ingenious puppets, sir, who live in a box and look out on the world only when it is gaping for amusement. We help to rule the nations and make the age as much as any other public men. We count ourselves on level benches with legislators. And a man who speaks effectively through music is compelled to something more difficult than parliamentary eloquence."

With the last word Klesmer wheeled from the piano and walked away.

Miss Arrowpoint coloured, and Mr Bult observed with his usual phlegmatic stolidity, "Your pianist does not think small beer of himself".

"Herr Klesmer is something more than a pianist", said Miss Arrowpoint, apologetically. "He is a great musician in the fullest sense of the word. He will rank with Schubert and Mendelssohn".

"Ah, you ladies understand these things", said Mr Bult, none the less convinced that these things were frivolous because Klesmer had shown himself a coxcomb.

Next day, when Catherine remonstrated mildly with him, Klesmer retorted:

"You would have wished me to take his ignorant impertinence about a 'mere musician' without letting him know his place . . . Even you can't understand the wrath of the artist: he is of another caste for you."

"That is true", said Catherine, with some betrayal of feeling. "He is of a caste to which I look up – a caste above mine."

Upon this hint Klesmer speaks. Catherine's words precipitate the proposal of marriage, which comes from her in one of the finest pages of the novel. The instant hostile reaction of her parents to what they regard as a mésalliance parallels the racial theme in the Deronda portion of the story. Mrs. Arrowpoint, the authoress of an essay on Tasso, was thrown into a pitiable state when

what she had safely demanded of the dead Leonora was enacted by her own Catherine. It is hard for us to live up to our own eloquence and keep pace with our winged words while we are treading on solid earth and are liable to heavy dining. Besides, it has long been understood that the proprieties of literature are not those of practical life . . . While Klesmer was seen in the light of a patronised musician, his peculiarities were picturesque and acceptable; but to see him by a sudden flash in the light of her son-in-law gave her a burning sense of what the world would say.

Mrs. Arrowpoint's first suggestion on learning of the engagement is to have Klesmer horsewhipped off the premises.

> "Every one will say that you must have made the offer to a man who has been paid to come to the house – who is nobody knows what – a gypsy, a Jew, a mere bubble of the earth."
> "Never mind, mama", said Catherine, indignant in her turn. "We all know he is a genius – as Tasso was."

Holding firm in her most un-Victorian rebellion, Catherine finally compels her parents to acknowledge this most un-English husband she has chosen.

If Klesmer appears seldom after his marriage, the ethics he advocated in social relations and in the arts pervade the whole novel. He calls on Mirah to ask her to sing at a party at their house in Grosvenor Place, for which, we are told, she received £100. He also plays her accompaniment when she sings at Lady Mallinger's. From the few passing references he seems to be firmly established in London, "a patron and prince among musical professors". But the more vivid impression is the earlier one of the brilliant young pianist with a peppery tongue, easily stirred to defend the vocation of the dedicated artist. No character in the book is more convincing. Henry James wrote that Klesmer "comes in with a sort of Shakespearian 'value', as a painter would say". Shakespearian characters, he explains, are "characters that are born out of the *overflow* of observation, characters that make the drama seem multitudinous, like life". It is a fine tribute to George Eliot's achievement.

Some critics were reluctant to believe that an author by imagination alone could create such a character and insisted on looking for an original from whom he could have been copied. Franz Liszt has been generally accepted as the model for Klesmer since 1885, when Lord Acton in his review of Cross's

Life of George Eliot asserted that "Liszt became Klesmer". The opinion has been repeated and improved upon; Blanche Colton Williams in her biography of George Eliot (1936) called Klesmer "a nearly perfect portrait of Liszt". George Eliot made Liszt's acquaintance in 1854, when she went to live with George Henry Lewes at Weimar. Lewes, having known him in Vienna fifteen years earlier, called to renew the acquaintance, and Liszt returned the call the next day, inviting them to lunch at the Altenburg, where he lived with the Princess Sayn-Wittgenstein. During the rest of their stay at Weimar the Leweses saw him frequently. In an unsigned article entitled "Liszt, Wagner, and Weimar" which she wrote for *Fraser's Magazine* (July 1855), George Eliot says of him:

> Most London concert-goers, for whom Liszt has "blazed the comet of a season", think of him as certainly the archimagus of pianists, but as otherwise a man of no particular significance; as merely an erratic, flighty, artistic genius, who has swept through Europe, the Napoleon of the *salon*, carrying devastation into the hearts of countesses. A single morning's interview with him is enough to show the falsity of this conception. In him Nature has not sacrificed the man to the artist . . . if Liszt the pianist were unknown to you, or even did not exist, Liszt the man would win your admiration and love. See him for a few hours and you will be charmed by the originality of his conversation and the brilliancy of his wit; know him for weeks or months, and you will discern in him a man of various thought, of serious purpose, and of a moral nature which, in its mingled strength and gentleness, has the benignest influence on those about him.

Her journal describes in greater detail the impression he made on her during their first day together:

> My great delight was to watch Liszt and observe the sweetness of his expression. Genius, benevolence, and tenderness beam from his whole countenance, and his manners are in perfect harmony with it. A little rain sent us into the house, and when we were seated in an elegant little drawing room, opening into a large music-salon . . . came the thing I had longed for – Liszt's playing. I sat near him so that I could see both his hands and face. For the first time in my life I beheld real inspiration – for the first time I heard the true tones of the piano. He played one of his own compositions – one of a series of religious *fantaisies*. There was nothing strange or excessive about

his manner. His manipulation of the instrument was quiet and easy, and his face was simply grand – the lips compressed and the head thrown a little backward. When the music expressed quiet rapture or devotion a sweet smile flitted over his features; when it was triumphant the nostrils dilated.

Sweetness, tenderness, gentleness, benignity – none of these are qualities one could attribute to the irascible Klesmer. Nor is there any resemblance between the long, Dantesque face of the forty-three-year-old Liszt, familiar to every one from Scheffer's portrait, and the massive, square countenance and "grand features" of young Klesmer. He is "the German, the Sclave, and the Semite", whose Jewishness forms an important part of the novel's structure. But Liszt was a Hungarian, born a Catholic; after some scandalous decades with the countesses, he was reconciled to the Church, taking minor orders in 1865 – the year in which *Daniel Deronda* is laid – to appear, tonsured and in clerical garb, as the Abbé Liszt. That he could not have sat for Klesmer George Eliot made clear by a direct allusion in Chapter 22: As the Arrowpoints thought of him, "Klesmer was not yet a Liszt, understood to be adored by ladies of all European countries with the exception of Lapland; and even with that understanding it did not follow that he would make proposals to an heiress. No musician of honour would do so."

Though Lord Acton was wrong about Liszt, George Eliot did meet at Weimar a musician in whom can be seen more plausibly the germ from which the character of Klesmer grew. At the table d'hôte in the Erbprinz Hotel 18 September 1854 Liszt presented to the Leweses a young Russian pianist and composer named Anton Rubinstein, whose one-act opera *The Siberian Huntsmen* he was about to produce at the Weimar Theatre for the Duchess's jubilee on 9 November. George Eliot's journal mentions him only once, but there can be no doubt that she saw him frequently at the Erbprinz, where she and Lewes also took their meals, and during their visits to the Altenburg. Rubinstein fits precisely her description of "the German, the Sclave, and the Semite". His mother, a native of Prussian Silesia, was a Jewess named Kalèria Levenstein; his father, a Russian Jew from Berdichev. Anton, born in the Russian province of Volhynia, lived his first years on a tract of land his father farmed in the village of Vichvatinetz; when he was four or five they migrated to Moscow, where his father tried to operate a pencil factory, which was equally unsuccessful. Till he was thirteen Anton was left in the hands of his teacher Villoing, wandering about Europe as a child virtuoso, and the valuable gifts received when he played before royalty were, on his return to Moscow, pledged as collateral for the failing business. If we may believe his *Autobiography*, Rubinstein knew both "abundance and penury, ay, even to hunger" in his early days. Klesmer's background is recalled in a single sentence. When he comes to the Meyricks' tiny house to hear Mirah sing, "He remembered a home no larger than this on the outskirts of Bohemia; and in the figurative Bohemia too he had had large acquaintance with the variety and romance which belong to small incomes".(chapter 39).

In physique and manner there is a strong resemblance between Rubinstein and Klesmer. The portraits show him as exceedingly handsome, with the massive features given to Klesmer, blue eyes (Klesmer's were brown), and the thick mane of hair, which he used to throw backward when he played in conscious imitation of his hero, "the king of musicians, Liszt". According to Grove's *Dictionary* Rubinstein could "play a simple piece by Haydn or Mozart so as to bring tears into his hearers' eyes; on the other hand, he would sometimes fall prey to a strange excitement which caused him to play in the wildest fashion" – a mood we recall when Klesmer plays with "the torrent-like confluences of bass and treble . . . like a convulsion of nature". The trait in which the two most closely resemble each other is their brusqueness. The same tone of vehement, unaccommodating candour with which Klesmer pulverizes Gwendolen's hopeless plan for a career on the stage can be heard in all Rubinstein's writings. His *Autobiography* (1890), *A Conversation on Music* (1892), and his *Gedankenkorb* (1897) all bristle with tart comments on his contemporaries that rival in acerbity anything said by "the terrible Klesmer". Rubinstein spent a good part of his life at St. Petersburg, where he had early played for the Court and in later years was Director of the Conservatory of Music. Klesmer too has connections there. After his clash with Mr. Bult, resolved to leave England, he says: "I am neglecting my engagements. I must go off to St Petersburg".

One bit of documentary evidence confirms the relation between them. In May 1876, when Rubinstein was in London, Mrs. Frederick Lehmann invited the Leweses to dine with him and stay for the evening party, at which he was going to play. George Eliot, in the midst of writing the last book of *Daniel Deronda*, was worn out and discouraged by the lack of enthusiasm readers were showing for the Jewish elements of her novel. Though she had sternly resolved to accept no invitations till it was finished and had given some offence by her refusals, George Eliot broke her rule for this occasion. Lewes wrote to Mrs. Lehmann, "We shall so like to renew our acquaintance with Klesmer, whom we met at Weimar in '54! Therefore 'whisper it not in Gath' but expect us." And in a postscript he added, "Couldn't you bring Rubinstein here next Sunday?" The visit to the Priory proved impossible; but they met Rubinstein at the Lehmanns' dinner 15 May 1876, after which he played Beethoven, Chopin, Schumann, and some of his own compositions. "Stupendous playing!" exclaimed Lewes in his diary. They met again at the Felix Moscheles', where he played his sonata for violin and piano with Wieniawski, and on 27 May the Leweses went to his concert at the New Philharmonic, where he was the soloist in his *Concerto in D*. "Rubinstein played transcendently and roused quite a storm of enthusiasm", Lewes wrote. A year later when he returned to London George Eliot was suffering from kidney stone and could not go to the Moscheles' party, where Rubinstein played while Fraülein Redeker and Max Friedländer sang two duets from his sacred opera *The Maccabees*, which were illustrated by tableaux-vivants. She was doubtless gratified to think that her *Daniel Deronda* had helped create the patriotic interest in Jewish history that prompted the choice of this programme.

GEOFFREY TILLOTSON

Authorial Presence:
Some Observations

The questions posed by the presence of the teller in his tale are questions touching the nature of literature in general as well as of narrative literature. They concern the relation of writing and reader, and writer and reader. In this brief essay I propose to look at one or two of them.

We are dealing with narrative only on a big or fairly big scale, perhaps not even with the short-story, certainly not with parables, ballads, fables. For in reading short narratives there is never any question of our suspending our disbelief in the actuality of the action, and it is this suspension that is in question when the teller in the tale is being discussed. It is because it is held that the intrusion (to use a crude term) of the teller undoes that suspension that critics from at least Lamb's time have objected to it. We do not suspend our disbelief in the action of a short narrative because a short narrative is, or is felt to be, related to something else, either in the way of illustration or confirmation or questioning of an idea. A longer narrative allows the reader opportunity to lose himself in the story. But up to the late nineteenth-century narrators were expected to break into this suspended disbelief from time to time. The longer narrative, in other words, was a literary form that included the teller in his tale in something like the way that it included its hero in it. It included him as noticeably if not as constantly as it included the hero. The idea that a long narrative could be met with an unbroken suspension of disbelief had scarcely been thought of. That we have had many long narratives in the twentieth century in the reading of which disbelief remains suspended is a proof that there was room for a new literary form – say, that of *Mrs Dalloway*. It was a mistake, however, to assume that the discovery of this new form invalidated the old. Far from it. Indeed the old form may well come to be used again, perhaps to become the dominant form. For it had many convenient pockets, as it were, which make the new form rather resemble those so-called "utility" garments we knew in the war – garments devoid of all "extras", even in the way of pockets.

To look at one of these handy pockets that the old form provided as a matter of course. The other day I happened to read a story by that admirable writer of detective fiction, the late Cyril Hare. Into a fairly long short-story he introduces a certain professional "Expert Elocutionist", and begins by representing his exaggerated speech by means of a device of typography: "It will be an inter-r-esting compar-r-rison" and so on. A writer in the new form would presumably have to go on tediously reproducing the elocutionist's speech in this way. Hare, however, who was belatedly using the old form, avoids tediousness by interposing in brackets the welcome news that

it is useless to trouble the printer in an attempt to reproduce Mr Speckles's voice. It must be taken for granted, or half this tale would have to be printed [with hyphens].[1]

Reading that, I was reminded of Henry Kingsley, who in *Mademoiselle Mathilde* (which we shall look at again later) announces that he is translating into standard English the broken English spoken by the French aristocrats when they are living in England. How, one wonders, does a writer in the new form get over such inconveniences? He cannot interpose with an announcement of the obvious way of doing so.

And would it not be sometimes a help to a twentieth-century novelist if he did not have to entrust his own commentary on the action to the mouths of the personages themselves, whom he has to make like himself for the purpose? How seldom is the nineteenth-century author himself disguised as a personage in his story, and how often the twentieth-century author!

The new form seems to me to have owed its rise mainly to the need for a change that comes over every form sooner or later. There had been so much intrusion of the teller in the long novels of the nineteenth century that an obvious change for new writers to make would be that of throwing him out – the process took a long time, for almost to the end Henry James would use such intrusive phrases as "our heroine". They did so, however, on a mistaken view of the nature of fiction that a closer acquaintance with one critic in particular would have saved them from. For Johnson had dealt finally, in his Preface to Shakespeare, with the whole business as it affected plays, and so *mutatis mutandis* long stories. He pointed out that there was more happening in a spectator's mind when he saw a play than what Coleridge, working on hints in eighteenth-century criticism, was soon to call by the famous phrase I have been quoting. Johnson agrees that the mind of the spectators may be "wandering in ecstasy", but claims that, despite this,

> the spectators are always in their senses, and know, from the first act to the last, that the stage is only a stage, and that the players are only players.

Nor was he the first to note that if the murders being enacted were really believed in, the spectators would mob the stage. In other words, the mind of the reader includes more than suspended disbelief or "wandering ecstasy". For it is continuously judging the action, criticizing it, making a silent running commentary on the elaborate matter and art of the play or novel. And it is because of the presence of these other things in the reader's mind that from the earliest times onward the teller felt confident that intrusion would be welcome. He intruded on his tale because of the suitability of his formulating and voicing the reader's own running criticism. It was a happy state of things when the author was also the publisher and had his audience before him in the banqueting hall, as the comedian still has in the music hall. In those conditions he had the satisfaction of seeing his commentary in the act of being acceded to. Those old conditions, however, were not felt to be obsolete by the nineteenth-century novelist, who will speak of "my reader and I", as Charles Reade does, or who will give us the sort of thing Dickens gives us near the end of *Bleak House*:

> "Why, now", says the trooper [George Rouncewell], glancing round him and speaking in a lower voice, "I begin to understand how you come to think as you do think, mother. Rooms get an awful look about them when they are fitted up, like these, for one person you are used to see in them, and that person is away under any shadow, let alone being God knows where."
>
> He is not far out. As all partings foreshadow the great final one, so, empty rooms, bereft of a familiar presence, mournfully whisper what your room and what mine must one day be.

And when from time to time all the novelists appeal to the reader, perhaps even as a person, with "reader", or "gentle reader", or "irascible reader", or "bachelor reader" or what not, they are pretending that the old physical companionship is still in being. Sometimes the narrator shows the reader himself making the intrusion. Reade, who is the *enfant terrible* among the great English writers, actually goes so far as to make the reader's supposed comment take the form of "How so, Mr. Reade?" – he has just sprung a little surprise, and the reader requires an explanation, having been attending closely enough to see that one is called for. The commentary made by the narrator is simply expressing that of the reader. And because of this, it is always comment according to human nature. For however eccentric each reader may happen to be as a man he is always perfectly normal when he reads a story. All this means that commentary is elicited by the nature of fiction, and that the explicit comments of nineteenth-century novelists are one way of expressing them. There are other ways, and the nineteenth-century novelists made use of them too – all the devices of expression to which we give the names of "irony", "innuendo", "suggestion", "tone of voice", and so on. That the novelists of today prefer to use these only is no reason why other novelists should not have preferred to use more, indeed to use all.

Further, the reader is always given a personal presence along with a work of literature, though an unsophisticated reader may be scarcely aware of it. A reader who is sophisticated enough to be the sort of reader the writer had in mind discovers the presence of the author. Bagehot and A. C. Bradley were conscious of the "Shakespearean" in the plays, and wrote essays on Shakespeare the man. If that is true of our response to a play it is true *a fortiori* of our response to a novel. A dramatist, as far as words go, works entirely by speeches, and the speeches which are those of individuals are coloured by the characters he has imagined for them – very much coloured when Shakespeare is the dramatist. A novelist on the other hand, gives us narrative as well as speeches, and narrative is the author speaking in his own voice. We all pride ourselves, we sophisticated play-goers and novel-readers, on subscribing to Buffon's idea that the style is the very man, and the conditions of a novel make the personality of the novelist sharply clear. Start reading any novel and after a few sentences you have formed an idea of the writer's mind quite apart from any idea you have formed of what he is writing about. That this is so is another reason why the teller is inside his tale willy nilly. He is inside it because he has written it, and when as a nineteenth-century novelist he shows that he knows he is inside it, that is no more than an extension of Shakespeare's presence in the plays. The "intrusion" of the teller in all the long stories written before late Henry James (to use an English example) does not produce a change of kind, but only of degree.

We respond to the personalities of writers whether they are exhibited or not. Every reader goes in awe of George Eliot as an author as soon as she has completed a half dozen sentences merely of third-person description, and every reader warms to Mrs Gaskell as an author after the same thirty seconds. Our response is sharper still when the authors loudly exhibit themselves. One of the delights of reading nineteenth-century novels and of all tales before our own day, is that the personalities exhibited are or interest. Half the philosophy of Thackeray comes out in his personal commentary, and who would miss Reade, who flashes out important ideas of his own – and ours – by the dozen, especially ideas about the sexes, and has the power to say things like "But wedding flowers are usually well-watered in the private apartments" (which Thackeray must have envied as a brilliant instance of what he loved to do himself); or who will end a joyous chapter by breaking out into song, written out as notes on a stave; or cry "cursed jealousy!

it is the sultan of all the passions, and the Tartar chief of all the crimes", an exclamation which he introduces by invoking one of his personages, whom he immediately couples with his readers:

Ah! William Fielding, and all of you, "Beware of jealousy".

As for the personality of Henry Kingsley, the simplest thing to say is that it is to men novelists what Mrs Gaskell's is to women novelists.

I spoke above of the spectator's sense of the dramatist's art. How can he not sense it, the play often being in verse? Indeed a play is an opera "penny plain". Johnson knew that among other reasons the audience goes to the theatre to see and hear the acting – "They come to hear a certain number of lines recited with just gesture and elegant modulation", in the same way as the opera-goer goes to hear the soprano's top notes. In reading a novel we sophisticated readers are savouring every aspect of the art, and this is one reason why authorial intrusion when it is not for the purposes of moral comment is for the purposes of literary. The author will often discuss technique with the reader, who knows what is at stake. Trollope in a political novel will affect to protest that he cannot be expected to describe a Cabinet meeting. And Henry Kingsley, who sometimes poses as a writer for boys, will exhibit his wish that he could hand over a tender scene to a woman novelist.

And now, I think, we can see the English novel of the eighteenth century and nineteenth century as a variant of earlier narratives in that it carries one of the prime literary forms – that for long narratives – to an extreme, encouraged by circumstances, which include serial publication. It is the novel of Fielding and Sterne carried further so as to combine the abundance, and sometimes the coherence of plot given us by Fielding with the abundance of the comment given us by Sterne. We have to judge each novel on its merits as belonging to the particular variant of the form that it soon shows us it belongs to. Judged by the standard that has shown itself to be appropriate Trollope, I think, sometimes offends by failing to place his comments artfully. He is not given to intruding very much, and when he does he has sometimes allowed us to forget the strength of his authorial presence enough for us to be shocked by the suddenness of its further and plainer intrusion. When he tells us in an aside that he remembers once when he was dining with a friend that . . . and so on. That direct reminiscence would be quite acceptable in a novel of Reade's or Henry Kingsley's because these novelists have made us feel that we are always on the brink of having it given us. These two novelists write acceptably because they insist all the time that they are writing in the extremest form of the novel.

And for fear any reader thinks that that makes for crudeness of narration let me show him how Henry Kingsley for one, and on one occasion, introduces the author into his *Mademoiselle Mathilde*. I hope it will show too how crude has been my term "intrusion".

It is difficult to put one's finger on the precise moment when it really happens. Opening the book at the first page of the text we read under the heading "CHAPTER I." a subtitle in small caps:

A chapter which will have to be written several times again: each time in darker ink.

The author of that unusual chapter heading is felt to be near. But he has not yet intruded as it were physically. Then follows the beginning of the tale:

It was quite impossible, so Mademoiselle Mathilde D'Isigny concluded, that any reasonable being could dream of going out on such an afternoon. It was not to be thought of. Nevertheless, she began thinking at once about her sabots and her red umbrella.

The first sentence of the novel, then, records the thought by which the heroine finished off a series. Nothing could be further from an author intruding himself. Instead of that, he is deep in the mind of a personage. It might be the beginning of a novel by Virginia Woolf. The second sentence, however, is ambiguous in that it might record the thought of either the heroine or the author. The centre from which the writing is proceeding is trembling. In the third sentence it fixes on the author decisively.

In the next paragraph we get description of place:

A wild revolutionary-looking nimbus, urged on by a still wilder wind, which seemed, from its direction, to have started from America, had met the rapidly-heated and rapidly-cooled strata of chalk in the valley of the Stour in Dorsetshire. The nimbus, chased by the furious headlong American wind, met the chalk downs while they were cooled by a long winter's frost, and at once dissolved itself into cataracts of water; into cataracts more steady, more persistent, and, in the end, more dangerous, than any which ever came from the wildest and noisiest summer thunderstorm.

This is not plain description, however, but description coloured with the author because coloured by the theme of the novel. The nimbus is called "revolutionary-looking" and America is referred to because the novel is set in the year in which the French Revolution broke out, and the personages, some of which figure in history books, are very much part of it. The author is intruding into his description pertinently, his story being what it is.

Then follows the opening of the next paragraph:

It was quite impossible that any reasonable woman could go out on such an afternoon.

Again we are thrust back into ambiguity because those words might be recording the thought either of Mathilde or the author. In the rest of the sentence, however, the thought is plainly his alone:

still the sabots and red umbrella dwelt on her mind, for it might under certain circumstances become necessary, although impossible.

And that final sub-clause shows that he is again commenting as well as describing – he is adding a touch of the comic spirit to which the discrepancy between mind and action is laughable. From this point onward ambiguity reigns, and simply by being ambiguous delights. Whereupon, half a crowded page later, the ambiguity is further complicated by the beginning of the eighth paragraph:

Mademoiselle Mathilde may or may not have thought of these things.

Not only is the reader uncertain, then, but the author also! And this brings him very near, for an author in doubt is an author present very plainly. In the twelfth paragraph, therefore, we are not surprised to find him revealed, unashamed, and complete with his first person pronoun:

> Now, with all due deference to Mrs Bone and Sir Joshua Reynolds, Mathilde was not a *pretty* woman; any face more utterly unlike his lovely "Kitty Fisher" cannot be imagined; and I very much doubt if she ever had been.

Now at last the author is unequivocally inside his story.

Is it not clear already that this method of writing a novel is a subtle method, that intrusiveness as practised here at least does not thrust itself on the reader? Moreover, is it not also clear that we have been now fully informed as to the sort of novel we have embarked upon? Our novel has the teller prominently present in his tale, his presence being made felt by methods variously direct and indirect. Does it not, therefore, behove us to criticize it for what it is without odious reference to what it is not?

NOTE

1 "The Tragedy of Young Macintyre", in *Best Detective Stories of Cyril Hare*, ed. Michael Gilbert (Penguin Books, 1964), p. 51.

J. C. MAXWELL

The "Sociological" Approach to The Mayor of Casterbridge

Ian Gregor recently asked the question "What kind of Fiction did Hardy write?"[1] Before offering his own answer, he outlines three ways of looking at Hardy which have, successively though with overlaps, been current: the philosophical (Immanent Will and the like), that which takes its cue from Hardy's own formula, "novels of character and environment", and, most recently, that which treats Wessex "as actual social history" and credits the power of the novels to "their imaginative testimony to the gradual destruction of a stable agricultural community by the inroads of nineteenth-century industrialisation".[2]

This sketch does not, of course, claim to be exhaustive. It ignores, for example, one of Hardy's most stimulating critics, A. J. Guerard, whose Hardy bears an odd resemblance to the Dickens of Edmund Wilson. But the third of his three Hardys is certainly a figure to be reckoned with by any present-day critic. I have chosen to examine fairly closely what the leading champion of this Hardy, Douglas Brown, has made of the novel which he has discussed in the greatest detail, The Mayor of Casterbridge.

The Mayor has always been a highly respected novel and has sometimes been described as Hardy's greatest, especially by those who are not over-enthusiastic Hardyans.[3] It is not, moreover, in any obvious way a "difficult" novel: its qualities are plain and unmistakable in broad outline. There ought, then, to be no distracting subordinate problems in examining what Brown has to say of it, both in his separate monograph,[4] and in his earlier general book on Hardy.[5]

The two poles of Hardy's art, in Brown's view, are the "sociological" and the "fabular",[6] and of the latter he writes with great perceptiveness. The sociological emphasis, too, is readily understandable, and it is a useful corrective for those, if any still exist, who think of Hardy as spending most of his time brooding over Schopenhauer and Hartmann.[7] But to insist that Wessex as it was when he wrote, and as it had been in his boyhood, was a real flesh-and-blood concern to Hardy is one thing. To place this concern in the framework Brown devises is another. And *The Mayor*, as we shall see, presents special difficulties of its own.

Brown formulates the main thesis in *Thomas Hardy*, pp. 30ff. "The five great novels have a common pattern." The protagonists, "strong-natured countrymen, disciplined by the necessities of agricultural life", are brought into relation with "men and women from outside the rural world, better educated, superior in status, yet inferior in human worth". Eventually, "what the situation means becomes more evident: it is a clash between agricultural and urban modes of life". So far, this might be merely a fictive pattern, no doubt with some basis in reality, but appealing to Hardy principally for artistic reasons. But the next step in the argument is that "this pattern records Hardy's dismay at the predicament of the agricultural community in the south of England during the last part of the nineteenth century and at the precarious hold of the agricultural way of life", and that it has to be seen in the light, especially, of "the agricultural tragedy of 1870-1902".

This is clearly a far-reaching thesis as to what the novels are basically "about". And Brown is relatively cautious in his formulation. He offers nothing so crude as the statement by Arnold Kettle – "The subject of *Tess of the D'Urbervilles* is stated clearly by Hardy to be the fate of a 'pure woman'; in fact it is the destruction of the English peasantry"[8] – on which Ian Gregor aptly comments: "it is interesting, and rather characteristic, that a novel like this must first of all be shown to be socially and historically significant before it can be considered 'important'."[9] But Brown is prepared to go a good deal of the way with Kettle.

Referring to the latter's essay, he speaks of *Tess* as Hardy's "most tragic fable of agricultural defeat",[10] and refers to the "agricultural tragedy" as "the substance of his narrative art",[11] implying a contrast with something else that is, by comparison, superficial or secondary; and in discussing *The Mayor* in particular, he shows a tendency to play down the individuality of the protagonist – "he is agricultural man, defeated"[12] – and Guerard is rebuked for over-psychologizing him as the "damned and self-destructive individualist".[13]

I think there are very serious objections to be made to all this, and hope that an examination restricted to *The Mayor of Casterbridge* will at least show that it does not apply at all well to that novel.

Tess, however much we may dissent from what Kettle says about it, is at least not merely written during but set in the period of agricultural depression. In fact, criticism of it on the sociological side might take the line that it paints an insufficiently harsh picture of the life that Tess would in fact have lived at Flintcomb Ash.[14] But with *The Mayor*, Brown is faced with the special difficulty that the main action is played out during the eighteen-forties. This makes Brown understandably uneasy. Henchard, "agricultural man", falls at a time when, no doubt, many individuals came to disaster in a similar way, but it is hard to see his fate as epitomizing that of English agriculture. Brown is not too happy about the years from the repeal of the Corn Laws to 1870, and is reduced to writing of them as "two decades of apparent prosperity . . . (Farfrae's decades)".[15] It is hard to see how prosperity is made merely "apparent" by the fact that new conditions, especially the opening up of the wheat-growing areas of the New World, prevented it from being more than temporary. Yet without some such notion, Henchard cannot convincingly be given the representative role which Brown wants him to play. Difficulties multiply if we look not just at Henchard but at his relationship to his rival and supplanter, Farfrae.

It is easy to agree in general terms that something impressive and important about the relationship between different generations is being presented through these two characters. Julian Moynahan has, with some plausibility, seen Henchard and Farfrae in the roles of Saul and David,[16] and the main objection to this sort of interpretation is not that it is wrong but that it covers too much: that the "conflict between generations" is "so archetypal that it is omnitypal".[17] But for Brown, Farfrae must stand for something more sociologically distinctive than just the younger generation. In *Thomas Hardy*, the formula is fairly simple: "[Henchard's] story . . . enacts forcefully the tension between the old rural world and the new urban one. Farfrae is the invader, the stranger within the gates."[18] But there is some rethinking in *Thomas Hardy: The Mayor of Casterbridge*: "I used to identify Farfrae as the Invader, but I can no longer read *The Mayor* in that way. Farfrae comes from outside, but he joins; he is *for* the agricultural community, not a disrupter; he holds a hope of renovation in his skills and intelligence; created perhaps out of Hardy's truthful acknowledgement of local inadequacies."[19] Some such modification is obviously called for. Farfrae is certainly not in any literal sense an "urban" figure, and it would be a rather crude and patronizing stereotype to regard him as alien to the countryside just because he can adapt himself to changing conditions. But Brown modifies his picture of Farfrae without making corresponding adjustments to that of Henchard and what he stands for. If no longer so much an alien, still less an urban invader, Farfrae remains an intruder, and this is all right so long as we do not insist on seeing Henchard in a sharply antithetic role as a fully assimilated and representative member of the community. It is surely important that, as Howard O. Brogan says, "all of the main characters, male and female, are intruders into a community in which they do not really belong".[20] Brown is conscious of this when he is emphasizing the "fabular" side of the book, and writes of the "fairy-tale transformation" of Henchard "from skilled labourer migrant in the country to corn factor and mayor in the country town", but hastens to add, less convincingly, that "he is still the essentially *representative* protagonist".[21]

What is it to be "representative" in this sense? Literally, Henchard is a highly individual and very exceptional member of his community, whose fate is all the more impressive because it too is exceptional: the sort of thing that can happen, but very seldom does happen in such a spectacular form. For this purpose, it is important that in one way he should not be "representative". Hence, Hardy is right to set the action in a period of relative long-term agricultural stability and prosperity, though the plot requires what Hardy calls in his Preface "the uncertain harvests which immediately preceded the repeal of the Corn Laws". Yet Brown would have him also "representative" of a fate that is later – a good deal later – going to overtake the agricultural community as a whole. This is surely a very unsatisfactory kind of juggling both with time and with the relation between naturalism and something that can hardly be seen as falling short of allegory. Hardy's art just does not have the feel of being like this. It is odd that a critic who wants, rightly, to have him very firmly rooted in the real world of the nineteenth century should in effect remove him from it. This comes out particularly in a parenthesis in which Brown writes of *The Mayor* as "a novel much concerned with the drama of the Corn Law conflicts".[23] In any straightforward sense of being "concerned with", this is plainly untrue. Brown has to take a panoramic view of the whole period from the forties to the eighties in order to make out that Hardy is somehow giving a poetic rendering of the process of agricultural change. On the very next page, indeed, we read that "each of the great Wessex novels treats *in imaginative form* of the defeat of our peasantry and the collapse of our agriculture"[23] (my italics). Brown seems unable to make up his mind whether to interpret this in an extreme form, with Kettle – as an assertion that the novels are not "really" about the characters they claim to be about; or as a more modest assertion that Hardy's imagination works on the social setting as well as on the individual characters, and that the latter must be seen in the light of what Hardy implies, but does not spell out, about the former. Certainly a reader who can enter sympathetically and knowledgeably into Hardy's attitude towards the rural society of his own day, and that of the earlier period in which some of the novels are set, is likely to be a better reader than one who approaches them with no historical knowledge. In fact Brown seems to come to rest half way between these positions. He is unwilling to sacrifice the individuality of Hardy's characters, but he moves some way towards the more radical interpretation because of his belief that "human relations and human persons are represented less for their own sakes than for the clearer focusing of the invasion and the havoc".[24]

It might still be true that, even if Henchard is scarcely "agricultural man" in Brown's sense, there is a broad distinction between his way of life and that of Farfrae that reflects the distinction between the old rural world and the world of Hardy's own day. Brown, we have seen, is prepared to withdraw somewhat from his earlier contention that this is "the tension between the old rural world and the new urban one".[25] But he still lays stress on one element of modernity: Farfrae can cope with a market economy and Henchard cannot.[26] But Hardy's own Preface, which Brown ignores, suggests a very different attitude towards market fluctuations as an element in the story. The main reason for setting the action in the mid-forties is that the harvest was then much more of a gamble, and a temptation to speculation, than it later became: "the home Corn Trade, on which so much of the action turns, had an importance that can hardly be realized by those accustomed to the sixpenny loaf of the present date [1895], and to the present indifference of the public to harvest weather". The curiously perverse way in which Brown regards Henchard and Farfrae, and what they respectively stand for, can be studied in some detail in terms of his treatment of a particular episode.

He quotes[27] Farfrae's account to Lucetta of his dealings (chapter XXIII), which is later said to describe "the new market ethics Farfrae boyishly vaunted to Lucetta".[28] The quotation itself is preceded by the description of the innocuous sentence "A man must live where his money is made" (which in its context is simply an explanation of why Farfrae left his home) as his "candid declaration" which "is a submission to 'the market's' terms: accumulation of stock and finance-strategy not to fulfil a necessary role in trade; not to connect Caster-bridge with the agriculture of its countryside; but for its own sake, or for further reserves of financial power" – a formidable set of implications to be unrolled from a casual sentence. But it is on the following more extended quotation that Brown relies:

"Yet I've done very well this year. O yes. . . . You see that man with the drab kerseymere coat? I bought largely of him in the autumn when wheat was down, and then afterwards when it rose a little I sold off all I had! It brought only a small profit to me; while the farmers kept

230

theirs, expecting higher figures – yes, though the rats were gnawing the ricks hollow. Just when I sold the markets went lower, and I bought up the corn of those who had been holding back at less price than my first purchases. And then", cried Farfrae impetuously, his face alight, "I sold it a few weeks after, when it happened to go up again! And so, by contenting myself with small profits frequently repeated, I soon made five hundred pounds – yes! – (bringing down his hand upon the table, and quite forgetting where he was) – while the others by keeping theirs in hand made nothing at all!"

Brown's immediately following comment is: "The technique extends the traditional wariness of farming communities and reaches out towards the idea of finance corporations".

Now if Farfrae's methods were to be taken as representative of a new system, with concomitant dangers to an established way of life, one would expect them to be set over against a contrasting practice that fairly represented the healthy functioning of a traditional system and values. What is extraordinary is that Brown does not seem to have noticed how the old-style farmers are in fact described as having behaved. There is no need to idealize Farfrae – Brown's later "canny moderation, striking just the right equipoise between competing possibilities",[29] is fair enough. But if Farfrae is telling the truth – and we have no reason to doubt it – he has been behaving much better (even if for prudential rather than loftily moral reasons) by the traditional agrarian standards than the farmers: contenting himself with moderate gains, where they have, with short-sighted cunning and avarice, been trying to play the market; they are the lineal descendants of Shakespeare's farmer who hanged himself on the expectation of plenty.

The farmers of chapter XXIII are, of course, less important for their own sakes than as a foreshadowing of Henchard's more disastrous gamble a few chapters later, and it is in connection with this that Hardy elaborates on the point later to be made in the Preface, the dependence of this crucial part of his plot on the old order of things:

The time was in the years immediately before foreign competition had revolutionized the trade in grain, when still, as from the earliest ages, the wheat quotations from month to month depended entirely upon the home harvest. A bad harvest, or the prospect of one, would double the price of corn in a few weeks; and the promise of a good yield would lower it as rapidly. Prices were like the roads of the period, steep in gradient, reflecting in their phases the local conditions, without engineering, levellings, or averages. (chapter XXVI)

Nothing could be clearer. Far from choosing a period for his novel in which new market standards are invading a hitherto innocent agrarian economy, Hardy has chosen the *latest* period at which the uncushioned dominance of price fluctuations depending on the home harvest, which had existed "from the earliest ages", still persisted. Brown's treatment of this passage is extraordinary: "Hardy chooses to indicate the forces operating on the wheat markets at the time of his tale, as though to throw the whole weight of agricultural change behind Henchard's decline",[30] and Henchard is credited with "efforts to mimic the new capitalist techniques".[31]

It would be impossible for an intelligent critic to misrepresent his subject so badly if there were not some correspondence to reality in what he says. A broad contrast between old and new is certainly present in Henchard and Farfrae. One feels that something true and illuminating is being said about Farfrae when Brown remarks that "negotiation through trade union is not far off, one feels, and Farfrae will do well at it".[32] But this is more because Farfrae strikes us as adaptable to any changing situation than because he belongs specifically to the new world of Hardy's own day. It is, in fact, one of the skilful things about Hardy's portraiture of him that he is allowed to remain a very limited character, responding to the immediate challenge of the situation rather than creating a new situation – a good mayor of Casterbridge in a better than average year. In terms of Shakespearian parallels, if there is something of Lear in Henchard – "the oldest hath borne most" – there is also something of the pattern of *Richard II*, and as in that play, a too mechanical pattern of rise and fall is avoided by not giving Farfrae, the Bolingbroke of the novel, the same degree of prominence that belongs to the protagonist. Henchard – it is a commonplace of criticism – remains the unchallengeably dominating figure even in defeat and disaster.

Philip Larkin has expressed dissatisfaction about what has been written on Hardy with the appeal, "Wanted: Good Hardy

Critic".[33] I am not myself so pessimistic. I think we have had a number of good ones: Brown himself, whom Larkin does not mention, is, at his best, one of them: Guerard is another. I do not find it necessary to supplement this essay, limited and negative though it has been, with a reassessment of *The Mayor of Casterbridge*, because I think it has, on the whole, been justly appreciated, even if some of the commonplaces have worn rather threadbare. Larkin is right, however – it is Arnold Kettle on *Tess* that is immediately in question – in saying that "the reader feels uncomfortable rather than illuminated" by the sort of criticism that exhorts us to "trust the tale and not the teller".[34] True, one must with Hardy as with any other novelist be prepared to follow the tale if it is clearly determined to escape the monitory eye of the teller. But with a plain, intelligent, and articulate writer like Hardy, it is at our peril that we ignore lucid and explicit comments such as he makes in this book – I am thinking particularly of the passages discussed from the Preface and chapter XXVI. At least they are likely to be a safer guide than the critic's judgement of what the historical situation might or ought to have prompted the novelist to offer his readers.

Note on the Chronology of
The Mayor of Casterbridge

Two chronologies of the novel have recently been offered: by the late Carl J. Weber in the second edition of his *Hardy of Wessex* (1965), pp. 149-50, and by F. B. Pinion in *A Critical Commentary on Thomas Hardy's "The Mayor of Casterbridge"* (1966), pp. 56-60. Still more recently, Weber and Pinion have engaged in a "dialogue" in the *Library Chronicle of the University of Texas*, VIII.3 (Spring 1967), which contains a couple of pages (pp. 4-5) on the question. Weber there gives his reasons for, and also abandons, his absolute dating for the main action (1846-9), so that it need not here concern me. If we are to take the remark in the Preface about "the uncertain harvests which immediately preceded the repeal of the Corn Laws" as conclusive for the novel, then Henchard's fatal summer must be

1845, the only year in the period immediately preceding repeal which, in the violence of its fluctuations though not in their exact timing, fills the bill. On this basis, the internal chronology will be as follows. Susan and Elizabeth arrive in Casterbridge in September 1843, when Henchard's vow still has two years to go (chapter V). The marriage takes place the same November (chapter XIII), and Susan dies the following year. The "agreement entered into this sixteenth day of October" which Henchard dictates to Elizabeth Jane in chapter XX belongs to 1844. 1845 is the year both of the revelation of Henchard's past, and of the expiring of his vow, though events are rather crowded at this point, and Hardy may not have worked them out very carefully. Weber goes wrong in two respects. He makes the revelation of Henchard's past occur only one instead of two years after the arrival of Susan and Elizabeth Jane, and he makes a further year elapse before the expiry of the vow. Lucetta dies in 1846, and Henchard in 1848: when he left Casterbridge it was "almost two years earlier" that he had waited to tell Farfrae of Lucetta's illness (chapter XLIV). The only real inconsistency that I can see is that in chapter XLIV Henchard looks back to "five-and-twenty years" before, when it is in fact twenty-four. But this may be a round number: it is "a quarter of a century" a few pages later. Hardy evidently did not use a calendar. One crucial date, the 16 September on which the vow expires, is made to fall on a Sunday, which it did not in fact do between 1838 and 1849. (The next year when it did so is 1855, which is too late even for Mr. Pinion's chronology, to which I now turn.)

The chronology offered by Mr. Pinion departs even further from what I am proposing, in that it transfers the whole action to the 1850s. His arguments are of some weight. In the first place, Hardy in revising the opening sentence of the novel altered "before the present century had reached its thirtieth year" to "before the nineteenth century had reached one-third of its span", which certainly suggests a date between 1830 and 1833 for the opening (and hence 1851 and 1854 for the fatal year). It is in keeping with this that the museum of chapter XXII was not "in a back street" until 1851, and that a note by Hardy shows that he knew this. Mr. Pinion also points out that the phrase in chapter XXIII about "the years immediately before foreign competition had revolutionized the trade in grain" is not conclusive for a date before repeal, since "foreign competition did not *revolutionize* the trade in corn for nearly thirty years or more". This is, however, a two-edged argument, since a strict interpretation of "immediately" would then place the action not in the 1850s but in the 1870s. Hardy is, on any showing, writing rather loosely. On the whole, I am still inclined to prefer the mid-1840s as the date, though nothing in my main argument would be adversely affected by acceptance of Mr. Pinion's dating.

NOTES

1 *Essays in Criticism*, XVI (1966), 290-308.

2 *Ibid.*, p. 291.

3 For example, Frank Chapman, *Scrutiny*, III (1934-5), 30.

4 *Thomas Hardy: The Mayor of Casterbridge* (London, 1962): hereafter *T.H.M.*

5 *Thomas Hardy* (1954, 1961): hereafter *T.H.* I have used the 1961 edition. I am sorry that Brown's untimely death prevents this essay from being a contribution to a continuing dialogue.

6 *T.H.M.*, p. 14.

7 This name is misprinted Hauptmann in *T.H.*, p. 22.

8 *An Introduction to the English Novel*, II (1953; Greyfriars ed., 1962), 50.

9 Ian Gregor and Brian Nicholas, *The Moral and the Story* (London, 1962), p. 136.

10 *T.H.M.*, p. 43.

11 *T.H.*, p. 42.

12 *T.H.M.*, p. 62.

13 *Ibid.*, p. 38, citing A. J. Guerard, *Thomas Hardy: The Novels & Stories* (London, 1949), p. 148.

14 See William J. Hyde, *Victorian Studies*, II (1958-9), 51.

15 *T.H.M.*, p. 42; similarly *T.H.*, p. 32.

16 *PMLA*, LXXI (1956), 118-30.

17 George Wing, *Hardy* (Edinburgh and London, 1963), p. 64.

18 P. 65.   19 P. 31.

20 *ELH*, XVII (1950), 316.   21 *T.H.M.*, p. 15.

22 *T.H.*, p. 35.   23 *Ibid.*, p. 36.

24 *Ibid.*, p. 30.   25 *Ibid.*, p. 65.

26 *T.H.M.*, p. 43.   27 *Ibid.*, pp. 33-4.

28 *Ibid.*, p. 49.   29 *T.H.M.*, p. 50.

30 *T.H.M.*, pp. 49-50.   31 *Ibid.*, p. 50.

32 *Ibid.*, p. 53.

33 *Critical Quarterly*, VIII (1966), 174-9.

34 *Critical Quarterly*, VIII (1966), 174. I might also mention, as relevant to some of the points made in this essay, the article by Raymond Williams in *Critical Quarterly*, VI (1964), especially the last three pages (348-51), where Williams remarks that "the pressures to which Hardy's characters are subjected are the pressures from within the system of living, not from outside it . . . Henchard is not destroyed by a new and alien kind of dealing, but by a development of his own trade which he has himself invited" (p. 349). Though it is only indirectly relevant to the subject of this essay, any reader of *The Mayor* is likely to be interested in an article in the *Economic History Review*, 2 Ser. XX (1967), 280-92, by E. H. Hunt, "Labour Productivity in English Agriculture, 1850-1914". This contrasts the high-wage and high-productivity areas (which would include Farfrae's home) and the low-wage and low-productivity areas, in which the low wages, and consequent malnutrition, helped to perpetuate low productivity. Hardy knew what he was doing when he made Christopher Coney say to Farfrae: "we be bruckle folk here . . . so many mouths to fill, and God-a'mighty sending his little taties so terrible small to fill 'em with" (ch. VIII).

IAN GREGOR

Jude
the Obscure

[i]

If it is still tempting to quote E. M. Forster's remark, "that there is some vital problem that has not been answered, or even posed, in the misfortunes of Jude the Obscure",[1] this is not because of a reluctance to recognize some valuable discussions of the novel, but because the work has consistently defied satisfactory discussion as a whole. The success of the parts is a commonplace in criticism of the novel, but it is invariably offered as a datum, a tacit recognition that Hardy failed to make his material cohere. So we find A. J. Guerard in his perceptive study writing that the novel invites "enumeration" of the problems it deals with. He goes on to list them:

1. The socio-economic problems of educational opportunity for the poor and of class deracination.
2. The social problems of marriage, divorce and repressive moral censorship by public opinion.
3. The psychological problems of Jude's sexuality and his urge to self-destruction, and of Sue's epicene temperament and her moral masochism.
4. The religious problem of church reforms.
5. The ethical problems of naturalistic morality and of moral sanction independent of dogma.

237

6. The bio-philosophical problems of inherited family characteristics and of the new will-not-to-live.
7. The spiritual problems of modern unrest, modern introspectiveness, and modern melancholy and spiritual isolation.[2]

Leaving aside the accuracy of this "enumeration" and the fragmentation it implies, it will be readily conceded that Guerard is listing issues, which are raised in the novel. Generally brought in to support his criticism is Hardy's own remark in the Preface:

> Like former productions of this pen, *Jude the Obscure* is simply an endeavour to give shape and coherence to a series of seemings, or personal impressions, the question of their consistency or their discordance or their permanence or their transitoriness, being regarded as not of the first moment.

This is usually interpreted as Hardy taking out a novelist's license to cross metaphysical frontiers duty-free.

What I want to suggest in the paper that follows is that these familiar phrases constitute something much more precise than a novelist offering a general reminder about the nature of his art, or an anticipatory defence of a fragmentary work, but rather they serve as a clue, both as to the kind of totality that is present in Jude and why that totality has been lost in a miscellany of detail.

[ii]

The presentation of Hardy as a divided figure is common enough. John Holloway has pointed out how cheerfully commentators on the novels see him, both as "the chronicler of a ghastly world of planless and ironic fate and as recording all the interest and variety and even charm of rustic life", leaving unnoticed that "if these ever occur in a single book, Hardy is probably ridiculous as an artist".[3] It is more than the possible coincidence of these two views within a single book that should make us pause, it is that they should co-exist at all. It makes us wonder about Hardy's "views". That his attitude to life was a tragic one, however we define it, would seem incontestable and yet we know that Hardy, throughout his life, was deeply troubled by this response. We read in the autobiography that he felt critics approached his work "with an ignorant prejudice against his pessimism, which they allowed to stand in the way of fair reading and fair judgement".[4] Pessimism now seems to be an inescapable part of our reaction to Hardy, and yet if we think of him as the laureate of "crass causality" and "dicing time", we are neglecting entirely that impression of resilience which pervades the fiction. These ambiguities are suggested by that jaunty diary entry, which Hardy wrote for New Year's Day 1902, under the heading "A Pessimist's Apology":

> Pessimism (or rather what is called such) is, in brief, playing the sure game. You cannot lose at it; you may gain. It is the only view of life in which you can never be disappointed. Having reckoned what to do in the worst possible circumstances, when better arise, as they may, life becomes child's play.[5]

The wry acceptance is here but it is accompanied by a sardonic self-criticism, where the acceptance is seen as an indulgence, a bluff cynicism, "the sure game", "child's play". The route from a diary to fiction is never straight, but nevertheless the tone of that note is heard repeatedly in Hardy's tensed awareness of the multiple causes of the tragic element. Even in *Jude*, possibly Hardy's most unequivocally tragic novel, the nature of the tragedy is constantly interrogated:

> "We must conform!" Sue said mournfully. "All the ancient wrath of the power above us has been vented upon us, His poor creatures, and we must submit. There is no choice. We must. It is no use fighting against God!"
> "It is only against man and senseless circumstance", said Jude.
> (VI.iii)

Jude's attitude is amplified in his remarks elsewhere that "the time was not ripe for us. Our ideas were fifty years too soon . . ." (VI.x) and "it was my poverty and not my will that consented to be beaten. It takes two or three generations to do what I tried to do in one . . ." (VI.i). In responding to the cosmic and inevitable presence of tragedy in the novel, we have continually to remember his recognition of the contingent, the individual's failure to assess his vision in the light of particular circumstance.

Hardy's bifocal presentation of tragedy in *Jude* is paralleled by a similar presentation of ethics. From one point of view the novel would seem to be fiercely concerned with the cant and futility of conventional attitudes towards marriage and the church, the satire being as unsparing as it is unequivocal:

> ... standing before the aforesaid officiator, the two swore that at every other time of their lives till death took them, they would assuredly believe, feel, and desire precisely as they had believed, felt, and desired during the few preceding weeks. What was as remarkable as the undertaking itself was the fact that nobody seemed at all surprised at what they swore." (I.ix)

> "They are two clergymen of different views, arguing about the eastward position. Good God – the eastward position and all creation groaning." (VI.ii)

The sardonic tone of this is representative of considerable sections of the novel, and yet, considered as a whole, the book is remarkable for a tireless compassion, so that no matter whether we are confronted by egotism or sharp practice, hypocrisy or indifference, it seems quite irrelevant to think of the characters in terms of their being "good" or "bad". It is not that local criticism is assumed into a more inclusive, more generous view; it is the more puzzling situation of a detailed criticism, which remains pertinent and memorable, and yet extrinsic to the over-all view behind it. Hardy's "views", whether philosophical or ethical, seem part of a strange relationship between his "presentation of particulars" – as he calls them in the Preface to *Jude* – and his total outlook, a relationship which can be seen in perspective if we look at the changing emphases in his fiction as it developed.

[iii]

Even in his earliest work we find Hardy acutely sensitive to the extreme delicacy of the line to be drawn between animate and inanimate nature. Romanticism has long made us familiar with the idea of the earth as a sentient being, but Hardy's concern was not so much with nature as with man, trying to apprehend an element in him, which could best be seen by viewing nature as an organic whole. Perhaps the most striking visual example of this occurs at the opening of *The Return of the Native*:

> There the form stood, motionless as the hill beneath. Above the plain rose the hill, above the hill rose the barrow, above the barrow rose the figure. Above the figure was nothing that could be mapped elsewhere than on a celestial globe.
>
> Such a perfect, delicate, and necessary finish did the figure give to the dark pile of hills that it seemed to be the only justification for their outline . . . (I. ii)

"The figure" as a "necessary finish" for "the dark pile the of hills", poised motionless between the plain and the heavens, this is a quintessential "still" of Hardy's universe. Like the hills and the barrow, the figure is seen in terms of its form, a form which both integrates and justifies the scene. The pattern is all. But it is not a pattern into which the figure is assumed, in the manner of Wordsworth's Lucy:

> No motion has she now, no force,
> She neither hears nor sees
> Rolled round in earth's diurnal course,
> With rocks and stones and trees.

Rather, it is the figure, which seems to be the justification for the pattern. As soon as we put it like this, the unusualness of Hardy's position becomes clear. His sense of the uniqueness of the figure seems at total variance with the Wordsworthian view, but his apprehension of this uniqueness as part of a vast continuum of nature is something we think of as characteristically Wordsworthian.

This scene is static, but Hardy habitually sees things in terms of motion, in flux and reflux, fall and rally, and what he sees as positive in its motion is human adaptability to the particular task it is called upon to perform, to read the way things are going. Clym Yeobright and Eustacia are blind to such a reading. For Clym, Egdon is a haven from the modern world, for Eustacia it is a slough of despond. Neither see it as Hardy does, "a vast tract of unenclosed land", a neutral stage for human drama. If Egdon becomes malignant, it is because the human actors have transferred their feeling and attitudes to it. We are led into talking of "transference" because the Heath is much too simple for what Hardy is implying by it, it is too exclusively geographical, too literally external to convey an extra-personal life without oversimplifying it. Egdon converts drama into melodrama.

The remainder of Hardy's career can be seen as the gradual enclosure of that "vast tract of land" within the confines of the personal, yet never forgetting its extra-personal nature. In *The Mayor of Casterbridge*, history comes not to replace but to reinforce geography, and Egdon is found in the town of Casterbridge. This enables the life of the individual to be projected not simply as an isolated figure standing motionless on a hill, but as an inseparable part of a vast continuing process stretching back to the Romans and beyond them to the most primitive tribes, and forward to the changing world of machines and new ways of life. The clash between Henchard and Farfrae is only the latest arena in the inevitable process of change and misunderstanding between the hungry generations. As always in Hardy, the cosmic view must be counterbalanced by the circumstantial and contingent, so that for Henchard and Farfrae this is not the latest arena but their only arena, and from this point of view they emerge not as illustrative of a cosmic process, not even as contemporary representatives, but as deeply considered individuals of this time, of that place. For Hardy, these perspectives have their own autonomy, and it is this calculated disjunction which he assumes when he speaks as critic of society, and then as compassionate spectator of the universe. As the fiction develops, the two perspectives, while still retaining their autonomy are, in dramatic terms, brought closer and closer together. In *The Return of the Native*, the characters are made to cast long shadows across the heath; in *The Mayor of Casterbridge* we have an epic confrontation of Man with Man; in *Tess of the D'Urbervilles*, a single figure dominates the tale, and in her personal history, the cosmic and the circumstantial must be found. From one point of view, she is a dreaming milkmaid, a prey to illusions and misunderstandings; from another she is – like Henchard – caught in the collapse of a traditional rural community, with its time-honoured work, its tacit and unchallenged values; from yet another, she is the

Eternal Victim to Unseen Powers and she offers herself ritually on the sacrificial altar of the Druids. She is the apotheosis of the Wessex novels, in the sense that the motionless figure lying on the altar-tomb at Stonehenge is directly related to the motionless figure of Eustacia Vye standing on Rainbarrow Hill. The individual may give "finish" to the scene, but it is the scene which enables us to understand the individual. "Now I am at home", Tess remarks, and in an episode reminiscent of tragic ballet, the novel finds its climax, scene fading into person, and person into scene. *Tess* is also the apotheosis of the Wessex novels in that Hardy writes for the last time with a backward glance, and if the emotion is not recollected in tranquillity, it is recollected in intensity. As the black flag extends itself upon the breeze, it signifies the end not merely of Tess but of the long saga of Wessex novels:

> "Justice" was done and the President of the Immortals, in Aeschylean phrase, had ended his sport with Tess. And d'Urberville knights and dames slept in their tombs unknowing. The two speechless gazers bent themselves down to the earth, as in prayer, and remained thus a long time, absolutely motionless; the flag continued to wave silently.

But the novel does not end here, there is a final sentence to come:

> As soon as they had the strength they arose, joined hands again, and went on.

Here, in the last moment of the novel, we have Hardy refusing to end on a note of passive acceptance, but seeing, as always, that flux must precipitate reflux, the fall must initiate a rally, if the truth is to be told.

[iv]

Angel and 'Liza-Lu may "go on", but whether their creator could follow was another matter. With *Tess*, Hardy exhausted his exploration of Wessex, and the novel that follows stands apart from the rest of his work. That this has been inadequately recognized is due partly to the "succès de scandale" it shared with *Tess*, thus bracketing it with that novel, and partly to the fact that, being Hardy's last novel, it has been considered as marking the end of a line, rather than a significant alteration in direction. Where recollection was the imaginative mainspring of the Wessex novels, so that their action, however urgently it engaged us, seemed a part of all our yesterdays, Hardy turns in *Jude* to the present and the future. This shift in time affects not only the mood of the novel, but its themes and structure. Before developing this central consideration, it is a useful preliminary to see how different this novel is, even in its setting, from the novels that preceded it.

Egdon Heath is seen now, not in relation to the heavens and the surrounding valleys, but as a landscape framed by a railway carriage window. It is the railway, not tracks and roads, which divides this map of Wessex, and meeting places tend to be in "the fireless waiting rooms" of rural stations. It is the railway that connects the bleak open downs with Christminster, and it is that town, which provides the essential world of *Jude*:

> High against the black sky the flash of a lamp would show crocketed pinnacles and indented battlements. Down obscure valleys, apparently never trodden by the foot of man and whose very existence seemed to be forgotten, there would jut into the path, porticoes, oriels, doorways of enriched and florid middle-age design, their extinct air being accentuated by the rottenness of the stones. (II. i)

Jude, a stonemason, finds his living in the crumbling walls of the past. But, in Christminster, walls defeat rather than sustain him, "Only a wall divided him from those young contemporaries of his with whom he shared a common life . . . Only a wall – but what a wall!"(II.ii). (Poor inns and lodgings, this is the accommodation the novel habitually provides; everything is temporary and provisional, and the book echoes to farewells.)"Jude's face became so full of complicated glooms that hers was agitated in sympathy as she bade him adieu through the carriage window. And then the train moved on, and waving her pretty hand to him she vanished away."(III.v). The wall that divides, the claustrophobia of the railway compartments, these motifs are repeated in the houses, where the characters are often driven to separate rooms. Sue hides in a cupboard under the stairs with the spiders rather than sleep with her husband; Jude has his striking vision of Christminster from the narrow octagonal lantern in the Sheldonian; while their furniture is being taken away, Jude and Sue lock themselves in an empty room. It is not difficult to see that this sustained emphasis on "the cabin'd, cribb'd, confin'd" succeeds in creating the desolate and provisional room as the embodiment of loneliness, the self-created prison out of which the individual glances desperately before "vanishing away". Where the earlier novels had continually stressed the community of being, *Jude* stresses a wounding isolation, an exacerbated consciousness of self.

When we shift our consideration away from these atmospheric motifs, towards the general plan of the novel, we can see how largely it is preoccupied with this awareness and definition of self. The characteristic scene of the Wessex novels is that of the human figure seen in silhouette. Where there is conflict, it is conflict with a way of life, a social attitude, a cast of mind; in *Jude* the conflict is interiorized, one temperament with another, so that place becomes a matter of little significance, the essential landscape is of heart and nerves.

"How ugly it is here", Jude's reflection as a boy on the country that surrounds him, is typical of the way in which landscape is no longer a sentient being, but something to travel across and forget. Jude's boyhood is spent in a village where all community life is extinct, felled trees lie strewn across the green, a bright new Gothic church overlooks a churchyard full of cast iron crosses warranted to last five years. Obscure, unwanted, Jude longs increasingly to be delivered from this dead world to Christminster, the realm of his dream of learning, the new Jerusalem. He encounters only deception, first from a vagrant quack, who promises him books which never come, and then from Arabella. "Married is married", "pigs must be killed", Arabella's prescriptions are as final as they are lethal, and the section closes with Jude finding, in the wreckage of his marriage, his own wedding present being sold back to him by the auctioneer, "the frame is a useful one, if you take out the likeness. You shall have it for a shilling." Rejected by the village, by his wife, Jude's isolation in a world of indifference seems complete: he resolves to begin again and go to his new Jerusalem.

"I fancy we have had enough of Jerusalem . . . There was nothing first rate about the place or people, after all – as there was about Athens, Rome, Alexandria, and other old cities." (II.v). Sue's rejections gradually become for Jude part of the heady experience of living in Christminster. For him, it seems to promise everything that Marygreen lacked, "a unique centre of thought and religion – the intellectual and spiritual granary of this country".(II.vi). But, for Sue, the granary is a labyrinth of illusion and superstition, which she herself has escaped. With increasing fervour he moves out of his magic maze to follow her. Under her Voltairean spell, his Christminster ambitions collapse, she becomes the centre of his existence "nearer to him than any other woman he had ever met, he could scarcely believe, that time, creed, or absence would ever divide him from her". (III.iv).

It is a division, however, which Sue feels it imperative to maintain, and to secure it, she marries Phillotson. "But I am not really Mrs. Richard Phillotson, but a woman tossed about, all alone, with aberrant passions and unaccountable antipathies." (IV.i). If Jude was caught in a trap of Arabella's devising, Sue is caught in one of her own. Like the rabbit caught in the gin, she struggles hopelessly with her own nature and Phillotson, with magnanimity, sets her free. "For though as a fellow creature she sympathises with, and pities me, and even weeps for me, as a husband she cannot endure me . . . she loathes me, and my only manly, and dignified, and merciful course is to complete what I have begun."(IV.vi). And so, with the wreckages of their respective marriages behind them, Sue and Jude try to implement "their supreme desire to be together – to share each other's emotions, and fancies, and dreams". But only with the return of Arabella – their sex.

[v]

If we look back at the narrative from this point, we see how dominantly it is concerned with an internal quest for the reality of the self. As the narrative develops, it mines deeper into the meaning of this. Education, which begins as a matter of being "crazy for books", leads into trying to understand the nature of the human condition; sex, which begins as the casual seduction of a barmaid, is seen to be an integral part of this understanding. And these two forces – the conscious effort to become aware of our condition and the unconscious drives in its expression – dominate the last phase of the novel. Increasingly, it is Sue who extends its meaning. Jealousy of Arabella – "love has its own dark morality when rivalry enters" – prompts her to give herself to Jude. But it is a bond which she refuses to acknowledge publicly, knowing instinctively that if she did so, she would be committed to the reality of marriage. So the strange life of Jude and Sue continues, excluding the world outside, parrying and neutralizing the claims of the world within. Agricultural life, so dominant in the Wessex novels, appears only once, and that in the form of "a show", a revelatory moment in the interior life:

> "Happy?" he murmured.
> She nodded.
> "Why? Because you have come to the great Wessex Agricultural Show – or because *we* have come?"
> "You are always trying to make me confess to all sorts of absurdities. Because I am improving my mind, of course, by seeing all these steam-ploughs and threshing-machines and chaff-cutters, and cows and pigs and sheep." (V. iv)

Wessex life as "an improvement for the mind" is far from the themes of the earlier fiction, but to find it expressed in so equivocal a manner shows the great difference in tone. The happiness that Sue and Jude enjoy at the fair is fleeting. Public hostility grows against their manner of life and Jude is dismissed from his employment as an ecclesiastical stonemason. For the second time, he has to face the break-up of his home and the selling of his furniture. "You must fall back", Sue remarks sardonically, "upon railway stations, bridges, theatres, music halls, hotels – everything that has no connection with conduct". It is too great an exile from life, and Jude, intimating his death, returns to Christminster "to receive the reflection of the sunshine from its wasting walls".

Rain and thunder greet them on their return and in the crowded city, assembled for the Remembrance Day ceremony, they cannot find rooms. It appears a culminating rejection and Father Time becomes the terrible agent of the doom Sue feared

ominous

he is the only shadow"

would overtake them. "We must conform ... There is no choice", the destruction of the children comes as an unequivocal judgement to Sue, and she tries to expiate what she feels to be her crimes by returning to Phillotson as his wife. The letter must be seen to live, even if the spirit, which sustains it, is dead. "All wrong, all wrong", Jude said huskily. "It will be a fanatic prostitution – God forgive me, yes – that's what it will be." Arabella, for a long while an interested spectator of this conflict, now seizes her opportunity and dupes Jude into a re-marriage. As Jude's internal world darkens and fades, the external world, as if to emphasize its remoteness from him, brightens, and the sound of Christminster "en fête" punctuates his last hours. Sue, self-imprisoned at the schoolhouse with Phillotson, Jude dying in a dismal lodging in Christminster – both alone with themselves – and outside a world of gaiety and sunshine and flowers, the private and public world are now irretrievably apart. As a boy, Jude had felt that "all around you there seemed to be something glaring, garish, rattling and the noises and glares hit upon the little cell called your life, and shook it, and warped it".(I.ii). He has now become deaf to those noises, completely enclosed within his own cell, "all was still within", as "through the partly opened window the joyous throb of a waltz entered from the ball-room at Cardinal". (VI.xi).

The ostentatious counterpoint of these dramatic closing scenes is a characteristic feature of the book, and one about which Hardy himself was very conscious:

> Of course the book is all contrasts ... Sue and her heathen gods set against Jude's reading the Greek testament; Christminster academical, Christminster in the slums; Jude the saint, Jude the sinner; Sue the pagan, Sue the saint; marriage, no marriage; etc., etc.[6]

The significance of this heavily contrasted structure has been understood as a strategy in polemic, as if we were being invited to assess the validity of one view against another, resolving in the case of *Jude* into a question as to how far it can be considered a Christian or an anti-Christian work. Such considerations are beside the mark, in so far as the contrapuntal structure of the novel is to make us aware of process, not conclusion, of withdrawal rather than engagement. The detachment is not sardonic but compassionate, and, if anything is determined here, it is to offer a more inclusive view. But, for Hardy, inclusiveness of view demands attention both to the near and the far, it has to be a human view, and not man masquerading as the President of the Immortals. In the Wessex novels, the near and the far are framed within their setting in the past; in *Jude* the setting is the present and, accordingly, new bearings are taken. With the near, we are involved in satires of circumstance, with the world of the social critic, looking sceptically at education, at marriage, at religion – at the way we live now. With the far, we see that "the social moulds civilisation fits us into, have no more relation to our actual shapes than the conventional shapes of the constellations have to the real star patterns". "The social moulds", and "the actual shapes". Hardy sees that to stress one at the cost of the other is to present a half-truth. Consequently, we find in *Jude* Hardy seeking to convey this meaning through a multiple technique of character which can lay emphasis on the present and contingent and then on what, in *The Woodlanders*, he calls, "the great web of human doings weaving in both hemispheres from the White Sea to Cape Horn."

[vi]

In a novel deeply involved with the processes of time, it is not surprising to find the abstraction embodied directly in Father Time. If *Jude* has received widely varying critical estimates, there is certainly a consensus of opinion that the child is not a success, that he is a fugitive from another art, Lady Macduff's son unnervingly encountered on "The Great Western". What is more important, however, is to recognize Hardy's purpose here, a purpose as remote from presenting a child in naturalistic terms as Shakespeare's.

In a diary entry on London, Hardy observed that the city "appears not to see itself. Each individual is conscious of *himself*, but nobody conscious of themselves collectively . . . There is no consciousness of where anything comes from or goes to – only that it is present."[7] It is Father Time's role in *Jude* to present that collective consciousness. In the railway carriage on his way to meet Sue and Jude:

he seemed to be doubly awake, like an enslaved and dwarfed divinity, sitting passive and regarding his companions as if he saw their whole rounded lives rather than their immediate figures. (V. iii)

His choric role in the general drama is recognized by Sue and Jude:

The boy's face expressed the whole tale of their situation. On that little shape had converged all the inauspiciousness and shadow which had darkened the first union of Jude, and all the accidents, mistakes, fears, errors of the last. He was their nodal point, their focus, their expression in a single term. (VI. ii)

The presentation of Father Time is illustrative of Hardy's difficulty of presenting in a novel stripped of the immense suggestiveness of the Wessex landscape that extra-temporal dimension to the human drama so central to his imagination. In "Midnight on The Great Western", Hardy shows how much more comfortably the boy is accommodated within a poem:

> What past can be yours, O journeying boy,
> Towards a world unknown,
> Who calmly, as if incurious quite
> On all at stake, can undertake
> This plunge alone.[8]

The poem derives its strength from its omissions; we are ignorant of the precise journey, what is at stake and why "his plunge" is "alone"; the intensity of the lyric lies in questions which have no answer. But in the novel the boy has to retain his mythic poignancy and, at the same time, be fitted into the pattern of the narrative. They are mutually destructive, one element seeking to retain the mystery of "the term", the other "explaining" it away. But Father Time's role is central to Hardy's conception of tragedy, so that the radical awkwardness is eloquent testimony that the boundaries of Wessex coincided for Hardy with the boundaries of fiction. To be at home in a larger world he needed the idiom of poetry.

Sue Bridehead thinks of herself as being best expressed in the language of poets, but she is wholly a creation of The Novel. It is she who feels Father Time's presence most acutely, and she feels it because within her there is a remorseless conflict between her insatiable desire to transcend time, to belong to an ethereal order of beings and her rootedness within the idiosyncrasies of her own temperament and the attitudes of her own time. In her, Hardy seeks to embody what he feels to be the complementary truth to Father Time. Where he is a reminder of the before and after, she is of the present; he representing the collective consciousness, she so highly personalized that she cannot form a fully human relationship. Faced with Father Time's question about why she is going to have another child, she replies, "I can't explain". Ostensibly availing herself of Victorian reticence, she speaks truer than she knows. She can never "explain" and in this resides much of the brilliance of her characterization. Professor Heilman in a perceptive delineation of her character observes how deeply paradoxical a figure she is, appearing "as the special outsider on the one hand and as quite conventional on the other",[9] and he goes on to note how Hardy presents her continually in terms of "perverseness", "riddle", "conundrum", "unreasonable . . . capricious", "puzzling and unpredictable", "that mystery, her heart". Sensitive to suffering, yet often markedly indifferent to its effects, a rationalist with something approaching awe towards conventional sanctions, Sue emerges as a deeply considered individual, the product of a precise moment in our cultural history. A devoted follower of Mill, she is a study in depth of "the new woman", "the slight pale bachelor girl" as Hardy writes in his Preface, who begins to inhabit the fiction and drama of the closing decades of the nineteenth century, but who does not survive the First World War. Professor Heilman feels that the brilliance of her delineation must be ensured by her tragic status, but here, it seems to me, his analysis falters. He sees Hardy's sense of tragedy in too orthodox terms. Hence, he finds himself in an argument about Sue's "representativeness". For Hardy, Sue in her return to Phillotson was more ill than tragic, precisely because, in the pattern of the novel, she was the embodiment of the tragedy of the contingent, a victim of time and place. Jude's role after the death of his children is to become, as far as Sue is concerned, a baffled commentator on her behaviour, as she withdraws into a private world of her own terrible devising. In the last phase of the novel, Sue is presented as a tragic "case" and the case is part of the larger tragedy of the novel. Sue's tragedy can only be understood properly if it is taken in conjunction with the presence of Father Time, and with its effect on Jude. By means of a triple presentation of character – choric with Father Time, personal to the point of idio- syncrasy with Sue, representative with Jude – Hardy tries to catch, kaleidoscopically, that ever-shifting emphasis between the cosmic and the individual, which lies at the centre of his thought.

[vii]

It is Jude who gives the book its title, and it is to him that we must turn, finally, to complete its meaning. If he is described as a representative character, this should not be taken to imply a morality figure, a failed Everyman. Rather, it is because in Jude the rival but complementary truths about human existence suggested by Father Time and Sue converge. The moment of crisis comes for him when Time destroys his children, but to take its significance, we have to go back to earlier stages of the narrative.

The novel would seem to have emerged from a note, which appears in Hardy's diary in April 1888: "a short story of a young man – 'who could not go to Oxford' – His struggles and ultimate failure. Suicide . . .".[10] When he began to write, however, the novel changed its character and, in April 1894, Hardy wrote to *Harper's* offering to withdraw it from publication, regretting that "it was not the story he originally had in mind . . . but the characters had taken things into their own hands and were doing better work than he had anticipated".[11] The "better work" could be said to consist of exploring the implication of his formal theme. As Lawrence puts it, what Jude wanted from study was "not a store of learning, nor the vanity of education, a sort of superiority of educational wealth . . . he wanted . . . to find conscious expression for that which he held in his blood".[12] The quest to find expression is consistently presented by Hardy in a double-edged way. "He was a species of Dick Whittington, whose spirit was touched to finer issues than a mere material gain"(II.i) – "finer issues" certainly, but he belongs to the lineage of childhood-heroes, confident in their hopes, but bought of inexperience. He learns, but he becomes "a tragic Don

Quixote" (IV.i), noble in his ambitions, sadly naïve in their consequences. Above all, he is "obscure". In one sense, his obscurity is social. He is poor, an outsider, barred from the world of education and its accompanying privileges. But, though this theme may have precipitated the novel, it does not sustain it and, after the early sections of the novel, virtually disappears. Jude is "obscure" to himself and his development is to find his "actual shape" within "the social mould". It is at this level that his education takes place, conducted not with the aid of "the Fathers . . . Bede and ecclesiastic history . . . a smattering of Hebrew", but at the hands of Arabella and Sue.

Although they present an archetypal contract, Arabella and Sue share a common indifference to Jude's struggle for a formal education. Though their attitudes differ – for Arabella it is a distracting pastime, for Sue a misguided waste of spirit – they both see in Jude's "craze for books", a rival allegiance. And both demand, in their various ways, a total attention.

Father Time can be accommodated by neither woman. Arabella lives exclusively for the present. She seeds Jude, she knows at once that she must have him. "I want him to have me. I must have him. I can't do without him." Her relationship with him is instinctual and, as Lawrence says "she only wished to be aware of herself in contact with him".[13] It is a self, which she can find only in the moment and it is this which prompts her ruthless opportunism. Sue, on the other hand, sees in Jude a way of escaping the self, of transcending time. When Arabella is described in terms of primal energy and animal passion, Sue is "ethereal", "aerial", "a phantasmal, bodiless creature", and when Jude embraces her, his arms seem to pass through her. For Arabella, Jude is a sexual conquest, "a shorn Samson"; for Sue a spiritual instrument, "your freedom from everything that's gross has elevated me". Both women "must have" Jude, one to exclude the past and the future, the other to secure an "elevation" into a timeless world of spirit. It is the terrible action of Time, however, the natural son of Arabella and Jude, that destroys Sue, so that she replaces an isolated and isolating world of hope and joy, with a similar world of fear and self-destruction.

It is precisely through this action of his son, however, that Jude obtains an apprehension of time, to which Arabella and

Sue are blind. His desire to live reasserts itself over the death of his children. But it is a desire without a context. To return to Arabella is a death of the spirit, it is only his drunken body she can have. Sue has denied the body, and she covers her ears and kneels as Jude passes out of her life for the last time. Looking back to the death of his children, Jude sees that "Sue and himself had mentally travelled in opposite directions since the tragedy: events which had enlarged his own view of life, laws, customs and dogmas, had not operated in the same manner on Sue". He has accepted his paternity of Time as part of the cosmic process, and the terrible action that has followed, but his view of life has been "enlarged"; this is not the end of action, the paralysis of individual will. Sue, who was so close to him that "they seemed to be one person split in two" he sees as "a sort of fay or sprite – not a woman". For Jude, it is "man and senseless circumstance" that lie behind their tragedy, a tragedy that has taken place at Aldbrickham and Elsewhere. If Jude's end is uncompromisingly tragic, this is not because Sue lies in Phillotson's bed, in the way that Tess lies in Stonehenge with "the power of the ancient wrath above us", but because she has defiled and destroyed herself – and it is she who drives him back alone to the imprisoning room in Christminster. In a particular part of that town, where "boughs and coughs and consumption lurked", a series of seemings of great complexity is finally brought to its tragic end.

"A series of seemings" – that phrase can perhaps now be seen not as an artistic prescription but as central to Hardy's thought. If *Jude the Obscure* has often made the impression of a miscellany of subjects held together only by the tragic intensity of its mood, this is not the result of a novelist unable to find his theme, but rather from the recognition of the multiple ways in which that theme can be regarded. The ways were present in Hardy's fiction from the beginning, and Wessex, a region at once precise and local, timeless and universal, enabled the novelist to communicate his shifting truths. With that region removed from *Jude*, however, Hardy finds his extra-temporal dimension in the choric figure of Father Time, and his fidelity to the particular in "the puzzling and unpredictable" Sue Bridehead. Though "Wessex" was no longer adequate to what Hardy wanted to say, the polarization of his vision around

Father Time and Sue was taking his art in directions he felt neither inclined nor capable of travelling. It was to be left to the next generation of novelists to brood metaphysically on Father Time and explore the psychological depths of Sue. The outcome was to be a shift in the art of fiction, and with it a new totality of view. If Hardy stopped writing in the shadows of that fiction, it was not simply that its art was not his, but because his art was designed to resist such a totality, whether it was the inclusiveness of hope or the inclusiveness of despair. His "totalities" lay in the acceptance of disjunctions, and the epitaph he imagines for himself is an affirmation not of the connections of pattern but of "the series of seemings", which had haunted his fiction from its beginning:

> When the Present has latched its postern behind my tremulous stay,
> And the May month flaps its glad green leaves like wings,
> Delicate-filmed as new-spun silk, will the neighbours say,
> "He was a man who used to notice such things"?[14]

NOTES

1 *Aspects of The Novel*, London, 1949 (Pocket Edition), p. 90.

2 A. J. Guerard, *Thomas Hardy* (New Directions, 1962), p. 32.

3 *The Victorian Sage* (London, 1953), p. 245.

4 *Life of Thomas Hardy* (London, 1962), p. 402.

5 *Life*, p. 311.

6 *Life*, p. 42.

7 *Life*, pp. 206-7.

8 "Midnight on The Great Western", *Moments of Vision* (London, 1962).

9 "Hardy's Sue Bridehead", *Nineteenth Century Fiction*, Vol. 20 (1966), pp. 307-23.

10 *Life*, pp. 207-8.

11 Quoted in "The Genesis of *Jude the Obscure*", John Paterson, *Studies in Philology*, vol. 57 (1960), pp. 87-98.

12 D. H. Lawrence, "A Study of Thomas Hardy", *Phoenix* (London, 1961, pp. 499-500.

13 *Phoenix*, p. 500.

14 "Afterwards", *Moments of Vision*.

PETER URE

George Moore
as Historian of Consciences

It was in 1900, sitting in Dublin under his celebrated apple-trees, that George Moore was overcome by a feeling of his own goodness. "An extraordinarily clear and inflexible moral sense rose up and confronted me", he wrote in *Salve*, ". . . I had never been able to do anything that I thought wrong, and my conscience had inspired my books". The passage comes immediately after one which advocates polygamy; it is plain that Moore, lodged in the catholic puritan city, is at his exercise again. Conscience, he seems to be saying, is a process by which the individual's "ideas" or "thought" will shape his deeds; if they fail to, "if our deeds go down one set of lines and our ideas go down another", a life is wasted. For a novelist, this implies the possibility of tragedy or comedy according to which kind of story he chooses. In either case, a study in conscience is a study in the relation between "ideas" and deeds. Moore claims to detect this interest as early as his first novel, *A Modern Lover* (1883). Most of us would probably think of this book, better known in its revised version *Lewis Seymour and Some Women* (1917), as a study in consciencelessness and an early example of the room at the top syndrome; but it is comedy because there is no split in Lewis between what he does and his "ideas" for himself. Plainly, "ideas" in this context is as tricky a word as "conscience", for it does not mean simply notions or opinions but seems to include ambition, appetite, amour-propre, and

257

above all perhaps what Nature whispers to polygamous man.

The passage in *Salve* continues the tale of Moore's early novels:

> The Mummer's Wife declines, for she is without sufficient personal conscience to detach herself from the conventions in which she had been brought up. Alice Barton in *Muslin* is a preparatory study, a prevision of *Esther Waters*; both represent the personal conscience striving against the communal, and, feeling that I had learnt to know myself at last, I rose from the seat, and looked round, thinking that in Æ as in myself thought and action are at one. Alike, I said, in essentials, though to the casual observer regions apart . . . But everybody in Dublin thinks that he is like Æ as everybody in the world thinks he is like Hamlet.[1]

Æ and Hamlet have this in common: they stand, like E. M. Forster's singular Greek gentleman, at an angle to their universes, Mr Balfour's Ireland and Claudius's Denmark. Moore is choosing his ground. He is reminding us that while we may think of Hamlet as primarily a fine conscience whose ideas are not rightly related to his deeds, he is also – and is it secondarily? – one whose conscience strives against the rotten state. That latter theme is at least as important in Moore as it is unimportant in Henry James. He is on his mettle as Zola's ricochet in England; a primary impulse may have been the wish to infuriate the members of his own class by questioning their privileges and attitudes, but beneath the aesthetic foolery there is anger about Ireland and the poor. Nailing Claudius's guilt interests Moore as much in those three early novels as does imparting a fine grain to the characterization of their heroines. My purpose is chiefly to compare the three protagonists in the light of what Moore wrote in *Salve* about them; but no one is likely to find the books of great interest who imagines that sympathy for the victims of social injustice is separable from hatred for those who profit by it.

Any assessment is complicated by the existence of more than one version of each of the three works. It is characteristic of the whole Moorini mix-up that when Moore wrote in 1911 the passage just quoted from a late reprint of *Salve* there was no such book in existence as *Muslin*, which was first published in 1915. There was only *A Drama in Muslin* (1886), a work whose

enormous difference from its descendant requires exploration.
But the primary task is to consider how the novels relate to
one another in the light of facts which do seem clear: that *A
Mummer's Wife* (1884, radically revised in 1918) and *A Drama
in Muslin* are now in a much worse state than the half-forgotten
one to which Moore consigned *A Modern Lover* in *Salve*. They
are unlikely to have been read by anybody, except dedicated
specialists in Moore, under the age of forty; whereas *Esther
Waters* (1894, and never revised so radically as the other two)[2]
is still a famous book widely read in the 1960s, if we may judge
by the place which it holds in various popular series.[3] The
contrast between its fortunes and those of its two predecessors
is a steep one. That putative reader sinking into the infirmity
of age who has considered all three may be surprised and
puzzled by it. It is true that the period covered by them is a
long one, a decade during which Moore's artistic fortunes
oscillated a good deal – he could little bear in later years to
speak of the other novels which he wrote during it, nor shall we.
It is true also that the assessment of these books can be and
has been satisfactorily managed in terms of a movement from
Zola to Balzac by way of Gautier and Huysmans.[4] Such evolu-
tions are radical; yet the conviction may remain that a comparative study of the novels of the kind that the author himself
sketched beneath the apple-tree in Ely Place will show that they
share a deep-lying similarity of construction and design, and
that there is something odd about the way in which the third
has prospered at the expense of the other two.

The traveller who is determined to reach Moore Hall will
eventually, after wandering far from the Ballinrobe road, come
upon the reed-choked lake and the steep foursquare shell of
the Georgian mansion, its defiant chimneystacks rising up into
the desolate beauty of the Mayo plain. More evocative than
Lissadell even, the ruin would be a perfect setting for the
performance of Yeats's greatest ghost-play, but *A Mummer's
Wife* is a strange, hot, and alien book to have been composed in
so silent a place. The contrast suggests Moore's perverse or
virtuoso determination to turn himself into a European (that is
to say, a Zolaesque) novelist by fleeing as far as possible from
the natural source of his art. Yet the novel itself is not weak
from flight but vigorous with ambition. It is a study in the

corruption of a conscience inherited from the community and the ruin of the individual who embodies it. Kate Ede, married to a pathetic, shop-bound husband crippled by asthma, runs in association with her husband and his mother a dressmaker's business in Hanley in the Potteries. A liaison with her lodger, Dick Lennox, the manager of a company of actors touring the industrial North, is followed by an elopement. Kate, who is discovered to possess a good singing-voice, joins the company and becomes one of its stars. As its fortunes fail in strike-bound towns, her Bovaryesque nature (her soul rises to her lips at a sentimental word and her eyes become "liquid with love") grows sour with jealousy. The strain of a life that is no longer rooted in one narrow place is hard for her to endure; almost insensibly she begins the slide into alcoholism. The real disaster is the loss of her baby, who dies of cold in her cradle because Kate is in a brandy daze. Her new husband Lennox is, after his fashion, loyal and kind, but his habits, social and sexual, even his table-manners, are not those of Hanley, and he cannot check her insane bouts of jealous violence, which are compounded by drink and unemployability. The last third of the novel is set in London where "Sentimental Kate", as the prostitutes call her, finally dies of drink and exhaustion.

The apparent contradiction in this story is: how could anyone on whom Bohemianism (as it is frequently called, in the manner of the times) has such a destructive effect have brought herself to leave the narrow path of provincial virtue? As becomes a realist, Moore is volubly anxious to tag every effect with its cause (an anxiety which notably diminishes in the revised version), and the problem gives him a great deal of difficulty. In scene after scene in the first half of the novel we are offered a heroine whose behaviour does not make sense to herself (p. 145),[5] who is disgusted by the animality of the theatrical life and yet enthralled by its sensual melodies (p. 153), who longs to escape from Hanley as a "horrible place" and yet can't help regarding it as home (pp. 158-9), who hates the present and fears the future (pp. 162ff.). Moore has to create a character who is to break free from seven years of conditioning (her marriage to Ralph Ede and the dreary mother-in-law whose own conscience enacts itself in her inhibitory cry of "I'm a Christian woman") and yet to prove unable to adapt herself to her new life precisely because that conditioning has been so thorough. Moore's solution seems to be to stress not so much the passion for Dick Lennox as the sentimentality which earns Kate her sobriquet from the whores: her tendency to abandon herself to slack-bodied and indiscriminate reverie (pp. 29ff., 59ff.) even, or especially, in church (pp. 109ff.). There is a long passage at the beginning of chapter VIII in the unrevised version – it was later much reduced – which describes her return to the sentimental literature of her girlhood before she married Ralph Ede. In the face of the new horizon of experience opening before her in her liaison with the actor, Kate's impulse is to *go back*, and this is in character. She drifts, as it were, through the narrow barriers of her religion and conditioning "without internal struggle or analysis of mind" (p. 111) on a stream of sentiment, reverie, and vague longing for a sweeter life; but when she has dropped below stream from them, those barriers cast a dreadful shadow over all the rest of her journey, which does not, however, change its essential character of self-indulgent drifting.

In the second half of the book Kate at first blooms, for her dream had its element of actuality; but the languorous process by which she has arrived in this new world has its fatal counterpart in her failure to see the life which she now lives as wholly real. There are idyllic breakfasts (pp. 199ff.) and hazy evenings (pp. 229ff.) and in the end a disastrously sentimental and dreamy approach to looking after the baby (pp. 319ff.). Kate, therefore, does not suffer from "pangs of conscience" in the ordinary sense – "nothing beyond the mechanical conviction that she was a very wicked woman and deserved to be punished" (p. 199). There are other mechanical convictions which count for even less: the actors live by their wits, cheating landladies and defrauding railway companies when they get the chance, and Kate soon ceases to be shocked by this. But if nearly all the "conventions of her upbringing" drop from her, there is one cluster of inhibitions, that concerned with sexual behaviour, which remains. In choosing it, Moore showed some insight into the pathology of conscience. Kate's inappropriate strait-lacedness, her absurd (in the context) fastidiousness about the "moral [i.e., the sexual] question" is the tell-tale sign:

Anecdotes of clever swindles no longer wounded her feelings . . .

The middle-class woman, in a word, had disappeared, and the Bohemian taken her place; and had it not been for the anger with which she repulsed all levity of conversation, and the cold way she frowned upon the spicy little stories, the delight of theatrical supper-tables, the closest scrutiny might have failed to find a clue wherewith to trace her back to her origin. But regarding the moral question she seemed to grow daily more severe, and many were the disputes Kate and Dick had on the subject. For the smallest thing said in her presence she would challenge him with not respecting her. (pp. 243-4)[6]

The rest of *A Mummer's Wife* is essentially a study of how this element of her conscience, having bitten too deep, destroys its possessor by assuming the diseased form of jealousy. Kate's nervousness about "impropriety" perverts into psychotic anxiety about Dick's inevitable (because professional) associa-tion with other women: from jealousy to offended amour-propre, rage, brandy for calm and comfort and dreaming, the death of the baby, the wish to punish herself for that (p. 328) – the sequence is clear and plausible enough. In other ways, Kate's failure is of course a failure to adapt herself to the way she lives now: the collapse of the touring company worries her as it might worry any middle-class, unbohemian wife (p. 290), but it is hardly such worries that are going to destroy her.

This record of the falling to pieces in an alien atmosphere of a piece of "cheap Tottenham Court Road furniture", as Moore puts it with the studied cruelty of an aesthete or of a practitioner of the scientific novel, has at its heart, therefore, a reversal of the conventional patterns. Consciences such as Kate's neither humanize nor act as the agents for some divine strategy of punishment or reformation. The fault for which Kate suffers is, if anything, the wish to be punished. If she disapproves of her-self it is not because of rectitude but because of habit – a "mechanical conviction" – and the obverse of this is her drifting and dreaming and drinking. These are aspects of a personality which is habituated to using its dreams to cheat its inhibitions and vice-versa; if this process is identified we can glimpse the coherence that informs the apparent contradictions of her story.

There is something comically gallant in the spectacle of Moore returning to his pastoral and lacustrine solitudes in order to compose a book so foreign in material, if not in final moral insight, to the manners of County Mayo. But his next novel, *A Drama in Muslin*, came straight out of the drawing-room and demesne at Moore Hall. Whatever else it is, this book, as A. N. Jeffares has sufficiently indicated,[7] is one of the prime documents of the last phases of Anglo-Irishry, belonging to the group of which *The Real Charlotte*, some of Yeats's tragic poems, or Lennox Robinson's *The Big House* are worthy members. In his anxiety to avoid "telling", and to reduce the elements of hysteria, melodrama, and sexuality, Moore revised *A Drama in Muslin* much more destructively than even *A Mummer's Wife*, totally re-making it in the image of his 1915 self.[8] The effect is to insulate nerves which in the earlier version, as in its companion-piece *Parnell and his Island* (1887), were nakedly and offensively exposed. The articulations of *Muslin* flow so smoothly as to produce an effect of bonelessness. Its predecessor, without being at all inefficiently constructed, has raw patches on its surface which remind us of Moore's need to torment a community that was still living and blundering on. Another major result of his excisions is almost to demote Alice Barton from being the central awareness to merely acting as another participant, if the most important, in its social kaleidoscope.

A Drama in Muslin dramatizes the fortunes of a group of Galway Ascendancy families during two Dublin Castle seasons. The family central to the pattern is that of the Bartons of Brookfield, who are Catholics: two daughters, Alice the intellectual and Olive the prettier of the two, a dominant mother whose whole life is concentrated on disposing properly of her girls in the Dublin marriage-market, and a dilettante father who spends his idle, landlordly time in painting large and foolish historical pictures. Their neighbours are the Cullens: Lord Dungory, a perpetual guest at Brookfield, takes refuge there in the ambiguous ministrations of Mrs. Barton from the bullying of his two fanatical Protestant daughters. His third daughter, the crippled Cecilia, is Alice Barton's passionately attached friend. Then there are the Scullys, who are despised because their forebears kept a grocer's shop in Gort. The son, Fred, is a horse-riding lout of the kind described in *Parnell and his Island*, while the daughter, Violet, is Olive Barton's chief competitor in the marriage-stakes, especially for the person and fortune of the "little Marquis", Lord Kilcarney. Olive romps affectionately with another "hard-riding country gentleman", Captain Edward Hibbert; but he has no money, is compromised with a mistress, and is soon ordered out of the house by Mrs. Barton. After five months in a countryside shaken by the Land League campaign, these groups and one or two others go up to Dublin for the season. Here Alice Barton encounters an English intellectual or "literary shopboy", John Harding, who encourages her attempts to write. She learns to know her own mind better and to detach herself from an Ireland that continually enforces a painful contrast between the peasant's cabin and the big house, Dublin Castle and the Dublin slums. Her emancipation is signalized especially in the episode towards the end of the novel when she rescues her old schoolfellow May Gould from despair after she has become pregnant by Fred Scully and secretly helps her through her confinement with money which she has earned from writing stories for magazines. In her own sister she has an example of the harm wrought by the communal conscience and its institutions (such as the marriage-market): for Olive, after losing Lord Kilcarney to Violet Scully despite Mrs Barton's frantic campaigns on her daughter's behalf, tries to elope with Captain Hibbert, is stopped by his mistress, and, after a serious illness, ends the book still on the market. Alice herself, in the face of her mother's bitter enmity, marries the unpretentious English doctor who attends Olive; as they leave Ireland for Kensington their last sight of the country is of an eviction accompanied by all the traditional stigmata of brutality (a scene greatly modified in *Muslin*).

Although it is a hundred pages shorter than *A Mummer's Wife*, this novel is a work of greater and more numerous dimensions. In that one of its aspects which is most imperilled by the revision, it deals with the emotional and intellectual growth of Alice, that is to say, with the formation of her personal conscience. This puts it in the same category as other works concerned with a young girl's education, such as *The Tempest*, *Mrs. Warren's Profession*, *Saint Joan*, or *Roots*. This conscience is formed chiefly by what it sees, although for the ideas to come to life in confident action it requires the timely catalyst John Harding, who is the one educator who comes from outside to help. Moore does not discipline his own tongue and manages point of view but laxly; yet what Alice sees is more or less the entire contents of the novel, which thus contribute to Alice's slowly accumulating resistance to the values of her society. When we look back from the vantage-point of the final chapters we can see that Alice's total repudiation of her milieu is explained by all that has been described in the novel – from Mrs. Barton's syrupy manoeuvres to the disastrous tale of Olive, from Cecilia's Lesbian sickness (an education in the horrors of emotional disablement) to May Gould's incurably frivolous femininity (a lesson in woman's underrating of herself). Moore does not need, in the quest for a supposedly scientific explanation of the sort favoured in naturalistic theory, to draw upon half-baked notions, concocted outside the novel, about middle-class womanhood, as he does in *A Mummer's Wife*; instead, he can point to his whole story as the necessary cause of Alice's turning out as she does. Except in its final actions (the secret protection of May Gould, and the open defiance of her mother) Alice's conscience does not simply strive against the communal one – it is educated by it to reject it. In the same way, in the year of *Esther Waters*, Shaw was to make Vivie's role in *Mrs. Warren's Profession* one of both repudiating and being educated into awareness by her wicked mother, who is the emblem of the communal conscience as it decays. Vivie and Alice have other things in common. While Vivie is brisk and Alice spiritual and Pre-Raphaelite (p. 296),[9] both have a certain aura of coldness. Although her author constantly assures us of the warmth of her temperament and her longing for marriage, Alice's union with the stout Dr. Reed and her retreat to a house adorned with yellow porcelain by William Morris is satirically handled in a way that reminds us of Paula De Stancy's remarks at the end of Hardy's *A Laodicean* as she contemplates a similar fate:

> "And be a perfect representative of 'the modern spirit'?" she inquired; "representing neither the senses and understanding, nor the heart and imagination; but what a finished writer calls 'the imaginative reason'?"[10]

Alice's is a rescue operation limited to herself; she cannot drag anyone else out of the pit that is Ireland. To this extent her conscientious resistance takes on a probably unintended air of selfishness. Even her work for May Gould does not much modify this; and in the final pages she can offer her sister Olive, who seems virtually broken by her experience, only cold comfort and the promise of a long stay in Kensington.

As we approach the task of setting *Esther Waters* in the light of the other two, it seems that the much greater fame of the third is not easily to be accounted for by proportionate superiorities in construction and style. Here again is a book over which the ruined shell in County Mayo conspicuously broods, for Woodview is plainly Moore Hall transplanted to the Sussex downs. The horse-racing element which centres on Woodview and the King's Head has its counterpart in the *mœurs* depicted in the other novels – play-acting in the industrial North and marrying and giving in marriage amongst the Ascendancy families. The formula is the same: a heroine confronting a destiny affected by a social phenomenon of a fairly recondite sort. *Esther Waters* disturbs us much less than the others with passages which are coldly assertive or melodramatically crude; but if the revised versions of the first two (which are presumably the ones commonly read, if read at all) were to be compared with the (naturally much less revised) third, it would be hard to prove that the advantage lies with *Esther Waters*, in respect at any rate of quality of composition and texture.

It is only common justice to Moore to observe that he does not resemble those novelists who are the realists' legacy to our own day – those who merely exploit recondite manners for their own sake, contentedly furnishing them with character stereotypes in order to convert what is really history or sociology into instant fiction. Here, if anywhere, the advantage lies with the first two books. There is much in the King's Head betting scenes and the famous study of Derby Day that looks like ballast, whereas in *A Drama in Muslin*, as we have seen, Moore has contrived that everything that he shows us constitutes in the end the substance of the "ideas" by which Alice acts and judges. In *A Mummer's Wife*, despite the Zolaesque high relief in which much of the detail is drawn, there is surprisingly little feeling that the characters are merely stalking-horses for the manners. Though Moore may think of his characters as typical and sometimes lectures us on the middle-class woman and similar topics with the prescribed objectivity, their social roles are countervailed by their individualities. The individualities do not range very widely. There is a Moore heroine of whom Kate, Alice and Esther are only avatars. But this heroine, although partly begotten by Moore's French masters, is an invention and not just a stereotype.

Moore also seems from the first to have been accomplished at *pace*, at the achievement of a large and satisfying movement, or rhythm, through his books. They conform at least to his own criteria, formulated about this time, for the "avoidance of any disruptive sense of finality at the end of each episode or chapter" and for "rhythmical progression of events, rhythm and inevitableness (two words for one and the same thing)".[11] Rhythm entails iterative devices, a trick Moore often overworked (as in the numerous, repetitive descriptions, many of them excised for *Muslin*, of Mrs. Barton's appearance and gestures); but Esther's recurrent mental images of the racehorses at Woodview, or the stress in *A Mummer's Wife* on Dick's gluttony, are more successful examples. Rhythm also entails the reader's being carried forward through a larger movement, and here Moore's continuities of story help. We are kept always at Kate's elbow, and, although her story covers four years, there are no apparent breaks in it; Esther's lasts eighteen, and the same techniques are used. In *A Drama in Muslin* we note (more clearly than in *A Mummer's Wife*) the device of a central turning-point or watershed that is to be used also in *Esther Waters*. This occurs when the family groups go up to Dublin for the Lord Lieutenant's season, when Alice meets Harding, her sister fails with Kilcarney, and the lavish colours and contrasts of life in Dublin are shaped against the country scenes that precede and follow (in both books there is a deliberate rhythmic and symbolic interplay between town and country). In *Esther Waters* the novel reaches its crest when, after William's and Esther's chance meeting in London, Esther finally takes her decision to throw in her lot with her old lover and not with Fred Parsons, and changes from a servant-girl into a publican's wife.

The final maturity of this heroine's "idea" is, however, given expression in a later colloquy with Fred:

"You used to be a good religious woman. Do you remember how we used to speak when we used to go for walks together, when you were in service in the Avondale Road? I remember you agreeing with me that much good could be done by those who were determined to do it. You seem to have changed very much since those days."

For a moment Esther seemed affected by these reminiscences. Then she said in a low musical voice –

"No, I've not changed, Fred, but things has turned out different. One doesn't do the good that one would like to in the world; one has to do the good that comes to one to do. I've my husband and my boy to look to. Them's my good. At least that's how I sees things."[12]

"Them's my good" is one of those crystallizing moments, like "Nelly, I *am* Heathcliff" or Madame Merle's "Everything!" that the novel achieves less frequently than Elizabethan drama. It deserves to be written in the forefront of any criticism of *Esther Waters*, although its effects are perhaps muffled, as are many things in *Esther Waters*, by Moore's somehow unconvincing attempts at English demotic. This affirmation of the personal conscience is echoed in the structure of the book, which might otherwise be mistaken for an example of the moral duality which Brian Nicholas thinks it is.[13]

Esther does at first seem paradoxical enough. Her character combines puritanism with a vivid responsiveness to nature and man and a fiery amour-propre. After her child is born, the book sets her on the lowest rung of her community, in a posture of perpetual struggle against the selfishness and lack of conscience of those above her, employers, baby-farmer, and the rest. Her own fiery moral sense, which is never primarily abstract but directly expressed in her cherishing of Jackie against all the odds, is seen in her actions on his behalf and in an occasional outburst:

> two innocent children murdered so that a rich woman's child may be brought up. I'm not afraid of saying it, it's the truth; I'd like everyone to know it. (p. 142)

When she does attain a kind of equilibrium with Fred and Miss Rice, chance unbalances it[14] (the accidental meeting with William). Her decision to go to William emerges out of a muddle of motives, some rational, some purely affective; it is by no means certain whether Jackie's welfare is any more important than what Nature, through its various avatars, whispers to the suffering Esther. Once she has joined William at the King's Head, Esther's posture towards her social milieu – the pub, the racecourse, Soho – becomes one of acquiescence instead of resistance. She makes an occasional protest and an occasional prayer, in character, just as her counterpart Mrs. Barfield once did down at Woodview, but "them's my good" does become her guide in everything.

"Them's my good" – this is the clear and inflexible moral sense, the conscience which inspires Esther's actions. Although her attitudes to society (both that part of it which is deeply implicated with her own religion and the hostile ranks of the proud and careless) shift about, there is no inconsistency in her motives. She takes whatever action she deems must be, in order to accomplish an objective which is always the same. There is no split in Esther between her idea and her deed. Wrong is what may harm her good; she is resolute enough never to *do* anything which she *thinks* wrong. Because "them's my good" comes completely to override the conventions of her upbringing – her religious faith and duties – it is the very consistency of the motive that is pointed by the two conflicting postures of resistance and acquiescence. The means alter, but the end remains the same. It is not Esther's business to struggle against her society for the sake of her principles of religion; she does so only when "them's my good" requires it. And when "them's my good" so prescribes it is her business to compromise with those very principles which, measuring her society, tell her it is wicked and should be resisted. Esther must be one of the first characters in fiction to make so clearly Huck's choice – to put friends first and "virtue" second. That this choice has incremental gifts of the spirit for the chooser is suggested perhaps by the otherwise over-long case of Sarah Tucker at the end of the King's Head portion – Esther's charity begins to extend its range, just as that of the "Saint" enfolded all in her besotted house. It is the actions that follow from this choice that do of course in the eyes of most readers constitute Esther's virtue, although they might commonly choose a less regal word, such as integrity. The novel is none the less a mighty quibble on the idea of virtue as defined by Esther's puritanism and as defined by some term such as Wordsworth's "strength of love".

Esther Waters may be marginally a better work of art than

A Mummer's Wife or *A Drama in Muslin*. But the margin would be established on rather negative grounds; most of these Moore wiped away when, in revising the first two novels, he reduced the number of brash lecturettes and toned down the over-explicit. Even so, it seems likely that *A Drama in Muslin*, at least, would have done better if it had been left alone. The notion that Moore greatly improved the actual texture of his work, his style of writing, by his frequent recasting of sentences and rewording does not survive a thorough comparison of the various versions – the process was not radical enough for that, and may be best summed up as a mild, schoolmasterly attention to mistakes and inelegancies in the originals rather than to the imposition of the freshly woven (and altogether later) manner.

Perhaps the criticism of fiction will be able to evolve absolutely convincing techniques for demonstrating that *Esther Waters* deserves its pre-eminence just as much as the other two merit the relative oblivion to which they have been consigned. It does not appear to have done so yet. No doubt the reflex actions of the publishing business may account for much – a book once singled out tends to retain its place. It is even possible that, for a majority of those readers who can take a realist novel any way, one about London and Epsom seems necessarily more real than one about Galway and Dublin or Hanley and Blackpool. The factors are external and social rather than autonomous and internal. Is it, then, much too rough to say that *Esther Waters* is a world classic primarily because its heroine seems to us so much nicer than Kate Ede or Alice Barton? Esther acts nobly, as we think, Kate ignobly, and Alice merely sensibly. It is not possible to withold approval from the strength of love when it is expressed in the mother's determination to save the child or the wife's loyalty to the ailing husband. Approval is very easily transferred from the fictive being to the fiction itself. There is no other literary genre where it is so easy to control our approach to the artefact by manipulating our attitudes to the behaviour of the artificial character. It is the novel's privilege, or burden, that it will very often be singled out for popular approval in proportion to the liking accorded to its *personae*. The happy ending is not important in itself but only as a corollary of this.[15]

In writing *Esther Waters* Moore set out to enlarge his audience after he had been brought low by several failures.[16] Although he agreed that the novel had assured his reputation for his lifetime, he was full of doubt in later years. He is reported to have said that *Esther Waters* radiated goodness and had "done more good than any novel in my generation"; at other times he claimed to regard it as "worthless", a "bad" book. A moral and social "good" and a literary-critical "bad" are involved here. In his usual frivolous way Moore was putting a perfectly sober question to his posterity.

Appendix:
Muslin *and* A Drama in Muslin:
A Note on the Revision

[i] The part of Alice is very considerably reduced. In every contact which she makes with other characters there is a tendency to diminish the depths, variety, and intensity of the relationship. (My page references are to the Vizetelly 1st edition of *A Drama in Muslin*, London, 1886). Thus in the description of the first night at Brookfield, Alice's long reverie at the end of chapter II (pp. 30ff.) and the description of the contrasts in the room shared by the two sisters disappear; the contrast between Olive and Alice is consequently underplayed, and this contrast is generally less explicit in the 1915 version. Similarly, Alice's relationship with John Harding is greatly reduced (pp. 145ff., pp. 196ff.). Alice's isolation and difference from her family get less emphasis, and especially diminished is her half-successful understanding of her father (pp. 38ff.). The most dramatic reduction of this kind is in her friendship with Cecilia, from which the explicit note of sexual repression on Cecilia's part virtually disappears; this entails, amongst many minor tonings-down, the removal of a whole chapter of Cecilia's passionate distraction (Bk. III, ch. VI). Many of Alice's reflections on her experiences and on life in general vanish. She no longer reads Scott or compares herself to Amy Robsart (p. 53); the development of her religious scepticism is much less starkly described (pp. 66-7), her hostile meditations on the Catholic ceremony of the Mass disappear (p. 70) – indeed, the

whole scale of the church-going episode is altered, as are many of those involving Irish manners. The intensity of her feelings after the ball in chapter VI of Book I goes, as do her loneliness and despair (pp. 203ff.), her writings, her room and books (pp. 255ff.), her resentment over her own spinsterish state after the May Gould episode (p. 263), her feelings after Dr. Reed proposes (p. 312). The result of all this is virtually to demote Alice from being the consciousness that broods over the novel, in both its aspects as a family story and an account of Ireland in the 1880s.

[ii] Moore obviously desires to reduce the element of hysteria and melodrama and baleful political anger. Often in *A Drama in Muslin* he goes over the edge into the ridiculous in his attempts to describe intense feelings – not only those of Alice, but also of Cecilia. A striking example here is the complete excision of the meditations of the Marquis of Kilcarney (pp. 217-20) as he wanders through the streets of Dublin. No doubt another motive, apart from removing a passage of high excess, was the wish to avoid giving undue emphasis to a minor character. Much of the content of Kilcarney's meditations is political, and this connects with another major feature of the revision.

[iii] After the reduction of Alice Barton the most striking series of cuts affects the rendering of political and social conditions in Galway and Dublin. These are far less vividly rendered in *Muslin* and there seems little doubt that the removal or drastic modification of many passages of this sort constitute a major loss to the novel. Thus the vivid contrast between the "big house" life and the barren countryside (p. 51) is lost; the stress on the squalor of the peasantry during the church-going episode (and Alice's sympathetic reaction) is greatly weakened (pp. 70ff.); more suitable for excision was the description of Land League troubles and the Irish scene (pp. 94-102, the biggest cut of all except for the removal of Bk. III, ch. VI), which, unlike the scene in the chapel, is little more than rather inert journalism. There are big cuts in the description of social life in Dublin (pp. 156ff.), its poverty and ignorance and the shallowness of its tea-party view of political crisis; the well-known description of the aspect of the slums as seen by the Lord Lieutenant's guests proceeding in their carriages to the

Castle is greatly modified; a long passage on the state of Ireland
mixed up with the excitement aroused in ascendancy circles by
Violet Scully's impending marriage (pp. 264ff.) is cut out, and,
as has already been mentioned, the eviction with Alice and Dr.
Reed encounter as they leave Ireland is much cut and altered
(pp. 322ff.).

[iv] This by no means exhausts the tale of revision. For
example, Mrs. Barton is throughout much re-handled, and when
she is first introduced the cuts in the presentation of her (pp.
22ff.) give a probably unintended prominence to Lord Dungory.
Moore tried to "tell" less by making many reductions in his
renderings of settings, landscape, rooms and so on. There is
some rewriting and rearrangement of whole scenes (for
example, the picnic, the eviction), but on the whole Moore's
chief activity in 1915 was large scale reducing and minor
rewording. Of 343 pages in the 1915 *Muslin*, only 93 pages
have escaped unaltered from *A Drama in Muslin*.

NOTES

1 *Salve* (reprint, London, 1947), pp. 23-4.

2 This revision has been described by R. A. Gettmann in "George
Moore's Revisions of *The Lake, The Wild Goose,* and *Esther
Waters*", *PMLA*, LIX (1944), 540-55. It should be noted that
Gettmann omits all mention of Moore's biggest reduction: the
cut of seven pages in the 1894 edition from the story of the ruin
of Sarah Tucker, entailing the omission of the original's 34th
chapter and part of the 35th (see *Esther Waters* (1894), pp.
271-7); Moore is obviously trying to get under control what
remains in the final version a digressive disturbance to the
structure.

3 The version used in these series is that of 1920. In 1936 *Esther
Waters* was one of the first inclusions in the Penguin series (no.
23 in that history-making list); it is in Dent's Everyman and in
1965 was included in the Oxford World's Classics.

4   See the series of articles by M. Chaikin, in particular "A Mummer's Wife and Zola" and "Balzac, Zola and *A Drama in Muslin*", Rev. *de Littérature Comparée*, xxxi (1957) and xxix (1955); and Enid Starkie, *From Gautier to Eliot* (London, 1960), pp. 73-7.

5   Page references are to the unrevised version. I have used the second edition (London, 1885).

6   This passage does not appear in the revised version.

7   *Essays Presented to Amy G. Stock*, ed. R. K. Kaul (Jaipur, 1965), pp. 137-54.

8   See Appendix, pp. 271-73.

9   My reference is to the unrevised version, London, 1886.

10 *A Laodicean* (London reprint, 1926), p. 499.

11 Quoted in Kenneth Graham, *English Criticism of the Novel 1865-1900* (Oxford, 1965), p. 118.

12 P. 289; references are to the unrevised (1894) edition of *Esther Waters*.

13 Nicholas's severe account (ch. IV of Ian Gregor and Brian Nicholas, *The Moral and the Story* (London, 1962)) is the most important critique of *Esther Waters* known to me. A good deal of it is unarguable, but, if I understand it rightly, it appears to derive from three main ideas which do not seem to be fully supported by the text as I read it:
[i] that there is "an extreme contrast between [Esther's] known character and her behaviour". Esther's is a divided self at the beginning of the book, not unlike Kate Ede's. She is a good, "religious" girl but at the same time a Moore heroine with a strongly sensual side, a sensuous feeling for the world around her, and a fiery temper. There is more than one passage which tries to realize Esther's feeling for "Aprill with his shoures soote' (e.g., pp. 31ff., the opening of ch. VI). "Above [her] Protestantism", says Moore, "was human nature". This *double* self is her "known character". Her puritanism is therefore, for good characterological reasons, in abeyance when William seduces her; but the episode brings it out again overwhelmingly, together with her capacity for sullen fury (p. 71). She recovers from this, but remains extraordinarily scrupulous about admitting responsibility (p. 84) and at the same time is in love with William (p. 73). None of this is especially paradoxical or extraordinary.
[ii] that Esther is represented as both a victor over life and a

victim of it, and is therefore a psychological illogicality. It is true that Esther displays a strong will and purpose and at the same time has a tendency to claim at crises that "life" is too much for her. For Nicholas, it is chiefly this, if I understand him rightly, that vitiates the scenes in which she chooses William instead of Fred. He appears to exaggerate here: for example, the passage which he quotes on p. 105 shows Esther worrying about the danger of Fred encountering William and cursing her rotten luck at the possible upset to her plans for a life with Fred: she is not excusing herself for yielding, as life's victim, to William once more because she is at this point in time quite determined to have Fred. It seems doubtful if Esther's practice of saying that life's too much for her (when in another sense it obviously isn't) is more than an idiom or characterizing device – "What rotten luck I have!" It is of course the case that Esther, in eventually choosing William, is actuated by a mixture of rational prudential motives and irrational ones; she asks herself what is best for Jackie while at the same time experiencing her old sensations about William. Any bit of the dialogue with Fred (pp. 228-31) shows the two sets of motive at work in a way that reads like a convincing transcript of muddle and strain. Anyone who acts and talks in this way could be said both to choose and to succumb – but not in Esther's case to an external blameable "life" (though she often complains of this) so much as to a rooted predilection (as the story insists) springing out of a part of her nature.

[iii] that Moore presents Esther's religious principles as the source and sign of her virtue, or integrity, the true self which gives her ultimate validity as a pure woman and virtuous sufferer, and relies on this continued presentation in the hope that the reader will continue to take her virtue for granted despite her readiness to compromise (e.g., with racing, pubs, and sex). As I have tried to indicate above (p. 269), the sense of Esther's integrity is, I think, mediated to us in quite a different way.

14   Moore's willingness to admit chance may have been one of the features that distinguishes his work from pure naturalistic theory: see William Newton, "Chance as Employed by Hardy and the Naturalists", *PQ*, xxx (1951), 154-75.

15   Herbert Howarth is the only writer I have come across who considers that the ending of *Esther Waters* is an unhappy one, "a story of pointless courage and devotion": see *The Irish Writers 1880-1940* (London, 1958), pp. 46-7. Probably the determination of readers and critics that fictive personages whom they

admire should end happily has led them to overlook the many clues that give a very gloomy and foreboding character to the last pages of the book: see, for example, Graham Hough's reading, Introduction to the World's Classics edition (London, 1964), p. xi.

16 See Malcolm Brown, *George Moore: A Reconsideration* (Seattle, 1955), pp. 128ff.

Part Three

MARTIN PRICE

The Other Self:
Thoughts about Character in the Novel

[i]

At the beginning of his study of the nude in art, Sir Kenneth Clark asks "What is the nude?" and offers this answer:

> It is an art invented by the Greeks in the fifth century, just as opera is an art form invented in seventeenth-century Italy. The conclusion is certainly too abrupt, but it has the merit of emphasizing that the nude is not the subject of art, but a form of art.
>
> It is widely supposed [Clark goes on] that the naked human body is in itself an object upon which the eye dwells with pleasure and which we are glad to see depicted. But anyone who has frequented art schools and seen the shapeless, pitiful models that the students are industriously drawing will know this is an illusion. The body is not one of those subjects which can be made into art by direct transscription . . . the various parts of the body cannot be perceived as simple units and have no clear relationship to one another. In almost every detail the body is not the shape that art has led us to believe it should be.

Not only is the nude itself an invention, Clark points out, but each of the great poses of antique sculpture must be seen as inventions in their own right, new instances of "how the naked body has been given memorable shapes by the wish to communicate certain ideas or states of feeling".[1]

It is through this analogy that I propose to enter the problem of character. The analogy holds in certain obvious ways. We have a daily and intimate acquaintance with our naked body, and recognize that a sense of identity is somehow tied to it. As Merleau-Ponty has said, "The perceiving mind is an incarnated mind . . . For contemporary psychology and psychopathology, the body is no longer mostly *an object in the world*, under the purview of a separated spirit. It is on the side of the subject; it is our *point of view on the world*, the place where the spirit takes on a certain physical and historical situation."[2]

The counterpart of this awareness of the body is the equally familiar awareness of that stream of images, feelings, ideas, and fantasies that make up mental life. Just as we live within, through, and out from the body, so we live immersed in this stream of mental processes. Nakedness, Clark tells us, is not the nude; he calls his book "a study in ideal form", and it is in character that we find the psychic counterpart of the nude.

There are moments when we are required to stand outside ourselves. We are suddenly forced to consider the self we have known from the inside and to consider it in terms that are not our own familiar words for our feelings and hopes. We must describe ourselves in a language that applies to others as readily as to ourselves. We are cut off from the stream of private associations and personal history, and we must articulate what we have often felt but seldom needed to recognize, much less had to capture in categories that will make sense to others. How difficult this proves is an index of our self-awareness. There are some who have seen themselves largely in the terms of public language; there are others who rarely have done so. The latter will feel strangeness and inadequacy in what they can articulate.

This movement from immersion to reflection, from inside to outside, from subject to object, from I to he, becomes a problem of characterization. Boswell wrote at the head of his *London Journal*: "A man cannot know himself better than by attending to the feelings of his heart and to his external actions". The terms are striking. He is both actor and spectator, agent and observer; as we read on in the journal we see that he is experimentalist as well, creating situations in which he can surprise his feelings or test his actions. As he attends to the feelings of his heart or analyses his actions in light of their motives, he can find a way of describing himself, and to describe himself is, for

Boswell, a way of controlling himself. He is interested in making a character as well as recording one, but the two interests shift in importance. What makes Boswell remarkable is his openness, candour, and curiosity; he is as much fascinated by the problems he encounters in himself as he is by the discipline of shaping himself; and at times the interest of self-characterization supplants the concern with self-control. We can see three levels here: the raw experience; the detachment with which it is studied and recorded, often in moral terms; the moral effort to shape the self.

These two upper levels tend to shade into each other. Most of the inventories of self and attempts at self-characterization we commonly undertake are directed to some purpose. Questions like "Who am I?" are demands for a specific kind of answer. When we try to answer such a question, how shall we choose?

"One has before one, for reflection and comment, whether in one's own person, or in the person of another, always a whole person ... The distinctions that we make among ... features of a person's life, by regarding some as ultimate ends and others as subordinate means, will be, at least in part, distinctions of value; in laying emphasis on some and neglecting others, we will be marking that which we ourselves believe to be essential in human life."[3] The whole person is rarely accessible. If we contemplate, for example, our intellectual history, specific episodes may remind us that our intellectual life is not autonomous but rather affected, even shaped, by other elements of the self. Such episodes may undo the simplifications that our purpose imposes and allow us a momentary glimpse into the wholeness of the self. Yet our intellectual life does have a measure of autonomy, and our purpose requires that we limit our attention to the matter at stake.

This third level of purposiveness is the one at which we generally operate in self-scrutiny, and the self is rarely a simple, massive conception. More often we are drawing out of it those aspects that meet attention because they serve some immediate purpose. The purpose is usually a social one, that is, set by our relations with others, directed by the claims or demands of others. These aspects of the self that respond to social demands have been called roles, and social psychologists, who study the self as it performs in and is shaped by society, have given careful study to the problems of role-playing. One extreme position sees the self as nothing more than the structure of its roles:

> The learned repertoire of roles is the personality. There is nothing else. There is no "core" personality underneath the behavior and feelings; there is no "central" monolithic self which lies beneath the various external manifestations . . . The "self" is a composite of many selves, each of them consisting of a set of self-perceptions, which are specific to one or another major role, specific to the expectations of one or another significant reference group.[4]

Reference groups have been defined as "those groups to which the individual relates himself as a part or to which he aspires to relate himself psychologically". They serve "as major anchorings" for one's sense of identity. Much empirical study and subtle analysis have been given to the way in which a self is constructed of roles, or, in a more moderate view, the way in which a self orders the roles to which it is committed. "In carrying out roles", one theorist writes, "one is involved in a continual process of validation and modification", but it may also be claimed that one "leaves some mark, however faint, upon the cultural definition".[5] If the self has been built out of roles, it may in turn affect the roles it assumes.

George Herbert Mead traced the emergence of the sense of a self to participation in social activity. Mead uses as a model the game in which each player learns his own role through sensing the other players' expectations of him.

> A person is a personality because he belongs to a community, because he takes over the institutions of that community into his own conduct. He takes its language as a medium by which he gets his personality, and then through a process of taking the different roles that all the others furnish, he comes to get the attitude of the members of the community. Such, in a certain sense, is the structure of a man's personality . . . The structure, then, on which the self is built is this response which is common to all, for one has to be a member of a community to be a self. Such responses are abstract attitudes, but they constitute just what we term a man's character.

"It is a structure of attitudes, then, which makes a self, as distinct from a group of habits", and one becomes a true self as he includes "as elements in the structure or constitution of his self" not only particular attitudes of other individuals toward him but those of the "generalized other", "the social group as a whole to which he belongs". We may see in the "generalized other" the system of values involved in our conception of self. It is precisely against this submission to an impersonal other that existentialism protests – this surrender of the self as an initiating and free agent to the impersonal anonymity of merely social existence, the loss of authenticity in becoming an object for others to act through or upon. The self ceases to live but is lived by the impersonal other, the public or the mass, the whole system of awarding and imposing roles.[6]

Clearly the issues involved in role-playing are too great and too many to be considered here. One can discern the danger of the two extremes that Iris Murdoch has identified as "neurosis" and "convention", the first a turning in upon the self and a neglect of the reality of others, the second a passive reduction of the self to the roles that are assigned it by its culture; the first gives us self-enclosed works of high internal coherence, the second journalistic accounts of a life without true persons. It may be that we can be reminded of the substantive nature of the self, and of character, by the very conflict between roles, or between the full individual and a particular role he assumes. Peter Ure has written on this tension between "character" and "role" in Shakespeare:

> It is often because we are made aware of the gap, not the consonance, between the man and the office that the situation becomes profound and exacting, and permits rich inferences about what the hero's inward self is like. It is the character faced with his role, forced to decide about it, the quality of his response, that Shakespeare shows us, not just his performance in the role . . . He often allows history or tradition to define the nature of the role that is offered, the more sharply to bring out the spectacle of the individual fitting himself (or failing to fit himself) to it.[8]

With these reservations, we can still recognize that much of life is committed to the playing of roles and to apprehending others through their roles. Whether we seek to characterize ourselves or others, we follow a pattern of what E. H. Gombrich calls making and matching. We construct a somewhat vague image – often a particular role – with only so many attributes as we need at first, and gradually we test it against new experience, correcting it, filling it in, progressively differentiating it. Gombrich uses as an illustration the stick that a child makes into a hobby-horse. The stick may have a head, like that of a cane; and it can serve many purposes. It may be a harpoon, a sceptre, a hockey stick. Once the child has made it serve as a horse, he may give it ears, eyes, a rein, a tail: he supplies new details as its functions require them.[9]

Something like this takes place with the people we know. If the man we meet is going to do nothing but punch a ticket, he need not become more than an undifferentiated conductor. He remains accounted for by a simple role, and so do we for him. But as we come to know people whom we expect to see longer or know better, we want to go further towards comprehending them and towards revealing ourselves.

This is true of our experience of fictional characters. It would be possible to make long lists of all the attributes of characters that are never supplied. We do not know what most characters eat. We hear about servants in Jane Austen's novels, but we rarely see them. The things revealed about Emma Bovary are the very things ignored in Henry James's heroines. Rarely does a critic speculate about Robinson Crusoe's sexual frustration during his long years on the island. What of the missing attributes? The fact is that we do not miss them. Traits in a given character might readily lend themselves to explanation by depth psychology; but this kind of explanation is not required, and in fact it cannot be sustained as we turn to other characters in the same book. We can make surmises about the attributes that are missing, but we are hardly inclined to do so unless the novel invites it.

For we do not live all of our lives among complex personalities, nor do we live all of our conscious lives *as* complex personalities. We rely on other people maintaining their roles, and we feel an obligation to do the same. This does not, of course, preclude knowing that an individual is assuming a role, that we can look behind it when we wish, that we can drop our usual roles on occasion and resume them again with little difficulty. There is, in short, a flexibility in role-playing that makes it work without sheer dehumanization. But much of our lives depends on others' maintaining their roles and requiring of us only so much of a response as the role itself demands.

I have pursued the analogy of fictional character and our conceptions of self in order to emphasize two things. First, there is considerable artistry inherent in our normal behaviour, and the intensification and direction it gains in a work of art does not obliterate the continuity of art and life. Second, the flexibility of role-playing and the purposiveness of it, directed to and by a dramatic situation, prepare us to accept more readily the flexibility of characterization. It may range from mere sketching in of necessary roles to the most complex construction of a person revealed in the conflict of roles or in the successive adoption of roles. But, more important, the terms in which character is conceived and the level at which it is sought are governed by the larger purposes of the novel. The novel provides the society in which the individual character finds definition.

[ii]

The analogy between society and the novel will take us only a short way, however. A novelist with a keen sense of form, like Henry James, longs for a society that has a complex and lucid structure – like a novel. Balzac, James tells us, had the good fortune to live amid

> social phenomena the most rounded and registered, most organized and administered, and thereby most exposed to systematic observation and portrayal, that the world had seen. There are happily other interesting societies, but these are for schemes of such an order comparatively loose and incoherent, with more extent and perhaps more variety, but with less of the great enclosed and exhibited quality, less neatness and sharpness of arrangement, fewer categories, subdivisions, juxtapositions. Balzac's France was both inspiring enough for an immense prose epic and reducible enough for a report or a chart.

Balzac lived "in an earthly heaven so near perfect for his kind of vision that he could have come at no moment more conceivably blest to him", for he escaped the "fatal fusions and uniformities inflicted on our newer generations, the running together of all the differences of form and tone, the ruinous liquefying wash of the great industrial brush over the old conditions of contrast and colour".[10]

For a novelist whose subject is the conditions of social life, for whom "man is on the whole cruelly, crushingly, deformedly conditioned", a society with complex structure may provide the forms other novelists may need to invent. The novel not only claims, by virtue of offering itself as a work of art, a high degree of structure, but it is a structure which has some unifying end, some principle of composition. The unity of a novel is expressed most succinctly in thematic terms. This presupposes that a narrative is shaped so as to disclose a meaningful form, and to apprehend the form is to find some way of stating the meaning towards which it moves. Such a theme is rarely stated overtly in the work; to extricate it from the work is not to hold it up for contemplation in its own right but rather to see it as the general statement that is given intensity, precision, suggestiveness, and fullness of implication by the work itself. The theme is the starting point of our *study* of the work, for it is the most general principle of structure in the work; by turning it back upon the work, we can see a radiance in details and a resonance in parts.

If we start with theme, we can ask of each element: what is it for? The way in which an author conceives character is part of a unitary purpose. Nor should this be taken as a narrowly rhetorical view of fiction. I am not concerned with character as example. And I want to leave room for the unpredictable processes of composition. D. H. Lawrence makes the point most firmly. The novel "won't *let* you tell didactic lies, and put them over":

> You can tell me, Flaubert had a "philosophy", not a "purpose". But what is a novelist's philosophy but a purpose on a rather higher level? And since every novelist who amounts to anything has a philosophy – even Balzac – any novel of importance has a purpose. If only the "purpose" be large enough, and not at odds with the passional inspiration.[11]

This is to say, first, that the energy of what is imagined may undo the end for which it is created, and, second, that we always commit ourselves – in an act of imagination – to more than we fully recognize. We are all familiar with the mixed pleasure and horror an author can feel at finding his characters demanding lives of their own, shouldering aside his programme, or suddenly dying of inanition. And there are many authors who count on characters' taking over the direction of the work, as it were, once they come into fictional life. We need not credit every wilful surrender of the author as a real one. He may be sensitive to a deeper level of motive than he can summon at the start and wait for its emergence; the internal logic of his characters may force him to do what he did not allow himself to see that he intended. But the intention I am concerned with is the intention revealed by the structure of the work; to call it intention at all is only to claim some purposiveness, at whatever level of consciousness.

The purpose of a novel is to reveal life under a certain aspect, to shape it so as to make sense of a roughly formulable kind – the formulation is its theme. To do this the writer creates a model, a small-scale structure whose proportions or relationships have some analogy with the realities we know. The scale of a work of art, always seems smaller than that of life if only because what it presents is more intensively ordered, more transparently significant, more readily encompassed and studied, more sharply framed and closed than any segment of actual experience.[12]

Only through implying statements do novels achieve form. The tale is a naïve form whose shape is its very end. We delight in the fact that it comes out. It has a kind of symmetry, clear design, an artful building of suspense, and a satisfying resolution, like the resolution of a musical form. But the novel is more than such a tale. The resolution of its form is somehow consonant with the disclosure of meaning, and there are some novels whose only resolution is the disclosure of meaning. We have the expectation of meaning, and the novel which never quite fulfils the expectation still demands some effort to discover the meaning it does not freely yield. Its effect, whether the author wishes or not to achieve such an effect, is created in part by the very expectation that it will disclose meaning. But of course what interests us about the meaning is how it is earned. The statement may be, after all, somewhat banal, or at least familiar, once we articulate it as theme, just as a theatrical role may be all too familiar until we see a new actor invest it with remarkable meaning. The novel implies a statement, but it does not exist for the sake of its statement; rather, the novel makes a statement so that it can be a novel.

Character may be said to exist within a novel as persons in a society, but the "society" of the novel is one with intensive and purposive structure. We read the novel immersed in its complexity, it is true, but with confidence in its resolution and its ultimate significance. This sense of a total structure inevitably qualifies the attention we give to the characters; it need not diminish that interest, but it complicates it. Characters simply cannot be persons in the sense that we commonly know persons in life. It is clear enough that many characters we have read about are more vivid to us than persons we know in daily life, that in a certain sense these fictional persons are more "real" than most actual persons. But to say this conceals more problems than it clarifies. Actual persons are curiously open; they have lives yet to live, they impinge upon us in direct ways. We confront them; we can affect them. We see them as coming closer to us or receding, and if they recede we may miss them. In all these respects, and countless others, real persons have an urgency that the persons of fiction cannot have.

A fictional character lives within a work of fiction. He may spill over and demand a work of his own, as Falstaff does a play of his own. We may be able to invent new experiences for him beyond the range of those the author has invented, as Pamela Hansford Johnson has invented new scenes for Proust's characters. But if a character spills over from a literary work, it is not into our lives, but into another work. We may, it is true, see people we know in terms of fictional characters. We may imagine ourselves in terms that have been appropriate to fictional characters, in daydreams or in more serious moments. But, if characters are like persons, still we must recognize wherein they differ from actual persons and what makes them the peculiar kind of thing that is part of a work of fiction.

When we read a novel, whatever we need to know about a character is revealed to us in that work. By the end of the work our awareness of the character has come to some kind of resting point. We know by then all that we wish to know. All the questions or problems that are raised by the character are resolved. If they are not, if the novel deliberately leaves the character ambiguous, the very ambiguity is a resting point. This is where we are meant to be left, the point of what we have read. It is ambiguity to be taken as ultimate, not one such as in actual life we seek to get beyond. In that sense one can say that characters exist for the sake of novels rather than novels for the sake of character.

If characters exist for the sake of novels, they exist only as much as and in the way that the novel needs them. Jane Austen's world is a strikingly limited one.[13] It is a world of visits and conversations, which take place in houses and gardens. We do not see people at work; we do not directly encounter violent action or violent passion. The limits of what may be said are fairly narrow. We are given, in effect, a shallow and well-lighted stage where we can see the comedy of manners played out with great attention to speech and gesture. The point of this world becomes clear as soon as we see the full import that manners can hold. The shallow stage of Jane Austen is a scene where discrimination – tact, intelligence, self-awareness – can play out its part, unconfused by darker or deeper impulses. We are permitted to concentrate upon a limited portion of the full social scale, upon a limited portion of the full emotional range of people, upon a specific kind of action which involves feeling and intelligence. The feeling is never of the depth we see in Dickens or D. H. Lawrence, the intelligence is not the kind we see in George Eliot or Dostoevsky. The characters are differentiated to the degree that the story requires, and we can certainly extend their powers to the solution of other problems, but their powers are uniquely defined in the solution of precisely these problems, for it is these problems that have called those powers into being.

What I have been presenting is the framing effect of the novel. Its model of reality, by its very limits, creates a more intensive field than life can offer, and the co-presence of all the elements is felt more sharply. One of the ways in which this is felt is in ambiguity of figure and ground. Our need to unify our perceptions requires us, when we see an ambiguous two-dimensional picture, to resolve its difficulties by pushing one of the elements onto a deeper plane. We accept the complexity of a third dimension in order to simplify a puzzling awareness of two.[14] Something of the sort occurs in the novel as well. When a character speaks in terms that have been memorably used by the narrator, we are caught by the ambiguity of voices. Or when a character is presented in terms that are clearly applicable to the setting, we are again awakened to puzzle and artifice. Shall we see the character as somehow one with narrator or setting? What happens to the "reality" of the character as a person? Or what happens to the reality of Dickens's characters when each exemplifies, as in *Little Dorrit*, some dimension of the common plight of self-imprisonment? Are they somehow absorbed into one design, flattened as it were to one plane? Is there an iridescence of awareness: can we see them at once as persons and as parts of a design?

This ambiguity of figure and ground recurs in every aspect of the novel. Is a character a person living a free and spontaneous life or part of a plot, and can any plot fully resemble the untidy actuality of real life? Does the person dissolve into an agent of plot, or does the plot seem, at some level, the working out of the characters' inherent natures? Again, how shall we comprehend in one novel characters that are clearly seen as schematic or archetypal with characters who seem full and substantial? The ambiguity is like that of a film used as backdrop for stage actors or that found in a film which uses both photographed and cartoon characters. These are all familiar problems of artistic illusion, but it is important to recall that they operate in the novel and in our conception of character in the novel. One may substitute "character" in Dr. Johnson's famous remarks about the drama: "It will be asked how character moves, if it is not credited. It is credited with all the credit due to character."

[iii]

We have had a pendulum shift in the view of character over the last hundred years. Victorian critics found character more absorbing than the structures it inhabited – the plots of plays or novels, whether Sophocles and Shakespeare or the work of their own age – and created in turn that ultimate tribute to the mysteries and subtleties of character, the dramatic monologue.[15] But in that form alone we can see the movement through Pound and Eliot towards a symbolist mode, where character becomes at most the constellated form of image patterns, historical allusions, philosophical themes. Gerontion exhibits the burden of history and the loss of belief, and he has all but dissolved into the large themes he suggests. He remains a voice addressing someone – self, friend, lover, God, we can hardly say – recalling fragments of memory so discontinuous and elusive as to suggest at one moment isolated and tormented selves, at others the career of recent Western culture in its alienation from faith and its loss of coherence. Eliot's poem denies us the surface and texture of personality: we are deep within a self, ruminating, arguing, pleading, and we are immersed in a predicament that seems to shift from depth to depth. By any inclusive definition of the term. Gerontion is a character; yet he is at once less and more.

This pattern is diffused over much of "modern" literature. I use the quotation marks to indicate that the adjective has become one of those unstable names for a period style unlikely to survive because of its ambiguity. Unlike Gothic or baroque, which began as terms of abuse and remained as neutral designations, the term "modern" has too many other uses, and it will probably give way in time to "symbolist". There exists already the anomaly of a new distinction between "modern" and "contemporary", and there are invented terms, at once paradoxical and barbarous, like "post-modern", to meet the problem. Eliot's poem can stand for the tendencies in symbolism that have increasingly come under attack.

The attack has been directed to the symbolist novel in particular, for it is there that we encounter the problem of character most directly. (One might point in passing to poems by Randall Jarrell, Robert Lowell, and Philip Larkin for instances of the return to character in other forms.) Objections have taken several forms: that it denies social reality in excessive concern with personal sensibility; that it is overschematized and excludes the illogical, the untidy, the contingent; that it represents a neglect of persons in all their differences and distinctiveness. Angus Wilson, Barbara Hardy, W. J. Harvey, John Bayley, and Iris Murdoch have carried on the attack with intelligence and generosity, trying to reassert the power of the great nineteenth-century novels and their relevance to our own literature.[16]

The symbolist novel as these critics treat it (and not all of them so identify it, nor do all of them discuss the same writers) has a high degree of internal coherence. So intense is the coherence that characters are denied real freedom; they must exemplify patterns of meaning, and they must achieve virtual transparency to do so. They lack the substantial, opaque solidity of real persons. In fact, characters tend to dissolve into the elaborate verbal structure of the work, becoming nodes, as it were, of images or motifs; or they dissolve into aspects of one central character, dialectical forces within one situation or mind. The figure gives way to the ground, or at best there is a shimmering iridescence. Is Augustus Carmichael more substantial, more central in *To the Lighthouse* than the painting of Lily Briscoe or Mr. Ramsay's quotations from Tennyson and Cowper? Are characters allowed a full range of motive? Can they have true histories? Do the things they possess and handle have an independent reality, or are they symbolic stage-properties like the skull that Mrs. Ramsay covers with her scarf, the scarf that is fated to fall in the section called "Time Passes". And is the very existence of that section, where all the principal actors are off the stage, where the house itself enacts the themes of the novel, an indication of the low estate to which character has fallen?

The creation of character is a form of art as well as moral exercise, and the symbolist novel seems to have abjured this art for others, much as painting has shattered the portrait and disposed its elements in new ways. The losses are real, and we can sympathize with those who deplore them, but the attack has often taken a confusing turn. As against schematization we are offered truthfulness, as against the coherence of the work we are offered love for persons other than ourselves, as against artfulness we are offered empiricism, liberalism, and a warm response to the energies and contingencies of the actual. The symbolist work is taken to dramatize revulsion from the messy and uncontrollable; it is related to the abstraction that Wilhelm Worringer opposes to empathy, at once anti-humanistic and distrustful of the changes of history and the puzzles of the conditional.[17] Much of this may be sound diagnosis. But it obscures the problem of art and seems to oppose art to life, mere formalism to moral awareness. My object is to recover more clearly the inevitable artifice in the conception of character. The character we admire as the result of loving attention is something constructed by conventions as arbitrary as any other, and we can only hope to recover an art by recognizing it as art.

As soon as one asks for an admission of the contingent and accidental, one is left with the question of what to rule out. Clearly the contingency one asks of the novelist is a penumbra that surrounds the structure, out of which the structure seems to emerge as a statue emerges from marble or a Cézanne landscape from the discontinuous washes of watercolour and the white paper. How much of the marble can the statue sustain? Too much of the unworked material, and it seems fragmentary and sportive. Too little, and it seems clumsily encumbered by waste. Before the sculptor can find the appropriate balance he must have conceived the composition as a whole – worked and unworked stone together.

In a similar way, the contingency a novelist can admit is only relative contingency, and what makes it admissible, after all, is a thematic conception that requires it and therefore makes it relevant. Barbara Hardy cites the episode in Anna Karenina of Koznyshev's abortive proposal to Varenka.[18] It is an episode that might have been omitted, as these characters might have been omitted from the novel. But it is more than either an instance or a study of contingency. The proposal fails because neither character quite wants it, and all the accidental trivia that somehow rush to Varenka's lips have behind them her resistance to the exposure and pain of a new relationship. Koznyshev has pressed beyond his comfortable rationalizations to come to the point of proposing, but he is ready to withdraw, all too easily thrown off. Each of these characters represents a kind of half-life in the novel. Varenka's conventionality and denial of life once seemed to Kitty saintliness. Koznyshev's intellectuality and condescension had the power to shake Levin's confidence. But, in fact, each of these characters helps define the vitality of the central figures, who risk everything because they cannot endure something less than life; and we can also see links between Koznyshev's small relapse in this case and Karenin's in a greater, between Varenka's timid conventionality and Dolly's more moving counterpart. It is only as we see the theme of the novel, and its structure, in full dimension that these contingencies have their relevance as well.

If we turn to the problem of the social milieu of fictional characters, we can see it alternatively as figure or ground, as the situation for which these characters exist or as the means by which their natures are tested or conditioned. Manners, as we saw, are supremely important for Jane Austen because they are the field in which the moral self is revealed and defined. Manners are a form of role-playing. We use them to order our relations with each other; we can use them for disguise and deceit; or we can make them a game, an end in themselves, mere empty formalism. Jane Austen's characters reveal themselves by the way they use manners. Her novels contain noisy and rude people, some who are polite monsters, others who are gauche but generous. We learn that Lady Middleton's self-centred, complacent correctness is much worse than her husband's hearty officiousness, although at times her indifference is easier to bear than his disregard for others' privacy. Manners can be socially useful even when the motives that govern them are selfish, and living up to a code of manners has the value of making it possible to protect one's feelings. It is fortunate for Jane Austen's heroines that some things cannot be said and many need not be said: the novels are full of cruelty and vindictiveness that can only be met on neutral ground or in social forms.

Yet the cost of maintaining a role, of fulfilling the demands of manners, is often a high one: Elinor Dashwood and Fanny Price perform great "exertions" to conceal their own pain or to protect the feelings of others. It is finally when she commits an overt act of rudeness against poor, defenceless Miss Bates that Emma brings down the judgement she always fears and unknowingly wants, the disapproval of Mr. Knightley. It is his explicit rebuke that calls her back to what I shall call her "other self". He reminds her of all that at her deepest level of awareness – a level of moral conscience – she believes.

In George Eliot's *Middlemarch* a character like Lydgate needs a complex social world in which to be defined. The "realism" of the novel places Lydgate in a solid world of social structures, personal obligations, professional commitments, physical passions, and allows us to see his character revealing itself in each of those aspects. We are constantly aware of the resistance of

Middlemarch to Lydgate's innovations and of his impatience and lack of tact. We are aware of his extravagance and how it builds up obligations that will make him dependent on Bulstrode in ways he cannot anticipate.

In George Eliot's world the crucial moments are moral choices, but what they may reveal, as Iris Murdoch puts it, is "that the exercise of our freedom is a small piecemeal business which goes on all the time and not a grandiose leaping about unimpeded at important moments. The moral life, in this view, is something that goes on continually, not something that is switched off in between the occurrence of explicit moral choices."[19] To present such a view the novelist needs density of circumstances, which demand small unconscious decisions whose effect is irreversible. And the novelist needs the interplay of those roles which men contemplate singly: Lydgate's "intellectual passion" cannot survive the stubborn erosion of will that his wife imposes.

Lawrence's *Women in Love* provides the contrast of two pairs of lovers. The uneasy union of Gerald Crich and Gudrun Brangwen alternates between prostrate dependency and resentful cruelty. Each has an ego which cannot acknowledge, except in flashes of shame or prurience, the deeper passions that govern it; the ego tries to create stability through assertions of will. Each must control or dominate others in order to hold off the inward doubt or sense of emptiness. Gudrun fixes people in small, ironic sketches of sculpture; she sums them up, reduces their otherness to a manageable form and scale. Gerald controls others by becoming an efficient industrial magnate, ruthlessly mechanizing work till men feel that their selves are appropriately surrendered to the God of the Machine. Gerald and Gudrun, each wary and defensive, spy out the other's weaknesses. They come together in a terrible scene where a violent rabbit tears the flesh of Gudrun's arm and Gerald in turn clubs the terrified rabbit with his hand. They recognize in each other the perverse love of power, the desire both for cruel domination and for painful surrender.

The other lovers, Rupert Birkin and Ursula Brangwen, have a strong sense of self but a distrust of the ego's defences. They search for a way to get beyond the self, beyond personality, to reach a union in impersonal darkness from which each can return to "free proud singleness". They also are wary; Birkin seeks to throw off female domination, the claims of domesticity, the rule of the woman; Ursula rejects Birkin's demand for the surrender of her sense of identity, fearing the loss of self rather than its regeneration. Once Birkin and Ursula have achieved this union, or "star-equilibrium", where each is freed of the ego but retains a self, there follows a scene where they buy a chair at a street market. It is a handsome chair, well-proportioned, simple, with some vestiges of a beautiful surface. But it is also the past, the surrender of self to social conventions, the threat of a household and an inauthentic life. They give it away and resign from the world of work.

In Lawrence's novel it is Gerald and Gudrun who reach out to society and need it, whereas Birkin and Ursula move down below the ego defined by society, through the self to the dark impersonal powers which are the center of its being, which are Being itself. Against this metaphysical depth are set all the forms of retreat that society offers: the possession of chairs, the dead world of Breadalby, the Crich industrial empire, London Bohemia. Just as Jane Austen moves below the surface of manners to the moral urgencies which underlie it, so Lawrence moves below the surface of the ego to the reality of Being. In both cases the surface gives way to reveal depth, then reforms anew with our consciousness of all that lies below it. At some point the terms in which the self is presented give way to new terms; the apparent self gives way to the other self, which it may disguise or protect, whose energy it may pervert or direct.

In *Middlemarch* we see this transcendence of the apparent self in moments of expansion, of the movement out of contracted self-regard into sympathy and a sense of obligation. "Was she alone in that scene? Was it her event only?" It is with these questions that Dorothea Brooke moves to the window and sees "a man with a bundle on his back and a woman carrying her baby . . . Far off in the bending sky was the pearly light; and she felt the largeness of the world and the manifold wakings of men to labour and endurance." There is little in George Eliot that suggests the metaphysical dimension of man's existence unless it is the claim of duty, and even this is interpreted as the demand of sympathy. The other self is found in relatedness to fellow-men. In Jane Austen it is found in the purified world of manners, purified by the accord her heroines finally achieve between their moral sense and their social existence. In Lawrence the ego and society are constantly seen as assertions of the will, and the other self is only attained through an act of transcendence.

These remarks are too brief to be very useful unless they make clearer the way in which the dimensions of character the novelist presents are determined by something more than his love for the reality of other persons. The fullness of the characters we admire in George Eliot depends on the relevance of their social roles to the situation in which their meaning is realized. We may wish to encourage new novelists to pursue comparable themes, but we must recognize that George Eliot's world is as much adapted to her themes as any other novelist's, that it achieves its peculiar fullness of humanity by ignoring those dimensions that might impress us as no less significantly human in Jane Austen or in Lawrence.

NOTES

1   Kenneth Clark, *The Nude: A Study in Ideal Form* (New York, 1956), pp. 4-7.

2   Maurice Merleau-Ponty, *The Primacy of Perception*, ed. James M. Edie (Evanston, 1964), pp. 3, 5. This passage occurs in a prospectus of his work translated by Arleen B. Dallery.

3   Stuart Hampshire, *Thought and Action* (New York, 1960), pp. 91-2.

4   Orville E. Brim, Jr., "Personality Development as Role-Learning", in *Personality Development in Children*, ed. Ira Iscoe and H. W. Stevenson (Austin, Texas, 1960), p. 141; cited in J. Milton Yinger, *Toward a Field Theory of Behavior: Personality and Social Structure* (New York, 1965), p. 145 with Yinger's demurrer.

5   Yinger, *Toward a Field Theory of Behavior*, p. 108. See also Michael Banton, *Roles: An Introduction to the Study of Social Relations* (London, 1965), esp. pp. 127-50; and Anne-Marie

Rocheblave-Spenlé, *La Notion de Role en Psychologie Sociale* (Paris, 1962), esp. pp. 213-73.

6 *George Herbert Mead on Social Psychology: Selected Papers*, ed. Anselm Strauss (Chicago, 1964), pp. 226, 222. For a fuller text, see G. H. Mead, *Mind, Self, and Society*, ed. Charles W. Morris (Chicago, 1934), pp. 135-63. For the protest, see Edward A. Tiryakian, *Sociologism and Existentialism* (Englewood Cliffs, N.J., 1962), pp. 104ff.

7 Iris Murdoch, "The Sublime and the Beautiful Revisited", *Yale Review*, XLIX (New Haven, 1959), pp. 254-5, 264-5.

8 Peter Ure, "Character and Role from Richard III to Hamlet", in *Stratford-upon-Avon Studies*, v, *Hamlet* (London and New York, 1964), pp. 9-10.

9 E. H. Gombrich, *Meditations on a Hobby Horse and Other Essays on the Theory of Art* (London, 1963), pp. 1-11.

10 Henry James, *Notes on Novelists with Some Other Notes* (New York, 1914), pp. 112-3, 150-1, 159. The extracts are from two essays on Balzac, written respectively in 1902 and 1913.

11 D. H. Lawrence, "The Novel", in *Reflections on the Death of a Porcupine and Other Essays* (London, 1925), p. 104.

12 See the interesting remarks by Claude Lévi-Strauss, *The Savage Mind* (1962) (London and Chicago, 1966), pp. 20-2.

13 Cf. Henry James, "The New Novel", *Notes on Novelists*, p. 323: "Who could pretend that Jane Austen didn't leave much more untold than told about the aspects and manners even of the confined circle in which her muse revolved?"

14 On figure-ground relationships in art, see Rudolf Arnheim, *Art and Visual Representation: A Psychology of the Creative Eye* (Berkeley and Los Angeles, 1954), pp. 177-203; E. H. Gombrich, *Meditations on a Hobby Horse*, pp. 151-9; E. H. Gombrich, *Art and Illusion: A Study in the Psychology of Pictorial Representation* (2d ed., New York, 1961), pp. 242-87.

15 See Robert Langbaum, *The Poetry of Experience: The Dramatic Monologue in Modern Literary Tradition* (London, 1957), esp. pp. 160-81.

16 The most relevant works are: Angus Wilson, "Diversity and Depth", *Times Literary Supplement* No. 2946, 15 Aug. 1958, p. vii; Barbara Hardy, *The Appropriate Form* (London, 1964); W. J. Harvey, *Character and the Novel* (London, 1965); John

Bayley, *The Characters of Love* (London, 1960); Iris Murdoch, "The Sublime and the Beautiful Revisited", *Yale Review*, XLIX (New Haven, 1959), pp. 247-71.

17 Wilhelm Worringer, *Abstraction and Empathy: A Contribution to the Psychology of Style* (1908), trans. Michael Bullock (London and New York, 1953). Worringer's ideas gained considerable currency in England through their use by T. E. Hulme in the posthumous volume, *Speculations* (London, 1924).

18 Barbara Hardy, *The Appropriate Form*, pp. 190-2. The episode occurs in *Anna Karenina*, Book VI, ch. 4, 5.

19 Iris Murdoch, "The Idea of Perfection", *Yale Review*, LIII (New Haven, 1964), p. 373. Although Miss Murdoch sees this as a novelist's view, she does not ascribe it to George Eliot.

Conrad, James
and *Chance*

"Think what English literature would be like without Conrad and James . . . There would be nothing!"[1] Thus Ford Madox Ford; and we must at least agree that there would be markedly less. The roles of Conrad and James in the English tradition of fiction are parallel in many respects; aliens themselves, they brought, and mainly from France, a view of the novel form at once broader as regards subject-matter and more self-conscious as regards form, than had been current in Victorian England; and in so doing they became the recognized, perhaps the supreme, masters of what we are still calling the modern novel. When one further considers that James and Conrad knew each other fairly well for nearly twenty years, one anticipates a relationship of quite exceptional human and literary interest. Actually, though certainly not lacking an appropriately ironic complexity, the relationship is above all elusive and obscure.

This is mainly for simple lack of evidence. Conrad habitually destroyed his letters; James burned most of his papers before his death: and less than a dozen letters survive from what must have been a fairly large correspondence.[2] Even so, there was probably a good deal of ambiguity in the relationship itself.

[i]

Conrad read and admired James rather early, while he was still

301

at sea. Once he had decided to become a professional writer, and his second novel, *An Outcast of the Islands,* came out, he thought of sending it to James; but it was very difficult to pluck up courage. In one letter (16 October 1896) Conrad writes to his first literary mentor, Edward Garnett: "I do hesitate about H. James. Still I think I will send the book. After all it would not be a crime or even an impudence." Then, after two further letters from Garnett, Conrad finally announces (27 October 1896): "I have sent *Outcast* to H. James with a pretty dedication; it fills the flyleaf".[3]

Conrad's self-mockery about the "pretty dedication" only partly prepares us for the lacerating embarrassment of the letter to James which accompanied the book. It begins

> I address you across a vast space invoking the name of that one of your children you love the most. I have been intimate with many of them, but it would be an impertinence for me to disclose here the secret of my affection. I am not sure that there is one I love more than the others. Exquisite Shades with live hearts, and clothed in the wonderful garment of your prose, they have stood, consoling, by my side under many skies. They have lived with me, faithful and serene – with the bright serenity of Immortals. And to you thanks are due for such glorious companionship.[4]

The thanks continue, and the letter closes with Conrad asking James to accept his book and thus "augment the previous burden of my gratitude".

Psychologically one senses the paralysing apprehension of an insecure worshipper approaching a distant and redoubtable deity; or of a lover whose abject fear of rebuff almost invites humiliation. The laborious indirection of the prose has echoes of James's own reluctance to specify the referents of his pronouns; but the primary influence is French, not only in making "children" stand for "books", but in that special tradition of abstract and hyperbolic magniloquence which gushes from the Immortals of the *Académie Française* on ceremonial occasions.

Some months after receiving this effusion, James reciprocated by sending Conrad his just-published *The Spoils of Poynton,* with the inscription: "To Joseph Conrad in dreadfully delayed but very grateful acknowledgment of an offering singularly generous and beautiful".[5] Then, a week later, on 19 February

1897, Conrad announced jubilantly to Garnett: "I had a note from James. Wants me to lunch with him on Thursday next – so there is something to live for – at last."

The meeting probably took place in James's London apartment at 34 De Vere Gardens, Kensington – it is there that Conrad later remembered that he had chanced upon the Pepys epigraph for his next book, *The Nigger of the "Narcissus"*. But Conrad was then living in Essex, and occasion for the two to meet very often was lacking. Eighteen months later, however, James and Conrad were brought closer together. In the summer of 1898 James became the lessee, and later the owner, of Lamb House, in Rye; and in October, the Conrads moved to the Pent, a Kentish farmhouse some fifteen miles to the east, and fairly close to Sandgate, where H. G. Wells was living. The Fords soon moved nearby, and there followed a period of quite close literary frequentation, of which many picturesque episodes have been recorded: Wells tells of Conrad "driving a little black pony carriage as though it was a droshky and encouraging a puzzled little Kentish pony with loud cries and endearments in Polish";[6] Mrs. Conrad recalls Henry James taking the Conrad's small son on his knee, and forgetting "his existence, now and then giving him an absent-minded squeeze", while baby Borys, with an "instinctive sense of Henry James's personality . . . sat perfectly resigned and still for more than half an hour";[7] and one also hears of James, nearly sixty, accompanied by Edmund Gosse, bicycling some ten miles across the marshes to have tea with H. G. Wells.[8]

Few of the friendships then formed were destined to survive; and there is no Rye school of novelists to rival the Lake School of poets. Conrad's feelings toward H. G. Wells cooled soon after he had dedicated *The Secret Agent* (1907) to him, though the rupture was not as violent as that of Wells and James, nor even as the earlier quarrels of Wells and Ford. James, never very fond of Ford, broke with him completely at the time of his conspicuously messy divorce (1910); Conrad's relationship with Ford became a good deal less intimate after the years of collaboration; and although there was no breach, Conrad saw very little of James after 1906.

The collaboration between Conrad and Ford on *The Inheritors* (1901) and *Romance* (1903), and Ford's help on Conrad's fiction

303

between *The End of the Tether* (1902) and *Nostromo* (1904) is probably the most important, as it is certainly the best known, of the literary consequences of these contacts. But it is worth considering what literary importance the Conrad-James relationship may have had. James was fifty-four when they met, and had been publishing for nearly thirty years, so the debt would obviously be entirely on Conrad's side; and there is no question of Conrad's profound reverence for James's achievement. Conrad habitually addressed James, and James alone, as *"cher maître"*;[9] one imagines that for Conrad the veteran who had been the friend of Flaubert and Turgenev was a captain under whom he would willingly serve to learn the final secrets of the novelist's craft. James, for his part, seems to have been willing. He showed Conrad the prospectus of *The Wings of the Dove*; this, for so secretive a writer as James, indicates a special kind of confidence – Conrad was, as James later told Wells, the only writer who had ever been permitted to read "those wondrous and copious preliminary *statements* (of my fictions that are to be)".[10]

There was, then, an early period of considerable literary intimacy; but although F. W. Dupee is not alone in viewing Conrad as James's "greatest disciple",[11] as far as I know no one has investigated whether, or how, Conrad may have learned from James.

There is, it is true, a very percipient comparison of "James and Conrad" by E. K. Brown.[12] For Brown both novelists are alike, not only in their greatness, but in the fact that they focus our interest not on "what will happen, but rather with what the happening will mean to the principal character or characters"; they differ mainly because James's subjective interest in the "world within" tends, especially in the later novels, to place the characters in a void where the "world without" hardly exists, whereas Conrad, is "immensely strong" just where James is weak, in the representation of "the visible world"; although Conrad's attempt to convey the internal, subjective world as well seems often to involve him in great technical difficulties.

Brown does not touch on the matter of influence; my own guess is that it was probably James's example which, more than anything else, helped Conrad to evolve his mature technique at a crucial stage in his development. Ford suggests – in the most generous spirit – that it was he who worked out with Conrad the new techniques of the Impressionist Novel,[13] which is itself an attempt to convey states of mind – E. K. Brown's "world within" – through sense impressions of the visible world. But in 1898 Ford had written only one very youthful novel, whereas Conrad had read and admired James for many years before the collaboration began; and Conrad also met James some eighteen months before he met Ford.[14] It is significant that it was at this time, in the early years at Rye, that James, genial as never before, was producing the great works which precede *The Ambassadors* – *The Spoils of Poynton* (1896), *What Maisie Knew* (1897), and *The Awkward Age* (1898): novels in which the Jamesian method of narration through the registering consciousness of one or more narrators is already perfected. It may also be significant that these were the works which Conrad apparently most admired. Of *The Spoils of Poynton*, Conrad wrote to Garnett that "the delicacy and tenuity of the thing are amazing" (13 February 1897); and although he then thought it only "as good as anything of his – almost", Ford, who himself thought it "the technical high-water mark of all James's work", reports "the rapturous and shouting enthusiasm of Conrad over that story when we first read it together so that that must have been the high-water mark of Conrad's enthusiasm for the work of any other writer".[15]

Ford's testimony is a little misleading – Conrad had read *The Spoils of Poynton* long before he met Ford; but it at least confirms Conrad's enthusiasm for a work which J. W. Beach calls "the first absolutely pure example of the James method".[16] The dates of this enthusiasm are significant: in February 1897 Conrad, after finishing *The Nigger of the "Narcissus"*, was turning away from the French influence, notably that of Flaubert. James had moved away long before, his example and his teaching may well have helped Conrad to move in the same direction. At all events, in August 1897 Conrad completed "The Return", a story with a somewhat Jamesian subject – "the fabulous untruth" of a society husband's "idea of life"; and in a letter to Garnett Conrad analyses the failure of the story in somewhat Jamesian terms – "if I did see it [the reason for his failure] I would also see the other way, the mature way – the way of art".[17] Then, after Conrad had failed to make any progress with his continuation of *The Outcast of the Island*, *The Rescue*, partly because "I seem to have lost all *sense* of style and yet I am haunted, mercilessly haunted by the *necessity* of style"[18] (29 March 1898), but still well before the meeting with Ford, Marlow made his appearance: "Youth" was written in the summer; *Lord Jim* was begun; a story called "Dynamite", the probable germ of *Chance*, was projected in May; and *Heart of Darkness*, the fourth of the Marlow stories, was written that winter, in the earliest days of Conrad's association with Ford.[19]

The significance of Marlow has been much analysed, and it certainly cannot be evaluated briefly. Very roughly, it seems to me that it was through Marlow that Conrad achieved his version of James's registering consciousness. Conrad's version is, of course, very different from that of James. In a sense it is technically more extreme, since where Marlow occurs, Conrad largely gives up the use of direct authorial narrative, which James usually retained; on the other hand Conrad's method is more expandable – there can be several narrators – and more suited to concrete visualization – Marlow tells us what he saw and heard, and we can see him doing it. With Marlow, in fact, the narrative point of view is wholly scenic, dramatized; and yet its as completely adapted to the relation of inner states of consciousness as to descriptions of the external world.

Whether this change in Conrad's narrative direction was influenced by Henry James can hardly be proved; but if so Conrad must have been particularly pleased by a letter from James praising *Lord Jim*. The letter has not survived, but Conrad's delight at its tenour is evident in his report to Garnett (12 November 1900):[20]

I send you the H.J. letter. A Draught from the Fountain of Eternal Youth. Wouldn't you think a boy had written it? Such enthusiasm! Wonderful old man, with his record of wonderful work! . . . And to you alone I show it . . . P.S. Pray send the James autograph back – registered.

The friendship of James and Conrad, however, does not seem to have become any closer after 1900. The two men were never on christian-name terms; there are very few references to James in Conrad's correspondence after 1900; and even fewer references to Conrad in James's. One reason may be that James, long established in England, knew many more people, and inhabited a much grander and more fashionable world. One gets the sense of social distance very strongly from two letters of 1902[21] which James wrote to that complacent pillar of the Establishment, Edmund Gosse, about a plan to relieve Conrad's acute and endemic financial difficulties by an award from the Royal Literary Fund. In his covering private letter to Gosse James writes:

> I lose not an hour in responding to your request about Conrad – whom I had not in the least known to be in the state you mention. It horrifies me more than I can say . . .

James can hardly bring himself to say "poverty"; and it is perhaps because of James's special attitude to money that he was apparently one of the few friends Conrad did not tell about his recurrent financial crises; the acid test which distinguishes intimate friendship from cordial acquaintance often seems, sadly enough, to be the question: "Would I turn to him, or he to me, for a loan if need arose?"

In his official letter of support James is certainly "warm yet discrete", as he explains to Gosse, in his praise of Conrad's "charming, conscientious, uncommon work" which has "truly a kind of disinterested independent nobleness". It is "real literature, of a distinguished sort", and Conrad has been, for James, "one of the most interesting and striking of the novelists of the new generation." On the other hand the warmth of James's praise is curiously qualified by the distance of his tone.[22] However, it is always difficult to estimate the intention behind James's later style, if only because the use of abstract terms in personal relationships makes one suspect irony, or a defensive formality; so all one can be sure about from these two letters is that James admired and wished to help Conrad, but was not intimately involved in his affairs.

For his part Conrad not only gave James warm and perceptive praise in his letters to Garnett (13 February 1897) and Galsworthy (11 February 1899); he also wrote "Henry James: An Appreciation" (1905) for the *North American Review*. The ceremonious grandiloquence of the essay's style hardly enables Conrad to come within sighting distance, of, as the saying is, "the words on the page"; but it is a moving personal tribute, and at the same time suggests a profound inward understanding of James's moral world. As Conrad later wrote to John Quinn,[23] he intended only " 'An Appreciation'; nothing more – nothing less"; and more specifically, an appreciation of James's "art in a large relation, as a fellow writer . . . the sheer great art of it, where not so much the mind as the soul finds its expression".

Conrad begins by announcing that James's "books stand on my shelves in a place whose accessibility proclaims the habit of frequent communion"; and he continues with jocose urbanity:

> I do not know into what brand of ink Mr. Henry James dips his pen; indeed, I heard that of late he had been dictating; but I know that his mind is steeped in the waters flowing from the fountain of intellectual youth. The thing – a privilege – a miracle – what you will – is not quite hidden from the meanest of us who run as we read. To those who have the grace to stay their feet it is manifest. After some twenty years of attentive acquaintance with Mr. Henry James's work, it grows into absolute conviction which, all personal feeling apart, brings a sense of happiness into one's artistic existence.

Conrad's essay makes two main points about the nature of James's outlook: it is relativist and it is tragic. Relativist because

> the creative art of a writer of fiction may be compared to rescue work carried out in darkness against cross gusts of wind swaying the action of a great multitude. It is rescue work, this snatching of vanishing phrases of turbulence, disguised in fair words, out of the native obscurity into a light where the struggling forms may be seen, seized upon, endowed with the only possible form of permanence in this world of relative values – the permanence of memory.

Conrad defines the tragic quality of James's work in the characteristic formula: "Nobody has rendered better, perhaps, the tenacity of temper, or known how to drape the robe of spiritual honour about the drooping form of a victor in a barren strife". The sphere of heroic action in modern times, Conrad concedes, has much diminished, for "the earth itself has grown smaller in the course of ages"; but James is a heroic writer nevertheless:

... the struggles Mr. Henry James chronicles with such subtle and direct insight are, though only personal contests, desperate in their silence, none the less heroic (in the modern sense) for the absence of shouted watchwords, clash of arms and sound of trumpets. James's vision denies the desire for finality, for "which our hearts yearn".

James's vision denies "the desire for finality, for which our hearts yearn"; it asserts instead – and here Conrad places a familiar theme of later James criticism in a perspective that is at once highly general and deeply personal – the imperative of renunciation:

That a sacrifice must be made, that something has to be given up, is the truth engraved in the innermost recesses of the fair temple built for our edification by the masters of fiction. There is no other secret behind the curtain. All adventure, all love, every success is resumed in the supreme energy of an act of renunciation.

[ii]

After 1905 James and Conrad seemed to have seen much less of each other, although they continued to exchange their works, usually adorned with magniloquent inscriptions, and usually acknowledged in equally lapidary style. But the resonance of full human reciprocity is absent; instead there sadly comes to mind E. M. Forster's phrase, "a friendliness, as of dwarfs shaking hands, was in the air". For instance, when Conrad sent *The Mirror of the Sea* to James in September or October of 1906, he wrote (in French) that he was "very sure of the friendship with which you honour me"; nevertheless he also, as if not wholly sure of the book's welcome, repeated a deprecatory phrase he had used earlier in sending *The Nigger of the "Narcissus"*: "the book has at least the merit of being short". James responded promptly (1 November 1906) with:

No one has *known* – for intellectual use – the things you know, and you have, as the artist of the whole matter, an authority that no one has approached. I find you in it all, writing wonderfully, whatever you may say of your difficult medium and your *plume rebelle*. You knock about in the wide waters of expression like the raciest and boldest of privateers.

Conrad, one surmises, may have winced at the faintly con-
descending colloquialism of "knock about", and at the nautical
metaphor, which had the effect of relegating him to a separate
novelistic domain from James's. Yet we would be wrong to
make too much of the implicit reservations: for James, a saucily
colloquial trope was the fatal Cleopatra for which the world of
explicit human communication was well lost; James certainly
admired, and may have envied, Conrad's breadth of experience;
and his praise is – for him – remarkably direct and unqualified,
as he concludes with a uniquely impressive and eloquent tribute:

> You stir me, in fine, to amazement and you touch me to tears, and I
> thank the powers who so mysteriously let you loose with such
> sensibilities, into such an undiscovered country – *for* sensibility.
> That is all for to-night. I want to see you again.

Early the next year, in 1907, the Conrads went abroad, and
when they returned it was to move away from Kent into
Bedfordshire. It is from there that Conrad's last published letter
to James is written (12 December 1903), to thank him for the
first six volumes of the New York Edition. Conrad "gloats
over the promise of the prefaces" and, after reading that of *The
American*, tells how he "sat for a long while with the closed
volume in my hands . . . thinking – that's how it began, that's
how it was done".

In 1909 the Conrads moved back to Kent, to a house a dozen
or so miles away from Rye, but there was no personal contact
with James for some four years. The silence was apparently
mainly on James's side; he was much preoccupied, saddened by
the death of his brothers, gloomy about the public's neglect of
his writings; and his visit to America, combined with a long and
serious illness, meant that he remained out of touch even with
close friends for several years. Conrad was not among the two-
hundred and seventy or so friends who presented James with a
golden bowl on his seventieth birthday, 15 April 1913;[24] which
may only mean that the sponsors did not think of him as a close
friend, or that Conrad had failed to answer a letter.

Later that year, however, Conrad apparently made some
friendly overture; and James responded, from London, in a
supreme example of the later epistolary indirection (19 June
1913):

I always knew you were a shining angel, and now, under this
fresh exhibition of your dazzling moral radiance (to say nothing of
other sorts), my natural impulse, you see, is to take advantage of
these sublime qualities in you up to the very hilt. Thus it is that I
throw myself upon the use of this violent machinery [the letter was
dictated and typed] for at last, and in all humility, approaching you;
because I feel that *you* will feel how I must have some pretty abject
personal reason for it. That reason, to deal with it in a word, is
simply that, having so miserably, so helplessly failed to do what I
was, during all the dreadful time, unspeakably yearning to – which
was neither more nor less than to get again into nearer relation with
you by some employment, however awkward, of hand or foot – I
now leave each of these members as just damnably discredited and
disgraced, and seek the aid of nimbler and younger and more vivid
agents than my own compromised 'personality' has proved itself able
to set in motion. In other (and fewer) words, I just sit here muffled
in shame for the absolute *doom* of silence – in all sorts of directions
too than the beautiful Kentish, and the insidiously Polish, and the
triumphantly otherwise *magistrale* – that, beginning, horrible to think,
something like four years ago at least, was so long to disfigure the
fair face of my general and constitutional good intention. For the
moment I merely lift the edge of the crimson veil of contrition to say
to you, peeping, as it were, from under it, that I don't despair of helping you to lift it almost altogether off me when once we shall really
be within mutual reach.

Not having yet exhausted the resources of syntax and metaphor to prolong the agonies of separation, James addresses
himself to the possible modalities of reunion:

I hear with fond awe of your possession of a . . . miraculous car,
the most dazzling element for me in the whole of your rosy legend.
Perhaps you will indeed again, some July afternoon, turn its head
to Lamb House, and to yours, my dear Conrad, and your Wife's
all far more faithfully than you can lately have believed even by
whatever stretch of ingenuity, Henry James.

Conrad paid a call; but he seems to have been told that the
Master was not at home. There was nothing exceptional in the
fact itself; Conrad himself apparently once had the great Lord
Northcliffe turned away from his door when he had called un-
invited;[25] as for James, though he delighted to receive his friends

he was often away; and if he was busy, sick, or expecting guests, his servants were no doubt accustomed to shield him from the importunities of callers by the hallowed mendacities of social decorum.[26] After considerable delay James yet again proposed a meeting, in terms even more elaborately disingenuous (13 October 1913):

> Will you conceive of me as approaching you as the most abject of worms, most contrite of penitents, most misrepresented – by hideous appearances – of all the baffled well-meaning and all the frustrated fond? If I could but *see* you for an hour all would become plain, and I should wring your heart with my true and inward history.

The cause of this particular "reaching out" in what James terms "the suppliant's flat-on-my-belly, the crawling with-my-nose-in-the-dust, posture" is to make amends for Conrads'

> generous signal to me by your afternoon call of some weeks, horribly many weeks, ago. You will be able to say nothing, however, that will reduce me to softer pulp than I already desire to present to you every symptom of . . .

The combination of "afternoon call" with the earlier phrase "most misrepresented by hideous appearance", seems to exclude the simplest explanation – that James had actually been out; but no further explanation is given. Instead the baroque banter continues as James wonders if Conrad

> mercifully and magnanimously can: come over to luncheon with me, by an heroic effort – and believe that I shall thereby bless you to the (perhaps not very distant) end of my days. If you tell me that this is impossible through the extremity of inconvenience, I will then arrange – that is, heaven forgive me! propose and aspire to – something less onerous to you.

There follows a review of possible methods of transportation: Conrad's fabled motorcar; that failing, James might "recklessly procure one for the occasion myself"; and there are trains "rather happily available". Any specific proposal, however, is delayed until the postscript, which invites Conrad . . . "*any* day after this week that you may kindly name for luncheon and if you can stay your stomach to 1:45".

All things considered we might have expected James to consider waiving the customary lateness of his midday collation; but he was old and set in his ways. To anyone assured of James's regard, the letter as a whole would have been taken merely as one of James's increasingly elaborate jokes; and Conrad no doubt so took it. Writing after James's death he told John Quinn "in our private relations he has been always warmly appreciative and full of invariable kindness. I had a profound affection for him. He knew of it and he accepted it as if it were something worth having. At any rate, that is the impression I have. And he wasn't a man who would pretend. What need had he? . . . even if he had been capable of it."

One detects, alas, a note of guarded doubt: Conrad speaks of James "accepting" Conrad's "profound affection", not of his reciprocating it. This, taken with Conrad's apologetic deference in sending *The Nigger of the "Narcissus"* and *The Mirror of the Sea*, and with the way that the delays in replying seem all to be on James's side, makes it likely that it was Conrad who sought to maintain the friendship, rather than James. It also seems probable that the elaborate formality of their intercourse, at least after the early days, had been a more-or-less conscious protection, by two proud but highly-civilised men, both against any overt acknowledgement of the inequality of their reciprocal sentiments, and against the intrusion of matters where they might disagree. Conrad for instance apparently felt that from *The Ambassadors* on, James had become the prisoner of his own technique;[27] while James must have had many reservations about Conrad's work, apart from *The Nigger of the "Narcissus"*, *Lord Jim* and *The Mirror of the Sea*.

In any case the mere passage of time was bound to change their relationship. At first James had been able to see Conrad mainly as a curiosity – Wells reports that to James, Conrad was "the strangest of creatures";[28] James referred to Marlow as "that preposterous Master Mariner";[29] and although one cannot doubt the exceptional sincerity of James's praise in the passages cited, they are all concerned with Conrad as a sea-writer or as an exotic (as in the letters about *Lord Jim* and *The Mirror of the Sea*). But, beginning with *Nostromo*, Conrad had increasingly encroached on the more normal and terrestrial domains of fiction; and by then Conrad's sales and reputation were steadily increasing, while James's continued to diminish. This contrast in their respective situations is vividly evoked in an interchange as early as 13 February 1904, related by Olivia Garnett: "Conrad, for once gleeful, exclaimed: 'I am at the top of the tree' H.J. replied: 'I am a crushed worm; I don't even revolve now, I have ceased to turn'."[30]

By 1913 it had become apparent to many critics that Conrad was James's chief rival for the title of the greatest contemporary novelist; and then in *Chance* Conrad made his closest approach to a Jamesian novel.[31] John Cowper Powys, for example, comments that "No work of Conrad's has so close an affinity with the art of Henry James . . . the disturbing vibration, the intense malice of provoked curiosity . . ." And – as we shall see – *Chance* has many other Jamesian elements; including the irony that Conrad's most Jamesian novel should have achieved a popular and financial success such as had for thirty years now eluded James, and at the same time provoked James to strike the last sad note in his dealings with Conrad.

[iii]

We do not know whether Conrad finally had lunch with James, though the two men probably did meet again. But later that year James proposed to the *Times Literary Supplement*[32] an article which was to contain his only published critique of Conrad. It appeared under the title "The New Generation" (19 March and 2 April 1914), and was reprinted in *Notes on Novelists* under the equally misleading title of "The New Novel".

The article – which is not James at his best, and which also provoked James's breach with Wells – divides the novelists into the very young, and the not-so-young. Among these latter James lists Maurice Hewlett, John Galsworthy, H. G. Wells, Arnold Bennett, and Conrad. All but the last of them are presented as following what James calls the "fatal error" of Tolstoy, "the great illustrative master-hand . . . of disconnexion of method from matter" – they all think only of their matter not of their art. Conrad, on the other hand, is presented as the prime – and unique – example of the other extreme:

It is doubtless fortunate that at the very moment of our urging this truth we should happen to be regaled with a really supreme specimen of the part playable, for our intenser interest, by a case of the exhibition of method at any price. Mr. Conrad's "Chance" places the author absolutely alone as the votary of the way to do a thing that shall make it undergo most doing. The way to do it that shall make it undergo least is the line on which we are mostly now used to see prizes carried off; so that the author of "Chance" gathers up on this showing all kinds of comparative distinction.

James's main objection to the narrative method of *Chance* is that it compromises the reader's sense of the reality of the events by drawing attention to the narrators rather than to the narrative: Conrad

> sets in motion more than anything else a drama in which his own system and his combined eccentricities of recital represent the protagonist in face of powers leagued against it, and of which the *dénouement* gives us the system fighting in triumph, though with its back desperately to the wall . . . This frankly has been our spectacle, our suspense and our thrill; with the one flaw on the roundness of it all the fact that the predicament was not imposed rather than invoked, was not the effect of a challenge from without, but that of a mystic impulse from within.

This view of *Chance* seems to me not to take account of Conrad's aims, and since James singles out the novel's ending for special attention, I would like to suggest that the method of narration here is in fact a response to the "challenge from without", to the imperatives of the story itself.

Very briefly, *Chance* is told through three major informants. The primary narrator, whose words constitute the novel, is an unnamed "I" who reports his conversations with Marlow. Though technically a secondary narrator, it is Marlow who is chiefly responsible for assembling the stories of the fictional protagonists: the Fynes, Flora, her father, De Barral, and her lover, Captain Anthony; Marlow's interminable colloquies also interpret the psychological and moral dimensions of the story, in what James felicitously terms "a prolonged hovering flight of the subjective over the outstretched ground of the case exposed". Then there is the third narrator, Powell, who meets the first two narrators at the beginning by chance, and who was second mate of Anthony's ship when the events of the last half of the novel occurred.

In the denouement it is Powell who happens to observe De Barral putting poison in Anthony's nightcap of brandy and water. Powell warns Anthony in time; Anthony, totally misinterpreting the situation, and thinking Flora put the poison in, says he will let her off at the next port; Flora announces "I don't want to be let off"; they embrace; out of jealousy De Barral drinks the poison himself; and Anthony, resolving that "I am not going to stumble now over that corpse", at long last consummates his marriage with Flora while her father lies dead in the next cabin.

James, presumably, would have focused the whole narration on the sensibility of Flora, as he did with Fleda Vetch, Maisie Farange and Nanda Brookenham, who are in some ways similar figures – innocent and only superficially contaminated victims of adult corruption. But Conrad often used reciters, partly to avoid the posture of psychological omniscience, and partly to dramatize the difficulty of understanding human values and motives. In the present instance both these reasons seem particularly apposite; and in addition it is surely evident that the rather gamey melodrama of the final scene would be much too obtrusive if it were related through Flora's consciousness. Instead it comes to us indirectly, and very selectively, through the recital of Powell; having no knowledge of the events that led up to the harrowing emotional deadlock between the lovers, or of its final resolution, he merely reports a few surface manifestations whose real significance is reconstituted through Marlow's imagination and the reader's; nowhere, I imagine, can subject matter have called more strongly for externality and indirection of presentation.

But this scene, though the end of Powell's narrative, is not quite the end of the novel. For in the last few pages of *Chance*, we are surprised to discover the reason why Powell, four years after the death of Captain Anthony, is haunting the particular Thames-side inn where narrators one and two are doing a little holiday sailing. Since *Troilus and Criseyde* the remarriage of widows has called for supreme authorial tact; and in *Chance* Conrad has recourse to his "eccentricities of recital" to bring about a neatly postponed recognition and resolution combined. Marlow finally discovers that Flora lives nearby, which accounts for Powell's presence in the first place; and the two are going to marry. The system thus "fights back in triumph" by relegating what might have been the anticlimax of Flora's remarriage into an artfully mundane, and structurally secondary, framework for the more vivid romantic colours of the central part of the story, the love of Flora and Anthony.

Much may be said against *Chance* and its narrative method: some obtrusive artificiality, a tendency to sentimentalize, and moments of fatiguing garrulousness; but the charge that its mode of recital is gratuitously imposed seems itself to be gratuitous.

James and Conrad must have looked at the treatment of *Chance* in the "New Generation" essay from very different points of view. James would certainly have felt that he was innocent of envy or malice, and he could point to passages where Conrad was implicitly accorded a higher literary status than any other author treated: Conrad alone is called a "genius"; and *Chance* is described as the work of "a beautiful and generous mind" with "a noble sociability of vision". But, as Conrad must have seen, what James gives with one hand he takes away with the other, and in much more detail. Imperceptive about the reasons for the method of *Chance*, James, no doubt impelled by the rhetorical requirements of his polar opposition between Conrad's concentration on method, and the infatuation with mere matter of the other contemporary novelists, does not mention earlier works in which Conrad might have figured as offering happier examples of harmony between form and content. And it was surely stretching the prerogatives of age when, from the height of his 71 years, James placed Conrad, at 57, in the "younger generation" (as he already had earlier in his 1902 letter to Gosse); especially when Conrad was actually nine years older than the next oldest novelist treated, H. G. Wells. It must also have been especially bitter to Conrad when James brought out his friend Edith Wharton, the only American novelist discussed, as his "eminent instance . . . most opposed to that baffled relation between the subject matter and its emergence which we find constituted by the circumvallations of *Chance.*" And when, finally, we notice that James cites his own *The Awkward Age* as a further salutary demonstration of how "the novel may be fundamentally organised", only one conclusion seems possible: in what Edith Wharton noted as "his increasing preoccupation with the structure of the novel",[33] James is leaving as his literary legacy: "My life-work for the art of fiction has failed; nor can I acknowledge Conrad as a successor – even poor Edith Wharton has learned my lesson better".

In a letter to John Quinn, Conrad wrote that James's treatment of *Chance* was "the *only time* a criticism affected me painfully".[34] But it did not alter their personal friendship which continued to the end: when, in the summer of 1915, James solicited a contribution for a war charity anthology, Conrad replied with all the old warmth to his *"cher maître"* (24 July 1915). But one understands how it must have hurt, not only that James didn't like *Chance* better, but that he went out of his way to say so in print, especially after his own public praise of James in the *North American Review*. For Conrad, rightly or wrongly, the obligations of friendship outweighed those of literary criticism: Curle tells of hearing Conrad "say of some living author, 'I like him and I don't want to talk about his books' "; in public, at least, if Conrad could not praise he preferred to remain silent.[35]

But, as Conrad knew, James was quite different; he had never been known to spare the critical rod even for his closest friends. With an intimate, such as Edith Wharton, James had been savage enough in private criticism:[36] for some reason – perhaps Conrad's devotion to him, or his disarming politeness – James had not, probably, been as frank with Conrad, and his reservations clamoured for expression somehow. In the end it comes down to an invincible difference of temperament. The impulse to love and be loved was not as close to the surface in James as in Conrad; it was there, but always at the mercy of many other conflicting impulses; above all, the truth about what mattered most – the art of the novel; and it was difficult to disentangle this felt truth completely from other more personal impulses – the urge to dominate, to get other people in your power, to achieve in fact the absolute satisfactions of the Godhead, or of its latter-day embodiment, the critic. And this, in the end, is surely the functional strategy of the later Jamesian style and point of view: that formidable digestive instrument really does produce a "baffled relation between the subject-matter and its emergence", because the subject-matter – people – can only emerge in subordination to James's detached analysis of them in abstract terms of his own choosing.

It was a subordination which came to dominate his life as well as his fiction. "Our poor friend" is the implied stance which James adopts for Conrad, as well as for Strether and for his later fictional protagonists; and it is difficult not to see it, ultimately, as a strategy of patronage: in his last letters, Conrad as a person, and even James's feelings about him, seem to have become merely pretexts for prose, artifacts to be manipulated by an Omniscience with a capital "O".

It is not, I think, a question either of emotional insincerity or of intentional patronage on James's part. To anyone at all self-conscious about literary expression and personal relationships, the difficulty of writing a letter increases in exact proportion to the writer's awareness of the recipient's awareness of these things. James would have felt he was insulting Conrad, as well as betraying his real self, if he remained at the level of the usual epistolatory banalities, from the opening "Sorry I haven't written before", through the central "let's get together", to the final "regards to your wife". Instead James felt bound to encompass in a unified rhetorical structure everything from the immediate business at hand – the hackneyed items of apology, invitation and salutation – to the remoter and yet intimate presences of past relationship and present feeling. So ambitious and all-enveloping a compositional imperative inevitably pushes towards abstraction and indirection; and in the process the sense of mutuality and naturalness is fatally compromised. As James came to live more and more for his art, other people, in the letters, as in the novels, became the victims, not of any conscious patronage, but, purely incidentally, of James's confidence in a finally-achieved stylistic mastery over his material.

Conrad's powerful critical mind may have proffered some such redeeming explanation; but the disappointment at what he called being "rather airily condemned"[37] must have rankled. As Conrad had worked his painful way through the literary jungle it had been from James's voice that he most hoped for recognition; but when the voice finally spoke out it did not accept him as a peer.

The final muted footnote on the relationship follows closely enough along the lines of how Marlow, in *Heart of Darkness*, kept his own counsel after Kurtz's death. As an obituary tribute the *North American Review* reprinted[38] Conrad's "Henry James: An Appreciation", though without his knowledge.[39] It is as if, in a final gesture of fidelity towards James, chance itself were enacting Conrad's affirmation in *Under Western Eyes*: "A man's real life is that accorded to him in the thoughts of other men by reason of respect or natural love".[40]

NOTES

1 Letter to Herbert Read, 19 March 1920 (*Letters of Ford Madox Ford*, ed. Richard M. Ludwig (Princeton, 1965), p. 127).

2 Of the six letters from Conrad to James known to me, two are published in *Lettres françaises*, ed. G. Jean-Aubry (Paris, 1929), and two in G. Jean-Aubry, *Joseph Conrad: Life and Letters* (London, 1927). I am indebted to Professor Frederick R. Karl, who is editing Conrad's letters, for copies of the originals; as also for his generous assistance and advice in other respects. I gratefully acknowledge the permission of the Trustees of the Joseph Conrad Estate to publish portions of these letters, and the gracious help of the Librarians of the Houghton Library at Harvard, the Beinecke Library at Yale, and the Academic Center Library at the University of Texas.

Of James's letters to Conrad, three were published in *Twenty Letters to Joseph Conrad*, ed. G. Jean-Aubry (London: The First Editions Club, 1926); one of them is reprinted in *Selected Letters of Henry James*, ed. Leon Edel (London, 1956). I gratefully acknowledge Professor Leon Edel's help, and his permission, as editor of the James correspondence, to reprint portions of these letters here.

3 *Letters from Conrad, 1895-1924*, ed. Edward Garnett (London, 1927), pp. 50, 54. It seems likely that James was the only author whom Conrad singled out in this way.

4 The letter is dated 16 October 1896, the day of Conrad's first letter on the subject to Garnett; Conrad presumably kept it at least until 25 October, the date of his second letter to Garnett.

5 Jean-Aubry, *Life and Letters*, I, 201, N.2.

6 H. G. Wells, *Experiment in Aubobiography* (New York, 1934), p. 527.

7 Jessie Conrad, *Joseph Conrad as I Knew Him* (London, 1926), p. 48.

8 Wells, *Experiment in Autobiography*, p. 508.

9 *Lettres françaises*, pp. 34, 77.

10 15 November 1902 (*Henry James and H. G. Wells*, ed. Leon Edel and Gordon Ray (London, 1959), p. 83).

11 *Henry James* (London, 1951), p. 281.

12 "James and Conrad", *Yale Review*, xxxv (1945), 265-85.

13 F. M. Ford, *Joseph Conrad: A Personal Remembrance* (London, 1924), pp. 174-215.

14 In September 1898 (Jocelyn Baines, *Joseph Conrad: A Critical Biography* (London, 1960), p. 215).

15 Ford Madox Ford, *Portraits From Life* (Chicago, 1960), p. 11.

16 Joseph Warren Beach, *The Method of Henry James* (New Haven, 1916), p. 233.

17 *Letters from Conrad*, pp. 94, 98.

18 *Letters from Conrad*, p. 127.

19 Baines, *Joseph Conrad*, p. 210; and *Joseph Conrad: Letters to William Blackwood and David S. Meldrum*, ed. William Blackburn (Durham, North Carolina, 1958), pp. 21, 36-7.

20 *Letters from Conrad*, pp. 173-4.

21 26 June 1902 (British Museum, Ashley MS 4792.) I am very grateful to David Thorburn for providing me with the transcripts.

22 There is a rather similar ambiguity towards Conrad in a letter James wrote to Gelett Burgess. James's price for "a short tale" which Burgess has asked for, as an editor of *Ridgway's Militant Weekly*, had proved too stiff; but Burgess had acquired *The Secret Agent* for serialization; and in a postscript James commented: "I rejoice for you in your having something from the interesting and remarkable Conrad!" (23 September 1906. I am grateful to Professor Joseph Backus for informing me of this letter, and for providing a transcript.)

23 24 May 1916. I am indebted to the Manuscript Division of the New York Public Library, and the Trustees of the Joseph

Conrad Estate, for permission to quote this letter, from the John Quinn Papers, Vol. I.

24 I am indebted to the Colby College Library for photocopies of the correspondence and list of subscribers. Gosse's management of the affair caused "the most awful fuss", according to Hugh Walpole (Rupert Hart-Davis, *Hugh Walpole: A Biography* (London, 1952), p. 99).

25 According to Joseph H. Retinger (*Conrad and His Contemporaries* (London, 1941), p. 68).

26 Jacques-Émile Blanche, indeed, speaking of how James protected himself from casual visitors, reports that much earlier Conrad had called without previous notice at the Reform Club, and been told that James was out (*Mes Modèles*, Paris, 1928, p. 176).

27 Richard Curle, *The Last Twelve Years of Joseph Conrad* (London, 1928), p. 119.

28 Wells, *Experiment in Autobiography*, p. 525.

29 Ford, *Joseph Conrad*, p. 161.

30 Cited by Simon Nowell-Smith, *The Legend of the Master* (London, 1947), p. 135. I am very grateful to Mr. Nowell-Smith and to Professor Moser for giving me the date of this diary entry.

31 John Cowper Powys, "Chance", *A Conrad Memorial Library* (New York, 1929), pp. 219-20.

32 Letter of James to Bruce Richmond, 19 December 1913 (*The Letters of Henry James*, ed. Percy Lubbock (London, 1920), II.350-2.

33 Edith Wharton, *A Backward Glance* (New York, 1934), p. 323.

34 24 May 1916.

35 Richard Curle, *Last Twelve Years of Joseph Conrad*, p. 16.

36 "His tender regard for his friends' feelings was equalled only by the faithfulness with which, on literary questions, he gave them his view of their case when they asked for it – and sometimes when they did not."(Wharton, *A Backward Glance*, p. 181).

37 Letter to Quinn, 24 May 1916.

38 April 1916.

39 In his letter to Quinn thanking him for sending the article, Conrad wrote that he had "forgotten it completely" 24 May 1916).

40 Dent Collected Edition (London, 1947), p. 14.

CLIFFORD LEECH

The Shaping of Time: Nostromo and Under the Volcano

Until this century, the action of a drama was plotted in what we can call a straight line. If we saw Event B on the stage after Event A, we were expected to assume that it came later in time. Aristotle's demand, of course, was that B should arise out of A "by probability or necessity", but even the most carefree and romantic of playwrights would adhere to the principle that succession in presentation implied succession in action. What we get from such writing is a series of present moments correspondent indeed to our normal and superficial concept of actual experience. Memory and anticipation are not ruled out, and memory plays a particularly important part in those dramas where the Unity of Time is observed: Tamburlaine and Henry V can begin by dreaming of the conquests they will later achieve; *Oedipus Rex*, *The Wild Duck* and *The Tempest* can use memory so fully that, while the explicit action moves always onward, the spectator's mind is busily constructing a past which is no longer moving because complete. In these last instances it is worth noting that the past in such a play is commonly removed from the play's action by a substantial tract of years. The past that matters for Oedipus is comprised of events that terminated with his marrying Jocasta and becoming King; for Gregers Werle and Prospero the special burdens they carry are not related to what happened only yesterday. Thus commonly – though not uniformly, the linked history plays of the Elizabethan years being among the exceptions – there is a sharp sense of difference between what is presented and what is referred to as anterior; and almost always the principle of temporal succession is adhered to. It is true that it was possible to use a framing device, with for example the dramatized action functioning as something recalled by a narrator – by Gower in *Pericles*, by Madge in Peele's *The Old Wives' Tale*, by Bohan in Greene's *James IV*. Yet I know of only one instance, even in such cases, where time is treated lightly inside the action thus framed. In *James IV* Bohan is presenting the play to Oberon in order to demonstrate the condition of things in the world that long ago made him turn recluse: the dramatist at one point allows Oberon to intervene in the action to save one of Bohan's sons from execution. Here magic is enabled to transform the past, but Greene's example was not followed in the plays of his successors, and thus remains a curious exception to an otherwise uniform adherence to linear time in dramatic action.

This may at first sight appear strange. The Elizabethan dramatists are notorious for playing certain tricks with time: they could move from midnight to dawn within a few minutes, as in the first scene of *Hamlet*, and they could use inconsistent references to duration, as most liberally in *Othello*. But there was dominant in play-writing a dichotomy between a completed past and a present that was shaping itself in relation to, and perhaps under the full control of, that past. This is in conformity with a total view that sees things ultimately "working out"; the present is subsumed into the past; the idea of the past held by us in the present possesses, as we have seen, a character of completeness, but our actions in the present are continuously adding to the structure; a moment comes which crowns the work, when there is no more future, when the past is subsumed into a static present. This is symbolized in the terminal point of a play (or of any piece of narrative fiction cast in the same mould of thought): Time triumphs, as it is asserted in the sub-title of Greene's *Pandosto*; the whirligig of time brings in its revenges, as Feste tells Malvolio at the end of *Twelfth Night*; when Edmund in *Lear* recognizes that for him Fortune's wheel has come full circle, he employs the traditional emblem to signify that a pattern in his life, previously hidden from him, has now reached total being and become plain. But such terminal points in plays and early novels are symbols of a larger idea.[1] For the individual man, the moment of completion is death, which gives a wholeness to his life, makes his total being ready for judgement. And for the universe, as seen by writers for whom the Christian tradition is strong, there will also come a moment when succession evaporates, when becoming yields to being. Marlowe makes Mephistophilis anticipate such a condition:

> when all the world dissolves
> And every creature shall be purify'd,
> All places shall be hell that is not heaven. (V. 125-7)[2]

Thus we can understand that in a fictional presentation the principle of temporal succession would be normally adhered to without conscious questioning: Greene could make Oberon intervene in an event belonging to the past, but *James IV* is not a very serious play and the King of the Fairies could for once be permitted to enjoy a bizarre extension of the powers normally credited to him. Such a thing could not happen in a purposeful holding up of the mirror to nature, and even in comedy of the lightest sort it remains, as far as I know, a unique departure.[3]

But suppose our view of the world is of a different sort, not one in which becoming yields ultimately to being, in which a pattern is finally established, but one in which a man's death is no more and no less than a single incident in his life, in which time does not triumph or bring in its just revenges – in which indeed hero and villain and common man are equally "caught" in what we call the "end", in which justice does not exist except in the mind of man, in which causation itself is a concept to be handled gingerly. We may hear of a friend dying in a painful and grotesque fashion, and our immediate reaction is to let that fact colour our whole sense of his being: for the moment each step in his experience seems only to have been bringing him nearer to that final happening which is felt to shape all that went before. But when the initial shock of the news has passed, we may work closer to a freedom from that traditional response, and our recollection of the man as he was in separable moments before death will assume something approaching autarky. It is even, perhaps, possible for a man about to die to see his death thus, as only one incident among others. Katow in Malraux's *La Condition humaine*, walking towards the railway-engine where he was to be thrown into the furnace, could say to himself: "Allons! supposons que je sois mort dans un incendie." That of course exhibits a degree of self-command that makes us catch our breath, but the point that is especially important here is that, not only was there an absence of justice in Katow's end (and, in the writer's view, nothing beyond that end in the way of compensating experience), but the end itself did not negate Katow's life. He died terribly, but that is a separable fact from his having lived, and with a kind of splendour. Such a view of things, when not felt at a deeper level, can lead to a complacency as offensive as any facile notion of ultimate compensation. In Jean Anouilh's play *L'Alouette* the story proceeds to the burning of Joan of Arc, and then the commentator asserts that Joan's story was nevertheless a triumphant one and the play will therefore end with a re-enactment of her moment of success when the Dauphin was crowned at Rheims: so time in the theatre, as often nowadays, is made to turn backwards and we see one of the play's earlier scenes repeated, we see Joan smiling once more, and we leave the theatre glad for the success of French arms in rebutting the invader. On the way home we may resent the trick that has been played upon us. The situation is indeed different with Malraux: he does not spare us a sense of the agony awaiting Katow, and in another of his novels, *La Voie royale*, he makes one of his characters, watching the painful death of his friend, feel a longing that there were indeed gods to whom he could cry in his anger that no hope of heaven, no promise of reward can justify the end of any human life. For Malraux, death is terrible because it brings to an end and because the struggle against non-being can be agony; but it does not govern the pattern, it does not invalidate the life that has been. Here the finely articulate Malraux gives utterance to a view of things which in our century has gained ground and which has incidentally led some dramatists to a freer use of temporal patterns than their predecessors thought of.

The novel in its earliest phases was almost as fully wedded as the drama to the principle of succession. Philosophically there could be no difference indeed between the two modes: in narrative fiction time had its triumphs as regularly as in tragedy and comedy. But for technical reasons there is an important difference. In the drama a clear distinction exists between what is narrated and what is presented: the former is conveyed through a set speech (either by a chorus-figure or by one of the *dramatis personae*) or on occasion through an interchange between two or more speakers, while the latter is acted out before our eyes; the recollected and the immediate belong in different worlds of discourse correspondent to the separate notions of past and present. But in the novel all is narrative: there commonly is an immediate story-line, but when one of the characters talks about the past or where the omniscient narrator (like a chorus in a play) interrupts the story-line in order to apprise us of things we need to know concerning events that have led up to those with which we are to be primarily concerned, the interposed narrative will not necessarily differ in its mode of presentation from the main story-line itself. Thus the story of the Paphlagonian King in Book II, chapter X, of the *Arcadia* and the story of Mr. Wilson in Book III, chapter III, of *Joseph Andrews* present events of the past in a mode only partially distinct from that of the adventures of Musidorus and Pyrocles or of Parson Adams and Joseph. There is indeed a degree of distinction in these instances, for in Sidney the narrative is sufficiently short for us to remain conscious of the presence of Musidorus and Pyrocles, who are listening to it, and Fielding goes so far as to make Adams interrupt Wilson from time to time or at least silently register his response to what is being narrated. To that degree a past-present dichotomy is maintained in a fashion inherent in the dramatic writings contemporaneous with these novels. But when the inset narrative is substantial in length and the novelist allows it to be self-contained, the distinction evaporates. Moreover, a writer of narrative will frequently have more than one character as a centre of attention, as Spenser has when Una and her knight are separated, as Cervantes has when Sancho goes to his island: he will then commonly find himself in the position of having to travel back in time in order that we may learn what has happened in the interim to the character who for a time has been neglected. "We last saw our hero when he was taking a sad farewell of the beauteous Isabel, little knowing of the danger that was to threaten her at home while he was far away." We have already been given a narrative of Isabel's misadventures, and now we go along with the hero until once again we get to the point of time, or thereabouts, where she in her turn has been left. This of course can be tedious, and many a reader of lesser Victorian fiction has yawned at meeting such words as I have here put together to illustrate the use of the device at its most elementary. Even in this small way, however, the novel's long-established freedom in its use of time is evident.

There is, moreover, a subtler distinction between drama and narrative fiction which is relevant here, and that concerns the nature of a "present moment" in the two modes. In drama what is present is and must be something discrete. It is a man stabbing or kissing or dying, a man saying the words "To be or not to be". In the novel there is frequently no such sharpness of effect. For one thing, all is in the past. The indications of action are nearly always in the past tense, unlike the stage-directions which a reader of a play is given. For another, the presence of the narrator, even at his most reticent, is brought to mind at least in such necessary formulae as "said John". And there is the use of the characterizing adverb, or the frequent indication that what a character is saying is in complex relation with his condition of mind. At every instant there is a doubleness of viewpoint: the experience presented is seen both through the eyes of the character or characters involved (and for him or them it is immediate, present) and through the eyes of the narrator (for whom it has taken its place in a total fabric of narrative and thus belongs to the past). Clearly the drama approaches the condition characteristic of the novel when a framing action is used, but even then the fact that we watch real people acting makes what they do and say possess a high degree of self-containment. In the novel we are always, to a greater or lesser degree, aware of the present as simultaneously past. We are aware too of the complexity of each moment, of its associations within a series. Drama at its simplest has the quality of a rite, in which each act and word has a hieratic function. Narrative, on the other hand, puts us into the flux. Among writers earlier than the late nineteenth century, it is Sterne who avails himself most fully and self-consciously of the freedom that narrative thus allows. He can expand the moment, prolonging it by holding its many facets before us in turn; he can turn on his tracks, making the past once again present; he can insist on the complexity of response that a group of characters may display to a single happening; he will delight to break his narrative to add his own particularizing and generalizing comments.

But in the writing of recent generations even Sterne's degree of freedom has become an established thing.[4] The novel has shown itself to be the mode most appropriate to the modern consciousness of the nature of living. Drama has won a large measure of freedom, but its inversions of the temporal sequence have often about them something of the perversity of an anti-ritual. The novel and the film, on the other hand, have become the basic media of the twentieth century when it is taking itself most seriously in the field of fully articulate expression. The drama is capable of strong and poignant gestures in the deliberate rejection of its historic mode. Indeed the drama remains fully necessary in its function of explicit denial. Nevertheless, novel and film are predisposed to temporal freedom, and in the rest of this paper I wish to discuss two major examples of a free manipulation of event – Conrad's *Nostromo*, first published in 1904, and Malcolm Lowry's *Under the Volcano*, first published in 1947.

In common they have a setting in America south of the United States – *Nostromo* in an imaginary republic called Costaguana, facing the Pacific, *Under the Volcano* in Mexico – and a concern with the tragic event. In other respects it might appear they are as far apart as *The Winter's Tale* and *The Tempest* – the one ranging freely over a wide tract of time, from that moment when the Gould family were first made to assume the burden of the silver mine to a future only hinted at, when the Goulds' success is once more brought into question; the other giving us (after a retrospective opening chapter) the anguished events of a single day. Of course, the Shakespeare analogues are not exact: *The Winter's Tale* follows the line of temporal progression, *Nostromo* repeatedly comes back to the same moment of crisis before finally taking off into more or less plain narrative; the conclusion of *The Tempest* is poised between the completed and the open-ended effects, displaying and simultaneously questioning the point at which time has triumphed, while the opening chapter of *Under the Volcano* takes away from the Consul's death, at the end of the novel, some part of its finality. Nevertheless, just as the two Shakespeare plays combine strong technical differences with a similarity in mood and viewpoint, so the two novels exemplify different ways in which the twentieth-century writer may show his readiness to treat time with disrespect, to see death as an incident, to assert the validity of the thing that is as, and because, it happens.

The first chapter of *Nostromo*, like the beginning of *The Return of the Native*, gives a static description of the setting: the Placid Gulf, with the "insignificant" Punta Mala on one side and the peninsula of Azuera on the other (one ominous in name, the other through its legend of men lost in a search for treasure), the islands called the Isabels forming a barrier against the open sea, and the location of the Sulaco plain and its relation to the republic of Costaguana. Isolation is emphasized, the mercantile adventurers being kept away by the prevailing calm of the gulf and the mountains beyond the plain preserving a quasi-independence for Sulaco, but the hints of ill omen on either side of the gulf, the gauntness of the islands, and the implicit suggestion that steamships, soon to replace sail, will not be so easily deterred – all mark this as a setting for tragic events. It seems we are to witness the destruction of a Utopia. But we soon learn that that is to see things too simply: Costaguana is a republic already torn, subject to the historical tensions of the nineteenth century even before the Placid Gulf ceases to be a deterrent; dictatorship, federalism, liberalism, take their turns in the country's mode of government; semi-isolation is no guarantee against violence, corruption, intrigue; all it effects is to keep these things local, domestic.

In the second chapter we are taken to a point in Costaguanan history to which the novel returns again and again – the defeat and flight of the liberal head of state Ribiera. The novel is divided into three Parts – "The Silver of the Mine" (giving the ideas of both romance and "material interests"), "The Isabels" (forbidding in view of the opening account of the islands, dramatically the turning-point for Nostromo and Decoud), and "The Lighthouse" (symbolic of the new link with the outside world, and the scene of Nostromo's end – the end of the complete individualist being appropriately part of the narrative which brings Sulaco into the North American orbit). Ironically, Sulaco becomes independent of the rest of Costaguana and is received into the larger mercantile world, a valuable scrap in a larger system of dependencies. At the end of the book we are reminded that this too is not a static condition, that inimical political forces are beginning to gather strength, and the San Francisco millionaire will not always be the mine's remote landlord.

Conrad's characteristic movements backwards and forwards in time are profoundly functional here. The story could have been told straight on, the rise and fall of rival powers being exhibited in normal progression, the people growing old and in turn dying, the romantic, infertile marriage of the Goulds slowly withering, Antonia suddenly diminished by Decoud's death, Decoud the visionary liberal being disposed of some time before the tougher, ideology-free Nostromo found that his small (though large for him) raid on "material interests" did not free him from time and chance. The book is dedicated to Galsworthy, and in a sense the people of Sulaco are Conrad's analogues to the Forsytes that Galsworthy was later to chronicle, struggling with their load of silver, living and dying within the context of an historical process. But an analogue closer in quality to Conrad's work is Thomas Mann's *Buddenbrooks* of 1902, which, like *The Forsyte Saga*, uses the method of straight narrative to show the operations of time. A major book, even in the twentieth century, does not have to juggle with the time-scheme.

Yet we have seen that the point in Conrad's narrative to which we are first taken is repeatedly returned to. After Part I, chapters II-IV, has told us of Ribiera's defeat and the good deeds accomplished by Nostromo at that time, the remainder of Part I moves backwards. First, in chapter V, we learn of events eighteen months before, when Ribiera's government was precariously shedding the light of liberalism over the country and the Goulds' mine, and then in the remaining three chapters of Part I we are taken further back, to the brutal dictatorship of Guzman Benito, the saddling of Gould's father with the burden of the mine, the resolution of Charles Gould (romantically taken at the time of his courtship) to make the mine flourish, his time of growing success with American help, and then in chapter VIII, at the end of Part I, we are back to the story of Ribiera's defeat. Part II has also eight chapters, and the first seven of these likewise move towards the same moment of crisis in Costaguanan fortunes as had been the subject of the opening and concluding chapters of the narrative in Part I. Only Part III moves definitively forward beyond that point, though often turning back upon itself to juxtapose present with past more ironically, and, with particular force, giving us Decoud's death (though it happened earlier) as part of the narrative leading to the fulfilment of his dream of independence for Sulaco, an independence achieved only through an entry into a larger subjection. The retrospects of Parts I and II are different in tone and theme: that of Part II is more intimate, concerned far more with personal relations: the small, gracious figure of Mrs. Gould in Part I becomes more fragile, more poignant and resigned (yet stronger too) as her husband's concern with the mine grows under our view from a romantic enterprise (appropriately linked with his wooing of her) to an obsession that she cannot share, that puts a silence between them. And we come closer to Antonia and Decoud and Dr. Monygham and, of course, Nostromo in Part II, sharing with them all that strange half-calm in Sulaco that was made possible while Ribiera ruled and the implications of North American patronage were not fully evident. The relation of the book's three parts provides the basis for a superb structure, the lingering with the past in the first two-thirds of the narrative hinting at a reluctance to plunge into the characteristic world of the twentieth century, the free movement between past and present placing an insistence on the *fait accompli*, on the entrammelling of fully alive individuals within a partially hidden progression which, however enterprising they may be (Charles Gould in legal, Nostromo suddenly in illegal, adventure, Decoud in his political vision and his love), is not within their control. The political and mercantile events are part of the world's pattern at that time, and, in echo of Tolstoy, Conrad makes his smaller Napoleons into marionettes controlled by something that operates of its own momentum, whether because it is so destined or because the cards have fallen at that moment in that way.

We may still ask why it is Ribiera's defeat that is the point so often returned to. It was, surely, the end of a dream, the dream of liberal self-government for a community, with the fantasy informing it that violent men can be reasoned with and thus controlled, that financial help from outside can be wholly beneficent. The aftermath of the defeat is first a period of unleashed violence (within which Nostromo's crime is understandable and congruent) and then a period of ominous success for the Gould enterprise and the power that from afar shapes it. The irony of Part III is made clear in chapter XI, where Mrs. Gould comes to realize that

> There was something inherent in the necessities of successful action which carried with it the moral degradation of the idea.

To this is juxtaposed, in the preceding paragraph, her own vision of the good life:

> It had come into her mind that for life to be large and full, it must contain the care of the past and of the future in every passing moment of the present. Our daily work must be done to the glory of the dead, and for the good of those who come after.

That is a possibility for Mrs. Gould; hardly for Antonia, whose life after Decoud's death is an empty looking back and a devotion to good works in the present; not at all for Charles Gould, with his eye fixed on building the fortune of his mine; or for Dr. Monygham, for whom recollection is torment, the future of no account, and the present a matter of painful, wholly disinterested love for Mrs. Gould. She, as much as Nostromo, is in the book's centre, the figure of affirmation who, with a barrier between her and the husband she loves, quietly defies process in her vision of a present which is lived in full respect for what precedes and what follows. Whatever the past has been and the future will be, they are for her things which the present, otherwise barely existent, must serve. But the goodness is in the service: it will not bring good into new being or banish grief; the dead must be honoured despite the anguish of memory; the world and its people must be cultivated, though nothing tarnishes more obviously than the realization of an aim.

This is no occasion for an adequate study of this major novel, but it is hardly possible to turn from it before noting some of the recurrent motifs that help to give depth to its treatment of human beings within a tract of time. The fact that old Viola had served with Garibaldi links the story with that historical example of a triumph tarnished. The use of the nickname "Nostromo" by the upper-class liberals is a hint of possessiveness that goes along with Charles Gould's exploitation of the mine, his mere acquiescence in his wife's love, his unaware betrayal of Sulaco into the power of the old man of San Francisco.[5] The pathetic cooperation of the outlaws in "freeing" Sulaco counterpoises the dependence of the Goulds and their friends on "our man" the Capataz. The presence of Hirsch in the boat carrying its load of silver, Decoud's and Nostromo's astonishing avoidance of capture, the chance that Nostromo was misunderstood by Viola when he went to ask for Giselle as his wife, the chance that Viola shot Nostromo in mistake for Ramirez – these things, like so much in the book, defy "probability or necessity", though they are all congruent with the people concerned. Even the moment of panic which made Nostromo speak ambiguously to Viola when he said "I have come to ask you for . . . my wife!" fits within the context that has been established: Nostromo the thief is subdued in the presence of the single-minded fighter for republican liberty. Yet in the concatenation of events it is chance that operates, giving indeed to the whole concept of time a more terrifying quality.

Lowry's *Under the Volcano* is at first sight a book with a much narrower compass. Apart from chapter I, the events directly presented occur between an early morning and the same day's dusk. There are only three characters whose fortunes we follow throughout: the Consul (no longer a consul), his wife Yvonne, his younger brother Hugh. They move about in or near the town of Quauhnahuac, never out of sight of the twin volcanoes that dwarf the men at their feet and contain within themselves the threat and promise of destruction. In the main line of narrative there is no movement back and forth, apart from the retrospective chapter I. The day's action occurs in 1938, but in chapter I it is a year later than that: Dr. Arturo Díaz Vigil and M. Jacques Laruelle remember, as they drink together, the dead Consul, the dead Yvonne, the bereft Hugh. Yet Lowry is strangely inexplicit in this opening chapter. We are never firmly told about the deaths of the husband and wife until we come to the end of the book, and many a reader has gone on to chapter II, and far beyond, in the belief that the main narrative follows, not precedes, the conversation of the two men with which the book begins and the musings of Laruelle that form the remainder of chapter I. What Lowry may intend here is to give a fuller sense of life to his main characters by not simply asserting in advance what happened to them on their day of disaster, while at the same time making Vigil's and Laruelle's comments ominous enough. Moreover, the inexplicitness makes the Consul and the others seem alive when they are being referred to in chapter I, and this is a mode of defying the operations, even the fatal operations, of time. To have lived and to be the subject of anguish in recollection is in some sense to be living still. Perhaps, however, a very perceptive reader may get the time-scheme right at once: my own experience was not that, and is borne out by that of other readers I know.

In the rest of the book there are passages of recollection, of course, as there are in any substantial novel, but attention is centred on the events of the day. Outside this centre there exists an extensive periphery. Because it is 1938, the war in Spain is going on and the Nazi threat, strong over Europe, finds sympathetic reverberations among the small bullies of Mexican officialdom. What Lowry also does is to make us aware of the cultural complexity of a human being's store of memory. A man of our time may think in terms of Dante, for example, of the Elizabethan dramatists, of (especially in 1938) German films of the 1920s, early "westerns" from Hollywood: strangely, the trivial and the masterwork can function similarly in providing the skeleton for thought, the interpretative symbol. When Yvonne and Hugh go riding in the morning, the great ravine they cross and skirt is called the "Malebolge", because Dante provides the suggestions of depth and corruption and miscellaneous horror: it is this ravine into which the Consul is thrown, where he dies as he descends. Repeatedly we hear of the film *Hands of Orlac* being shown at the cinema in Quauhnahuac, a poor film with Peter Lorre acting in vain, a re-make of a German silent film in which Conrad Veidt had played: that, too, was poor enough. The Lorre version is already old, poignant therefore as a reminder of lost time, but it provides also a chance link with the 1920s, a time when the characters were younger and Europe was not yet wholly dark: it acts therefore as a double filter for memory. Moreover, the melodramatic idea of the film – of the musician who lost his hands in an accident and had a dead murderer's hands grafted on in their place –

335

becomes a symbol of the duality of the human being, making and fearful of destroying, led on to destruction by the very instruments with which he makes. It is Hugh's love for Yvonne that leads him to betray his brother's trust; Yvonne's strong wish for a stable relationship with her husband that makes her despairing and promiscuous; the Consul's power of perception that makes him destroy his marriage, refuse Yvonne on her return, and finally acquiesce in the violence offered him. Any "present" moment, when experienced in full consciousness, is a focal point not only for a patterning of memories but for an interpretation of both personal and political life in terms of cultural experience. So much so that one can never respond simply to what the moment itself offers. In chapter IV Hugh and Yvonne are riding: the day is not yet hot, the country is gracious, the man and woman are in sympathy with each other:

> Earlier it had promised to be too hot: but just enough sun warmed them, a soft breeze caressed their faces, the countryside on either hand smiled upon them with deceptive innocence, a drowsy hum rose up from the morning, the mares nodded, there were the foals, here was the dog, and it is all a bloody lie, he thought.

Hugh goes on to recognize an appropriateness in the fact that this is a day of solemnity for the Mexicans, a day given over to honouring the dead, who "come to life" for the occasion – like the memories of betrayal in one's own life. Even so, this is life at its best:

> Another thought struck Hugh. And yet I do not expect, ever in my life, to be happier than I am now. No peace I shall ever find but will be poisoned as these moments are poisoned.

A little later he almost forgets:

> Christ, how marvellous this was, or rather Christ, how he wanted to be deceived about it, as must have Judas, he thought – and here it was again, damn it – if ever Judas had a horse, or borrowed, stole one more likely, after that Madrugada of all Madrugadas, regretting then that he had given the thirty pieces of silver back – what is that to us, see thou to that, the *bastardos* had said – when now he probably

wanted a drink, thirty drinks (like Geoff undoubtedly would this morning), and perhaps even so he had managed a few on credit, smelling the good smells of leather and sweat, listening to the pleasant clopping of the horses' hooves and thinking, how joyous all this could be, riding on like this under the dazzling sky of Jerusalem – and forgetting for an instant, so that it really *was* joyous.

He too could forget "for an instant, so that it really *was* joyous". The moment just after this, when he and Yvonne come to the brewery and drink the cold dark German beer and Yvonne hankers after buying the armadillo as a pet, is the book's idyllic moment, but *we* are never allowed to forget the recurrent personal betrayal, the burden of the mind's obligation to interpret, the large-scale disaster of the Spanish war, the coming extension of international strife, the hostility of nature to man. Only at a glance was the armadillo gentle:

> Each time the armadillo ran off, as if on tiny wheels, the little girl would catch it by its long whip of a tail and turn it over. How astonishingly soft and helpless it appeared then! Now she righted the creature and set it going once more, some engine of destruction perhaps that after millions of years had come to this.

The human mind has a further mode of self-tormenting. It is not easy to forget that – "even now, now, very now" – things are happening in the world that mock at a present joy. So Hugh is recurrently conscious that, as he talks and journeys through the day, the battle of the Ebro is being fought and lost. But the special plague is not merely that we are doing nothing, can do nothing, to prevent the disaster far away: it is also that we believe each act of ours contributes to a total pattern that ensures the future: because one raises or puts down a glass, the battle of the Ebro will be lost; if one had acted, even in a trifle, differently, a different future would have been ordained. This is not rational, but is part of our deep-seated sense of a total developing pattern, imposing a responsibility on us for all that is to happen. Yet there is no power along with the responsibility: only in retrospect are we convinced that, if we had not done such-and-such a thing, the future would not have been doomed: we should have broken through the straitjacket of destiny. The more aware we are of what is happening in the world outside our immediate view, the more fully this kind of self-tormenting, this sense of total responsibility with a total absence of power, will impinge on our present moments.

Yet in another way this book insists on a multiplicity of futures. There is what will happen, regardless. There is also the future we can imagine, and this is as much part of our experience as the thing that must be. The Consul and Yvonne dream recurrently of a free life by the woods and waters of British Columbia, the more idyllic because of its remoteness alike from Mexico and from the more thronged stages of the world. Lowry himself, of course, spent much of his last years in British Columbia, and he is making no claim in this novel that even the natural splendour of Canada's west coast is a guarantee of contentment. But for Yvonne and the Consul it could appear to be, and the dream was part of their last day. The most precarious of dreams, of course: as Yvonne in chapter IX sees in her mind the house above the beach she might share with her husband, she cannot fully concentrate on the simple image:

> Why was it though, that right in the centre of her brain, there should be a figure of a woman having hysterics, jerking like a puppet and banging her fists upon the ground?

And there is, too, the future beyond one's own death, which we have seen in personal terms in chapter I, and which in chapter XI, near the fact of death for the Consul and Yvonne, becomes extended beyond the time when this or that person of our "now" can be remembered. The night sky will be observed so long as man lasts, and always the basic questions concerning purpose and cause will be raised. Then even Yvonne's infidelities and the Consul's drinking, even the battle of the Ebro and the things done in our time in the name of race or for gain's sake, will be forgotten: there will be only recurrence, of delight and fragile hope, of shame and loss, of questioning and failure to answer.

Meanwhile there is the present, charged full with memory and ambivalent response. An instant is indeed of copious content: under contemplation its extent can become enormous, as the stream-of-consciousness novelists have long made us know. Lowry has reinforced this by packing the one-day's sequence of chapters II-XII with action and movement. It might appear that the intense activity could not have been borne by the three people concerned. The Consul begins the day hung-over and still drinking, Yvonne and Hugh have travelled overnight. Yet after her first sad encounter with her husband, she is seeing how her garden has become a wilderness, and then sets out with Hugh on their ride through the morning sunlight outside the town. Later they visit Laruelle, enter into the town's festivities on this day of solemnity, and then travel to Tomalín on the bus for the bullthrowing. Even then the journey is not over: there is the twilit road to Parián to be covered, where in the end the horse waits for Yvonne and the ravine for the Consul. When one thinks how little one does on most days, when one thinks of the dust and the heat and the nervous tension and the drinking, this day in a novel is frightening. Yet there are days that most of us have known, especially those days when tension has been at an extreme, which have strangely filled themselves with activity beyond normal endurance. In the result we are not wholly incredulous that the novel's people could have managed it, but we are conscious that such days are commonly days of crisis and shadow forth the characteristic depth of the existential moment. Yvonne in chapter IX follows a boy's gaze into the sky as he looks for an airplane he can hear: "she made it out for herself, a droning hyphen in abysmal blue". That is an image for the momentary in its ungraspability, fugitiveness – in relation both to what we call "now" in its strictest sense and to the lives we live in the whole context of time. But the hyphen drones, which suggests continuity, extension. The day, the individual's life, are also brief, but they take shape, they stretch profoundly by virtue of one's store of consciousness. What gives this extension is made up of personal relations and the nexus of cultural experiences. There is a lifetime in the moment, in the day of crisis. It is this that gives peculiar power to the novel or the drama that observes the Unity of Time, but this "Unity" in its fullest employment is not one of mere restriction: it encompasses the all that a man knows.

Conrad and Lowry have used different technical methods. Paradoxically, the book called *Nostromo* is far less centred in the personal than the book called *Under the Volcano*. Lowry, with the apparently more restricted canvas, has also given the

broader sense of historical event and geographical setting. By
Conrad's standards, *Under the Volcano* is at times untidy, careless: not every detail is finely enough meshed with the growing
pattern; there are times when the writer seems to argue with
himself that everything, even a menu card, is of high interest
because it exists. But both these novels are of major stature;
both are remote from simple progression in their narrative;
both explore the moment and see it within the total process;
both are tragic writings which juxtapose the human consciousness with the irresistible operations of time and chance; both
sharpen our sense of the immediate moment while insisting on
that moment as only a point of intersection. This coheres with
what we, the readers, know. For, like the modern novelist's
material, our experience of past and future is being continuously
shaped: our minds do the shaping now.

NOTES

1 In "Shakespeare and the Idea of the Future", *University of
Toronto Quarterly*, xxxv (1966), 213-28, I have suggested that the
use of such symbols of finality in drama does in practice go along
quite often with a continuing preoccupation with the unfolding of
event.

2 Text from *Doctor Faustus*, ed. John D. Jump (The Revels Plays),
1962.

3 There is a hint of something similar in Medwall's *Fulgens and
Lucres*, where the players A and B decide to take part in the
action, which belongs to a period before their time, but the action
is not substantially modified by their presence.

4 So much so that the new mode can be itself mocked in a novel.
Günter Grass can write thus in *The Tin Drum*, published in 1959:
You can begin a story in the middle and create confusion by
striking out boldly, backward and forward. You can be modern,
put aside all mention of time and distance and, when the whole
thing is done, proclaim, or let someone else proclaim, that you

have finally, at the last moment, solved the space-time problem. (Tr. Ralph Manheim.)

5   The nickname also signifies, of course, that in the larger sense Nostromo, like Lord Jim, is "one of us".

.

LOUIS L. MARTZ

Portrait of Miriam

A STUDY IN THE DESIGN OF
Sons and Lovers

[i]

The girl was romantic in her soul.

And she was cut off from ordinary life by her religious intensity which made the world for her either a nunnery garden or a paradise, where sin and knowledge were not, or else an ugly, cruel thing.

And in sacrifice she was proud, in renunciation she was strong, for she did not trust herself to support everyday life.

"You don't want to love – your eternal and abnormal craving is to be loved. You aren't positive, you're negative. You absorb, absorb, as if you must fill yourself up with love, because you've got a shortage somewhere."[1]

With very few exceptions, the commentators on Lawrence's *Sons and Lovers* have tended to accept the view of Miriam's character as thus described by the narrator and by Paul Morel. Mark Spilka, for example, in his stimulating book, bases his interpretation of the novel on the assumption that Miriam has "an unhealthy spirituality", is truly "negative", that she really "wheedles the soul out of things", as Paul Morel says, and that "because of the stifling nature of Miriam's love, Paul refuses to marry her" – justifiably, since "Miriam's frigidity is rooted in her own nature".[2] But I believe that the portrait of Miriam is far more complex than either Paul or the narrator will allow,

343

and that a study of her part in the book will cast some light upon the puzzling and peculiar technique of narration that Lawrence adopts when he comes to the central section of his novel, the five tormented chapters (7-11) running from "Lad-and-Girl Love" through "The Test on Miriam".

As everyone has noticed, Part I of the novel (the first third of the book, concluding with the death of William) is written in the manner of Victorian realism: the omniscient narrator, working with firm control, sets forth the facts objectively. The countryside, the mining village, the family conflicts, the daily life of the household – all is given in clear, precise, convincing detail. The use of local dialect, the echoes of biblical style, the short, concise sentences combine to create in us a confidence in the narrator's command of his materials. His fairness to everyone is evident. If the father is predominantly shown as brutal and drunken, in those savage quarrels with the mother, he is also shown in his younger glory as a man who might have flourished with a different wife: "Gertrude Coppard watched the young miner as he danced, a certain subtle exultation like glamour in his movement, and his face the flower of his body, ruddy, with tumbled black hair, and laughing alike whatever partner he bowed above".(pp. 9-10). Even when the wife has turned away from him she can enjoy his music:

> Quite early, before six o'clock, she heard him whistling away to himself downstairs. He had a pleasant way of whistling, lively and musical. He nearly always whistled hymns. He had been a choir-boy with a beautiful voice, and had taken solos in Southwell cathedral. His morning whistling alone betrayed it.
>
> His wife lay listening to him tinkering away in the garden, his whistling ringing out as he sawed and hammered away. It always gave her a sense of warmth and peace to hear him thus as she lay in bed, the children not yet awake, in the bright early morning, happy in his man's fashion (p. 18)

We watch Morel's relish in getting his breakfast and his joy in walking across the fields to his work in the early morning; we learn of those happy times when Morel is cobbling the family's boots, or mending kettles, or making fuses; we recognize his faithful labour at his gruelling job; and particularly we notice the love for him felt by the youngest child Arthur: "Mrs. Morel was glad this child loved the father".(p. 47). All these things give a sense of balance and proportion to Part I, making it clear that Paul's view is partial, unfair to the father, ignoring his basic humanity.

Paul's blindness towards his father's very existence as a human being is cruelly shown in the scene where Morel emerges from the pit to hear of William's death:

> "And William is dead, and my mother's in London, and what will she be doing?" the boy asked himself, as if it were a conundrum.
>
> He watched chair after chair come up, and still no father. At last, standing beside a waggon, a man's form! The chair sank on its rests, Morel stepped off. He was slightly lame from an accident.
>
> "Is it thee, Paul? Is 'e worse?"
>
> "You've got to go to London."
>
> The two walked off the pit-bank, where men were watching curiously. As they came out and went along the railway, with the sunny autumn field on one side and a wall of trucks on the other, Morel said in a frightened voice:
>
> " 'E's niver gone, child?"
>
> "Yes."
>
> "When wor't?"
>
> The miner's voice was terrified.[3]
>
> "Last night. We had a telegram from my mother."
>
> Morel walked on a few strides, then leaned up against a truck side, his hand over his eyes. He was not crying. Paul stood looking round, waiting. On the weighing-machine a truck trundled slowly. Paul saw everything, except his father leaning against the truck as if he were tired. (p. 137)

"Paul saw everything, except his father." Only the omniscient narrator reveals the man Morel, battered from his work, frightened for his son's life, sunk in dumb agony at the news, while his intimate dialect plays off pitifully against the formal language of Paul, to stress the total division between the two.

Part I, then, is a triumph of narration in the old Victorian style. It is a long prologue, in which the issues are clearly defined, and in which, above all, the mother's overpowering influence is shown in the death of one son, while she turns toward Paul as her only remaining hope: " 'I should have watched the living, not the dead', she told herself".(p. 140).

Meanwhile, as William is engaged in his fatal courtship, the figure of Miriam has been quietly introduced, in the natural, harmonious setting of the farm: "Mother and son went into the small railed garden, where was a scent of red gillivers. By the open door were some floury loaves, put out to cool. A hen was just coming to peck them. Then, in the doorway suddenly appeared a girl in a dirty apron. She was about fourteen years old, had a rosy dark face, a bunch of short black curls, very fine and free, and dark eyes; shy, questioning, a little resentful of the strangers, she disappeared".(pp. 124-5). Shortly after this follows the vivid incident in which the brothers jeer at Miriam for being afraid to let the hen peck the corn out of her hand:

"Now, Miriam", said Maurice, "you come an' 'ave a go."
"No", she cried, shrinking back.
"Ha! baby. The mardy-kid!" said her brothers.
"It doesn't hurt a bit", said Paul. "It only just nips rather nicely."
"No", she still cried, shaking her black curls and shrinking.
"She dursn't", said Geoffrey. "She niver durst do anything except recite poitry."
"Dursn't jump off a gate, dursn't tweedle, dursn't go on a slide, dursn't stop a girl hittin' her. She can do nowt but go about thinkin' herself somebody. 'The Lady of the Lake.' Yah!" cried Maurice. (p. 126)

We are bound to align this with the later incident of the swing, both of which might be taken "as revelations of Miriam's diminished vitality, her tendency to shrink back from life, whether she is making love, feeding chickens, trying to cope with Mrs. Morel's dislike of her, or merely looking at flowers".[4] But we should note that immediately after the passage just quoted Paul witnesses another aspect of Miriam:

As he went round the back, he saw Miriam kneeling in front of the hen-coop, some maize in her hand, biting her lip, and crouching in an intense attitude. The hen was eyeing her wickedly. Very gingerly she put forward her hand. The hen bobbed for her. She drew back quickly with a cry, half of fear, half of chagrin.
"It won't hurt you", said Paul.
She flushed crimson and started up.
"I only wanted to try", she said in a low voice.

346

"See, it doesn't hurt", he said, and, putting only two corns in his palm, he let the hen peck, peck, peck at his bare hand. "It only makes you laugh", he said.

She put her hand forward, and dragged it away, tried again, and started back with a cry. He frowned.

"Why, I'd let her take corn from my face", said Paul, "only she bumps a bit. She's ever so neat. If she wasn't, look how much ground she'd peck up every day."

He waited grimly, and watched. At last Miriam let the bird peck from her hand. She gave a little cry – fear, and pain because of fear – rather pathetic. But she had done it, and she did it again.

"There, you see", said the boy. "It doesn't hurt, does it?"

She looked at him with dilated dark eyes.

"No", she laughed, trembling. (p. 127-8)

The scene shows more than timidity; it shows, also, her extreme sensitivity, along with her shy desire for new experience: she wants to try, she wants to learn; if rightly encouraged she will and can learn, and then she can respond with laughter and trembling excitement. This first view of Miriam, seen through the eyes of the objective narrator, is astir with life: for all her shyness and shrinking she is nevertheless capable of a strong response. The whole initial sketch is suffused with her "beautiful warm colouring" and accompanied by her "musical, quiet voice". She is a girl of rich potential.

[ii]

As Part II opens we become at once aware of a drastic shift in method. The first two pages are given over to an elaborate interpretation of Miriam's character before she again appears, "nearly sixteen, very beautiful, with her warm colouring, her gravity, her eyes dilating suddenly like an ecstasy".(p. 144). No such extended analysis of anyone has appeared in Part I; there the characters have been allowed to act out their parts before us, with only brief guiding touches by the objective narrator. But here we sense a peculiar intensity in the analysis: the narrator seems to be preparing the way for some new and difficult problem, and in so doing he seems to be dropping his manner of impartiality. He is determined to set our minds in a certain direction, and this aim is reflected in the drifting length and involution of the sentences. The style of writing here seems designed to reflect the "mistiness" of the character he is describing, her remoteness from life:

> Her great companion was her mother. They were both brown-eyed, and inclined to be mystical, such women as treasure religion inside them, breathe it in their nostrils, and see the whole of life in a mist thereof. So to Miriam, Christ and God made one great figure, which she loved tremblingly and passionately when a tremendous sunset burned out the western sky, and Ediths, and Lucys, and Rowenas, Brian de Bois Guilberts, Rob Roys, and Guy Mannerings, rustled the sunny leaves in the morning, or sat in her bedroom aloft, alone, when it snowed. That was life to her. For the rest, she drudged in the house, which work she would not have minded had not her clean red floor been mucked up immediately by the trampling farm-boots of her brothers. She madly wanted her little brother of four to let her swathe him and stifle him in her love; she went to church reverently, with bowed head, and quivered in anguish from the vulgarity of the other choir-girls and from the common-sounding voice of the curate; she fought with her brothers, whom she considered brutal louts; and she held not her father in too high esteem because he did not carry any mystical ideals cherished in his heart, but only wanted to have as easy a time as he could, and his meals when he was ready for them. (pp. 142-3)

She is also a girl who is "mad to have learning whereon to pride herself"; and for all these causes she neglects and ignores her physical being: "Her beauty – that of a shy, wild, quiveringly sensitive thing – seemed nothing to her. Even her soul, so strong for rhapsody, was not enough. She must have something to reinforce her pride, because she felt different from other people." At the same time, her misty emotions lead her towards a desire to dominate Paul: "Then he was so ill, and she felt he would be weak. Then she would be stronger than he. Then she could love him. If she could be mistress of him in his weakness, take care of him, if he could depend on her, if she could, as it were, have him in her arms, how she would love him!"(p. 143).

In all this the narrator is anticipating the views of Miriam frequently expressed by Paul himself: that she is too spiritual, too abstract, that she shrinks away from physical reality, and that she has a stifling desire to absorb and possess his soul. The incident of the swing that follows shortly after (pp. 149-51)

would seem to bear out some of this: she is afraid to let Paul
swing her high, and Lawrence phrases her fear in language that
has unmistakable sexual overtones: "She felt the accuracy with
which he caught her, exactly at the right moment, and the
exactly proportionate strength of his thrust, and she was
afraid. Down to her bowels went the hot wave of fear. She was
in his hands. Again, firm and inevitable came the thrust at the
right moment. She gripped the rope, almost swooning."
(p. 151). Yet she has led Paul to the swing, and she is fascinated
by his free swinging: "It roused a warmth in her. It were
almost as if he were a flame that had lit a warmth in her whilst
he swung in the middle air." Who can say that Miriam is unable
to learn this too, as she has learned with the hen, and as she is
later shown to overcome her fear of crossing fences?

> Occasionally she ran with Paul down the fields. Then her eyes blazed
> naked in a kind of ecstasy that frightened him. But she was physically
> afraid. If she were getting over a stile, she gripped his hands in a
> little hard anguish, and began to lose her presence of mind. And he
> could not persuade her to jump from even a small height. Her eyes
> dilated, became exposed and palpitating.
> "No!" she cried, half laughing in terror – "no!"
> "You shall!" he cried once, and, jerking her forward, he brought
> her falling from the fence. But her wild "Ah!" of pain, as if she were
> losing consciousness, cut him. She landed on her feet safely, and
> afterwards had courage in this respect. (p. 154)

Certainly she wants to learn; only a few lines after the swing
episode we find this all-important passage:

> But the girl gradually sought him out. If he brought up his sketch-
> book, it was she who pondered longest over the last picture. Then
> she would look up at him. Suddenly, her dark eyes alight like water
> that shakes with a stream of gold in the dark, she would ask:
> "Why do I like this so?"
> Always something in his breast shrank from these close, intimate,
> dazzled looks of hers.
> "Why *do* you?" he asked.
> "I don't know. It seems so true."
> "It's because – it's because there is scarcely any shadow in it; it's
> more shimmery, as if I'd painted the shimmering protoplasm in the
> leaves and everywhere, and not the stiffness of the shape. That seems

dead to me. Only this shimmeriness is the real living. The shape is a dead crust. The shimmer is inside really."

And she, with her little finger in her mouth, would ponder these sayings. They gave her a feeling of life again, and vivified things which had meant nothing to her. She managed to find some meaning in his struggling, abstract speeches. And they were the medium through which she came distinctly at her beloved objects. (p. 152)

It seems as though she is learning to reach out towards the "shimmeriness" that is the "real living"; with his help she is coming out of her "mist" towards a distinct sight of "her beloved objects". *She* is learning, while *he* shrinks away from her intimate, shimmering eyes ("like water that shakes with a stream of gold in the dark"). She senses the meaning of his "abstract speeches", she gets "so near him", she creates in him "a strange, roused sensation" (p. 153) – and as a result she enrages him for reasons that he cannot grasp. Is it because he is refusing to face the shimmer that is really inside Miriam?

So, when he sees her embracing her youngest brother "almost as if she were in a trance, and swaying also as if she were swooned in an ecstasy of love", he bursts out with his irritation:

"What do you make such a *fuss* for?" cried Paul, all in suffering because of her extreme emotion. "Why can't you be ordinary with him?"

She let the child go, and rose, and said nothing. Her intensity, which would leave no emotion on a normal plane, irritated the youth into a frenzy. And this fearful, naked contact of her on small occasions shocked him. He was used to his mother's reserve. And on such occasions he was thankful in his heart and soul that he had his mother, so sane and wholesome. (p. 153)

One senses, as Miriam does at a later point, an alien influence here, twisting the mind of Paul and the narrator away from Miriam. Two pages later we see a dramatic juxtaposition of two warring actualities:

He used to tell his mother all these things.
"I'm going to teach Miriam algebra", he said.
"Well", replied Mrs. Morel, "I hope she'll get fat on it."

When he went up to the farm on the Monday evening, it was drawing twilight. Miriam was just sweeping up the kitchen, and was kneeling at the hearth when he entered. Everyone was out but her. She looked round at him, flushed, her dark eyes shining, her fine hair falling about her face.

"Hello!" she said, soft and musical. "I knew it was you."

"How?"

"I knew your step. Nobody treads so quick and firm."

He sat down, sighing.

"Ready to do some algebra?" he asked, drawing a little book from his pocket. (p. 155)

Who is sane and wholesome, we may well ask? And whose thoughts are abstracted from life? We are beginning to learn that we cannot wholly trust the narrator's remarks in this central portion of the book, for his commentary represents mainly an extension of Paul's consciousness; everywhere, in this portion of the book, the voice of the narrator tends to echo and magnify the confusions that are arising within Paul himself. These are the contradictions in which some readers have seen a failure or a faltering in the novel, because "the point of view is never adequately objectified and sustained to tell us which is true".[5] But I feel rather that Lawrence has invented a successful technique by which he can manage the deep autobiographical problems that underlie the book. We are watching the strong graft of a stream of consciousness growing out of the live trunk of that Victorian prologue, and intertwining with the objectively presented action. The point of view adopted is that of Paul; but since confusion, self-deception, and desperate self-justification are essential to that point of view, we can never tell, from that stream of consciousness alone, where the real truth lies. But we can tell it from the action; we can tell it by seeking out the portrait of Miriam that lies beneath the over-painted commentary of the Paul-narrator. This technique of painting and overpainting produces a strange and unique tension in this part of the novel. The image of Miriam appears and then is clouded over; it is as though we were looking at her through a clouded window that is constantly being cleared, and fogged, and cleared again. It is an unprecedented and inimitable technique, discovered for this one necessary occasion. But it works.

How it works, we may see by looking once again at the

frequently quoted passage where Miriam leads Paul, despite his reluctance ("They grumble so if I'm late") into the woods at dusk to find the "wild-rose bush she had discovered".

> The tree was tall and straggling. It had thrown its briers over a hawthorn-bush, and its long streamers trailed thick, right down to the grass, splashing the darkness everywhere with great split stars, pure white. In bosses of ivory and in large splashed stars the roses gleamed on the darkness of foliage and stems and grass. Paul and Miriam stood close together, silent, and watched. Point after point the steady roses shone out to them, seeming to kindle something in their souls. The dusk came like smoke around, and still did not put out the roses.
>
> Paul looked into Miriam's eyes. She was pale and expectant with wonder, her lips were parted, and her dark eyes lay open to him. His look seemed to travel down into her. Her soul quivered. It was the communion she wanted. He turned aside, as if pained. He turned to the bush.
>
> "They seem as if they walk like butterflies, and shake themselves", he said.
>
> She looked at her roses. They were white, some incurved and holy, others expanded in an ecstasy. The tree was dark as a shadow. She lifted her hand impulsively to the flowers; she went forward and touched them in worship.
>
> "Let us go", he said.
>
> There was a cool scent of ivory roses – a white, virgin scent. Something made him feel anxious and imprisoned. The two walked in silence. (pp. 159-60)

What is this "something" that makes him "feel anxious and imprisoned"? Is he like the hawthorn-bush, caught in the trailing streamers of the rose-bush? Is it because she has insisted on a moment of soul-communion which represents her tendency towards "a blasphemous possessorship"?[6] The narrator seems to be urging us in this direction. Yet in itself the scene may be taken to represent, amid this wild profusion of natural growth, a moment of natural communion in the human relationship, a potential marriage of senses and the soul. This is, for Miriam, an "ecstasy" in which nature is not abstracted, but realized in all its wild perfection. Paul breaks the mood and runs away towards home. And when he reaches home we may grasp the true manner of his imprisonment:

Always when he went with Miriam, and it grew rather late, he knew his mother was fretting and getting angry about him – why, he could not understand. As he went into the house, flinging down his cap, his mother looked up at the clock. She had been sitting thinking because a chill to her eyes prevented her reading. She could feel Paul being drawn away by this girl. And she did not care for Miriam. "She is one of those who will want to suck a man's soul out till he has none of his own left", she said to herself; "and he is just such a gaby as to let himself be absorbed. She will never let him become a man; she never will." So, while he was away with Miriam, Mrs. Morel grew more and more worked up.

She glanced at the clock and said, coldly and rather tired:

"You have been far enough to-night".

His soul, warm and exposed from contact with the girl, shrank. (pp. 160-1)

Miriam offers him the freedom of natural growth within a mature relation, though Paul soon adopts the mother's view of Miriam's "possessive" nature. He cannot help himself, but there is no reason why readers of the book should accept the mother's view of Miriam, which is everywhere shown to be motivated by the mother's own possessiveness. The mother has described only herself in the above quotation; she has not described Miriam, who is quite a different being and has quite a different effect on Paul. The fact is that Paul needs both his mother and Miriam for his true development, as he seems to realize quite early in the conflict: "A sketch finished, he always wanted to take it to Miriam. Then he was stimulated into knowledge of the work he had produced unconsciously. In contact with Miriam he gained insight; his vision went deeper. From his mother he drew the life-warmth, the strength to produce; Miriam urged this warmth into intensity like a white light."(p. 158). Or earlier we hear that Miriam's family "kindled him and made him glow to his work, whereas his mother's influence was to make him quietly determined, patient, dogged, unwearied".(p. 149).

But the mother cannot bear to release him. Miriam must be met by her with cold, unfriendly curtness, while the married woman, Clara, may receive a friendly welcome from the mother. Clara offers no threat: "Mrs. Morel measured herself against the younger woman, and found herself easily stronger".(p. 321).

"Yes, I liked her", she says in answer to Paul's inquiry. "But you'll tire of her, my son; you know you will."(p. 329). And so she encourages the affair with Clara: the adulterous relation will serve the son's physical needs, while the mother can retain the son's deeper love and loyalty. Mrs. Morel senses what she is doing, but evades the facts:

> Mrs. Morel considered. She would have been glad now for her son to fall in love with some woman who would – she did not know what. But he fretted so, got so furious suddenly, and again was melancholic. She wished he knew some nice woman – She did not know what she wished, but left it vague. At any rate she was not hostile to the idea of Clara. (pp. 242-3)

The mother's devices are pitiful, and at the same time contemptible, as we have already seen from the painful episode in which she overwhelms her son with raw and naked emotion:

> He had taken off his collar and tie, and rose, bare-throated, to go to bed. As he stooped to kiss his mother, she threw her arms round his neck, hid her face on his shoulder, and cried, in a whimpering voice, so unlike her own that he writhed in agony:
> "I can't bear it. I could let another woman – but not her. She'd leave me no room, not a bit of room –"
> And immediately he hated Miriam bitterly.
> "And I've never – you know, Paul – I've never had a husband – not really –"
> He stroked his mother's hair, and his mouth was on her throat.
> "And she exults so in taking you from me – she's not like ordinary girls."
> "Well, I don't love her, mother," he murmured, bowing his head and hiding his eyes on her shoulder in misery. His mother kissed him a long, fervent kiss.
> "My boy!" she said, in a voice trembling with passionate love. (p. 213)

"At your mischief again?" says the father, "venomously", as he interrupts this scene of illicitly possessive passion. Mischief it is, corrosive and destructive to the marriage that Paul needs, the full relationship that Miriam offers, with her intimate love for nature.

It will be evident that I do not agree with the view that Spilka and others have taken of that flower-picking episode with

Miriam and Clara, the view that takes the scene as a revelation
of a basic flaw in Miriam: "she kills life and has no right to it".[7]

> "Ah!" cried Miriam, and she looked at Paul, her dark eyes dilating.
> He smiled. Together they enjoyed the field of flowers. Clara, a little
> way off, was looking at the cowslips disconsolately. Paul and
> Miriam stayed close together, talking in subdued tones. He kneeled
> on one knee, quickly gathering the best blossoms, moving from
> tuft to tuft restlessly, talking softly all the time. Miriam plucked the
> flowers lovingly, lingering over them. He always seemed to her too
> quick and almost scientific. Yet his bunches had a natural beauty
> more than hers. He loved them, but as if they were his and he had a
> right to them. She had more reverence for them: they held some-
> thing she had not. (p. 237)

The last clause has a wonderful ambiguity. If we take Paul's
point of view, we will say that she is "negative", that she lacks
true life. If we ponder the whole action of the book, we will say
that what she lacks is the full organic life of the flower, sexually
complete within itself. She cannot grow into her full life without
the principle that Paul, with his masculine creativity, here displays. The passage shows a man and a woman who are true
counterparts, in mind and body. When, a little later, Paul
sprinkles the flowers over Clara, he is performing an exclusively sensuous ritual that threatens more than a pagan love-
death:

> Her breasts swung slightly in her blouse. The arching curve of her
> back was beautiful and strong; she wore no stays. Suddenly, without
> knowing, he was scattering a handful of cowslips over her hair and
> neck, saying:
>
> > "Ashes to ashes, and dust to dust,
> > If the Lord won't have you the devil must."
>
> The chill flowers fell on her neck. She looked up at him, with
> almost pitiful, scared grey eyes, wondering what he was doing.
> Flowers fell on her face, and she shut her eyes.
> Suddenly, standing there above her, he felt awkward.
> "I thought you wanted a funeral", he said, ill at ease. (pp. 238-9)

It is Paul, under his mother's domination, who kills life, by
refusing to move in organic relation with Miriam:

He would not have it that they were lovers. The intimacy between them had been kept so abstract, such a matter of the soul, all thought and weary struggle into consciousness, that he saw it only as a platonic friendship. He stoutly denied there was anything else between them. Miriam was silent, or else she very quietly agreed. He was a fool who did not know what was happening to himself. By tacit agreement they ignored the remarks and insinuations of their acquaintances.

"We aren't lovers, we are friends", he said to her. "*We* know it. Let them talk. What does it matter what they say."

Sometimes, as they were walking together, she slipped her arm timidly into his. But he always resented it, and she knew it. It caused a violent conflict in him. With Miriam he was always on the high plane of abstraction, when his natural fire of love was transmitted into the fine steam[8] of thought. She would have it so. (pp. 172-3)

The last sentence is a fine example of the way in which the commentary of the Paul-narrator can contradict the tenor of the action: "she slipped her arm timidly into his". Clara knows better and tells Paul the truth in that revealing conversation just before "the test on Miriam". Paul has been describing how Miriam "wants the soul out of my body": "I know she wants a sort of soul union".

"But how do you know what she wants?"
"I've been with her for seven years."
"And you haven't found out the very first thing about her."
"What's that?"
"That she doesn't want any of your soul communion. That's your own imagination. She wants you."
He pondered over this. Perhaps he was wrong.
"But she seems —" he began.
"You've never tried," she answered. (pp. 277-8)

This is not to deny that Miriam is shy, intense, spiritual, and, as a result of her upbringing, fearful and evasive of sexual facts. All these qualities belong to her character, for she is young, sensitive, and modest. My point is that her portrait does not consist simply of a static presentation of these aspects: her portrait is being enriched dynamically and progressively before our eyes, over a long period of years, from her early adolescence, through an awakening and potential fulfilment, to the utter extinction of her inner life and hope.

The truth of Clara's view has been borne out long before, as far back as that scene where Paul accuses Miriam of never laughing real laughter:

"But" – and she looked up at him with eyes frightened and struggling – "I do laugh at you – I *do*."

"Never! There's always a kind of intensity. When you laugh I could always cry; it seems as if it shows up your suffering. Oh, you make me knit the brows of my very soul and cogitate."

Slowly she shook her head despairingly.

"I'm sure I don't want to", she said.

"I'm so damned spiritual with *you* always!" he cried.

She remained silent, thinking, "Then why don't you be otherwise". But he saw her crouching, brooding figure, and it seemed to tear him in two. (p. 188)

And then, on the next page, as Paul repairs the bicycle tyre, we have an unmistakable glimpse of the vital image of Miriam, her strong physical feeling for him, and her true laughter:

"Fetch me a drop of water in a bowl", he said to her. "I shall be late, and then I s'll catch it."

He lighted the hurricane lamp, took off his coat, turned up the bicycle, and set speedily to work. Miriam came with the bowl of water and stood close to him, watching. She loved to see his hands doing things. He was slim and vigorous, with a kind of easiness even in his most hasty movements. And busy at his work, he seemed to forget her. She loved him absorbedly. She wanted to run her hands down his sides. She always wanted to embrace him, so long as he did not want her.

"There!" he said, rising suddenly. "Now, could you have done it quicker?"

"No!" she laughed.

He straightened himself. His back was towards her. She put her two hands on his sides, and ran them quickly down.

"You are so *fine!*" she said.

He laughed, hating her voice, but his blood roused to a wave of flame by her hands. She did not seem to realise *him* in all this. He might have been an object. She never realised the male he was. (p. 189)

Those last three sentences, the outgrowth of his torment, and the earlier remark, "so long as he did not want her", provide clear examples of the way in which the overpainted commentary tends to obscure the basic portrait of Miriam. It is the same in the episode at Nethermere: "He could not bear to look at Miriam. She seemed to want him, and he resisted. He resisted all the time. He wanted now to give her passion and tenderness, and he could not. He felt that she wanted the soul out of his body, and not him."

> He went on, in his dead fashion:
> "If only you could want *me*, and not want what I can reel off for you!"
> "I!" she cried bitterly — "I! Why, when would you let me take you?" (p. 194)

His bursts of anger and "hate", his feeling that Miriam is pulling the soul out of his body, are only his own tormented reactions to the agony he feels in being pulled so strongly away from his mother, as Daniel Weiss has said: "It is that for the first time in his life he is facing a mature relationship between himself and another woman, *not* his mother, and that a different mode of love is being demanded from him. It is Miriam's refusal to allow him to regress to the Nirvana, the paradisal state of the infant, her insistence that he recognize her, that fills him with anguish."[9]

As though to warn us against accepting Paul's responses and interpretations, Lawrence inserts in the middle of the crucial chapter, "Strife in Love", a long, vigorous, attractive, and surprising scene where the father is shown totally in command of the household, on a Friday evening, when the miners make their reckoning in Morel's house. Complaining with warm, vigorous dialect about the cold room, as he emerges from his bath, Morel draws even his wife into laughter and reminiscent admiration:

> Morel looked down ruefully at his sides.
> "Me!" he exclaimed. "I'm nowt b'r a skinned rabbit. My bones fair juts out on me."
> "I should like to know where", retorted his wife.
> "Iv'ry-wheer! I'm nobbut a sack o' faggots."
> Mrs. Morel laughed. He had still a wonderfully young body, muscular, without any fat. His skin was smooth and clear. It might

have been the body of a man of twenty-eight, except that there were, perhaps, too many blue scars, like tattoo-marks, where the coal-dust remained under the skin, and that his chest was too hairy. But he put his hand on his sides ruefully. It was his fixed belief that, because he did not get fat, he was as thin as a starved rat.

Paul looked at his father's thick, brownish hands all scarred, with broken nails, rubbing the fine smoothness of his sides, and the incongruity struck him. It seemed strange they were the same flesh.

"I suppose", he said to his father, "you had a good figure once".

"Eh!" exclaimed the miner, glancing round, startled and timid, like a child.

"He had", exclaimed Mrs. Morel, "if he didn't hurtle himself up as if he was trying to get in the smallest space he could".

"Me!" exclaimed Morel – "me a good figure! I wor niver much more n'r a skeleton".

"Man!" cried his wife, "don't be such a pulamiter!"

" 'Strewth!" he said. "Tha's niver knowed me but what I looked as if I wor goin' off in a rapid decline."

She sat and laughed.

"You've had a constitution like iron," she said; "and never a man had a better start, if it was body that counted. You should have seen him as a young man", she cried suddenly to Paul, drawing herself up to imitate her husband's once handsome bearing.

Morel watched her shyly. He saw again the passion she had had for him. It blazed upon her for a moment. He was shy, rather scared, and humble. Yet again he felt his old glow. And then immediately he felt the ruin he had made during these years. He wanted to bustle about, to run away from it. (p. 197)

Paul is the "outsider" here, the one who does not enter into the family warmth, as we have seen a few lines earlier from his cold comment on his father's vigorous exclamations ("Why is a door-knob deader than anything else?"), and as we see a little later from the way in which he turns "impatiently" from his books and pencil, after his father has asked him "humbly" to count up the money. And at the close of the episode he dismisses his father viciously: "It won't be long", he says to his mother. "You can have my money. Let him go to hell." (p. 201). Morel does not deserve this, we feel, after all the warmth and vigour of his action here. Paul is cruel to anyone who threatens his mother's dominion, however briefly.

This Miriam feels instinctively, a few minutes later, when

she looks at the stencilled design that Paul has made for his mother:

> "Ah, how beautiful!" she cried.
> The spread cloth, with its wonderful reddish roses and dark green stems, all so simple, and somehow so wicked-looking, lay at her feet. She went on her knees before it, her dark curls dropping. He saw her crouched voluptuously before his work, and his heart beat quickly. Suddenly she looked up at him.
> "Why does it seem cruel?" she asked.
> "What?"
> "There seems a feeling of cruelty about it", she said.
> "It's jolly good, whether or not", he replied, folding up his work with a lover's hands. (p. 201)

He has also made a "smaller piece" for Miriam; but when he sees her fingering the work "with trembling hands" he can only turn with embarrassment to tend the bread in the oven, and when she looks up at him "with her dark eyes one flame of love" he can only laugh "uncomfortably" and begin to talk "about the design". "All his passion, all his wild blood, went into this intercourse with her, when he talked and conceived his work. She brought forth to him his imaginations. She did not understand, any more than a woman understands when she conceives a child in her womb. But this was life for her and for him." (p. 202). But, as the imagery of conception ironically implies, such talk is not all of life for either of them.

Immediately after this, the physical scuffle and flirtation with Beatrice shows another need, which Miriam recognizes and would like to satisfy: "His thick hair was tumbled over his forehead. Why might she not push it back for him, and remove the marks of Beatrice's comb? Why might she not press his body with her two hands? It looked so firm, and every whit living. And he would let other girls, why not her?"(p. 207). A moment later, as usual, Paul tries to "abstract" their relationship into a French lesson, only to find that her French diary is "mostly a love-letter" to him:

> "Look," he said quietly, "the past participle conjugated with *avoir* agrees with the direct object when it precedes."
> She bent forward, trying to see and to understand. Her free, fine

curls tickled his face. He started as if they had been red hot, shudder-ing. He saw her peering forward at the page, her red lips parted piteously, the black hair springing in fine strands across her tawny, ruddy cheek. She was coloured like a pomegranate for richness. His breath came short as he watched her. Suddenly she looked up at him. Her dark eyes were naked with their love, afraid, and yearning. His eyes, too, were dark, and they hurt her. They seemed to master her. She lost all her self-control, was exposed in fear. And he knew, before he could kiss her, he must drive something out of himself. And a touch of hate for her crept back again into his heart. He returned to her exercise. (p. 209)

Miriam does not bear the slightest blame for the failure of this relationship: she is "like a pomegranate for richness", like the bride in the Song of Solomon; she combines a pure beauty of sensuous appeal with all the soul that Paul the artist needs for his further development. And like that bride she is not passive, she tries to draw Paul out of his imprisonment, tries to draw his attention towards the wild beauty of "the yellow, bursten flowers". His response is to level at her the most cruel of all his desperate charges:

"Aren't they magnificent?" she murmured.
"Magnificent! it's a bit thick – they're pretty!"
She bowed again to her flowers at his censure of her praise. He watched her crouching, sipping the flowers with fervid kisses.
"Why must you always be fondling things!" he said irritably.
"But I love to touch them", she replied, hurt.
"Can you never like things without clutching them as if you wanted to pull the heart out of them? Why don't you have a bit more restraint, or reserve, or something?"
She looked up at him full of pain, then continued slowly to stroke her lips against a ruffled flower. Their scent, as she smelled it, was so much kinder than he; it almost made her cry.
"You wheedle the soul out of things", he said. "I would never wheedle – at any rate, I'd go straight."
He scarcely knew what he was saying. These things came from him mechanically. She looked at him. His body seemed one weapon, firm and hard against her.
"You're always begging things to love you", he said, "as if you were a beggar for love. Even the flowers, you have to fawn on them –"
Rhythmically, Miriam was swaying and stroking the flower with

her mouth, inhaling the scent which ever after made her shudder as it came to her nostrils.

"You don't want to love – your eternal and abnormal craving is to be loved. You aren't positive, you're negative. You absorb, absorb, as if you must fill yourself up with love, because you've got a shortage somewhere."

She was stunned by his cruelty, and did not hear. He had not the faintest notion of what he was saying. It was as if his fretted, tortured soul, run hot by thwarted passion, jetted off these sayings like sparks from electricity. (p. 218)

The shortage is in Paul; and she fondles the flowers so warmly because they offer solace from his ruthless rejection of her natural being. Her closeness to flowers throughout the book shows her as an innocent Persephone who needs only to be carried away by the power that Paul might possess if he were a whole man. But he is not. He is a child, with a child's limited outlook. His mother's influence has reduced all other human beings to unreality. This the narrator makes plain in one of his rare moments of illumination:

He had come back to his mother. Hers was the strongest tie in his life. When he thought round, Miriam shrank away. There was a vague, unreal feel about her. And nobody else mattered. There was one place in the world that stood solid and did not melt into unreality: the place where his mother was. Everybody else could grow shadowy, almost non-existent to him, but she could not. It was as if the pivot and pole of his life, from which he could not escape, was his mother. (p. 222)

So then for Paul the warm reality of Miriam must fade away into spirituality and soulfulness, and she must suffer the cruel accusation summed up in the falsely composed letter that he writes at the end of the chapter, "Defeat of Miriam" – a letter of stilted, inflated rhetoric, false in every way:

"May I speak of our old, worn love, this last time. It, too, is changing, is it not? Say, has not the body of that love died, and left you its invulnerable soul? You see, I can give you a spirit love, I have given it you this long, long time; but not embodied passion. See, you are a nun. I have given you what I would give a holy nun – as a mystic monk to a mystic nun. Surely you esteem it best. Yet you

regret – no, have regretted – the other. In all our relations no body
enters. I do not talk to you through the senses – rather through the
spirit. That is why we cannot love in the common sense. Ours is not
an everyday affection. As yet we are mortal, and to live side by side
with one another would be dreadful, for somehow with you I cannot
long be trivial, and, you know, to be always beyond this mortal
state would be to lose it. If people marry, they must live together as
affectionate humans, who may be common-place with each other
without feeling awkward – not as two souls. So I feel it." (p. 251)

So she feels it too, and the hopeless rejection of her true character gives a death-blow to her inner vitality. " 'You are a nun
– you are a nun.' The words went into her heart again and
again. Nothing he ever had said had gone into her so deeply,
fixedly, like a mortal wound."

After such a wound, his later effort to carry on sexual relations with her is bound to be a failure. She tries, as she always
has tried, but her inner life is ebbing. This is not the marriage
that she yearns for, not the union that he needs. Paul hardly
knows that she is there, as a person; indeed he does not want
to know her as a human being. "He had always, almost wil-
fully, to put her out of count, and act from the brute strength of
his own feelings." (p. 290). The title of the chapter, "The Test
on Miriam", is bitterly ironic, for what the chapter presents is
the test on Paul's ability to free himself from the imprisonment
which he feels, but does not understand. This is clear from
Paul's stream of consciousness at the very outset of the chapter:
"There was some obstacle; and what was the obstacle? It lay
in the physical bondage. He shrank from the physical contact.
But why? With her he felt bound up inside himself. He could
not go out to her."(p. 278). His only refuge is to turn towards
a sort of mindless evasion of his torments, a rejection of his own
humanity:

> He courted her now like a lover. Often, when he grew hot, she put
> his face from her, held it between her hands, and looked in his eyes.
> He could not meet her gaze. Her dark eyes, full of love, earnest and
> searching, made him turn away. Not for an instant would she let
> him forget. Back again he had to torture himself into a sense of his
> responsibility and hers. Never any relaxing, never any leaving him-
> self to the great hunger and impersonality of passion; he must be

brought back to a deliberate, reflective creature. As if from a swoon of passion she called him back to the littleness, the personal relationship. (p. 284)

So Paul, near the end of this chapter, is reduced to pitiful, even contemptible, littleness. Miriam, in her violent despair, at last cries out the essential truth: "It has been one long battle between us – you fighting away from me".(p. 298). His response is shock and utter amazement: in his self-absorption he has never even begun to see it from her point of view. And he turns at once towards a painful series of self-justifications, throwing the blame on her: "He was full of a feeling that she had deceived him. She had despised him when he thought she worshipped him. She had let him say wrong things, and had not contradicted him. She had let him fight alone . . . She had not played fair."(p. 299). Yet at the very end of the chapter, the bitter truth of what he has done to her emerges poignantly out of his self-deception:

> "She never thought she'd have me, mother, not from the first, and so she's not disappointed."
> "I'm afraid", said his mother, "she doesn't give up hopes of you yet".
> "No", he said, "perhaps not".
> "You'll find it's better to have done", she said.
> "*I* don't know", he said desperately.
> "Well, leave her alone", replied his mother.
> So he left her, and she was alone. Very few people cared for her, and she for very few people. She remained alone with herself, waiting. (p. 300)

[iii]

Now all the tension of that doomed affair is over, and for the last four chapters of the book the method of the objective narrator may be resumed. With the opening of chapter XII everything comes back into clarity and firmness. Paul is making progress with his designs, he believes in his work, and the clear tone of this conclusion is struck at once as we read: "He was twenty-four when he said his first confident thing to his mother" about his art. Had Lawrence been a more conventional craftsman, he might have put the heading "Part III" at the top of this chapter, so that we could see clearly the essential structure of the book, that of a triptych, with the major scene of suffering in the centre, and two smaller scenes on either side, focusing our eyes towards the centre of the drama.

The portrait of Clara Dawes is not in any way designed to rival that of Miriam. Clara is second-best, and second-hand, for all her beauty. "Some part, big and vital in him, she had no hold over; nor did she ever try to get it, or even to realize what it was. And he knew in some way that she held herself still as Mrs. Dawes." (pp.360-1). Their physical passion is significant, not for itself, but for the clarifying, purgatorial effect upon both of them, leading them to find a truth that lies beyond those times when they "included in their meeting the thrust of the manifold grass-stems, the cry of the peewit, the wheel of the stars".(p. 353). This sort of immersion in mindlessness plays an essential part in Lawrence's later philosophy of love; but it is only a part, and it is here shown to be utterly insufficient. For Paul, the immediate result of the affair is the feeling that Clara is "not much more than a big white pebble on the beach". "What does she mean to me, after all?" he asks. "She represents something, like a bubble of foam represents the sea. But what is *she*? It's not her I care for."(pp. 357-8).

It has been, from the beginning, a flawed relationship, with unpleasant overtones of the mother-substitute.[10] During that trip to Lincoln with his mother, we recall, Paul had complained bitterly of his mother's aging: "Why can't a man have a *young* mother?" he cries.(p. 242). So now he has her, in Clara, only six or seven years older than he, a woman married, like his mother, to a rough workman who has, she says, treated her badly. There is a striking resemblance between Baxter Dawes and Paul's father – their use of dialect, their roughness, and their collapse into drunkenness and apathy, with outbursts of violence. Clara is "reserved" and "superior", like his mother; and she has the mother's deep discontent, her independent spirit, her sharp tongue, her bitterness against life and against men. This is an affair which, as the ominous flower ritual has prophesied, carries in itself the sources of its own death; and the affair dies as the mother is dying: "She [Clara] was afraid of the man who was not there with her, whom she could feel

365

behind this make-believe lover: somebody sinister, that filled her with horror. She began to have a kind of horror of him. It was almost as if he were a criminal. He wanted her – he had her – and it made her feel as if death itself had her in its grip." (p. 387). For Paul, at its best, the affair has been a blind rushing, an escape from thought, like being swept away in the torrent of the Trent: "Gradually, the little criticisms, the little sensations, were lost, thought also went, everything borne along in one flood. He became, not a man with a mind, but a great instinct." (p. 363).

Yet the result of this immersion is a new clarity of vision in Paul and a consequent clarity and precision in the remarks of the narrator. The whole effect is summed up in the remarkable self-understanding that Paul displays in chapter XIII, in the luminous conversation with his mother about his feeling for Clara: "You know, mother, I think there must be something the matter with me, that I *can't* love . . . I feel sometimes as if I wronged my women, mother."

> "How wronged them, my son?"
> "I don't know."
> He went on painting rather despairingly; he had touched the quick of the trouble.
> "And as for wanting to marry", said his mother, "there's plenty of time yet."
> "But no, mother. I even love Clara, and I did Miriam; but to *give* myself to them in marriage I couldn't. I couldn't belong to them. They seem to want *me*, and I can't ever give it them."
> "You haven't met the right woman."
> "And I never shall meet the right woman while you live", he said.
> She was very quiet. Now she began to feel again tired, as if she were done. (p. 351)

His growth in understanding, his realization of the importance, the bigness of the human relationship, is shown in his sympathy for Dawes, in his deepened understanding of the basic relationship between his mother and father (p. 317), and in his final reconciliation of Clara and her husband. In this way, perhaps, he can make amends to his father, by reconciling the surrogates of father and mother. And finally, the superb clarity of the whole objective vision now is shown in the long passage of the mother's dying, where she becomes in death a youthful bride in Paul's eyes, and Paul says his long farewell to his only love.

But for Miriam, nothing can be done, as we see in that last sad interview, after the mother's death: "Still, the curls were fine and free, but her face was much older, the brown throat much thinner. She seemed old to him, older than Clara. Her bloom of youth had quickly gone. A sort of stiffness, almost of woodenness, had come upon her."(p. 416). She is the walking ghost of her former self. He knows what he has done to her, but he cannot help her, for she no longer attracts him. The mother's influence has stifled the vitality in Miriam that once drew them together. Inevitably, he rejects her pathetic proposal with the mother's reasoning: "But – you love me so much, you want to put me in your pocket. And I should die there smothered." (p. 417).

" 'Mother!' he whimpered – 'mother!' " we read on the book's last page. It is the clearest judgement of the book. For *whimpered* is precisely the right word[11] to describe the bondage that has held him from Miriam. Yet there remains in him his mother's tough, unyielding will; maimed and damaged as he is, "he would not give in". The phrase has been three times applied to the mother in her fatal illness, and the words are perfectly in line with the whole tragic story. Whatever happens to others, he will survive: his mother's will drives him on into a pilgrimage of pain. But there is no reason to feel that his pilgrimage, however painful to him, will always be only destructive to others. His growth in self-knowledge offers a better hope. Paul has within himself a vital, creative spark; when that energy is frustrated, the results are bitterly destructive; but when, however briefly, that energy can be released, the results may be beneficent and beautiful. He has still, potentially, an artist's vision that can bring all things into harmony:

"What a pity there is a coal-pit here where it is so pretty!" said Clara.

"Do you think so?" he answered. "You see, I am so used to it I should miss it. No; and I like the pits here and there. I like the rows of trucks, and the headstocks, and the steam in the daytime, and the lights at night. When I was a boy, I always thought a pillar of cloud by day and a pillar of fire by night was a pit, with its steam, and its lights, and the burning bank, – and I thought the Lord was always at the pit-top." (p. 320)

NOTES

1 Quotations are taken from the first English edition of *Sons and Lovers* (London, 1913), but page references are made to the currently available editions in the Modern Library and Compass Books (Viking Press), where the texts are numbered 1-420 (older editions in these two series have different pagination, along with a somewhat more reliable text). The above quotations come from pages 142, 148, 215-16, 219.

2 Mark Spilka, *The Love Ethic of D. H. Lawrence* (Bloomington, 1955), pp. 45, 51, 56, 66. A notable exception to this view is presented by Graham Hough, *The Dark Sun: A Study of D. H. Lawrence* (New York, 1956), pp. 39-47, where Hough sees "the co-presence in the Paul and Miriam parts of *Sons and Lovers* of two different kinds of experience – more or less simple recollection, checked and assisted by Jessie Chambers; and a later interpretation of the whole sequence of events". The very early Freudian interpretation by Alfred Booth Kuttner also shows clearly the way in which Paul is being unfair to the character of Miriam: see the reprint of this essay of 1916 in the valuable collection edited by E. W. Tedlock, Jr., *D. H. Lawrence and Sons and Lovers: Sources and Criticism* (New York, 1965); see especially pp. 81-6. For the later Freudian study by Daniel Weiss, see note 9 below.

3 This important line is omitted in the current texts of the Modern Library and Compass Books.

4 Julian Moynahan, *The Deed of Life: The Novels and Tales of D. H. Lawrence* (Princeton, 1963), p. 17.

5 Mark Schorer, "Technique as Discovery", in *The Modern Critical Spectrum*, ed. Gerald and Nancy Goldberg (Engelwood Cliffs, 1962), pp. 76-7; the essay originally appeared in *The Hudson Review* (1948). See also the interesting essay by Seymour Betsky in *The Achievement of D. H. Lawrence*, ed. Frederick J. Hoffman and Harry T. Moore (Norman, 1953), esp. pp. 138-40.

6   The phrase is applied to Miriam by Dorothy Van Ghent on the later occasion when Miriam is caressing the daffodils and draws down Paul's harshest charges: see *The English Novel: Form and Function* (New York, 1953), p. 256.

7   Spilka, pp. 51-3.

8   Many later editions read "stream".

9   Daniel A. Weiss, *Oedipus in Nottingham: D. H. Lawrence* (Seattle, 1962), p. 53. Though Weiss sees Miriam primarily as "a static figure . . . the Ophelia, the virginal side of the maternal image" (p. 82), his book is excellent for the light it throws on the causes of Paul's misunderstanding.

10 Weiss's book is excellent on this point too, particularly in its treatment of the significance of the similarity between Clara's husband and Paul's father. See especially pp. 26-37.

11 The current Modern Library, Compass, and Penguin texts all erroneously read "whispered": see the comment on this textual crux by Harry T. Moore in Tedlock's collection, p. 63. (The older printings in the Modern Library and in Compass Books, however, retain the plates that read "whimpered".)

The Marble and The Statue:

THE EXPLORATORY IMAGINATION OF

D. H. Lawrence

> . . . you know that the perfect statue is in the marble,
> the kernel of it. But the thing is the getting it out
> clean.

It took Lawrence five separate novels, and two long essays, to capture *The Rainbow* and *Women in Love*. My first object in the paper that follows is to trace out this evolutionary process. The second, an inseparable part of the first, is to consider the relation of Lawrence's thinking to the novels during this period of intense creativity, particularly the *Study of Thomas Hardy* and *The Crown*. The third object, arising from the other two, is to argue for what seems to me a necessary approach to the nature of Lawrence's imagination.

[i]

Lawrence's two greatest works emerged from the same "flippant", even "jeering"[1] little "pot-boiler",[2] begun in order to distract him from a serious novel which was getting out of hand. In mid-January 1913 at Gargnano, he abandoned the idea of a novel based on the life of Burns, and began *The Insurrection of Miss Houghton*, which eventually became *The Lost Girl*.[3] He thought this "great – so new, so really a stratum deeper than I think anybody has ever gone . . . all analytical – quite unlike *Sons and Lovers*, not a bit visualised";[4] and even as he laid it

371

aside after 200 pages, it still lay "next my heart".[5] But it was
"*too* improper".[6] So he began instead, about the middle of
March, *The Sisters*, "a queer novel which seems to have come
by itself".[7] It was flippant because "it was meant to be for the
jeunes filles", it was jeering because both sisters were Frieda:
"*me*, these beastly, superior, arrogant females! Lawrence *hated*
me just over the children . . . so he wrote this!" But it did
Lawrence "good to theorise myself out, and to depict Frieda's
God Almightiness in all its glory",[8] to release his rebellious
feelings about her combination of the Prussian aristocrat, the
Magna Mater, and Pallas Athene in plaits. "That was the first
crude fermenting of the book", he wrote when it was well
advanced, "I'll make it into art now".[8] At quite an early stage
however the pot-boiler had already become "earnest and painful",[9] because Lawrence was incapable of remaining flippant for
long. "I can only write what I feel pretty strongly about, and
that, at present, is the relation between men and women."[10]
We glimpse what it is like to find one's work changing and
deepening under one's hands. "I am doing a novel which I have
never grasped. Damn its eyes, there I am at page 145 and I've
no notion what it's about . . . it's like a novel in a foreign language I don't know very well."[11] He finished before 11 June[12] and
left for a visit to England a few days later, returning to Germany
at the beginning of August.

As soon as he could, he began *The Sisters* again, making two
false starts, but eventually finding a new basis.[13] Back in Italy,
having written 340 pages, he felt that "The Laocoon writhing
and shrieking have gone from my new work, and I think there is
a bit of stillness, like the wide, still, unseeing eyes of a Venus of
Melos . . . There is something in the Greek sculpture that any
soul is hungry for – something of the eternal stillness that lies
under all movement, under all life, like a source, incorruptible
and inexhaustible. It is deeper than change, and struggling. So
long I have acknowledged only the struggle, the stream, the
change. And now I begin to feel something of the source, the
great impersonal which never changes and out of which all
change comes."[14] A new title, *The Wedding Ring*, indicates a
new direct concern with marriage.[15] By 10 January 1914 it was
"nearly finished";[16] but at the end of the month Garnett's
criticisms of the first half brought his own dissatisfaction to a

head and he laid the manuscript aside unfinished, to begin all over again. "It was full of beautiful things but it missed – I knew that it just missed being itself. So here I am, must sit down and write it out again. I know it is quite a lovely novel really – you know that the perfect statue is in the marble, the kernel of it. But the thing is the getting it out clean."[17]

This time there were at least seven false starts before the third version was properly under way, at much greater length than before. (These, with the two earlier versions, amounted to "quite a thousand pages that I shall burn".)[18] By 22 April, however, Lawrence was sure not only that his relationship with Frieda had "come through", but that the novel had too, and that there was the closest connection. "I am sure of this now, this novel. It is a big and a beautiful work. Before, I could not get my soul into it. That was because of the struggle and the resistance between Frieda and me. Now you will find her and me in the novel, I think, and the work is of both of us."[19] On 9 May he recorded her wish to change the title from *The Wedding Ring* to *The Rainbow*,[20] and by 16 May it was finished.[21] On 8 June they left for England where they were married.

Lawrence thought of the work as complete at this stage. Pinker had negotiated a lucrative contract with a new publisher, Methuen. Lawrence signed on 1 July[22] and submitted the manuscript, typed by his friend Dunlop who was British Consul at La Spezia, not only to Methuen, but also to Kennerley, with a view to publication in the U.S.A.[23] On 15 July he asked Marsh to lend him Thomas Hardy's novels and Lascelles Abercrombie's book on Hardy, because he hoped "to write a little book on Hardy's people".[24]

Early in August came a shattering blow. Methuen returned the manuscript as "it could not be published in its then condition".[25] The future was already casting a long shadow. Lawrence was aghast: "Here is a state of affairs – what is to become of us?"[26] Quite apart from his feelings about the novel itself, financial security had changed in a moment to embarrassment. The war had broken out. It seemed impossible to go back to Italy. Yet Lawrence seems never to have considered rewriting to satisfy Methuen. On 5 September he wrote to Pinker: "What a miserable world. What colossal idiocy, this war. Out of sheer rage I've begun my book about Thomas Hardy."[27] He told Amy Lowell on 18 November that it was "supposed to be on Thomas Hardy, but in reality a sort of Confessions of my heart", and that he was just finishing.[28]

It is easy to see what attracted Lawrence to the author of *Tess*, and more especially, *Jude*. He had told Garnett that the germ of his novel had been, even in the first *Sisters*, "woman becoming individual, self-responsible, taking her own initiative".[29] But in the same letter he explained that, although the first *Sisters* had been "flippant, and often vulgar and jeering", he was primarily "a passionately religious man, and my novels must be written from the depth of my religious experience". In January 1913, before he began the first *Sisters*, he had written an extraordinary "Preface" to *Sons and Lovers*, never intended for publication, which is only about *Sons and Lovers* in the same sense that the *Study of Thomas Hardy* is about Hardy. It is actually a first attempt to find a formulation for Lawrence's deepest religious convictions, by rewriting Christian theology in terms of the relation between man and woman. It announces his belief that the Flesh is made Word to dwell among us; that Woman lies in travail to give birth to Man, who in his hour utters his Word. "And God the Father, the Inscrutable, the Unknowable, we know in the Flesh, in Woman. She is the door for our in-going and our out-coming. In her we go back to the Father, but like the witnesses of the Transfiguration, blind and unconscious." But, as the bee moves between the hive and the flower, so man must move in a continuous creative rhythm between the source of his renewal, and his utterance, "the glad cry: 'This is I – I am I'. And this glad cry when we know, is the Holy Ghost the Comforter."[30]

In the *Study of Thomas Hardy*, Lawrence's religion and his fiction begin to come together. It is a sustained attempt to work out the meaning of his earlier intuitions into what could be called, not improperly, a "theology" of marriage – a study of creativity embarked on under the first impact of war. Only then was he able to write *The Rainbow*, the History, or even "Bible", in which that theology is embodied, tested, and further explored imaginatively, in terms of human relationships.

[ii]

Without the manuscripts of the first three novels, we cannot hope to measure fully how far the *Study* took Lawrence beyond *The Wedding Ring*. Fortunately, however, fragments of *Sisters* I and *Sisters* II survive; and Lawrence inserted a section of *The Wedding Ring* into the autograph manuscript of *The Rainbow*.[31] From these we can learn rather more of the growth of the work than the letters tell us.

The first *Sisters* seems to have been an "Ur"-version of *Women in Love*. Lawrence planned a novel of 300 pages. The remaining fragment is numbered 291-6. Gudrun, pregnant with Gerald's child, confronts both Gerald and Loerke in her lodgings in England. Gerald now wants to marry her, but she suspects it may be only because of the baby. Loerke has already offered himself. Even from a bald account, one can see what Lawrence meant by saying the novel was "for the *jeunes filles*", and the style is still a little novelettish, though the flippancy has quite gone. It ends:

> "I shouldn't have cared for any other man's child", she said, slowly. He kissed her hands, and they sat still. There was a good deal that hurt still, between them. But he was humble to her. Only, she must love him — she must love him, or else everything was barren. This aloofness of hers — she came to him as the father of her child, not as to a lover, a husband. Well he had had a chance, and lost it. He had been a fool. Now he must make the best of it, and get her again. But it hurt that she did not seem to want him very much. It hurt keenly.
>
> Then while he was thinking, with his forehead hard with pain, she kissed him, drawing him to her, (?murmuring) "My love!"

Lawrence's theme, in the Gerald/Gudrun story, seems to have been the conventional Englishman's inability to submit himself to love with its sacrifice, its tenderness, its suffering. Loerke — "a decent fellow, really" — accuses Gerald of trusting to his position to play with women, and to his strength to threaten men. Gerald is forced to see the German's face "broken into lines of real agony, all distorted". He insists again and again that he "didn't *know*" whether he could love Gudrun. But in this scene he shows a "queer abstraction", an "unseeing look in his eyes, as of a creature that follows an instinct blindly,

375

thoughtlessly as a leopard running on in the sunshine, for the sake of running", which his sister Winifred finds "fascinating". Now he can accept humiliation before Loerke, and find tears of tenderness. "He was something he feared he never could be: he had got something he had pretended to disbelieve in. And, breathing hard, he knew that this was his life's fulfilment, and a wave of faith, warm, strong, religious faith, went over him." Only, he is also forced to measure and accept the damage which his inability to love has caused.

The story of the other "superior flounder" was, however, almost certainly the more important, though both were modelled on Frieda. Presumably, the "jeering" was directed through Ella's lover. (A remark in the letters indicates that this story was written in the first person.)[32] Ella was certainly positive, not to say opinionated, since Frieda refers to one of her own tart and sweeping generalizations as "Ella-ing". But the portrait seems to have become more and more significant to Lawrence, and it was the problem of understanding how Ella came to be as she was, through some hurt in her past, that constituted the growing-point.

Thus the second *Sisters* seems to have been the "Ur" – *Rainbow*. The fragment is numbered 373-80. Yet it is early in Ella's relationship with Birkin. The second *Sisters* was not then a rewriting of the first, but rather an attempt to get behind it, into the past. Ella is leaving Birkin's rooms in the Mill, after an encounter that has left her "trembling, flushed, ashamed", rebellious, and "as yet free of him"; while Birkin is "raging". Later, after her parents and the smaller children have gone on holiday to Scarborough, Ella dreams and meditates, searching her heart to understand Birkin and her own feelings. He comes to see her when Gudrun is out at a tennis party. The "new basis" of the novel can be detected not only in the concern with how Ella's past has shaped her present, but also in the style. The writing has developed a rhythmic quality, a steady cumulative rhythm quietening the somewhat melodramatic conception of the scene, a new "inner" dimension.

> Then he seemed to be coming to her. Summoning all her self-restraint she put her hand on his arm and said, pleadingly, pathetically:
> "No – no".

He stood still, silent. She felt his living arm beneath his sleeve. It was torture to her. Suddenly she caught him to her, and hid her face on his breast, crying, in a muffled, tortured voice:

"Do you love me?"

She clung to him. But his breast was strange to her. His arms were round her tight, hard, compressing her, he was quivering, rigid, holding her against him. But he was strange to her. He was strange to her, and it was almost agony. He was cold to her, however he held her hard in his power and quivered. She felt he was cold to her. And the quivering man stiffened with desire was strange and horrible to her. She got free again, and, with her hands to her temples, she slid away to the floor at his feet, unable to stand, unable to hold her body erect. She must double up, for she could not bear it. But she got up again to go away. And before she reached the door, she was crouching on the floor again, holding her temples in agony. Her womb, her belly, her heart were all in agony. She crouched together on the floor, crying like some wild animal in pain, with a kind of mooing noise, very dreadful to hear, a sound she was unaware of, that came from her unproduced, out of the depth of her body in torture. For some wild moments the paroxysm continued when she crouched on the ground with her head down, mad, crying with an inarticulate, animal noise. Then suddenly it all stopped. It was gone. Her head was clear. And then she was confused with shame . . . (Birkin) stood white to the gills, with wide dark eyes staring blankly. His heart inside him felt red-hot, so that he panted as he breathed. His mind was blank. He knew she did not feel him any more. He knew he had no part in her, that he was out of place. And he had nothing to say. But gradually he grew a little calmer, his eyes lost their wide, dark, hollow look. He was coming to himself.

"What did I do?" he asked.

It has of course less to do with Birkin, than with the coming to the surface of the deep bruise inflicted on Ella's inner being, by her earlier love affair. At the same time she is aware "that something was taking place, implicating her with him, which she could never revoke or escape. And blindly, almost shrinking, she lapsed forward". Birkin, too, is afraid. "It seems", he writes, "that everything has come toppling down . . . and here I am entangled in the ruins and fragments of my old life, and struggling to get out. You seem to me some land beyond." At the end of the fragment the two girls, walking by the shore, catch sight of Ella's former lover, Ben Templeman. "A wave of terror, deep, annihilating, went over her. She knew him without looking: his peculiar, straying walk, the odd separate look about him which filled her with dread. He still had power over her; he was still Man to her. She knew he would not see her, because he was rather short-sighted." It seems clear, however, that the novel was to end with Ella and Birkin finding their true selves, "the eternal and unchangeable that they are", ceasing to be "strange forms, half-uttered".[33]

The criticisms from Garnett which led to the abandonment of this novel, seem to have been that the character of Ella was inconsistent; that the affair with Templeman was "wrong"; and that what Lawrence called the "exhaustive method" meant that the "artistic side" was "in the background", the scenes not "incorporated" enough.[34] Lawrence agreed with the first point. He explained that he had made the mistake of "trying to graft on to the character of Louie the character, more or less, of Frieda". For the young Ella he had used the rather different personality of the girl to whom he had once been engaged, and whose father and family were to serve as models for the Will Brangwens.[35] He also agreed with the second point, while insisting that Ella could not be the girl she had to be "unless she had some experience of love and of men . . . Then she must have a love episode, a significant one. But it must not be a Templeman episode". He refused however to agree to the criticism of the novel's imaginative mode. He had realized that he could no longer write like *Sons and Lovers*, "in that hard, violent style full of sensation and presentation".[36] He felt that the new style, even if its "flowers" were "frail and shadowy", was true to himself in a period of transition. "I prefer the permeating beauty . . . it is not so easy for one to be married. In marriage one must become something else. And I am changing, one way or the other."[37] The new style had to feel, like the new man, for the hidden forces behind the surface drama.

The Wedding Ring brought the second *Sisters* nearer to *The Rainbow*, though it still went well on, into what is now *Women in Love*. The section that Lawrence thought enough of to incorporate into the first draft of *The Rainbow*, runs from Ella's first day as a teacher, to the family's removal to Beldover. It was more simply naturalistic than it is now, not so thematically heightened, but in essence the same. Unfortunately, however, since it lies outside the relationships with both lovers – though "Charles" Skrebensky is mentioned – it tells us little about the development of the imaginative mode. Its usefulness is rather that its pagination allows us to guess at the new length and what the novel may have contained. It is numbered 219-84, and represents sections 3-5 of chapter 10 of *The Wedding Ring* and sections 1-4 of chapter 11. We know that the novel was a good deal longer than the second *Sisters* which was planned for roughly 400 pages, autograph.[38] We can deduce from a letter[39] that there were about 150 typescript pages from near the end of the earlier episode with Skrebensky to the final failure. (The 65 pages of typescript must come near the beginning of this section.) There must then have been a link between the break with Skrebensky and the meeting with Birkin. Another letter[40] tells us that there were then a further 80 pages to the point where Lawrence decided to end *The Wedding Ring*. This looks like a novel of 475-500 pages, folio typescript, depending on the length of the linking section between the two love affairs. The significant point would therefore be that two-fifths of the novel would seem to have been devoted to Ella's childhood and girl-hood – a high proportion. The most likely explanation is that *The Wedding Ring*, seeking to extend the concern with marriage which had suggested the title to Lawrence near the end of the second *Sisters*, may have begun to build up an account of the marriage of Ella's parents as a contrast both with her failure, and with her success. Since the end-point was presumably the marriage of Ella and Birkin, the rainbow symbol probably pointed chiefly to the dissolution of the bad old world and the promise of the "land beyond". (The idea of the new title arrived when the novel was nearly complete.)[41] *The Wedding Ring* may have included, then, the story of Ella's parents, her child-hood and youth, the first girlish affair, Brinsley Street School, the Schofields, University and the second affair with Skre-bensky, a return to schoolteaching, and the final finding of themselves of Ella and Birkin. Of the episodes that may have caused the banning of *The Rainbow*, we can say definitely that the last relationship between Anna and Will, and Ursula's relationship with Winifred Inger,[42] were not in the novel; and that the handling of the affair with Skrebensky had not struck

Lawrence as indiscreet,[43] so that he was dumbfounded at the reaction of his new publisher.

[iii]

We may now consider the impact, on this apparently completed novel, of the *Study of Thomas Hardy*. The *Study* was almost finished by 18 November 1914. In late November Lawrence began his novel all over again.[44] By early January he realized that the work would be too vast to remain in one volume.[45] At the beginning of February he was claiming that there would be "no very flagrant love passages". At the end of the month he knew that there would be trouble with Methuen and that the novel would have to be fought for.[46] He finished on 2 March,[47] and when he received the typescript from Viola Meynell,[48] he revised the whole thing extensively once more. What had happened?

Through studying Hardy's art and Hardy's people Lawrence had found a language in which to conceive the impersonal forces he saw operating within and between human beings; involving a new clarification of what the novel he had been trying to write was really *about*; and the discovery of a "structural skeleton" on which to re-found it in a new dimension. The full implications only dawned gradually, but that it was a new dimension is beyond doubt.

Lawrence was impressed by the way that Hardy's figures moved against a vast impersonal landscape. "There is a constant revelation in Hardy's novels: that there exists a great background, vital and vivid, which matters more than the people who move upon it . . . This is the wonder of Hardy's novels, and gives them their beauty. The vast unexplored morality of life itself, what we call the immorality of nature, surrounds us in its eternal incomprehensibility, and in its midst goes on the little human morality play."[49] Its true "moral" is that man "at last must learn to be at one, in his mind and will, with the primal impulses that rise in him".[50]

Hardy must consequently have reinforced his understanding of his own new style. Before he began the *Study* he had already made a well known defence of the "psychology" of *The Wedding Ring* in answer to Garnett. "You mustn't look in my novel for the old stable *ego* of the character. There is another *ego*, according to whose action the individual is unrecognisable, and passes through, as it were, allotropic states which it needs a deeper sense than any we've been used to exercise, to discover are states of the same single radically unchanged element . . . the characters fall into the form of some other rhythmic form, as when one draws a fiddle-bow across a fine tray delicately sanded, the sand takes lines unknown."[51] The "characters" in Hardy exist in terms of being and consciousness, rather than the conduct of "the old stable ego".[52] In *Sons and Lovers* Lawrence's people had already opened into dimensions of being, but had retained a recognisable density springing partly from autobiography, and partly from the mode, "that hard, violent style full of sensation and presentation". The development of *The Wedding Ring* out of the first *Sisters* had taken Lawrence steadily further away from autobiographical material, and *The Rainbow* was to take him further still. His reading of Hardy must have taught him a great deal about the presentation of beings, related to the great background of nature, embodied in concretely rendered physical existence and consciousness, yet capable of revealing the "allotropic" play of the impersonal forces that were to be the deepest concern of *The Rainbow*. The first of its three stories, and the deepest dimension of the other two, could not have been achieved before the *Study*.

As he pondered "Hardy's people", moreover – Eustacia, Tess, Angel, Alec, and especially Arabella, Jude, and Sue – his whole understanding of the impersonal forces that operated within and between men and women began to be clarified, extended, deepened. He took up the intuitions of the "Preface" to *Sons and Lovers* and made a sustained effort to explore them imaginatively. The *Study* is not a philosophical work, nor a work of literary criticism, since Hardy is only what started it off. It is primarily a work of "religious" imagination, and secondarily an essential stage in the discovery of what he had been trying to write about since *Sons and Lovers* – the creativity of marriage.

Lawrence tries to formulate in the *Study* a way of looking at every personality and all relationships as the outcome of conflict between two radically opposed forces, impersonal, and universal.[53] Both are vital to creative growth; and though they are separable for the sake of understanding, they are ultimately one, as the movement at the rim of a wheel and the stillness at its centre are one. He continually refers to these forces as "Male" and "Female", but we must not simply translate into "Man" and "Woman". The *Study* sometimes invites confusion, being exploratory, but it is clear enough that "Male" and "Female" both exist and conflict within every man and woman, as well as between them. We need also to be clear that sex is essentially a religious mystery to Lawrence, the one way he knows and believes in, by which human beings can contact "the beyond": "the sexual act . . . is for leaping off into the unknown, as from a cliff's edge".[54] Sexuality as such is not essential. "What we call the Truth is, in actual experience, that momentary state when in living the union between the male and the female is consummated. This consummation may be also physical, between the male body and the female body. But it may be only spiritual, between the male and female spirit."[55] In order to avoid confusion, and register the religious dimension of Lawrence's imagination, we would be well advised to use his own alternative terminology. The "Female" is the force of *Law*, of *God the Father*. The "Male" is the force of *Love*, of *God the Son*.

Through the lives of all men and women there operates a creative conflict between these two great impersonal forces. God the Father is immutable, all-embracing, one. By his Law, life is pure being, in complete unity with the universe of created things. Man exists in the flesh, in nature, in sensation. All creation is one whole. To exist is to be in togetherness. But equally there operates throughout creation the force of God the Son, which is Love. Love however does not mean what we expect it to mean. It is the impulse to move from being to knowing, from undifferentiated oneness to perception of what is not-self, and to define the self by this process into individuality. So Love is the force of differentiation into the many, into separateness, into consciousness, and ultimately into self-expression and art. The ideal of Love is to move into ever more complete individuation.

These two forces are necessarily locked in eternal conflict. There can be no final victory, and no assertion that one is better than the other, for the conflict is necessary to growth. It is, in other words, not dualistic but implicitly dialectic, since it always implies a state beyond every successive clash of thesis and anti-thesis. Beyond God the Father and God the Son, and the battle between Law and Love, is God the Holy Spirit, the Comforter. There is not only collision but consummation, marriage. Now "that which is mixed in me becomes pure, that which is female in me is given to the female, that which is male in her draws to me, I am complete, I am pure male, she is pure female, we rejoice in contact naked and perfect and clear, singled out into ourselves, and given the surpassing freedom. No longer do we see through a glass darkly. For she is she and I am I, and clasped together with her I know how perfectly she is not me, how perfectly I am not her, how utterly we are two, the light and the darkness, and how infinitely and eternally not-to-be-comprehended by either of us is the surpassing One we make. Yet of the One, this incomprehensible, we have an inkling that satisfies us." That this is a theology, the next sentence will suffice to show: "Through Christ Jesus I know that I shall find my Bride when I have overcome the impurity of the Flesh. When the Flesh in me is put away, I shall embrace the Bride, and I shall know as I am known."[56]

There can however be no stasis, only a never-ending process. Lawrence sees all the inner history of mankind in religion and art as a set of variations on the same eternal dialectic. Within marriage, the whole point is that the lovers should open up for each other an infinite unknown, an infinite beyond. Lawrence vilified the "one-flesh" idea of marriage precisely because it suggested completion, the merging of opposites. Conflict remains vital; if one force ever wins or the other collapses the consummation is crippled. There must be neither submission nor over-assertion, neither too-female being nor too-male knowing. Battle is the condition of growth but the aim is to "come through", ever *beyond*.

What we watch is Lawrence in the act of trying to formulate a "theoretical" basis for his whole intuitive view of marriage, and in the process beginning to clarify what it was that his fiction had been trying to express. But we can also see him reaching in the *Study* for a new form, as well as a more articulate grasp of his subject. As his "theology" reinterpreted Judaism and Christianity, so he found in the sacred history in which their theology had been embodied, a hint of the shape his own "bible" ought to have, and a hint of the point at which it should end. "Always the threefold utterance: the declaring of the God seen approaching, the rapture of contact, the anguished joy of remembrance, when the meeting has passed into separation."[57] Refining on this, he cites the story of David as an example of the first phase, Solomon for the second, Job for the third. Then in discussing Solomon he shows that the rapture of contact turns into rupture, because the man is too weak and the woman conquers; but since there had been real contact, "the living thing was conserved, kept always alive and powerful, but restrained, restricted, partial".

This is why the new novel had to have three stories or "testaments": a beautiful but partial old world, in Old Testament style; a world of transition in which fulfilment is fused with failure, and the promised land is seen but not entered; a new world of maximum separation almost unto death, but retaining in extremity the memory of an abiding covenant. The *Study* would eventually show Lawrence where to end *The Rainbow* by removing all the Birkin material, changing a conclusion of affirmation to near-tragedy, but retaining an anguished joy in separation. It showed him where to begin, with a new story of a world dominated by God the Father, that his understanding of Hardy's art must have helped him to handle. *The Rainbow* was almost certainly written backwards; the story of Tom and Lydia being the last to take shape, with the others being filled out thematically against its perspective. That is why, after cutting all the *Women in Love* material, the novel is so much longer than *The Wedding Ring*. The *Study* also shows us why there is such continual reference to the Bible – (particularly the Noah story, the journeying Israelites, and the search for a son of God by a daughter of Man); why there is also such a wealth of theological language; and why *The Rainbow* reinterprets Biblical history and theology in so very different a light.

Before we leave the *Study*, however, we should also note the significance of Lawrence's application of his theory to Art. It too must contain a dialectic of opposites, a real conflict in which both sides are allowed to assert themselves fully, and the scales are never weighted. Furthermore it must both Be and Know – must contain, as it were, a continual "systole and diastole" of poetry and analytic prose, exploration and understanding. Most of all, the Supreme Art must move through thesis and antithesis to try to see beyond. There is an Art "which recognises and utters (a man's) own law", that is, his own being; and an Art "which recognises his own and also the law of the woman, his neighbour, utters the glad embraces and the struggle between them, and the submission of one", that is, where a man pits his own vision against an antithesis, which it overcomes. "But the supreme art is one which knows the two conflicting laws, and knows the final reconciliation, where both are equal, two in one, complete." This, he says, "remains to be done. Some men have attempted it and left the remains of efforts. But it remains to be done."[58] *The Rainbow* is an attempt at a supreme fiction, aiming at a wisdom which will not criticize one side of any conflict and not the other. Lawrence is critical of both Anna and Will, cogently critical of Ursula when we read him sensitively, not only of Skrebensky. Similarly, the imaginative exploration of Birkin in *Women in Love* aims at mature self-criticism, not mere self-assertion, and the treatment of Gerald and Gudrun is fully complex, cutting, and tender.

This in turn helps to make an essential point about the relation of the *Study* to the novel it enabled Lawrence to write. The *Study* allowed him to see that "every novel must have the background or the structural skeleton of some theory of being, some metaphysic";[59] for that is exactly what he had provided for himself. On the other hand, having also understood how essential it is that the highest form of art should be a true unweighted conflict, an exploration not an assertion, his next sentence goes on to insist that "the metaphysic must always subserve the artistic purpose *beyond the artist's conscious aim.* (my italics). Otherwise the novel becomes a treatise." The *Study* is the "structural skeleton" of *The Rainbow*; but it is not a skeleton key and must not be misused as one. It is the greatest of commentaries on what the novel is fundamentally *about*, but it is a treatise, and *The Rainbow* is not. When its "ideas" come to be embodied in human relationships, the basic insight is tested out, explored, and extended, with an enormous increase in subtlety and complexity. Lawrence was a novelist, not a philosopher, and the *Study* turned out to be only a stage, if a very important one, in the growth of a novel. *The Rainbow* discovers new themes, like that of death and resurrection: the way that the marriage of opposites involves a "death" of the pre-existing selves and a rebirth into a new state, the Resurrection, or Paradise, or the Heavens. (Though the "pale Galilean" had played an essential role in the *Study*, curiously His death and resurrection had not.) The novel is thus more explicitly dialectic than the treatise had been. Most obvious of all: when the imagination of Lawrence the novelist is liberated in its proper medium, he creates people and situations whose density extends far beyond the categories of his "thinking".

[iv]

The evolution of one of *The Rainbow*'s greatest scenes, the episode in Lincoln Cathedral, will show how the imaginative exploration grows out of the *Study*. At a very late stage in composition, moreover, the novel remains fluid in Lawrence's imagination, which finds it necessary to move on, by its own kind of "logic", to a stage quite beyond the scope of the treatise.

The Cathedral scene was not in *The Wedding Ring*, since we can watch Lawrence in the first draft of *The Rainbow* struggling to get hold of it, and failing at first.[60] He had grasped the contrast between the marriage of Tom and Lydia and the young married life of Anna and Will, and had summed it up in terms of his dominant image: in one case, the pillar of fire and the pillar of cloud locked into an arch, creating freedom, and a gateway to the beyond; in the other, the rich woman possessing her husband, settled on Pisgah, still within sight of the rainbow and the promised land, but capable only of being a threshold from which her children can set forth, because she has conquered.

Lawrence must have felt, however, that he needed to explore the religious dimension of the marriage further, beyond merely personal relationship – even when "personal" is defined at the depth of a chapter like "Anna Victrix". In the *Study*, as part of a long account of the spiritual dialectic in art, he had briefly remarked on the mediaeval cathedrals:

> The worship of Europe, predominantly female, all through the
> mediaeval period, was to the male, to the incorporeal Christ, as a
> bridegroom, whilst the art produced was the collective, stupendous

emotional gesture of the Cathedrals, where a blind collective impulse rose into concrete form. It was the profound, sensuous desire and gratitude which produced an art of architecture, whose essence is in utter stability, of movement resolved and centralized, of absolute movement, that has no relationship with any other form, that admits the existence of no other form, but is conclusive, propounding in its sum the One Being of All.

There was, however, in the Cathedrals, already the denial of the Monism which the Whole uttered. All the little figures, the gargoyles, the imps, the human faces, whilst subordinated within the Great Conclusion of the Whole, still, from their obscurity, jeered their mockery of the Absolute, and declared for multiplicity, polygeny.[61]

Lawrence's first attempt to realize this within the response of his human characters was, as one might expect, rather gushing and repetitive, allowing his imagination free rein. Will's response is a good deal longer than it is now, aiming again and again at the same target. The church is a great darkness and silence, a "dark rainbow", a "link of darkness' between the eternity before birth and the eternity after death. It is "away from time, always away from life". The repetition is not however merely repetitive; for Lawrence tries to create a succession of passionate leapings up from the "plain earth" to the "stud of ecstasy" at the roof, that point of tension where the "immemorial darkness" is both thrust up, and weighs back – again, and again, and again as the eye passes down the nave towards the "other mystery" of the altar.

In the same manuscript, he revised extensively with a new conception. Now the church is not outside life, it is the womb within which all life is implicit. Light begins to enter, a twilight, yet "the embryo of all light". The church lies

like a seed in silence, dark before germination, silenced after death. Containing birth and death, potential with all the noise and transition of life, the cathedral remained hushed, a great involved seed whereof the flower would be radiant life inconceivable, but whose beginning and whose end lay in the two extremes of silence. Like a shadowy rainbow, the jewelled gloom spanned from silence to silence, darkness to darkness, fecundity to fecundity, as a seed spans from life to life and death to death, containing the secret of all folded between its parts.[62]

He cut about a page and a half, began to discipline, condense, heighten.

The more significant growth however is in the response of Anna. We can tell little about the first version, since all but a few sentences were deleted[63] and replaced when Lawrence revised Will's response, but "she too was overcome", though she resisted. In revision, she is at first carried away almost as much as Will; only she is not fulfilled. For her soul longs to "be cast at last on the threshold of the unknown", at the altar, but always she is made to leap "to the ecstasy and the isolation and the agony up there". That night, she becomes increasingly dissatisfied, seeing the experience as a kind of crucifixion of self-knowledge. And again she longs for the march of the great pillars down the nave to the threshold of the unknown. She dreams of angels, flaming in praise around the presence of God. But when they go back to the cathedral the next day, there is no getting beyond self-realization, no transfiguration of the stigmata of self-knowledge, no door to the beyond. She is shut in. Even if she thinks of the smallness of man's ego against the "whole rotunda of day or the dome of night" there is no help, for "which star should she choose?" In the cathedral the altar is "a dragged nest, the Mystery was gone". She longs to take off like a bird, "to rise into the gladness of light . . . to escape from the builded earth, from man's day after day. Was man and his present measure to be forever the measure of the universe? But she must grasp at some resistance before she could thrust off. It was so difficult." So she grasps at the little faces.

At his second attempt, then, Lawrence has used the images thrown off in a remark in the *Study* – "the column must always stand for the male aspiration, the arch or ellipse for the female completeness containing this aspiration"[64] – but has made the "male" aspiration of Anna aspire beyond the "completeness" which satisfies Will. The march of the columns is succeeded by the flight of the bird from the dragged nest, towards the sun. The trouble is that the opposition is simple, and furthermore, by making Anna go through Will's experience before rejecting it, Lawrence has weighted the scales in her favour. She seems to know more than he does. There had been at the end of the previous chapter a similar tendency to lay too much stress on the failure of Will. As Lawrence had corrected that, so he now

labours to correct this, and to complicate and intensify the
oppositions while leaving the balance unweighted.

So in the final manuscript of *The Rainbow* he begins to introduce opposites within Will's response, as well as tightening the
style into greater cogency. The sentence I quoted from the first
draft now becomes:

> Spanned around with the rainbow, the jewelled gloom folded music
> upon silence, light upon darkness, fecundity upon death, as a seed
> folds leaf upon leaf and silence upon the root and the flower, hushing
> up the secret of all between its parts, the death out of which it fell,
> the life into which it has dropped, the immortality it involves, and the
> death it will embrace again.[65]

He also removes altogether the march down the aisle, so that
Will's response is now wholly concerned with the ecstasy of
the arch, the "female" completeness and inclusiveness of God
the Father, in which, as in the natural seed, all is One.

But he transforms Anna's response. She is now resentful from
the very first, in greater opposition; and she opposes to him not
the "blue vault" of the sky nor the "dark dome" of night, "but
a space where stars were whirling in freedom, with freedom
above them ever higher". She resists the march to the altar, and
catches at the little faces not as something to thrust off from,
but as something "which saved her from being swept headlong".
She resolves the opposition within her in a far more anti-
religious fashion. The faces which had been merely human
"with their nice and nasty traits" become "wicked", the
serpent of Knowledge in the Eden of God the Father. And she
becomes like them, jeering, malicious, but more so: she
triumphs not only in multiplicity, but in destruction.

It has become a far more complex conflict, and deeper. We
no longer take sides. Both lovers have half the truth, but their
conflict is destructive, for they do not marry their oppositions
and go through, beyond. Will's arches, his rainbow, contain
conflict resolved, but on too limited a level. Anna aspires to a
higher freedom and space, greater multiplicity and separateness, but she seeks to destroy her opposite. The new dimension
Lawrence has achieved also allows us to balance the contrast
with Tom and Lydia more fairly. We can measure how much
more "paradisal" the earlier marriage had been; how Tom and

Lydia rejoiced in the "otherness" of each other; but how they were also prepared to "die" to each other in marriage, and be reborn into a new world beyond. On the other hand, we can now see more clearly that the new intensities of Anna and Will, while making the marriage of opposites more difficult to achieve, also show up the limitations of Tom and Lydia. Will's religious and aesthetic intensity, Anna's rational intelligence and self-awareness, represent a greater range of human possibility as well as difficulty. So the growth of the Cathedral scene shows us Lawrence's exploratory imagination feeling for one of his great achievements, beginning from the insights and categories of the *Study*, but creating a richness and complexity beyond the scope of the treatise.

In the novel as we have it, however, the relationship between Anna and Will passes through yet another stage, in which we can see Lawrence reaching for a new kind of insight altogether. These episodes were not only not in *The Wedding Ring*, they were not in the first draft of *The Rainbow* either. There, Lawrence spoke only briefly of "some months" in which Anna

> let herself go, she gave him also his full measure, she considered nothing. Children and everything she let go, and gave way to her last desires, till she and he had gone all the devious and never-to-be-recorded ways of desire and satisfaction, to the very end, till they had had everything, and knew no more. Whatever their secret imagination had wanted, they had. And they came through it all at last cleared, resolved, freed. They were not ashamed of any of it. They were now resolved into satisfaction. They had taken every liberty, were prisoners to no more lurking desires. The marriage between them was complete and entire.[66]

In the final draft of *The Rainbow*, a page or two expand into half a chapter.[67] Will's escapade with the factory girl in Nottingham is new, and there is an odd new dimension in the treatment of the change between Will and Anna.

From the stage of the second *Sisters* at least, Lawrence had been becoming more and more aware of the importance of *impersonality* for his conception of marriage. In the *Study* he had discovered a language for talking about the impersonal forces that operated within and between human beings. In the Tom and

Lydia story, successful marriage had depended to a great extent on the utter strangeness and foreignness of the lovers to each other, and their delight in the battle of "others", opening the door to the unknown. In the Anna and Will story, Will is at first utterly strange too, like another form of life, a cat, a hawk; but by the end of "Anna Victrix" he is known, possessed. He can no longer open out the unknown.

Now, through the adventure of writing the "dark" relationship between Ursula and Skrebensky when he returns from Africa, Lawrence had achieved a new insight into what he would call the "African Way" of relationship in *Women in Love*. He must have seen, in that last sketched-in relationship of Anna and Will, an opportunity both to complete the range of their story, and to emphasize with a new insistence, and in a new way, the essential significance of "otherness" and "impersonality". It is the peculiarity of the insistence that has made this last relationship seem odd to critics; but if imagination may be spoken of as having a "logic", it is a logical extension of a growing insight.

The point of the episode with the warehouse girl is that the two are utterly alien, with nothing in common except sexuality, and that Will cares nothing about the girl as a person. Just because of this, a new word begins to be used. "He was himself, the *absolute*, the rest of the world was an object that should contribute to his being." "And his hand that grasped her side felt one curve of her, and it seemed like a new creation to him, a reality, an absolute, an existing tangible beauty of the absolute." The girl will not give herself to him, but in the roused state she has excited he suddenly becomes again to Anna "a strange man come home to her". At last, and on a new level, "she replied with a brilliant challenge . . . she challenged him back with a sort of radiance, very bright and free, opposite to him . . . It was as if he were a perfect stranger, as if she were infinitely and essentially strange to him." They become discoverers, and what they discover is "Absolute Beauty".

This new relationship is, however, sharply distinguished from their relation as lovers. It exists entirely in terms of lust. It begins in pure sexual challenge, abandoning morality, responsibility, above all, personality. It issues in "a sensuality violent and extreme as death. They had no conscious intimacy, no tenderness of love. It was all the lust and the infinite, maddening intoxication of the senses, a passion of death." Their lust not only now explicitly embraces the shameful and unnatural, but also finds in this a "sinister tropical beauty", a "heavy, fundamental gratification". (Wilson Knight is clearly correct in claiming that imagery and language identify the "unnatural" element as anal.[68]) It is a relation in "pure darkness", quite different from the marriage of opposites that is central to the book.

Lawrence clearly does not endorse this in the way he endorses the marriage of Tom and Lydia. Yet, equally significantly, he cannot be said to condemn it either. Whatever the private reactions of readers may be, it is important to notice how this relationship achieves things for Will and Anna that their loving relationship, in its partial failure, had withheld. They discover absolute beauty; become explorers. They find themselves without destroying each other; and for the first time they set each other free. Anna is recalled from her trance of motherhood to live more in herself, not through her children, and to take an interest in the outside world; and Will is not only more founded in himself but actually liberated into public activity. He not only takes up his art again but becomes a teacher, with a role in society. The first draft of the novel briefly sketched in these results, but we have now been provided with a somewhat startling reason for them.

The beauty is absolute as opposed to relative, because it is impersonal, pursued for its own sake. It has nothing to do with the personality. Anna and Will not only find it, but create it together, as a third thing beyond themselves. Will ceases to be a known, finite being to Anna. She meets him on equal terms at last; does not try to overcome or destroy him; is as ready to abandon herself to him as he to her. There is no defeat or victory, dominance or subservience. There is discovery, and there is freedom. We see how absolutely central to Lawrence his concern for the freedom of the individual turns out to be, and how far he is prepared to go to insist on it. Because they meet at last as distinct individuals, enriching themselves from each other rather than merging or battling for supremacy, even this relation in pure darkness can have beneficial results never achieved by the two as lovers.

Which is not to say, of course, that we are meant to see it as an equal alternative. In pure darkness there can be no marriage of total opposites, and hence there can be no transformation. Anna and Will are only more firmly settled into their existing selves; they are not transfigured, inheriting a promised land of re-creation. They "die" and are renewed, but it is "pure death" purely dark, and a renewal of the dark side of themselves only. A great part of their total personalities has to be excluded. Using the "carbon" metaphor with which Lawrence defended his new psychology against Garnett, we might say that the relation of lust is, to the relation of love, as jet is to the diamond that is produced by the interaction of black carbon with intense flame. Nevertheless, in this limited relationship, Will and Anna can confront each other in *some* of the ways essential to Lawrence's conception of a fruitful relationship, as they seemed incapable of doing as lovers. Because of this, the relation in lust can enrich and set free. Perhaps there is more concern with sexuality itself than elsewhere; but this, too, is a precise pointer to the limitation of the Dark Way. Even here it is a Way, a means to an end. It is still the end, of individual growth and individual freedom, that is the main concern.

[v]

As the *Study* was the growing point between *The Wedding Ring* and *The Rainbow*, so *The Crown* links *The Rainbow* with *Women in Love*. *The Crown* begins as a reformulation in new terms of the *Study*'s insight into creativity; but it goes on to develop a new insight into "corruption".

As Lawrence drew near the end of *The Rainbow* in its first draft, he conceived the idea of rewriting "the book I wrote – mostly philosophicalish, slightly about Hardy".[69] He finished the novel on 2 March, and immediately told Viola Meynell, who was taking care of the typing, that he was "going to begin a book about Life – more rainbows, but in different skies – which I want to publish in pamphlet form week by week – my initiation of the great and happy revolution".[70] He had met Lady Ottoline Morrell in January 1915, and through her Bertrand Russell, with whom he began to correspond about "revolution" – a new basis for society. The idea of Rananim, the select company of souls who could start a new corporate life together, also begins to figure in his letters from January.

From March to early July the completion of the old and the conception of the new work went on side by side. Viola Meynell sent back the typescript in batches, which Lawrence revised extensively in March and April (and possibly May),[71] before submitting the manuscript to Methuen on 1 June. In the light of the refusal of *The Wedding Ring* he had cause to worry about several scenes in *The Rainbow*, but he changed only a few phrases and sentences for that reason, and added the last relationship between Anna and Will. In July he corrected proofs and made further improvements, but told Pinker that although he had cut phrases, he could not alter passages or paragraphs. "There is nothing offensive in them, beyond the very substance they contain . . . And I can't cut them out, because they are living parts of an organic whole."[72] *The Rainbow* was published on 30 September. The police called on Methuen on 3 November, and the novel was banned at the Bow Street Magistrates' Court on 13 November.

Meanwhile he had begun rewriting his "philosophy" in the first half of March, and in April began to send what he had written to Koteliansky, who had agreed to type it for him.[74] In May he decided to type himself,[75] and on 8 June sent Russell "the first quarter".[76] On 20 June, while Russell was week-ending with them at Greatham, he sent Lady Ottoline what he had finished, and announced that he and Russell were planning a series of lectures in the autumn, in which Russell would talk about Ethics, and Lawrence "on Immortality".[77] But in early July he decided that the basic terminology of his own thinking would have to be changed. Russell seems to have convinced him that he had been "much too Christian", and had sent him to the early Greek philosophers. "These early Greeks", he wrote, "have clarified my soul. I must drop all about God."[78] Having used Christian theology and the Bible as a language he could adapt to his own insights, he was realizing that he could do without their underpinning. Shortly afterwards, however, he annoyed Russell by scrawling acrid comment over an essay he had been sent to read, and there were the first hints of disillusion with Russell and Lady Ottoline. In mid-September he penned Russell a savage denunciation, though the relationship subsequently improved again for a while. The plan for the lectures lapsed, but in early September he had conceived an alternative idea with Middleton Murry and Katherine Mansfield of publishing a little magazine, to be called *The Signature*. On 20 September he sent to the printer the manuscript of the first issue, containing the first essay of *The Crown*.[79] By 2 October he had "done my six papers",[80] one for each issue as originally planned, but the magazine only appeared three times, on 4 and 18 October and 4 November. The remaining three essays were not published until *Reflections on the Death of a Porcupine*. Lawrence moved to Cornwall at the end of December, and the Murrys arrived for their ill-fated tenancy of the adjacent cottage early in April. By 26 April[81] Lawrence had embarked on "the second half of *The Rainbow*".[82]

The Crown, then, shows us Lawrence moving from the world of *The Rainbow* to the world of *Women in Love*. For it was with a terribly heightened sense of polarization, the universal opposition of creation and destruction, that he turned again to the pages of the original *Sisters*. Although *The Rainbow* bears in its later stages the imprint of the war, much of its conception belonged to a pre-war world, and its growth had taken Lawrence imaginatively backwards from 1910. Moreover it was essentially a religious novel about the significance of marriage, though it had important things to say about what had happened to English society since 1840. But Lawrence felt that he had spent the months from August 1914 to January 1915 "in the tomb. And now I feel very sick and corpse cold . . . The War finished me: it was the spear through the side of all sorrows and hopes."[83] If there was something desperately idealistic or hysteric in his plans for revolution and utopia in early 1915, it was owing to his horror at what was happening, and his certainty that the world he had written *The Rainbow* for, was gone for ever. In September, a zeppelin in the London sky seemed a revelation of the Last Days: "it seems our cosmos has burst, burst at last . . . So it is the end – Our world has gone, and we are like dust in the air. But there must be a new heaven and a new earth."[84] (The treatment of his novel, that product of a religious imagination seeking the significance of the deepest human relationship, was only another example of the anti-life insanity he saw all round him.) Lawrence could not accept merely political, economic, or strategic explanations of the war. Such a cataclysm could only be explicable in terms of a rottenness at the heart of society and within the human soul.

Therefore, although *The Crown* was a rewriting of the *Study*, the differences go even deeper than the attempt to replace Christian language, pare away the whole apparatus of history, art criticism, and literary criticism, and write in more popular terms for a public audience. The essential difference is that the *Study* was positive, an account of the proper conditions for human growth, while *The Crown* is an attempt to diagnose disintegration.

The move from the world of the *Study* and *The Rainbow* to the world that would produce *Women in Love* can be detected in the third essay, "The Flux of Corruption". The first two essays are largely a rewriting of the *Study* in new terms. Instead of God the Father, God the Son, and God the Holy Ghost, we have the Lion and the Unicorn fighting for the Crown – or rather, fighting beneath it, producing it out of the clashing of the opposites, the Beginning and the End, Love and Power, Light and Darkness. From the crashing waves, the clashing cymbals, the interfusing elements, are born the foam, the music, the irridescent rainbow, absolute, while time swirls the opposites away. But the crowning glory is not a prize, for there can be no victory or defeat. The Crown is the *raison d'être* of all existence. It is what the opposites are there for.

Already there are differences from the *Study*. The treatment, particularly of light and darkness and the imagery from nature, is more consistently poetic, less conceptualized. There is a new realization, that has come from the writing of *The Rainbow* as well as from the war, that sometimes there is only a meaning-less swirling where no creation takes place; and that sometimes the Lion or the Unicorn go mad, turn in on themselves, seek to triumph in their own partiality, and become destructive. But these opening chapters are largely a restatement of the same dialectic theory in terms of a new elemental, non-Christian symbolism.

In "The Flux of Corruption", however, Lawrence begins to analyse the process of disintegration which, he now sees, must always follow consummation if the theory is to be truly dialectic.

> This is the terror and wonder of dark returning to dark, and of light returning to light, the two departing back to their Sources. This we cannot bear to think of. It is the temporal flux of corruption, as the flux together was the temporal flux of creation. The flux is temporal. It is only the perfect meeting, the perfect interpenetration into oneness, the kiss, the blow, the two-in-one, that is timeless and absolute.[85]

The flux of corruption seems terrible to us, caught as we are in the perspective of time; but in itself it is not evil. It is necessary. Yet evil begins "when that which is temporal and relative asserts itself as consummate and complete". The rest of the chapter, and the three which follow, explore the difference between a "flux of corruption" that is part of a divine process, and a vile and evil hardening into death that can know no rebirth.

It is important to note that the word "corruption" itself carries no overtones of judgement. "Destruction and Creation are the two relative absolutes between the opposing infinities. Life is in both. Life may even, for a while be almost entirely in one, or almost entirely in the other. For life is really the two, the absolute is the pure relation which is both. If we have our fill of destruction, then we shall turn again to creation."[86] So we have to learn a new kind of language, respond to a new kind of symbolism, very different from anything in the *Study* or *The Rainbow*. For,

> the process is that of the serpent lying prone in the cold, watery fire of corruption, flickering with the flowing-apart of the two streams. His belly is white with the light flowing forth from him, his back is dark and brindled where the darkness returns to the Source. He is the ridge where the two floods flow apart . . .[87] the swan is one of the symbols of divine corruption with its reptile feet buried in the ooze and mud, its voluptuous form yielding and embracing the ooze of water, its beauty white and cold and terrifying, like the dead beauty of the moon, like the water-lily, the sacred lotus, its neck and head like the snake, it is for us a flame of the cold white fire of flux, the phosphorescence of corruption, the salt, cold burning of the sea which corrodes all it touches, coldly reduces every sun-built form to its original elements. This is the beauty of the swan, the lotus, the snake, this cold white salty fire of infinite reduction.[88]

But "corruption, like growth, is only divine when it is pure, when all is given up to it". There are two ways in which the human *will* can distort "pure" corruption into vileness. Consummation is in the dimension of infinity outside time, but on earth everything is, and must be, carried past the point of consummation by the swirl of time. If man wills to arrest the process, to assert the old consummation beyond the point of its necessary disintegration, rottenness follows. The image Lawrence develops from the *Study* is that of the cabbage whose outside may still look healthy, but whose inside is threshed rotten by the thwarted force of inevitable disintegration. To try to turn the supreme moment of being into a possession, prolonged in time, is not only to become vile but to thwart the advent of new creation; for only when the previous consummation has entirely disintegrated back to the elementary opposites, can the creative process begin again. So when men determine to preserve old forms of society or relationship or value, rottenness results from the thwarting of divine process. The second kind of vileness comes from the will enclosing itself within the flux of corruption, declaring this to be the only form of life, and seeking its satisfaction from increasing consciousness of the process. When the self thus deludes itself that it is absolute, "all that remains is thoroughly to explore it. That is, to analyse it. Analysis presupposes a corpse." The soul then becomes "analytically" reductive, like an insect enclosed within a glassy envelope of nullity, *enjoying* the process of disintegration in "sensational gratification" of the flesh, or of the mind. Human relationship becomes a friction of ego upon ego, in which no union is possible, but pleasure is taken in mutual reduction. The climax of this is the death-wish, when the only sensation left to be explored, the only avenue for final disintegration, is the sensational brush with death, and eventually, willed death and destruction. For Lawrence, the war has come about for both reasons. To arrest a divine process is to become carrion-foul, like a vulture that used to be an eagle and could have been again; or it is to live within a sepulchre that might have been a womb. England and Germany, in fighting to preserve old forms, are the lion become dog and the eagle become vulture – both states of the animated sepulchre. On the other hand, "as far as there is any passion in the war, it is a passion for the embrace with death" – the war is the product of the death-wish of a generation.

398

The "God-quick" which is still present in the going-apart can, however, be liberated if the barren egoism of the will can be smashed. If men will only give themselves up to the forces that operate within them, there can be no evil. "Neither destruction nor production is, in itself, evil. The danger lies in the fall into egoism, which neutralises both." Only perpetuation is a sin. Man must be prepared to let go of the old; when corruption is necessary, all must be given up to it; for then there can be the beginning of the creative process again, a new dawn, a new earth, a new heaven.

[vi]

The new novel was written in a remarkable burst of sustained creativity between late April and the end of October 1916, in four drafts.[89] The first came easily: "I have not travailed over it. It is the book of my free soul."[90] Once again the formulation of a "structural skeleton" of "ideas", images and language had revealed a basic "shape". Yet it is vital to make the same reservations about the critical usefulness of *The Crown* as were necessary with the *Study*, for the novel was no less exploratory. When Lawrence returned to the original *Sisters* it was inevitably to rewrite in a new dimension altogether, but the way he had spoken of his first venture is strangely re-echoed. "I have begun a new novel: a thing that is a stranger to me even as I write it. I don't know what the end will be."[91] He had virtually finished the new *Sisters* in two months, by the end of June,[92] but it took him a further four months of rewriting before he was satisfied. The idea of calling it *Women in Love* is recorded on 13 July,[93] but towards the end of September he is thinking in terms of *The Latter Days*,[94] and at the end of October Frieda wanted it called *Dies Irae*.[95] The apocalyptic dimension of the novel was growing all the time, and the vision grew in other ways not less essential.

In the isolated cottage in Cornwall, Lawrence's feelings about the war became even more intense, and he began his novel in a mood of bitter misanthropy with no thought of publication. Indeed his Prologue, much of which dealt with the unadmitted sexual feeling between Gerald and Birkin, defiantly put publication out of the question.[96] But "more than that, it is beyond all possibility even to offer it to a world, a putrescent mankind like ours. I feel I cannot *touch* humanity, even in thought, it is abhorrent to me. But a work of art is an act of faith, as Michael Angelo says, and one goes on writing, to the unseen witnesses.''[97] The original *Sisters* was partly written in the first person. Now again, significantly, and unlike the previous three novels, the new work contained a character modelled on Lawrence himself. In the first drafts, not unnaturally, Birkin tended to be a mouthpiece, voicing Lawrence's world-hatred and his hopes for Rananim, preaching sermons from the unpublished chapters of *The Crown*, and insisting on a new post-*Rainbow* theory of the need for male leadership and female submission. But the strength of *Women in Love* as we have it now, and one basis for its claim to be regarded as a supreme fiction, is the way that Lawrence succeeds in dramatizing Birkin, surrounding him with a context of criticism, diagnosing his sickness, and bringing him through to greater maturity. In the growth of the novel we can measure something of the difficulty of self-scrutiny in that most terrible of years, which found its climax in the Battle of the Somme. So, this time, we not only watch a novel embodying the insights of a treatise in a richer and more complex world of human relationships, and a growth beyond *The Crown* as *The Rainbow* had moved beyond the *Study*; we also watch Lawrence shedding his sickness. He clarifies Birkin's deathliness, pins down the prig, the preacher, the would-be Salvator Mundi in him, and the element of pretentiousness in his language. He dramatizes him objectively, using Ursula with increasing cogency to point to his deficiencies. The first *Sisters* started by jeering at Frieda; the last uses her imaginatively to criticize himself. But in the process he also learns to understand more truly what can pass through the crucible of conflict and emerge, tested, to be affirmed. *The Crown* will map the battlefield; but it bears the same relation to the human history and significance of the battle as a general's map might do.

There is no less significant a growth in the story of Gerald and Gudrun. *The Crown* will help us to plot the differences among the various tragedies: why Gerald's differs from Gudrun's; what there is in common between them and the Fleurs du Mal – Hermione, the drinkers in the Pompadour,

Loerke – but also how each embodies a different kind of modern illness. As rewriting follows rewriting we can watch Lawrence's insight becoming more precise, and more appalling. It is not for nothing that he begins to think in terms of the Last Judgement; finding himself, and placing us, in a position to watch his characters choosing the Last Things, Life or Death, Heaven or Hell. But he decided not to call his novel *Dies Irae*, and in its final form it is not a cry of wrath and hatred for "putrescent mankind". The *last* judgement finely blends justice with imagination. *The Crown* will not show us how Lawrence achieved the complexity of his characters – will not account, for example, for the vitality in shrewdness and gaiety, as well as corruption, that pulses through even Loerke, and makes him a "wizard" as well as a "rat". The author of *The Crown* longed to smash the heads of his vultures. The author of *Women in Love* has more imaginative wisdom, finer sensibility, deeper humanity. Its very form demands of us an attentiveness that destroys categorization. Instead of the three big canvases of *The Rainbow*, we must attend continuously to a complicated system of variant contrasts, and respond to description imagery and dialogue, so that all the characters and situations are balanced against one another in growing understanding. When at last the characters begin to separate out, as it were, on our right hand and on our left, it is in irreducible complexity. *The Crown* will not show us how Lawrence learnt to dramatize, to hold the apocalyptic in that odd tension with the colloquial, often slangy dialogue, that makes *Women in Love* such a startlingly different experience from *The Rainbow*. *The Crown* will provide a very useful interpretative basis; a full study of the manuscripts would show us the effort of imaginative exploration that went into the novel's growth; but only literary criticism of the finished work, proceeding from both of these, could hope for adequate understanding.

I have space for only a bare indication of growth within the last two drafts; and I want to follow the same procedure as with *The Rainbow*, choosing first an example of how the insights of the treatise are more fully realized and clarified in the novel, and then an example of how the imagination moves on to a new kind of insight. The *Study* spoke of the need for art to proceed by a kind of dialectic of imagination and understanding. *Women in Love* does this: at its deepest level it grows through a series of imaginative plunges, each followed by an effort to understand what has been captured. The greatest of these, imaginatively the heart of the book, is the scene that gives "Moony" its title. The manuscripts show us Lawrence struggling to clarify his basic theme in the second half of that chapter, trying to give the insights of *The Crown* a more precise focus for the understanding of different characters. Later, they show him moving on another stage, as happened in *The Rainbow*, by the "logic" of his imagination, to a significant but peculiar rewriting of the climax of the Ursula/Birkin story.

The scene by the pond has already been captured in the penultimate draft, and so has the fleeting moment of truth and tenderness which follows. But then, inevitably, the process of conflict has to begin again. In this draft Birkin insists that Ursula should accept him "as a leader", she responds with a touch of the fishwife, and the scene breaks up in rather childish rage. Our response is likely to be wholly with Ursula, but an uneasy suspicion remains that it is not altogether meant to be.

> "Ultimately – ultimately, I know better than you – that's why you should pledge your allegiance", he said. "I may be wrong a thousand times, and you may tell me so. But ultimately I *know*, and you do *not know* – at least in your consciousness. Therefore you should serve with unquestioning allegiance and be glad you can serve."
>
> "Ha!" she laughed. "If I *could* serve you, I would be glad. But I don't believe in your ultimate wisdom, thank you. As soon as you begin to talk about ultimates, I am wary of you, my fine friend, I mistrust you completely. Let me hear a little humility from you, and I'll believe in you a little more readily."
>
> "And now", said he in a fury, "will you please go away and rid me of your presence."
>
> "I'm going", said she, hurt in spite of her hotness against him. They went down the bank in silence. Already he had taken the silence and the space to himself again, she was not there for him. He wrapped himself round with a grateful and rich solitude, of which he had at last the gift.[98]

But throughout the last draft, Lawrence had been liberating himself from the "leadership" theory which had been blocking his own, and not merely Ursula's, understanding of what marriage should be. As he rewrites,[99] he sees that what is really important is that *both* lovers should give themselves, their egos, their separate wills, away in "proud indifference". Birkin's case is strengthened, but at the same time Lawrence writes in Ursula's denunciation of the "Sunday school teacher" and the charge that it is he who cannot let go. The scene becomes fully dramatic, with more "right" on both sides. And now Lawrence makes it reorchestrate the symbolic scene which preceded it. The conflict ebbs away; peace returns, with tenderness, and even humour – that rare quality in Lawrence. Then, because Birkin is being investigated more searchingly, conflict starts again on a new plane. He realizes that there is an inconsistency in himself, in his confused fear of and longing for "dark" sexual passion. Suddenly Lawrence's imagination responds with a new leap: the description of the beetle-woman, the West African statuette. In grasping the significance of this, he succeeds for the first time in clarifying the nature of the different "reductive" Ways to be pursued by Gerald and Gudrun, and the creative Way that Birkin and Ursula will follow. "Leadership" is replaced by the ideal of freedom and "individual singleness" that had governed *The Rainbow*, but at a new depth and without the residual restrictiveness of the symbol of the arch. So, in the last draft, the African Way, the Arctic Way, and the Way which he is about to designate as "star equilibrium" become really clear to Lawrence, and will govern the remainder of the book. Out of the great imaginative leap of the moon scene, and the challenge to understand its significance by dramatizing the conflict between his two people, has come both a clarification and a refinement of the basic insights of *The Crown*. Obviously the basic "ideas" matter far less than the richness and variety of the imagination that thus distils them.

So imagination and understanding proceed in dialectic; but from his new standpoint, Lawrence realized that a new climax of the Ursula/Birkin story was called for. After the battle in "Excurse", the penultimate draft had a betrothal scene in the Saracen's Head, with some byplay about the three engagement rings and the need for a fourth, the wedding ring.[100] (I suspect that a version of this may have been the conclusion of *The Wedding Ring*, and that it may even have had an earlier prototype as the end of the Ella story in the original *Sisters*.) It is done mainly from Birkin's point of view. Ursula is like a frightened flower, opening up again to the sun, but "strained with years of tension". As Birkin's "fingertips went delicately, finely, over her face", his gentle love removes her fear "like removing a veil", and creates in her a "dazzle of released, golden light". Birkin, too, has been frightened, but becomes happy for the first time in his life "as flowers are happy, as the heedless things of the earth are happy. He had known ecstacy and delight before, but now for the first time he knew the grace of happiness, the strange, immortal serenity." After the writing of the resignations, however, he begins to feel again a seething sexuality. He fears it; wants desperately to hold on to the new gentleness; and forces Ursula into the false position o having to decide one way or the other. She doesn't know what she wants, and despite the new certainty of their love, the chapter ends, in the penultimate draft, with a dying fall.

"This is peace, peace of soul – only peace. And this peace is the greatest reality, even if we make war – isn't it?"
But her eyes were full of sad tears, and she did not answer.

In the last draft, however, having clarified the three "Ways", Lawrence is able to grasp the essence of "Star-equilibrium", and convey his certainty that once the essential relationship is right, the starry way can both include and transcend the darkness, as in the final chapters Ursula and Birkin will know and move beyond the snow. The way he proceeds to rewrite has puzzled, annoyed, or amused many critics; but once we see something of the "logic" of the imagination, criticism can at least proceed from a necessary understanding.

Lawrence alters the perspective, choosing to write now mainly from Ursula's point of view.[101] He is in fact returning to the vision of *The Rainbow* and its insistence on the primary importance of "otherness". Now at last a daughter of Man confronts a son of God: "one of these strange creatures from the beyond". (We have to remind ourselves of the meaning of the *Study*'s language.) But he is also taking further his discoveries in the last relation of Will and Anna. There, the essential factor in the coming together was impersonality; now, it must involve a strangeness of life that is beyond even manhood or womanhood.

The "strange mystery of his life flow" comes from the base of Birkin's spine because Lawrence is insisting that it is not reducible to sexual feeling, it is "deeper than the phallic source". He had come increasingly to see sexuality as a residue of human incompleteness – as though the front of a human being proclaimed its need for a complementary half. But what Ursula discovers and responds to is Birkin's *complete* otherness, his wholeness in himself, by touching the fulcrum of his movement as an independent being. It would be farcical to call this "anal" because it is precisely there to insist that what Lawrence is talking about is non-sexual in the usual sense; "sexual" only in Lawrence's sense of the meeting of utter opposites, the light and the darkness in and between both beings. The significance of the coming together of man and woman is that this is the one way to contact the beyond, and the particular nature of the "sexual" act is consequently of very minor importance. Lawrence emphasizes this by making his climactic moment depend on the touch of fingertips in a public room, waiting for tea. The marriage of opposites again involves a "death", a "perfect passing away for both of them", and "at the same time the most intolerable access into being, the marvellous fulness of immediate gratification". The individual is left "quite free", "free in complete ease", a "complete self". Thus the scene is peculiar both because it is "mystic", only to be understood in Lawrence's religious sense of the marriage of opposites; and because it is "physical", since Lawrence will acknowledge no dichotomy between the flesh and the spirit. The oddness springs from his need to create an adequate physical expression for a mystic relationship – an embodiment that will be "finally, mystically-physically satisfying".

The daughter of Man, then, finds her son of God in a consummation that for the first time, with two sophisticated modern individuals, achieves all the conditions of the marriage of opposites. It is paradisal like the marriage of Tom and Lydia, but without their limitations. It has the greater intensities of spirit and intelligence of Will and Anna, without their failure, and includes also the impersonal dimension of their last relationship to a higher degree, beyond sex. (It also gives Ursula a new "public" freedom; "She was usually nervous and uncertain at performing these public duties".) It begins from the singleness of being into which Ursula had "died" at the end of *The Rainbow*, but achieves a constellation of two stars in a greater freedom than that of the arch.

So the Rananim dream can be criticized with new accuracy, if still tenderly. The only truth in it had nothing to do with utopian places or communes, but lay in the perception that new growth could begin only in "perfected relation" between men and women. There is still the need to renounce the old selves and social functions, but the rest is "only travel" – the answer doesn't lie in Garsington or Italy or Florida.

The scene now however requires a further stage, because of Lawrence's need to urge that in perfected relation there can be no partiality. If the basic relation is right, it must be capable of including the whole being, all desires, all possibilities. In the Saracen's Head the radiance was not enough, "not altogether". So the consummation in the public place is followed by the car journey into the utter darkness, and the physical, sexual consummation which comes second, but is equally necessary. Many critics have made fun of the Egyptian Pharoah and his suave loins of darkness at the wheel of the car, and Lawrence's lack of both tact and humour is obvious enough. But the trouble comes mainly from the use of a symbolic short-hand, which we ought at least to try to decipher before we laugh. The car, and the way Birkin drives it, are there because Lawrence wants a quick suggestion that the new relationship can include the whole mechanical civilization into which Gerald plunged reductively, but can direct it to the destination of richer human Being. Birkin drives like an Egyptian because the relationship can include and transcend the whole African Way. In that most peculiar insistence of all, Birkin's Egyptianness remains secondarily Greek, with a "lambent intelligence" still playing "above his pure Egyptian concentration in darkness", because the marriage of opposites is never ultimately partial or reductive. After the radiance of the Saracen's Head, the Dark Way is temporarily the medium, but its opposite is still present. The lovers come together again in complete darkness, sensually, sexually, but what is confirmed in them is that "*star*-equilibrium which alone is freedom".(my italics). The two halves of the scene are complementary, the marriage of opposites is all inclusive.

To attempt to explain these scenes is not of course to explain their oddity away. In Lawrence's greatest writing, our imaginative response carries its own conviction, and the significance is distilled, if we will let it, by its own inevitable momentum. Here one feels that the art, for all its power, is esoteric, the language private. But we can at least try to clarify the nature of the vision that is operating, and why the "logic" of the imagination creates that particular kind of difficulty. Without some grasp of the inclusiveness of the Ursula/Birkin relationship, moreover, we shall hardly understand the "reductiveness" of the other Paths.

[vii]

It is not, however, only the esoteric places in the novels that can be illuminated by understanding the exploratory nature of Lawrence's imagination. We have some idea now of what the word "exploratory" means, against the perspective of the whole process of creation from the first *Sisters* to *Women in Love*. We have also seen that his theory of art was essentially a theory of process, and how amply the evolution of his greatest novels enacted that theory. But I want now to argue that "process" is absolutely central to Lawrence's imagination itself: that we shall not respond fully to his best work until we learn to read in terms of process. There is a tendency to give too static an account of Lawrence's "symbols". Even in highly sophisticated accounts of scenes like the episode with the horses in *The Rainbow* and the moon scene in *Women in Love*, one can detect that the basic question has been "What do the horses, or the moon, stand for?" or, more subtly, "What *are* they?" I want now to argue, in relation to both scenes, that criticism on such a basis can only establish part, and that not the essential part, of the imaginative vision that is operating.

Ursula's story in *The Rainbow* has shown her embodying all the "opposites" of her family at peak intensity, but forever trying to resolve her contradictions by pursuing one element of herself to the exclusion of others, never managing to find a way of marrying them – "always the shining doorway was a gate into another ugly yard, dirty and active and dead". She has ended by destroying Skrebensky, destroying even his potential for the Dark Way in which alone he could find fulfilment. Her remorse over her own selfish destructiveness is justified; but in seeking, in reaction, to reduce herself to her mother's domesticity, she denies the deepest most aspiring impulse of her own being. She has tried all the wrong ways. Only the right way remains, and Lawrence proceeds to confront her with its challenge in the inevitable climax of the book, that mysterious, difficult, but intensely powerful and haunting scene with the horses.

To ask "what" confronts Ursula is certainly to tap a part of the scene's rich significance, though even here no adequate answer will emerge from trying to expound the horses alone. The scene confronts the girl who is ready to deny the elemental forces in herself and settle for the ordinary civilized world of domesticity, with the powerful presence of those forces and their eternal challenge. The sophisticated, intelligent, educated, self-conscious daughter of Man, of the Prospect, and the City, is faced with the forces of the unitary Landscape of Nature, of God the Father: the big wind through which her grandfather walked, the earth and its roaring trees, the teeming rain, the looming power of the animal world that Tom so confidently mastered, the fire from their nostrils. But the summons is not to the simply elemental; it is to the complexity of the marriage of opposites. The bird-soul of the aspiring girl comes to the great Hall of the Warriors, attesting the eternity of battle; but she searches also for a lost stability beyond conflict and flux. If we then look through Ursula's eyes, we begin to see what Lawrence has embodied in the horses: She becomes

> aware of their breasts gripped, clenched narrow in a hold that never relaxed, she was aware of their red nostrils flaming with long endurance, and of their haunches, so rounded, so massive, pressing, pressing, pressing to burst the grip upon their breasts, pressing forever till they went mad, running against the walls of time and never bursting free. Their great haunches were smoothed and darkened with rain. But the darkness and wetness of rain could not put out the hard, urgent, massive fire that was locked within these flanks, never, never.[102]

What the elemental world embodies and reveals is the eternal clash of opposites in all created things. The horses are an intensity of conflict that cannot be denied or reduced – and must not be, in Ursula. Always the rain tries to put the fire out; always the fire must remain unquenched, battling against the rain. It is the opposition that makes the horses what they are, gives them their looming, monumental energy. But the horses are also gripped, clenched, unfinished. Their opposing energies are trying to get free. And if the fire could once pass right through the rain, and the rain right through the fire, there would be . . . a rainbow. So the horses re-state imaginatively to Ursula, and to us, the whole challenge to marry the Opposites that were embodied in the novel's opening pages.

Yet this is only part, and not the essential part, of the scene's power and meaning. For if we allow Lawrence's imagination to lead us, we shall see that the main question is not "what confronts Ursula?" but "what *happens* to Ursula?" To answer it, we have to respond to what is essentially a process. What happens, happens stage by stage, and if we respond to its "rhythmic" development, what we watch is Ursula confronting the challenge, and failing to meet it. In its simplest terms the challenge is, as ever, to meet the Other and pass through into the Beyond, but this must also mean a marriage of opposites in oneself that involves a kind of death and a kind of rebirth. Now, in the first "movement" of the scene, Ursula does succeed in going through, bursting the barrier of the Other. We have, however, to note the condition for this success. She walks with bent head, not looking, not thinking, not knowing. She simply follows her feet blindly and instinctively. Only in that way does she succeed in coming through the crucible, where her nerves and veins "ran hot, ran white hot, they must fuse, and she must die". This is the condition of Tom and Lydia, the old dispensation, unconscious, unaware. But, in the act of bursting through, the modern woman is forced to *know*, and the repetition of the words "know" and "aware", over and over again, marks the crucial point. We have seen continually in Ursula's story how it is her conscious awareness of her intensities that has made her predicament the hardest of all in the novel. So it proves here. As she passes the horses, and they pass her again, she is forced to know them. As they work themselves up for a climactic confrontation, she will be forced, this time, to go through in full awareness. And she cannot do it. She is terrified, her limbs turn to water, she climbs the tree, and collapses.

Instead of going through, she lapses into the element of water alone, becomes unconscious, inert, unchanging, unchangeable, like a stone at the bottom of the stream. This is her "Flood". She fails, and failing almost dies literally, as well as inwardly.

On the physical and psychological level this is adequately explained. She has suffered a terrible shock, and exposure, and miscarries. This is also "symbolically" appropriate, that the child of Ursula and Skrebensky should be an abortive birth. But on a deeper level Lawrence is asserting that Ursula has failed, not only because of the inadequacies of Skrebensky, but because she herself is incapable of the marriage of opposites. She has to "die" to her assertive will, to burst all the "rind" of unrealities and false relations within which her egotism has enclosed her, to trust herself as a naked kernel does to the elemental forces, before a "true" self can be born. The world she is then born into is the mysterious work of divine creation, and she lands on its boundary after crossing chaos: an "undiscovered land" where she recognizes only "a fresh glow of light and inscrutable trees going up from the earth like smoke". She is only on the outmost perimeter, but she is there, on the first Day of her Creation. She must no longer try to manipulate herself or others or relationships; she must wait for the coming of a son of God, from the infinite and eternal to which she now belongs, "within the scope of that vaster power, in which she rested at last". The covenant of the rainbow can only be seen by the reborn soul that has "died" to its old self in the Flood.

The scene that gives "Moony" its title[103] is as central to *Women in Love*, and if ever a scene was an imaginative leap, it is this. But it, too, can only be grasped in terms of process. We may once again begin "symbolically", but must not end so.

The darkness and the light are the two fundamental opposites of both *The Crown* and *Women in Love*. The darkness embodies the world of the senses and the flesh, of the unconscious, the world of the lion. The moon is the world of the unicorn, defender of virgins, of Diana, of the self-sufficient woman who needs no man. Ursula has been in a contemptuous state, "luminous with repudiation", and at the end of the chapter we will see this Diana self-sufficiency again in the "evil" of Gudrun and Ursula, banded together against the male in their father and in Birkin. The moon as Diana is obviously Birkin's enemy, to be destroyed. But he calls it Cybele, the "accursed" Syrian perversion of Venus, who emasculated her acolytes: woman the sexual destroyer, like the Ursula of the beach. The moon as Cybele is also Birkin's natural enemy. Yet again, Ursula has been reacting against the moon as sinister because she longs for darkness and dissolution. She joins Birkin in hating its call to clarity and definition. Birkin's odd scraps of conversation show his quiet despair, the collapse of his faith in salvation through women. Relationship with women is only an antiphony of lies, an entanglement with Diana and Cybele, yet "what else is there?" The dead flowers on the water make their comment on those other flowers he threw, in the scene which marked the beginning of his relationship with Ursula.

The scene that follows is an answer to the question "what else is there?"; but it is an answer not in terms of static symbol but essentially in terms of a process, revealing, imaginatively, the way of salvation. This is why one instinctively knows that this is the heart of the novel, against which everything else has to be defined. If we trust ourselves to the fiction, we *experience* an enactment, stage by stage, first of the process of death and rebirth through the marriage of opposites, which Ursula never achieved in *The Rainbow*; and then of the whole process of re-creation through disintegration, infinite going-apart, that is central to *Women in Love*. The moon of hard, clear definition, of self-sufficiency and assertion, is destroyed by the flooding-in of darkness and unconsciousness. This is the first stage of the Lawrentian account of the religious mystery of marriage. But its point is that the moon should re-form, gather itself together, refuse to be destroyed (for opposition is eternally necessary), be born again out of its "death". Birkin is "satisfied of so much". But then he throws stone after stone, exploding the world of the pool into a rocking, crashing, shattering chaos and confusion, again, and again, and again. We experience (as no mere account can convey) a breaking-apart, a smashing fragmentation, to the very last "broken flakes" of light. And we experience the coming together, out of that ultimate separation, into moon-equilibrium, polarity, constellation. The moon that had been sinister and deadly in self-sufficiency grows into a radiant rose – incandescent fire constellated in the dark water.

The whole scene is, once again, easily explicable in immediate emotional and psychological terms; we can see how Birkin and the watching Ursula work off bitterness, anger, repudiation, despair, the urges to death and destruction. Only, "Was it hate?" Or any other purely psychological urge? The deepest imaginative experience of the process tells us rather why we should welcome both the disintegration and the tenacity of the coming together of the rose-in-darkness, "to get over the disfigurement and the agitation, to be whole and composed, in peace".

If one regards these novels as "supreme fictions", it is not simply because of the huge imaginative effort that went into their shaping, or the courage and honesty of the self-examination, or even the rich power of embodying, testing, and exploring "ideas" in fiction. It is chiefly because Lawrence aspired to, and achieved in the greatest moments of these novels, an imaginative vision inclusive enough to allow *all* opposites play. He saw reductiveness as the only evil. The aim of the exploratory theory and the finest achievement of the exploratory process, was to battle through partialities, to become objective enough to make his "statues" stand free, complete.

NOTES

My thanks are due to Laurence Pollinger Ltd. and the Frieda Lawrence Estate, to the Academic Centre Library of the University of Texas, and to Messrs. William Heinemann Ltd, for permission to quote from the manuscripts and works of D. H. Lawrence; and to the University of Kent at Canterbury for enabling me to go to Texas. It has also been my good fortune to find myself working to some extent in friendly parallel behind Professor George H. Ford. His remarks on the developments out of *The Sisters* may be found in his *Double Measure* (pp. 41-2n. 140 and note 4 p. 232; 164-8 and notes 5-11 p. 234) as well as the Introductions to the cancelled chapters of *Women in Love* cited in my footnotes.

1 *The Collected Letters of D. H. Lawrence,* ed. Harry T. Moore (London, 1962), I.223, 273. (Hereafter referred to as "L.M.").

2 *The Letters of D. H. Lawrence,* ed. Aldous Huxley (London, 1932), p. 115. (Hereafter referred to as "L.H.") Also, L.M., I.197. (Letters printed in both editions will be referred to as "L.H. p. . . .; L.M. . . . .")

3 L.H. p. 92; L.M. I.178. Surviving fragments of the Burns novel are printed in Edward Nehls, *D. H. Lawrence: a composite biography* (Madison, 1957), I.184-95.

4 L.H. pp. 111-2; L.M. I.193.

5 L.H. p. 118; L.M. I.200. Aldington's misreading of this crucial letter in his Introduction to the Heinemann edition of *The Rainbow* has caused much confusion between Lawrence's differing attitudes to the two pieces.

6 L.H. p. 115; L.M. I.197.

7 L.H. p. 118; L.M. I.200.

8 L.M. I.207-8.

9 L.H. p. 115; L.M. I.197.

10 L.H. p. 118; L.M. I.200.

11 L.H. p. 119; L.M. I.203.

12 L.H. p. 124; L.M. I.209.

13 L.H. pp. 136-7; L.M. I.223.

14 L.M., I.241.

15 L.H. p.172; L.M. I.259.

16 L.H. p. 174.

17 L.H. p. 179; L.M. I.264.

18 L.H. pp. 186-7; L.M. I.269.

19 L.H. p.189; L.M. I.272.

20 L.H. p.193; L.M. I.276.

21 L.M. I.276.

22 L.H. p. 200; L.M. I.284.

23 See Lawrence's letters of 18 September and 18 November, in S. Foster Damon, *Amy Lowell. A chronicle* (Boston, 1935), pp. 270, 279.

24 L.H. p. 205; L.M. I.287.

25 See the report of proceedings at the trial of *The Rainbow*, *Sunday Times*, 14 November 1915, p. 13. (I am indebted for this reference, and much helpful criticism, to John Worthen.)

26 L.H. p. 207; L.M. I.289.

27 L.H. p.208; L.M. I.290.

28 Damon, *Amy Lowell*, p. 279.

29 L.H. p. 190; L.M. I.273.

30 L.H. pp. 100, 101.

31 In the D. H. Lawrence manuscript collection of the University of Texas; *cf.* Warren Roberts, *A Bibliography of D. H. Lawrence* (London, 1963), p. 353, entry E441b; p. 346, entry E331a. I identify the first fragment as belonging to *Sisters* I both on internal evidence of style and pagination, and because it is written on unusually large folio paper of poor quality, presumably Italian and like that of the manuscript of the "Preface" to *Sons and Lovers*, which is dated Gargnano, January 1913. I identify the second fragment as belonging to *Sisters II* because of the mention of Ben Templeman. The typescript inserted into the autograph manuscript of *The Rainbow*, pp. 219-75 and 279-84, renumbered 548-604 and 608-13, must come from an earlier stage because of the references to Ella and "Charles" Skrebensky, and the writing in of reference to Winifred Inger. *The Wedding Ring* is the only previous version we know to have been typed, by Dunlop, and this typescript is faint enough to be a second carbon. Typescripts of *The Wedding Ring* were submitted both to Methuen and to Kennerley.

32 L.M. I.208.

33 L.M. I.242.

34 See Lawrence's reply, L.H. pp. 177-8; L.M. I.263-4.

35 See George H. Ford, *Double Measure* (New York, 1965), pp. 116-7.

36 L.H. p. 172; L.M. I.259.

37 L.H. p. 178; L.M. I.264.

38 By deduction from L.H. p. 144; I.230; and L.H. p. 172; L.M. I.259. On the greater length of *The Wedding Ring*: L.H. p. 193; L.M. I.275.

39 L.H. p. 219. This is based on the assumption that Lawrence can roughly predict the final length because he is working from *The Wedding Ring* in the knowledge that *The Rainbow* will end shortly after the final failure with Skrebensky. Page 449 of the autograph manuscript of *The Rainbow* concludes the kissing scene in the church. My calculations of course can only be guesswork.

40 L.H. p. 189; L.M. I.272.

41 L.H. p. 193; L.M. I.276, 9 May 1914.

42 The last relationship between Anna and Will is written, in autograph, into the final typescript of *The Rainbow*. Reference to Winifred Inger had to be inserted into the typescript from *The Wedding Ring* incorporated into the autograph manuscript.

43 As late as 1 February 1915, six months after the rejection of *The Wedding Ring*, and when he had written 450 pages of *The Rainbow*, Lawrence assures Pinker that there will be "no very flagrant love passages in it (at least to my way of thinking)", L.H. p. 219. This *might* suggest that the beach scene had not yet occurred to him either.

44 He had written "the first hundred or so pages" by 5 December 1914, L.H. p. 212; L.M. I.296.

45 L.M. I.306.

46 L.M. I.316, 322.

47 L.M. I.327, 328.

48 The typing was done by two people, Viola Meynell farming out part of it to a Miss K. Lee in Harrow. (See the note on the back of p. 495 of the autograph manuscript.)

49 *Phoenix – The Posthumous Papers of D. H. Lawrence*, ed. Edward D. McDonald (London, 1936), p. 419.

50 *Phoenix*, p. 418.

51 L.H. pp. 198-9; L.M. I.282.

52 See Ian Gregor, "What kind of fiction did Hardy write?", *Essays in Criticism* (Vol. 16, No. 3 (1966), pp. 290-308.

53 H. M. Daleski, *The Forked Flame* (London, 1965), is the first account of the importance of the *Study* for the interpretation of the novels. I disagree to some extent with its method and conclusions, but this seems to me an important book.

54 *Phoenix*, p. 441.

55 *Phoenix*, p. 460.

56 *Phoenix*, p. 468.

57 *Phoenix*, p. 450.

58 *Phoenix*, pp. 515-6.

59 *Phoenix*, p. 479. See also the interesting aside about Hardy and his "metaphysic", L.H. p. 120; I.204, as early as the first *Sisters*.

60 Autograph manuscript, pp. 298-310, University of Texas Collection (Roberts, *Bibliography*, p. 346, entry E331a).

61 *Phoenix*, p. 454.

62 Autograph manuscript, p. 300.

63 See the foot of Autograph manuscript, p. 302.

64 *Phoenix*, p. 460.

65 Penguin edition, pp. 201-2. (This reprint of the "banned" first edition is much the best text available.)

66 Autograph manuscript, p. 341.

67 Penguin edition, pp. 227-39.

68 Wilson Knight, "Lawrence, Joyce and Powys", *Essays in Criticism* Vol. 11, No. 4 (1961), pp. 403-17.

69 L.M. I.323, 24 February 1915.

70 L.M. I.328.

71 The final typescript, in the University of Texas collection (Roberts, *Bibliography*, p. 346, entry E331b) is dated "April"; but Viola Meynell was still typing on 29 May (L.M. I.345), when Lawrence speaks of having "only to revise it and let you have it". He may therefore have revised a previous batch in May.

72 L.H. p. 242; L.M. I.356.

73 See Harry T. Moore, *The Intelligent Heart* (Rev. ed., Penguin, 1960), p. 254.

74 L.M. I.331, 333.

75 L.M. I.345.

76 *D. H. Lawrence's Letters to Bertrand Russell*, ed. Harry T. Moore (New York, 1948), p. 49.

77 L.H. p. 239; L.M. I.350.

78 L.M. I.352. (See also L.H. pp. 235, 237, 240; L.M. I.351, 353. The order and dating of these letters is obscure.)

79 L.H. p. 257.

80 L.H. p. 259. The new "philosophy" which Lawrence was writing between 5 January and 25 February was probably the ill-fated *Goats and Compasses*, advertised in Heseltine's circular in late February. (See Nehls, I.349 and footnote.)

81 L.H. p. 347.

82 L.M. I.449.

83 L.H. p. 217; L.M. I.309.

84 L.H. p. 253; L.M. I.366.

85 *Reflections on the Death of a Porcupine and Other Essays* (Bloomington, 1963), pp. 36-7. (Hereafter referred to as *The Crown*.)

86 *The Crown*, p. 78.

87 *The Crown*, p. 47.

88 *The Crown*, pp. 75-6.

89 There were further corrections and revisions in 1917. The relationship among the drafts of *Women in Love* is a very complicated problem which I hope to discuss on another occasion.

90 L.M. I.454.

91 L.M. I.451.

92 L.H. p. 354; L.M. I.457.

93 L.M. I.463.

94 L.M. I.477.

95 L.H. p. 372; L.M. I.480.

96 This Prologue has been reprinted by George H. Ford, *Texas Quarterly* Vol. 6, No. 1 (1963), pp. 98-111. Professor Ford has also reprinted the original second chapter, "The Wedding", in the University of Texas *Studies in Language and Literature* Vol. 6, No. 2 (1964), pp. 134-47. Both have very useful Introductions.

97 L.M. I.449.

98 Final typescript, in the University of Texas collection (unrevised text), p. 399 (Roberts, *Bibliography*, p. 353, entry E441e).

99   The Modern Library edition (New York, 1948), pp. 285ff.; Penguin edition (London, 1960), pp. 282ff. (The Modern Library edition, reprinted from the first American trade edition, is the best text now available; avoiding both the mistakes of the first English edition and the confusions then forced on Lawrence by Heseltine's threat of legal action.) For a study of the variants in the printed editions, see Eldon S. Branda, "Textual Changes in *Women in Love*", The University of Texas *Studies in Language and Literature* Vol. 6, No. 3, (1964), pp. 306-21.

100 Final typescript (unrevised text), pp. 496-510.

101 Modern Library edition, pp. 357ff.; Penguin edition, pp. 352ff.

102 Penguin edition, p. 488.

103 Modern Library edition, pp. 279ff.; Penguin edition, pp. 276ff.

Joyce's *Ulysses:*
Symbolic Poem, Biography, or Novel?

Is James Joyce's *Ulysses* a novel – interpret the term with as much latitude as you like? Or is it a kind of ragbag of Joyce's personal memories, inspired doodlings, speculations, private jokes, and scattered observations on Dublin life as it was lived in the early nineteen hundreds? Some of Joyce's Dublin acquaintances and friends, like Oliver St. John Gogarty (transmogrified in the novel into Buck Mulligan) have contended that to look for any consistent or over-all meaning is silly. Those that do so are "victims of a gigantic hoax, of one of the most enormous leg-pulls in history". But the general view has been quite otherwise. In that view, *Ulysses* is an ordered and intricately organized masterpiece. Indeed it is usually accorded the treatment given to a sacred book. A painfully careful exegesis is regarded as appropriate to these Joycean scriptures, which have been diligently searched in order to discover proof texts, to recover hidden meanings, to unravel cryptic allusions, and, more ambitiously, to develop a systematic symbolism.

The appearance of Robert M. Adams' *Surface and Symbol* a few years ago raised a good many questions about the consistency of the symbolism of *Ulysses*. As Richard Ellman has said, after Adams' exploration of the relation of fact and fiction in this work, "everyone will have to reconsider his position about *Ulysses*".

What Adams shows is that "there is no proper fictional

reason for some of the things that are said and done" in *Ulysses*. Some of the items are found to lack any symbolic import whatever. For example, the winners in the bicycle race that is held on Bloom's Day are mentioned by name and some commentators have tried to find special meanings in the names that Joyce chose for them. Is, for example, the name of the winner, J. A. Jackson, an "enigmatic allusion" to the author himself, viz. James Augustine Joyce, the son of Jack Joyce? Such an interpretation has been proposed. But Adams shows that Joyce copied the names from a newspaper account of a race that actually took place in Dublin on 16 June 1904. Adams is able indeed to prove that the newspaper that Joyce used was the *Irish Independent*, for the name of one of the riders, J. B. Jones, as printed in that paper, looks – probably because the type was dirty – "remarkably like 'Jeffs' ", the name that Joyce uses in *Ulysses*. In this instance, the symbol-hunter would be very much in the plight of the fabled cornet-player who was unfortunate enough to mistake a fly speck on his score for a musical note.

Usually, however, Joyce did not slavishly follow his sources but reworked the materials he derived from them very freely indeed. Yet the motive determining his alterations and transpositions is not always easy to discern. Often there seems to be no "fictional reason" served by the changes. There may be personal reasons: occasionally Joyce seems to be simply venting his dislike of a Dublin acquaintance as when, for example, he calls a priest whom he knew, and whom Adams is able to identify, "Father Purdon", assigning to him "deliberately, the name of a street in the red-light district of Dublin". In other instances the alterations serve to develop a private joke, and often a joke so private that only a Dubliner of the time and in the know would find it comprehensible. Adams, it should be said, is not particularly worried by Joyce's propensity to insert his signature thus into odd corners of his canvas or to work into it his little private ceremonies and rituals. Yet Adams does question, and properly, "a general principle of construction not very economical of the general reader's time, and not very neat so far as the economy of forces within the novel is concerned".

It is the latter point, of course, that is finally important. Conceivably the scholars some day may have succeeded in annotating all the private allusions and in solving all the riddles, but in so far as such material cannot be related to the import of the novel – in so far as it has no "fictional reason" behind it – then so much the worse for *Ulysses* as a work of fiction.

Because the prime critical sin of our day – certainly the currently fashionable sin – is "symbol-mongering", and because critics too often seize upon any item that seems invitingly "symbolic" or that evokes something remembered from *The Golden Bough*, we have had a proliferation of *Ulysses* "symbols", some of them clearly possessing no genuine relation to the work. Against this kind of reading, *Surface and Symbol* serves as a powerful counterblast. Adams has shown that some of the matter in *Ulysses* is mere connective tissue, some of it is not even healthy connective tissue. This or that suspicious lump, under his probing, turns out to be simply as excrescence, a wart, or, if deeper below the surface, a mere tumour, serving no function even though it may be harmless and benign. Such elements in *Ulysses* may represent bits of the author's private life, elements that he has not been able – or perhaps has not taken the trouble – to transmute into the fictional fabric. Or, to change the metaphor, such elements may be regarded as odd pieces of scaffolding, necessary perhaps for Joyce's rather peculiar method of composition, but once composition has been completed, serving no function, constituting no part of the total architecture, though still firmly attached to the permanent structure.

But the reader may ask, are you sure that you really understand Joyce's architecture? Isn't it possible that someone whose head was filled with preconceived notions about what a novel ought to be might mistake for bits of leftover scaffolding what are actually essential parts of the building? That indeed is the question. How does one determine what is integral and what is not? What is the organizing principle of *Ulysses*? Mr. Adams's essential contribution is to show that odd bits of scaffolding do remain – i.e., J. B. Jeffs for J. B. Jones – that some parts of *Ulysses* are merely surface and have no symbolic reference. Mr. Adams has also thrown suspicion on a still larger number of allegedly symbolic items by showing that the symbolic patterns they seem to suggest either peter out to nothing when one explores them further, or else require so much elaboration and so many esoteric references that the law of diminishing returns sets in.

On the more positive side, however, Adams is less helpful. He fails to discern some of the symbolic patterns that are really there. The section of *Surface and Symbol* entitled "Dog-God" is an instance. Adams begins this part of his book by referring to Joyce's well-known fear and hatred of dogs. He goes on to sum up what is known about the real life antecedents of the Citizen's dog Garryowen. The incident on the beach, recounted in the third chapter, in which Stephen sees the live dog sniff at the body of the dead dog is referred to Mulligan's earlier characterization of Stephen as a "dogsbody". Furthermore, Adams sees that the various references to dogs in *Ulysses* are connected in some way with spelling "God" backwards when the black mass is celebrated in the Circe chapter. The general inversion of the sacred rites converts "God" into "dog" – a matter most apposite to the pattern of Stephen's thoughts as developed in the earlier chapters of *Ulysses*.

In Adams's view, however, no really meaningful pattern emerges from the references to dogs; he finds the mention of them in *Ulysses* to be "surely random". The distant bark of a dog that is heard at the end of the Circe chapter may be read, Adams tells us, "if one wishes, as a pathetic picture of God in the modern world, where truth cries out in the streets and no man regards it". But Adams quite properly sees little point in pressing this particular notion. Even the fact that Rudy's conception is occasioned by Molly's sexual stimulation at seeing two dogs copulating doesn't seem to him to have any "crucial symbolic significance". If it does have, it is "buried in an oddly out-of-the-way corner of the book structure".

In his attempt to discover whether the references to dogs mean anything in particular in this novel, Adams considers the associations of Odysseus with the dog and with other animals, the pig and the fox. He is also driven back into speculations about what books on the subject Joyce might have read, including quite remarkable lexicons such as Selig Korn's *Etymologisch-symbolisch-mythologisches Real-Wörterbuch zum Handgebrauche für Bibelforscher, Archäologen und bildende Künstler* (Stuttgart, 1843) and Oskar Seyffert's *Lexikon der klassischen Altertumskunde*. Adams's conclusion is cautiously, but rather disappointingly, inconclusive. Joyce, he finds, digs up various traditional properties for Odysseus and Telemachus. For these he sometimes found "brilliant applications – parodic, serious, symbolic, superficial ... but sometimes he did not. Quite sensibly he continued to use them anyway, whether or no; and left the reader to find or neglect the application, according to his temperament."

I think that one can make more of Joyce's use of dogs than Adams has done and that one can show that the development of symbols and the interrelating of them are more coherent and even more traditional than a good deal of Joyce criticism would lead us to believe.

Though it is interesting to know that Joyce himself, like Stephen Dedalus, hated and feared dogs, the reader does not need to have this information in order to discover Stephen's attitude. The opening chapters of *Ulysses* reveal what the dog has come to stand for in Stephen's sensibility. Stephen's experience on Sandymount Beach (in the Proteus chapter) with the live dog and the dead dog is intimately related to his feelings about Buck Mulligan, to the recent death of his mother, and to his own sense of the importance of his vocation as an artist.

These are matters that are touched on in the very opening pages of *Ulysses*. And by beginning with them, we begin at the beginning, with the obvious, and not with the esoteric. For Stephen, who distrusts Buck Mulligan and who resents his having invited Haines to the tower, "dogsbody" and "beastly" are loaded terms to which Stephen overreacts. That his reaction is in excess of the occasion is plain enough if we are willing to read *Ulysses* "straight" – that is, as we might read any other novel. The reason for Stephen's sensitivity and bitterness also becomes plain enough, if, again, we read the first chapter with sufficient care to see that Stephen, in spite of his pose of callousness, has been powerfully affected by his mother's death. (Buck is quite right in seeing that Stephen is brooding over this hurt.)

Buck's merry travesty of the mass as he shaves also has its relevance to Stephen's mood. Holding up the bowl of lather, Buck intones *"Introibo ad altare Dei"* and then calls out to Stephen: "Come up, Kinch. Come up, you fearful Jesuit." But Stephen is not amused. We are told that Stephen is "displeased and sleepy" and looks "coldly" on Buck's antics.

When Buck, a few moments later, addresses Stephen as

"poor dogsbody", even though Buck speaks in a kind voice, the word *dogsbody* bears a meaning that for Stephen is edged. But before turning to inquire what the word conveyed to Stephen, we ought to determine what the term means in itself. Adams senses that "the overtones [of this epithet] are more important than the literal meaning", but he has not grasped the literal meaning. He writes that "the only recognized public meanings of the epithet, first applied to Stephen by Mulligan, are ludicrously irrelevant – midshipman or pease pudding. Even if we suppose it used loosely and in derision, the epithet in this sense has very little point." But "dogsbody" as currently used in Great Britain signifies a flunky of all work, a person on whom any kind of task can be imposed.

Midshipman, indeed, is or was one of the meanings of the word, but a midshipman is also called a "snottie". An illustrative quotation printed in the Supplement to the *Oxford English Dictionary* reads: "A midshipman is known . . . in the service as a 'snottie' . . . If he is a junior midshipman he is also a 'dog's body'." Joyce was evidently aware of the relation of "dogsbody" to "snottie", for when Buck, "thrusting a hand into Stephen's upper pocket", borrows his handkerchief, Joyce has him say: "lend us a loan of your noserag to wipe my razor . . . The bard's noserag. A new art colour for our Irish poets: snotgreen." The association would be "snotrag" – "snottie" – "dogsbody".

Stephen evidently understands the term to mean someone of no standing who can be saddled with any onerous or humiliating task, for a little later, noticing Buck's abandoned bowl of lather, Stephen observes to himself: "So I carried the boat of incense then at Clongoes. I am another now and yet the same. A servant too. A server of a servant." The Pope's proud title is the servant of the servants of God. It is in an ironically different sense that Stephen sees that he is the server of a servant. The man whom Stephen serves is in Stephen's embittered imagination himself a servant, truckling to and fawning over Haines, the Englishman. Stephen views himself as a dogsbody indeed.

The element "dog" in "dogsbody" has its own special and bitter meaning for Stephen on this morning. *Beast* and *beastliness* are very much on his mind, and the dog is perhaps the most familiar and least exalted example of the beasts. Doubtless this is why the common term of contempt is "son of a bitch" rather than son of a mare or son of a cow or son of a cat. When Buck Mulligan exclaimed to his mother some days earlier that his visitor was "only Dedalus whose mother is beastly dead", he was, of course, using *beastly* as a loose intensive. But when, challenged by Stephen, he undertakes to explain what he meant by the word, *beastly* takes on specific meaning: "You saw only your mother die. I see them pop off every day . . . and cut into tripes in the dissecting room . . . To me it's all a mockery and beastly. Her cerebral lobes are not functioning".

Yet what Buck Mulligan can accept with equanimity is to Stephen agonizing. Part of the agony stems, of course, from Stephen's own personal involvement: his mother's recent death. Of much greater importance is the fact that Stephen is keenly aware of the full consequences of the changed view of man that is implied. He knows what he has lost; he cannot accept palliatives and compromises. When Haines asks Stephen whether he is a believer, "I mean, a believer in the narrow sense of the word", Stephen replies: "There's only one sense of the word, it seems to me". Haines's "Yes, of course" assumes a community of feeling that is not there. He hastens to add: "Either you believe or you don't, isn't it. Personally I couldn't stomach that idea of a personal God. You don't stand for that, I suppose?" Stephen drily observes, "with grim displeasure", that Haines beholds in him "a horrible example of free thought".

If man is only a beast, then all priests of whatever religions are really "medicine men", and Buck, the medical student, who is preparing to be a genuine medicine man with effective medicaments, can see himself as the only true priest of the twentieth century. His mockery of the Mass asserts a claim which, even if made humourously by Buck, has to be taken seriously by Stephen. Stephen reacts to this assertion with active hostility, for Stephen himself claims to be the true priest of the modern world: the artist, the priest of the eternal imagination. Later on, in the middle of the library chapter, Best observes that "the sense of beauty leads us astray", John Eglinton replies: "The doctor can tell us what those words mean". The doctor in the group is, of course, Buck Mulligan. Stephen's comment to himself a propos of Eglinton's deference to science is: "Sayest thou so? Will they [the medical men] wrest from us [the artists], from me the palm of beauty?" Stephen is hypersensitive on this issue and allows his resentment of Buck to colour his whole notion of the relation of science to art, but that fact is scarcely the point here. To a very considerable extent *Ulysses* is "about" Stephen and his relationship to his world. At any rate, Stephen here plainly means to generalize the issue. His bitter remark to himself is not "Will Buck wrest from me the palm of beauty", but will "they" wrest it?

The collapse of religion has left science and poetry quarrelling over the spoils and jostling each other for place. It is thoroughly appropriate, therefore, that early in the first chapter Matthew Arnold should come into Stephen's thoughts. He has a vision of the neat quadrangle of an Oxford college, and in it, pushing his mower, "a deaf gardener . . . masked with Matthew Arnold's face". If Buck's proposal to "Hellenize" Ireland, and his playful hint of an Oxford-style debagging to be executed on the Oxonian Haines – if Haines misbehaves in the future – provide the immediate stimulus to this absurd vision, the relevance of Arnold to the general situation is nevertheless thoroughly appropriate. On the assumption that science had destroyed the "fact" to which religion was unfortunately attached, Arnold had prophesied that literature would assume the burden of promoting and dispensing values. Literature was fortunately not attached to the fact, was thus invulnerable to the corrosions of science, and for that reason "the future of poetry was immense". The point is not that Stephen's speculations necessarily duplicate those of Matthew Arnold. But the basic problem that faces him is that which Arnold had earlier faced, and Stephen at the end of the *Portrait*, just before setting out for Paris, had proclaimed himself a "priest of the eternal imagination", an Arnoldian solution of the problem.

On this morning, art is very much on Stephen's mind. He tells Buck that the "symbol of Irish art" is the "cracked looking-glass of a servant". A moment later he says to himself that Buck "fears the lancet of my art as I fear that of his". Stephen opposes to the surgeon's lancet the artist's "cold steelpen". As we have already observed, Stephen is distrustful of and irritated by Buck, not merely as a person, but for what Buck represents.

It is in this general context that the colloquy about "beastly dead" occurs. As we have seen, Buck has referred to Stephen as "poor dogsbody", and Stephen, a moment later looking at himself in the mirror, has asked himself. "Who chose this face for me? This dogsbody to rid of vermin." In this instance, "dogsbody" insists upon the "dog" element: viz. this "beastly" body – this contemptibly animal organism. The specific occasion for Stephen's irritation at Buck is, of course, Buck's relation to Haines. Stephen not only resents the presence of Haines and regards him as a "usurper", but has been badly frightened by Haines's conduct during the night before. Haines, caught up in a nightmare about a "black panther", had seized his rifle and fired a shot in the room. Stephen's first words to Buck on the next morning are an inquiry as to how long Haines is going to stay in the tower. Stephen tells Buck: "If he stays on here I am off". It is a threat which Buck does not take seriously, but which Stephen is to make good.

The black panther has its connections also with the theme of man as mere beast. In using the term *panther* Joyce may have had in mind the fanciful etymology (Greek *pan* meaning *all* plus *ther* meaning *beast*) which intimates that the nature of this animal includes somehow all the beasts. Perhaps so, perhaps not. If Stephen was familiar with the etymology, that fact might help account for the celebrated passage in the Proteus chapter where to Stephen's eye the dog on the beach imitates in his actions the whole animal kingdom – bounding like a hare, skimming like a gull, tripping like a buck, halting with stiff "forehooves". A little later, the dog rears up on his master with "mute bearish fawning", then lopes off "at a calf's gallop", sniffs at the carcass of a dead dog, then, ordered away by his master, runs down the beach and starts digging in the sand. Stephen watches the dog scraping "up the sand again with a fury of his claws, soon ceasing, a pard, a panther, got in spouse-breach, vulturing the dead".

Stephen's way of seeing the dog's action here is of course an amalgam of his own thoughts and associations. It is these associations that make the dog finally melt into a panther and that even give him the attributes of a bird ("vulturing" the dead). They also account for Stephen's curious observation that this monster was "got in spouse-breach".[1]

Stephen's notion that man is a mere animal, beastly born and later to be beastly dead, gives point to – as well as receives illumination from – the various references in the early chapters to panther, fox, and dog. These three animals have rather differing associations. The black panther is the terror of nightmare, but in Stephen's mind it associates itself with British colonialism – with the colonel who has served in India perhaps – and Stephen in applying the epithet to Haines thinks of him as a "panthersahib" also expects a fawning sensibility, for Stephen insists on seeing Buck as toadying to Haines. But we are not dealing with a rigid symbolism. When Stephen scornfully asks himself whether he is pining for "the bark of *their* applause", Buck and Haines are both dogs. The fox is peculiarly a type of Stephen himself, having to live by Stephens' credo of silence, cunning, and exile. He provides an analogue for Stephen's own apparent callousness toward his mother: "and on a heath beneath winking stars a fox, red reek of rapine in his fur, with merciless bright eyes scraped in the earth, listened". But Stephen is a dog too: he had called himself "poor dogsbody" as he gazed on his own face in the mirror, and now on the beach he applies the same term to the dead dog, the "one great goal" to which the live dog Tatters, "sniffing . . . eyes on the ground", moves. Mr. Deasy, an hour or so before, had remarked to Stephen that all "history moves towards one great goal, the manifestation of God". That great goal to which history leads, the manifestation of God, turns out to be the rotting mammalian flesh: "Here lies poor dogsbody's body".

Stephen, watching the dog digging in the sand of the beach, describes him as a "panther, got in spousebreach". Stephen knows that in the kingdom of the animals, as in heaven, there is no marrying or giving in marriage, and that among the beasts, there can hardly be adultery. Is it not a bit highfalutin to make the dog Tatters the bastard offspring of an adulterous union? Why, in his reverie, does Stephen do so? Because in some way the theme of adultery is tied in with man's mere beastiality and the emptying of any belief in the Christian story.

This is the primary stress when the theme of adultery first makes its appearance with Buck's rendition of "The Ballad of Joking Jesus". The Jesus who is the "I" of the ballad guarantees his divinity by claiming a divine father, a bird, the dove of the Holy Spirit. Joseph the Joiner is not his father, but in this poem which Buck chants in a "quiet happy foolish voice", this "queerest young fellow" is clearly a fraud, and the true story is not one of miraculous birth in which the divine becomes incarnate in human flesh, but a rather sordid account of adultery in which Joseph the Joiner has been deceived by his wife.

Stephen's Nestor, Mr. Deasy, touches the theme again. "A woman brought sin into the world. For a woman who was no better than she should be, Helen, the runaway wife of Menelaus, ten years the Greeks made war on Troy. A faithless wife first brought the strangers to our shore here. MacMurrough's wife and her leman O'Rourke, prince of Breffni. A woman too brought Parnell low." References to Helen of Troy and to Jesus in the matter of spouse-breach occur throughout *Ulysses* – most notably in the Circe chapter where Virag asserts that the real father of Jesus was a Roman centurion named Panther! Stephen thinks of Shakespeare, type of the artist, as a man deceived and cuckolded. Leopold Bloom is a cuckold and throughout the day remains uneasily conscious of Blazes Boylan's assignation with his wife. But at this point I am less concerned with Bloom and the later chapters in general than with seeing whether a pattern does begin to emerge in the opening pages of the novel.

Adultery, as we have seen, is associated in Stephen's mind with the disappearance of any supernatural claim and man's reduction to the status of beast. But it also has for him another powerful association. Doubtful paternity emphasizes the link between mother and child as the only certainty. In the second chapter, Stephen's meditations as he helps one of his students with his arithmetic problem enforces the point. As Stephen looks at the boy before him, "ugly and futile: lean neck and tangled hair and a stain of ink, a snail's bed", he reflects that "someone had loved him, borne him in her arms and in her heart . . . had loved his weak watery blood drained from her own. Was that then real? The only true thing in life?" These thoughts of course, are tangled with his thoughts about his mother. Stephen says to himself: "Like him was I, these sloping shoulders, this gracelessness". Stephen's sight of the old midwives on the beach reinforces the same thought: "One of her sisterhood", he reflects, "lugged me squealing into life. Creation from nothing. What has she in her bag? A misbirth with a trailing navelcord, hushed in ruddy wool. The cords of all link back, strandintwining cable of all flesh." Then after a brief interval comes the thought: "Wombed in sin darkness I was too, made not begotten". In the Nicene creed Christ was "begotten, not made, being of one substance with the Father". But Stephen ruefully assigns to his own creation only a biological making – made by "the man with my voice and my eyes and a ghost woman with ashes on her breath. They clasped and sundered, did the coupler's will."

Motherhood for Stephen is associated with the biological, and woman herself is the prime instance of the mammal: the creature that suckles its young. Fatherhood, on the other hand, is a mystical estate. As Stephen is to put in later on in the Library chapter, "fatherhood, in the sense of conscious begetting, is unknown to man. It is a mystical estate, an apostolic succession, from only begetter to only begotten. On that mystery and not on the madonna which the cunning Italian intellect flung to the mob of Europe the church is founded and founded irremovably because founded, like the world, macro- and microcosm, upon the void. Upon incertitude, upon unlikelihood. *Amor matris . . .* may be the only true thing in life. Paternity may be a legal fiction." For Stephen, Jesus as the son of God has become merely a fiction, though Stephen can still believe in a god of art, and view himself as standing in the apostolic succession of the priests of the imagination.

We do not, however, have to wait until the Library chapter for Stephen's full statement of the matter. The groundwork for this distinction is laid in the early pages of the novel. For example, in the Proteus chapter (p. 48), as Stephen watches the cocklepickers on the beach, he thinks of woman as the "handmaiden of the moon". The phrase echoes St. Luke's account of the Annunciation, where Mary replies to the Angel: "Behold, the handmaid of the Lord; be it unto me according to Thy word". Woman now has to be regarded as the handmaiden of the moon, subject to the biological process and bound to the cycle of menstruation and gestation measured off in lunar months. A moment later, Stephen thinks of her as one summoned to "Bridebed, childbed, bed of death, ghostcandled. *Omnis caro ad te veniet.*" The Latin sentence ("All flesh shall come to thee") is from Psalm 65. There the psalmist declares that all flesh shall come to Jehovah, but in the context of Stephen's present thoughts the deity to whom all flesh shall come is the vampire of death, "his bat sails bloodying the sea, mouth to her mouth's kiss". In a later chapter that deity will be seen as neither the dove of the Holy Spirit nor the bat-winged vampire, but as "the reverent Carrion Crow", as Stephen now envisages "the third person of the Blessed Trinity".

In some respects, the most brilliant instances of the reduction of the divine to the merely animal occur in the Circe chapter. The Black Mass in which the voices of all the damned utter "dog", reversing the syllable "God" uttered by the voices of the blessed, has been referred to. The other instance is that in which Stephen appears as the "Primate of all Ireland". When Stephen conjures one of the whores to "beware Antisthenes, the dog sage, and the last end of Arius Heresiarchus", Lynch observes: "All one and the same God to her". This exchange prompts Florry to say to Stephen: "I'm sure you are a spoiled priest. Or a monk." Lynch chimes in: "He is. A Cardinal's son." Stephen's comment, "Cardinal sin. Monks of the screw," calls up a vision of "His Eminence, Simon Stephen Cardinal Dedalus, Primate of all Ireland". He "appears in the doorway, dressed in red soutane, sandals and socks. Seven dwarf simian acolytes, also in red, cardinal sins, uphold his train, peeping under it . . . Round his neck hangs a rosary of corks ending on his breast in a corkscrew cross". Joyce (and perhaps Stephen too) is making use of the Elizabethan pun that turned on the fact that "cardinal" had come to be pronounced as "carnal". The word *monks* produces the "dwarf simian acolytes". They are seven presumably because of the number of the deadly sins, though here they are simply called "cardinal sins".

As we have observed earlier, "dog" is not used in *Ulysses* as a kind of mechanical counter: it is only one of the several symbols of the beastly. For the present instance Joyce has chosen the most nearly man-like of the animals, an anthropoid species, belonging to the highest order of the Mammalia. Stephen is doubly a primate: as the wisest of the beasts and as one of the highpriests of the eternal imagination, among clergy of that ilk, an archbishop and cardinal.

So much for the principal dog references as they concern Stephen. But does the dog really have any particular significance elsewhere in the novel? And specifically, what of its relation to Bloom? It is used significantly if only as helping to stress the polar contrasts between Bloom and Stephen. Bloom does not hate and fear dogs, but rather likes them, though not all dogs like him. He is chased by the Citizen's dog, Garryowen.

Bloom is perfectly content to belong to the highest order of mammals, not in the least dismayed to find man reduced to the naturalistic level. That the conception of his beloved little son Rudy was associated with the copulating of two dogs outside the Blooms' window does not trouble him. His memory of the event elicits from him no more than an elegiac sigh: "How life begins". There may be pathos and sadness in much of human life, but for Bloom the matter of concern is not that man is beastly born and will some day be beastly dead.

The appearance to Bloom of Paddy Dignam as a beagle, now that he is beastly dead and buried, makes good sense. But I must confess that I see little special meaning in the successive metamorphoses of the dog that Bloom meets in Dublin's night town. The fact that the dog is a retriever and then turns into wolf dog, setter, etc. accords with the general atmosphere of hallucination that hangs over this whole chapter. Perhaps nothing more is to be inferred. At any rate, Bloom is not terrified of the dog, whatever the breed he assumes. Bloom opposes cruelty to animals, loves doing good to others (including gulls, horses, and dogs), and readily gives the dog the tidbit that he bought to eat himself.

The distant bark of the dog in the Circe chapter certainly does not suggest "a pathetic picture of God in the modern world, where truth cries out in the streets and no man regards it". Adams has been quite right to reject this view of the matter. If God is, as Stephen earlier that morning told Mr. Deasy, simply a noise in the street, then the distant bark of the dog at this point in the novel makes good enough symbolic sense. But one need not insist on extracting a symbolic meaning; most of us will be willing to accept it as an incidental item in the description of the night scene.

The question put some pages earlier was whether *Ulysses* can be read as a novel. The reader's answer will depend upon whether he can discern a pattern of meaning that grows out of the thoughts and actions of the various characters. The first chapters, as I have tried to show, do yield a pattern of meaning, and one which, if it does demand a sensitive and careful reading, and if it does require that the reader should know something about the Mass, and that he have at least a bowing acquaintance with such historical figures as Matthew Arnold, Pyrrhus, Oscar Wilde, and Bishop Berkeley, does not require any encyclopedic scholarship. More important still, it does not require that the reader have the key or code to a private and esoteric set of "symbols".

Stephen's irritation at Buck and his resentment of Haines are indeed unreasonable, though understandable. The author has made it plain that we are not asked to agree with Stephen or to give him more than "dramatic" sympathy. Moreover, Stephen's gloomy thoughts and his bitter speculations are related to a more general state of affairs: they have relevance to the culture of our age, and they are used to throw light upon a climate of opinion that characterizes modern civilization.

The opening chapters of *Ulysses* give us a brilliant dramatization of, among other things, the alienation of the sensitive artist in our day. Stephen's case is, of course, special. It is related to his personal circumstances: his education by the Jesuits, his bitterness at his poverty, and his hurt at the recent death of his mother. But his case, special as it is, is related to general and universal problems including the relation of science, poetry, and religion seen in the post-Arnoldian world. Stephen has won a Pyrrhic victory. He has decided not to join Buck and Haines at The Ship at half-past noon and he has resolved not to return to the Tower that evening. He will break off his connection with Buck Mulligan. If this will cost him a place to sleep, so be it.

How is this pattern of meaning developed in the subsequent chapters? How is Stephen related to Bloom and what part does Bloom play in this emerging pattern of meanings? What finally is the total meaning of the novel? In a short essay, one can only sketch very general directions. Moreover, *Ulysses* is such a rich novel that one does not want to risk oversimplifying it or reducing it to an abstract theme. Perhaps the most concise way to indicate the pattern of meaning that develops in the novel is to make some comments upon the meaning of Stephen and Bloom. What occurs when these polar extremes are connected? What currents leap across from one to the other? Or does anything leap across? In my own view, no transaction takes place. The total meaning of the novel, so it seems to me, has to be one that accepts this obvious fact.

In spite of the many attempts to show that Stephen and Bloom achieve some sort of real communication, I think that the case is not proved. On this point I would agree with Harry Levin's early and excellent introductory study (*James Joyce*, 1941) and with Adams in his *Surface and Symbol*. There is no real communication between the two men. How could there be? Stephen and Bloom speak different languages. Indeed, these polar, antithetical men come closest to a meeting of minds in an incident that occurs in the Circe chapter. When Bloom and Stephen both look into the mirror in Mrs. Cohen's establishment, each sees not his own face but the face of Shakespeare, "beardless . . . rigid in facial paralysis, crowned by the reflection of the reindeer antlered hatrack." If one can accept the fact that they are "seeing things" in this chapter of hallucinations, there is perfectly good reason to account for their seeing this face. Stephen can see himself reflected in Shakespeare because for him Shakespeare is the type of the artist. Stephen conceives that Shakespeare, like himself, lacked appreciation, was betrayed, and had to live by Stephen's own code of silence, cunning, and exile. As for Bloom, Shakespeare, like himself, was a cuckold and a kind of commercial traveller.

The vision of Shakespeare that unites Stephen and Bloom has welled up, as it were, out of the subconscious, bypassing the medium of words. Yet the shared perception hardly amounts to communication, for presumably neither man knows that the perception is shared – that his opposite is seeing Shakespeare too.

Why is it that so many commentators have felt that Stephen and Bloom simply must have something to say to each other, something that will alter the lives of both? The demand has arisen from the very fact of polarity. Stephen and Bloom so completely divide the world of man between themselves that each obviously needs the other: either standing alone is incomplete. Yet the reader's sense that the two men ought to join forces or become atoned one with the other does not mean that they do. To argue that since an atonement is desirable it must occur takes the intent for the deed. In fact, it does more: it makes an assumption about the author's intent that cannot be supported by the author's text.

A complicating factor has been the prominence given in *Ulysses* to the theme of paternity. It has been argued that Bloom, throughout the day, is the only person who takes a fatherly interest in Stephen. Indeed, according to this argument Bloom proves himself to be Stephen's spiritual father. Yet it is a very obtuse special pleading that can make the argument that Bloom is the only person who is kind to Stephen during the day. Miles Crawford, the newspaper editor, Professor McHugh, Mr. Deasy the schoolmaster – all of them recognize Stephen's talent and express a wish to help him. Even Buck Mulligan, it is plain, thinks of him as a kind of genius and wishes him well.

Stephen does indeed need a father, but the father whom he has already chosen for himself is his namesake, Dedalus, the fabulous artificer. In any case, Bloom's efforts to engage Stephen's interests do not get very far. Stephen, tired and bored, rejects them politely, and finally, when Bloom suggests that Stephen spend the night with him, Stephen again politely but firmly rejects the invitation.

For the sake of argument, however, let us assume that the meeting of Stephen and Bloom is productive of something. What did it produce? Is there any evidence that Bloom's life has been changed by the meeting? It is true that in the Oxen in the Sun chapter, we are told that one of the dreams that Bloom has had argues that he is in for a change. But the only change that he finds when he returns home is a rearrangement of the furniture. He bumps into a walnut sideboard which is not in its accustomed place, thanks to Molly's altered notions of where it and other pieces of furniture should be. But apparently this is all that has been altered in the Bloom household. Bloom does request Molly to make breakfast for him the next morning, and several commentators have rather desperately interpreted this modest request as betokening that Bloom will become from now on master in his own house. It would be nice to think that the worm has finally turned, but the logic of the book would indicate that no real change in his relation to Molly has occurred or can occur.

Yet so insistent has been the urge to endow the meeting of Bloom and Stephen with significance that various expedients have been used to get over the obvious fact that they have nothing to say to each other and that nothing happens. One stratagem has been to point to "symbolic" communion or communication. In the kitchen of Bloom's house Stephen and Bloom have a cup of cocoa together. Since Joyce refers to the cocoa as "Epps's massproduct", it is evident to some readers that what really is being celebrated in the kitchen is a symbolic equivalent of the Mass, a rite of communion.

To take another instance: stepping out of the kitchen, Stephen and Bloom urinate in the garden, an act that is said to symbolize fertility. As they do so, they gaze upward and see the lighted window of Molly's bedroom. She is a kind of fertility goddess who presides over the scene. Stephen has found his true Muse and will become the writer that he ought to be. Thus, what does not occur in the thoughts and actions of the characters may still occur symbolically, and what occurs symbolically must be true.

A second strategy for proving that something does come out of the meeting of Stephen and Bloom is to make Stephen Dedalus and James Joyce interchangeable. The argument runs this way: since Stephen is an expression of Joyce as a young man, anything that happened to or was true of Joyce can be attributed to Stephen.

When Stephen leaves Bloom, after declining Bloom's offer of hospitality, where does he go? He has resolved not to return to the Tower. Where did he sleep that night? What happened to him? We are not told. The novel does not take his career any further. On the other hand, we know that James Joyce did indeed survive his experiences in Ireland, went to live on the Continent, and wrote *Ulysses*. Joyce did develop, was turned into a man by his marriage to Nora, and put away the rather brittle aestheticism of Stephen Dedalus. By a kind of illicit transfer from the realm of biography to that of fiction, various things that are true of Joyce can be attributed to Stephen Dedalus. W. Y. Tindall puts the matter quite explicitly in *James Joyce: His Way of Interpreting the Modern World*. He writes: "The encounter with Bloom has changed Stephen's inhumanity to humanity. The egotist has discovered charity, the greatest of virtues, and compassion for mankind . . . 'Pity', Stephen says in *A Portrait of the Artist*, "is the feeling which arrests the mind in the presence of whatsoever is grave and constant in human suffering and unites it with the human sufferer'.

He now discovers what this means, and, leaving Bloom, he goes away to write *Ulysses*." But the "he" who left Bloom with "*Liliata rutilantium*" still ringing in his head was Stephen, and the "he" who wrote *Ulysses* was James Joyce. For all we know, Stephen Dedalus never wrote any fiction at all.

What, then, is one to say about *Ulysses* as a novel? When one reviews the various attempts to elucidate the meaning of *Ulysses* it quickly becomes apparent that the red herring lying across the path is Joyce's own biography together with his own incidental comments about *Ulysses*. It is this material that has put most of the hounds off the true scent. One readily grants that *Ulysses* bears a very special relationship to Joyce's biography, and further that all sorts of parallels exist between Joyce and Stephen and between Joyce and Bloom, for that matter. I think also that one has to accept the fact that the structure is intricate, and that there are levels of meaning which will elude readers who are not in possession of certain specialized bodies of knowledge. Thus, in the earlier chapters the various heresies concerning the doctrine of the Trinity are used to comment upon Buck and Stephen and on the modern world generally. Averroes and Moses Maimonides, "flashing in their mocking mirrors the obscure soul of the world, a darkness shining in brightness which brightness could not comprehend", reverse St. John's account of the Logos, as a "light shining in the darkness" which the darkness could not comprehend. They also comment further upon the Christian scheme which has permeated Stephen's thought but which for him has now become emptied of reality.

Most readers will not be able or willing to pursue these more delicate ramifications. And they need not: the general import of the novel will come through even though the reader has to regard Aquinas, Averroes, and Aristotle as simply part of the equipment of Stephen's mind and thus dramatically appropriate to his brooding meditations. Furthermore, one has to concede the fact that *Ulysses* is a kind of private logbook and spiritual diary containing Joyce's own personal revenges on particular people, his private jokes, and allusions to incidents and happenings that had some particular meaning for him. On this general point, Adams's book has been decisive.

Yet when all is said and done, *Ulysses* is not simply a catchall into which Joyce stuffed such materials. Nor is it merely or even primarily a Joycean riddle. It is a novel, and yields, in spite of its special difficulties, the sort of knowledge about ourselves and about our world that any other authentic novel does yield.

Among other things, *Ulysses* is a novel about the rift in modern civilization – as reflected in the attitudes of an intransigent and sensitive and brilliant young artist, of a good-natured, rather bumbling, bourgeois citizen, and of a sceptical, practical, "natural" female like Molly Bloom, who is fascinated by men but who is also amused by them, and in some sense rather contemptuous of them and the elaborate intellectual structures that they insist upon raising. There is a great deal of comedy in *Ulysses*, though it does not bar out pathos. There is some very brilliant and searching satire.

The fabric of the book is intricate. The tone is of an equivalent complexity. Commentators, in their anxiety to find a happy ending, have insisted on the book's compassion and on its final optimism, have oversimplified and probably distorted its meaning. In any case, whatever conclusions about the meaning of this novel we are to draw will require testing against the fictional structure – will have to be matched with what can actually be found in the novel. Too often the commentator has argued in effect that the meaning of *Ulysses* is the development of James Joyce, and if we venture to ask why it is so important to learn about the artistic development of James Joyce, we are told that this is important because James Joyce was able to write *Ulysses*. The hopelessly circular nature of this argument needs no comment.

NOTE

1   The *Oxford English Dictionary* does quote from a mediaeval writer, Trevisa, the following incidence of the word: "Leopardus is a cruel beeste and is gendred in spowsebreche of a parde and of a lionas". The usage is so odd and the quotation is so apt to this passage in *Ulysses* that one finds it hard to believe that Joyce had not read this very passage in the *Oxford English Dictionary*. I suppose that he

had, and that his having done so probably accounts for his choice of this particular word here. But if Trevisa has extended the meaning of *spouse-breach* to include monstrous and unnatural union, its primary meaning of adultery is still present: etymology sees to that.

ANDREW RUTHERFORD

Waugh's
Sword of Honour

"You see, it is equally possible to give the right form to the wrong thing, and the wrong form to the right thing", says Lactantius in Waugh's *Helena*. The rhetorician's commonplace is anathema to critics who assume (as I do) an identity of style and meaning, of aesthetic form and moral content, yet such readers may be tempted to invoke a comparable formula as they find themselves relishing Waugh's consummate artistry while repudiating many of his values. ("His *bons mots* deserve to be repeated exactly", writes A. E. Dyson in a finely perceptive essay: "Take away the verbal precision, and you crash down too violently on the meaning".)[1]

That verbal precision, however, is itself a virtue, for the novelist as well as the mere craftsman. Lactantius, uncertain what to express, none the less "delighted in writing, in the joinery and embellishment of his sentences, in the consciousness of high rare virtue when every word had been used in its purest and most precise sense, in the kitten games of syntax and rhetoric". In Waugh such stylistic virtuosity contributes not just to its own peculiar pleasure, but to the exact registration and the subtle if at times eccentric valuation of experience. In the war trilogy which is his masterpiece, his concern for the niceties of linguistic usage underlies the excellence of dialogue, narrative, and auctorial commentary. The very organization of his sentences, with their conscious elegance of syntax, cadences, and punctuation, gives an effect of effortless superiority, of cool urbanity, of detached intelligence in supreme control of its material. And this technical expertise can be employed more daringly, more paradoxically, to convey sympathetic insight, as in the flashback to Virginia's past – to "her seduction by a friend of her father's, who had looked her up, looked her over, taken her out, taken her in, from her finishing school in Paris". The substance of a sensitive "woman's novel" is condensed by Waugh into a single sentence. For the first time we are given a deeper understanding of the "bright fashionable girl" Guy married; and the verbal clowning which seems at first sight to preclude a serious response shows the author withholding pity and indignation only to imply their necessity, and diagnosing a cynicism which is not his own but that of the family friend and the social group he represents. The "perfect blending of form and substance", which Conrad advocated, has become a common-place in discussions of plot, theme, and structure, but his plea for "an unremitting never-discouraged care for the shape and ring of sentences" is less obviously applicable to contemporary fiction: Waugh is one of the very few modern novelists whose phraseology and syntax are themselves a source of delight, illumination, and discovery.

The disposing intelligence which thus manifests itself in sentence structure and verbal wit also controls the organization of the trilogy as a whole. At first its close-knit unity was not apparent. When *Men at Arms* was published in 1952 its comic force was immediately recognized, and its authenticity as a picture of Army life. Moreover, the formality of Waugh's procedure, the conscious felicity of style, the progression from retrospective prologue to main narrative, the mannered (almost precious) subdivision of that narrative into three sections, "Apthorpe Gloriosus", "Apthorpe Furibundus", "Apthorpe Immolatus" – all this testified to the author's awareness of his novel as a work of art. Yet structurally it failed to satisfy. Apart from occasional loose ends in the plot, excessive attention seemed to be given to Apthorpe, while the hero's own progress from idealism to minor disillusion hardly seemed sufficient, thematically, to sustain the whole narrative structure. The dedication ("To Christopher Sykes: Companion in arms") tended to associate the author with his subject-matter, and this process was carried further by the dedication of *Officers and Gentlemen* to Major-General Sir Robert Laycock: Waugh's allusion to "those exhilarating days when he led and I *lamely followed*" came near to identifying himself with the limping hero, whose military fortunes so closely paralleled his own. Hence in spite of his assurance that this story is "pure fiction: that is to say of experience totally transformed" it seemed at this stage as if the transformation might be less than total – that this series might resemble one of those hybrids, half-fictional, half-autobiographical, more historical document than work of art, which proliferated after the First World War. And Waugh's assertion, in the first edition of *Officers and Gentlemen*, that he had thought at first that the story would run into three volumes but now found that two would do the trick,[2] suggested that the whole thing was being extemporized rather than designed.

Such suspicions, however, did less than justice to Waugh as an artist. His military service, which he later ranked with travel as a major stimulus to his imagination,[3] had provided him with themes in *Put Out More Flags* and *Brideshead Revisited*. In returning to it now he was exercising the privilege that his *alter ego* Pinfold envied painters – that of returning "to the same theme time and time again, clarifying and enriching until they have done all they can with it". The trilogy is his attempt to do all he could with his own war experiences and observations; and far from consisting of unshaped reminiscence, it embodies a grand design, the proportions and significance of which were not fully apparent until *Unconditional Surrender* was published in 1961. The earlier "less than candid assurance (dictated by commercial interest) that each [volume] was to be regarded as a separate, independent work" has since been repudiated by Waugh himself: he insists in his final recension of the trilogy that it was intended from the outset to be read as a single story.[4] When so read it gains not merely from the completion of an otherwise defective narrative, but from the reader's perception of structural relationships hitherto unapprehended, and of thematic developments startling in their implications.

The trilogy is a form specially appropriate for such progressive revelation. The old three-volume novel, as Professor Kathleen Tillotson has shown, was convenient for publishers, circulating libraries, and readers, but also for authors, presenting them as it did with a structural framework for their narratives. The trilogy is a radically different form, yet it too has artistic and commercial advantages. It provides three novels of normal length at suitable intervals, instead of a single monster which would price itself out of the market. It spreads income tax burdens. It keeps the author's name before the public (and whets readers' appetites so that the sales of individual novels reinforce each other), while relieving him of the strain of excessively prolonged gestation. But above all it suggests a way of patterning experience, of imposing clearly perceptible order on a large body of material. This may be overdone, as I think it is in the rigid structuring of *A Scots Quair*; or neglected, as in the flabbily experimental Tietjens series; but in Waugh's hands the full potential of the form is realized. Each novel records a distinct phase in the hero's emotional, spiritual, and military progress; each deals with a separate aspect and theatre of war; each forms (as Mr. Bradbury observes) "a distinctive experience". Yet they are closely linked by the continuity of the narrative, the recurrence of major themes, the reappearance of old characters in new roles, and by a formal parallelism:

> all three books begin in light spirit with a series of events in training, set in England, with Guy's mood a hopeful one, and all conclude with events in action abroad, where Guy witnesses and is involved in a betrayal, as a result of which he suffers in reputation, hope and faith.[5]

Each ends, one might add, with a return to England, and each contributes to the elaborate patterning of events, of recurring and contrasting motifs, which characterizes the trilogy as a whole. The resulting sense of unity in diversity is so satisfying, aesthetically and thematically, that one is tempted to speculate on the unique felicity of tripartite division in complex works of art.

Certainly, admirers of the trilogy in its original form will not readily be reconciled to Waugh's one-volume recension. We may discount a mere nostalgia for the actual physical form in which the books were first read: for the *aficionado* even the original dust-jackets had their charm, as did the dedications which rooted the narrative in biographical reality, or the

"Synopsis of Preceding Volumes" provided by the author himself in *Unconditional Surrender*, but excised from the one-volume version. More serious are the cuts in the text itself. These were simply intended, Waugh tells us, to remove "repetitions and discrepancies" and "passages which, on re-reading, appeared tedious",[6] they may also have facilitated presentation of the novel in this new handsome format; yet they are a grievous loss. Only an author prodigal of wit could have sacrificed so ruthlessly the comic extravaganza of a film of the '45, or the episode of the Loamshire officers suspected of being fifth-columnists; the disappearance of all references to Captain Truslove obscures the relation between Guy's boyhood reading and his romantic attitude to war; and the resentful reader misses many other passages which were relished on first reading and remembered long afterwards.[7] The formal structure of the novel is obscured too by the continuous narration; the three main phases of the action are less obviously distinguished; Guy's returns to England, for example, seem less significant as chapter endings than they did when marking the close of separate volumes. When all such protests have been made, however, it remains true that these are only minor changes: fundamentally, the main rhythm of the novel is unaltered and its significance unaffected by Waugh's revision. Discriminating readers may well refuse to accept this as the definitive text, but they will not be embarrassed in their interpretation by any changes of attitude, technique, or theme between the original trilogy and its "final" recension.

As a moralist Waugh has always been elusive or provocative. Critics who see literary greatness as dependent on moral insight tend to be ill at ease with comedies like his, which are only intermittently satiric. His refusal to comment on the outrageous content of his early novels can be seen as an extreme reaction against the intrusive narrators of Victorian fiction, and against the predictable moral norms which they invoked. His own cool abnegation of values made cynicism the passport to a world of comic irresponsibility, which must be justified in psychological rather than moral terms – in terms, we may say, of the therapeutic effect of an art-controlled emotional release, a comic catharsis. Nevertheless, Waugh's fiction also flirted with religion and morality: Father Rothschild in *Vile Bodies* makes some typical gestures towards Eternal Truth amid the flux of decadence, which Waugh seems to find both shocking and delightful. This ambivalence towards the world that he portrays is reflected in the ambiguity of *Vile Bodies* or even *A Handful of Dust* (which can be read cynically or satirically according to taste), and in his occasional self-deception about the nature of his own art. He sought to defend the eating of Prudence in *Black Mischief* as an episode showing "the sudden tragedy when barbarism at last emerges from the shadows and usurps the stage",[8] but this claim hardly counteracts the impression made by the pervasively flippant narration and amoral hero. Here as elsewhere the potential moral pattern is unrealized as the virtues are undermined and the vices mitigated by Waugh's sense of the absurd. We may certainly distinguish between a dead-pan narrative style that seems to be and is in practice cynical, and one that assumes the mask of cynicism to imply normative values which remain unstated. But often the distinction is a fine one, difficult to confirm without more pointers than Waugh's early narrative convention allows, while his own irony tends continually to erode the moral universe towards which he aspires from his native realm of comic anarchy.

In *Brideshead Revisited* we find the opposite extreme of dogmatic commitment and artistic overstatement, for the Catholic-aristocratic values which Waugh now asserts are untested (though not wholly untouched) by his once habitual irony. The fulsomeness with which they are presented is intensified by the narrator-hero's rich corrupt nostalgia, but the problem is not merely one of literary tact. Exquisitely as the vanished past is recalled – and Donat O'Donnell's allusion to Proust is far from inappropriate – we must feel uneasy about this Catholicism which "is hardly separable from . . . personal romanticism and . . . class loyalty",[9] this religion that figures as the glamorous adjunct to true aristocracy. Nevertheless, there was artistic courage of a kind in Waugh's writing, frankly and without defensive irony, a lament for the doomed English upper class, making public his own private myth of the aristocracy as "the unique custodians of traditional values in a world increasingly threatened by the barbarians".[10] The potent magic of his style induces an unwilling suspension of our disbelief for the moment: his elegiac romantic vision is persuasive and imaginatively compelling within the confines of the work itself. It shrivels only when confronted with reality. Hooper is an amusingly repellent character, but manifestly not representative in the way Waugh would have us believe. Brideshead itself is beautifully rendered – as is the dinner at Paillard's – but neither can sustain the symbolic value imposed on them by the narrator-hero. Complex truth, it would seem, cannot be told in the simplified terms of either myth or caricature, though these are among Waugh's favourite fictional devices.

For his trilogy he evolves a narrative method which includes both but transcends them, combining his old detached ironic manner with the passionate conviction of his later works, and fusing his comic with his tragic vision in an attempt to do full justice to the facts of war.

These are presented as "seen and experienced by a single, uncharacteristic Englishman",[11] who is uncharacteristic in ways that meet with Waugh's particular approval. There are obvious differences between author and observer-hero – differences in social origins, marital circumstances, and spiritual history – yet in many ways the two are very close. Guy may not be heroic, but he is neither an anti-hero like Paul Pennyfeather nor a picaro like Basil Seal. His undistinguished but honourable service parallels Waugh's own. His values, social, religious, and political seem identical with his creator's; and Waugh is well aware of how unrepresentative these are – how unacceptable to the majority of readers.

> News [of the Russian-German alliance] that shook the politicians and poets of a dozen capital cities brought deep peace to one English heart . . . [Guy] lived too close to Fascism in Italy to share the opposing enthusiasms of his countrymen. He saw it neither as a calamity nor as a rebirth; as a rough improvisation merely . . . The German Nazis he knew to be mad and bad. Their participation dishonoured the cause of Spain, but the troubles of Bohemia, the year before, left him quite indifferent . . . He expected his country to go to war in a panic, for the wrong reasons or for no reason at all, with the wrong allies, in pitiful weakness. But now, splendidly, everything had become clear. The enemy at last was plain in view, huge and hateful, all disguise cast off. It was the Modern Age in arms. Whatever the outcome there was a place for him in that battle.

The tolerance of Mussolini, the approval of Franco, the indifference to Munich, the loathing of Russia as much as Germany – these are deliberate affronts to liberal and left-wing orthodoxy. The idea of war as a Crusade in the cause of reaction outrages progressive and pacifist opinion simultaneously. Waugh intends his new value judgements to be as provocative as his old cynicism; and there is no suggestion here of any political divergence between hero and narrator. A traditionalist and cuckold like Tony Last, Guy too lives in a world of betrayal; but Broome provides a firmer base than Hetton for the reassertion of aristocratic values, while Catholicism offers more profound religious insights than Tony's ridiculous (though not wholly ridiculous) C. of E. The spiritual value of these two inherited traditions is embodied in Guy's father, whose deep piety and family pride flower – unexpectedly perhaps – in the charity that was so notably lacking in *Brideshead Revisited*. (It is hard to imagine Charles Ryder saying "Here's how" to Major Tickeridge, or showing kindness and courtesy to Miss Vavasour of the Marine Hotel.) The affectionate comedy that plays over Mr. Crouchback does nothing to discredit his goodness, which is a point of moral reference throughout the trilogy; his function being, as Waugh told Mr. Stopp, "to keep audible a steady undertone of the decencies and true purpose of life behind the chaos of events and fantastic characters", though he was also to figure as "a typical victim . . . in the war against the Modern Age".[12] To this complex of values must be added those of military tradition. After eight years of shame and loneliness since the failure of his marriage, Guy (like the hero of *Maud*) is again one with his kind when his country embarks on a just war; and he re-establishes full communion with his fellow-men in the comradeship of arms – first with the middle-class unfashionable Halberdiers, then with the upper-class friends of X Commando, the anachronistic "flower of the nation".

Such commitments are defensible, though suspect; but the interest of the trilogy lies less in Waugh's initial assertion than in his testing of the hero's values. By the end of Volume Two Guy can see that he began the war in a state of euphoric illusion; by the end of Volume Three his disenchantment is complete. The Crusade on which he set out proudly and happily becomes a pilgrimage of painful discovery, of humble expiation.

The author's foreknowledge of this is not shared, however,

with the reader. There are only a few hints, anticipations, which will be developed in the later sombre movements of the trilogy. It is significant that Sir Roger, at whose tomb Guy prays, was a Crusader who never saw the Holy Land but died in a local scuffle "with a great journey still . . . before him and a great vow unfulfilled": clearly Waugh foresaw from the outset his own hero's ultimate frustration. Nevertheless, the story of *Men at Arms* is told almost entirely from Guy's point of view, which the narrator seems to share, so that as we read we are fully involved in the process, immersed in the experiences that the hero undergoes.

At this stage, buoyed up by his romantic idealism, he takes war and soldiering light-heartedly: that is why the comic figure of Apthorpe bulks so large, whereas later episodes are dominated by ambiguous or sinister characters like Ludovic or Frank de Souza. Waugh relishes all the Army's idiosyncrasies of speech and behaviour, its taboos and shibboleths, its stereotyped or wildly eccentric personalities, its tragi-comedies of pettiness and muddle. But while working in a comic mode, Waugh's purpose transcends the satirical: this is not an exposure but an authentic record and joyous celebration of British regimental life. For those who have known such life, this novel provides the delight – aesthetically suspect but undeniably intense – of recognition; to the uninitiated it gives pleasure by revealing a new, uniquely entertaining social world; for both it quintessentializes an in-group experience known to many, but rarely if ever so well communicated. Robert Graves, for example, strikes a note of strident boastfulness in his account of the Royal Welch Fusiliers, which is hardly redeemed by the unconvincing irony that precedes and follows it – "And so here ends my very creditable (after eleven years) lyrical passage".[13] Kipling provides excellent vignettes of life in mess and barrackroom, but his own awareness of being an outsider leads to frequent faults in tone: "The talk rose higher and higher, and the Regimental Band played between the courses, *as is the immemorial custom*".[14] That last phrase overstresses what should have been left implicit, and when, a few lines later, Kipling describes the drinking of the Queen's health, his punning comparison between the sacraments of mess and mass inflates, rather offensively, the value of the military ritual. Such overemphasis is a recurrent defect in his portrayal of Army life, whereas Waugh brings to the same material a perfect blend of knowledge and detachment, of enthusiasm and stylistic tact, of love and irony. Guy rejoices in the Halberdiers because of their courage, efficiency, kindliness, and good fellowship, their traditions, their ceremonial, their sense of hierarchy. And Waugh rejoices with him, though retaining some awareness of the limitations of this mode of vision in an age of total war:

> At length when the cloth was drawn for dessert, the brass departed and the strings came down from the minstrels' gallery and stationed themselves in the window embrasure. Now there was silence over all the diners while the musicians softly bowed and plucked. It all seemed a long way from Tony's excursions in no-man's-land; farther still, immeasurably far, from the frontier of Christendom where the great battle had been fought and lost; from those secret forests where the trains were, even then, while the Halberdiers and their guests sat bemused by wine and harmony, rolling east and west with their doomed loads.

This is one of the few points where the narrator registers a sense of the inadequacy of the hero's responses: how inadequate they are we do not learn in full till *Unconditional Surrender*, but even now, with the Halberdiers representing an ideal of chivalric order, we are warned of adjustments to be made (alas) all too soon:

> Those days ... he realized much later, were his honeymoon, the full consummation of his love of the Royal Corps of Halberdiers. After them came domestic routine, much loyalty and affection, many good things shared, but intervening and overlaying them all the multitudinous, sad little discoveries of marriage, familiarity, annoyance, imperfections noted, discord.

That discord is as fully rendered as the harmony. Waugh excels in his portrayal of the grit in the military machine – the stupidities, "flaps", inefficiencies, rivalries, personal antagonisms – culminating in the injustice Guy suffers after Apthorpe's death and his estrangement from the Corps.

Yet it is important to note the limits of his disillusion. The Halberdiers may fall short of the perfection he had once attributed to them, but they remain a good regiment, efficient, disciplined, and brave, and these are virtues Waugh was never to repudiate. Writing in 1951 to an historian of the sad campaign in Crete, he mentions "the heartening appearance on the last day when discipline everywhere was low, of a small detachment of the Welch Regiment under a captain, marching in with their equipment in perfect order".[15] In that nether world of Crete as Waugh so brilliantly portrays it – that Inferno of defeat, disorder, shame – the Halberdiers preserve their honour untarnished. Amid the chaos Colonel Tickeridge and his companion are "cleanshaven . . . , all their equipment in place, just as they had appeared during battalion exercises at Penkirk"; "everything was in order" in the Halberdiers' defensive position, where we glimpse them fighting a model holding action; and although after X Commando they seem rather lacking in sophistication, their limitations and strengths are intimately related. (" 'They say it's *sauve qui peut* now', said Fido. 'Don't know the expression', said Colonel Tickeridge.")

Courage for Waugh remains one of the cardinal virtues, and cowardice an unforgivable sin – Fido Hound lying his way ruthlessly towards safety, Ivor Claire deserting his own men, the Yugoslav partisans failing to support Ritchie-Hook in his last battle. In this world of evil, treachery, and cowardice, the Halberdiers' is the life of Do Well, and it is a malignity of Fate that prevents Guy three times over from accompanying them into battle, so that he is left to face other, deeper crises in which their virtues are of no avail.

These crises involve agonizing reappraisals of his own habitual assumptions and beliefs. For nearly two years the war's infinite complexity of pain and pleasure had been accompanied for Guy by an overbalance of enjoyment. For X Commando he had come to feel a deep affection not untouched by what Edmund Wilson calls the "beglamored snobbery" of *Brideshead Revisited*.[16] His brother officers seemed the living embodiment of an obsolescent but noble aristocratic ideal: " 'The Flower of the Nation', Ian Kilbannock had ironically called them. He was not far wrong." And for Guy their fineness was epitomized in Ivor Claire:

[He] remembered Claire as he first saw him in the Roman spring in the afternoon sunlight amid the embosoming cypresses of the Borghese Gardens, putting his horse faultlessly over the jumps, concentrated as a man in prayer. Ivor Claire, Guy thought, was the fine flower of them all. He was quintessential England, the man Hitler had not taken into account, Guy thought.

Bernard Bergonzi aptly compares Guy's mood and idiom here with Charles Ryder's in some of the least inhibited passages of *Brideshead*, but the author stands now in a different relation to his hero, and the syntax of that final sentence shows the narrator hinting that Guy's certainties may be unfounded. Cherished prejudices on the relation between heroism and breeding are being jettisoned, however reluctantly. Sarum Smith, who was as socially detestable as Trimmer, behaves rather well in Crete ("He was not a particularly attractive man, but man he was"); while Ivor's cowardice shatters an illusion dear to Waugh as well as to his hero – the belief in a peculiarly aristocratic virtue.[17] This individual failure is soon swamped, however, in the general dishonour of Britain's alliance with Russia. Now, for Guy, the clear moral issues of the war have been confused, its just cause contaminated. He had thought of it as a Crusade:

> Now that hallucination was dissolved, like the whales and turtles on the voyage from Crete, and he was back after less than two years' pilgrimage in a Holy Land of illusion in the old ambiguous world, where priests were spies and gallant friends proved traitors and his country was led blundering into dishonour.

Dishonour is indeed more widely prevalent than Guy yet realizes. The narrator's standards throughout *Officers and Gentlemen* have again been close to the hero's, but the story has been told less exclusively from his point of view. We have been shown many episodes of which Guy is unaware. We know, as he does not, the full extent of Major Hound's disgrace. We have seen Virginia sink to taking Trimmer as a temporary lover. We know how Ivor's betrayal of the values of his caste is paralleled by Ian Kilbannock's: the journalist-peer's cynicism, amusing at first, is revealed as hateful and corrupting when he becomes the main agent of Virginia's final degradation, forcing her against her will into a prolonged liaison with Trimmer. The latter's contemptible commando "raid" stands in obvious contrast to Guy's patrol at Dakar or the agony of Crete (though his scramble for the boat is an ironic forecast of Ivor Claire's). And his build-up as a national hero is symptomatic – we suppose – of the replacement of truth and honour by propaganda as the Modern Age girds on its arms.

It is through this darker world that Guy moves in *Unconditional Surrender*. On completing *Officers and Gentlemen* Waugh "knew that a third volume was needed" but "did not then feel confident that [he] was able to provide it";[18] indeed more than five years were to pass before he began on *Unconditional Surrender*. His doubt and delay may be attributed in part to his distaste for the material he knew he had to handle in this volume – Crouchback's experiences in Yugoslavia, the final defacing of his own romantic images of war, the deeper probing into his hero's motives and ideals. The atmosphere is one of melancholy verging on despair. The knight's sword of the prologue to *Men at Arms* is replaced by the Sword of Stalingrad, symbolic tribute to what Guy sees as a cruel and evil ally. (The trains in the secret forests had rolled east as well as west with their doomed loads.) Theories of conspiracy, which provided material for farce in earlier volumes, assume sinister significance as Sir Ralph and his communist associates begin to influence the aims and conduct of the war. Treachery and betrayal of trust are now almost commonplaces of behaviour, and even men of honour like Brigadier Cape find themselves having to acquiesce in deeds of shame. The prevailing darkness is of course continually lightened by sardonic comedy, but the only real alternative to despair is offered by Guy's father:

> "The Mystical Body doesn't strike attitudes and stand on its dignity [he writes to Guy]. It accepts suffering and injustice. It is ready to forgive at the first hint of compunction . . . Quantitative judgments don't apply. If only one soul was saved that is full compensation for any amount of loss of 'face'."

These words, acquiring new solemnity from Mr. Crouchback's death and funeral, go on reverberating in Guy's mind until he finds their application to his own life. In remarrying Virginia, down and out now and with child by Trimmer, he is reversing all conventional ideas of individual and family honour.

"Knights errant [he says in self-justification] used to go out looking for noble deeds. I don't think I've ever in my life done a single, positively unselfish action. I certainly haven't gone out of my way to find opportunities. Here was something most unwelcome, put into my hands; something which I believe the Americans describe as 'beyond the call of duty'; not the normal behaviour of an officer and a gentleman; something they'll laugh about in Bellamy's."

His chivalric quest is directed no longer towards adventure, comradeship, and victory: it is now a lonely mission of self-sacrifice. Not the easy sacrifice of his own life in battle, but the sacrifice of his personal honour and the pure lineage of which his father was so proud. To give his name to Trimmer's bastard is the most unwelcome thing Guy could have dreamed of: he accepts it in the hope that the soul of the unborn child may thus be saved, for to his new way of thinking that would be "full compensation for any amount of loss of 'face' ".

In 1955 Waugh had announced that in the next volume he hoped to deal with "Crouchback's realization that no good comes from public causes; only private causes of the soul".[19] And for Guy the possibility of simple heroic action is now gone forever. The decline and death of his old hero Ritchie-Hook are emblematic of Waugh's altered vision. In Yugoslavia he finds himself helpless in face of the partisans' inertia, tyranny, and ignorant suspicion, their preoccupation with taking over the country rather than with fighting Germans. There are obvious temptations here to retreat into mere comfortable indignation, but confronted with the sufferings of the Jewish refugees, the archetypal victims of this war, Guy is forced to search his own heart more deeply and acknowledge the guilt he shares with Communist and Nazi:

"Is there any place that is free from evil [asks Mme. Kanyi]? It is too simple to say that only the Nazis wanted war. These communists wanted it too. It was the only way in which they could come to power. Many of my people wanted it, to be revenged on the Germans, to hasten the creation of the national state. It seems to me there was a will to war, a death wish, everywhere. Even good men thought their private honour would be satisfied by war. They could assert their manhood by killing and being killed. They would accept hardships in recompense for having been selfish and lazy. Danger justified privilege. I knew Italians – not very many perhaps – who felt this. Were there none in England?"

"God forgive me", said Guy, "I was one of them".

With this realization he

> had come to the end of the crusade to which he had devoted himself on the tomb of Sir Roger. His life as a Halberdier was over. All the stamping of the barrack square and the biffing of imaginary strongholds were finding their consummation in one frustrated act of mercy.

When that one act of mercy *is* frustrated – when all his efforts on behalf of the Jews result only in their becoming Displaced Persons in Italy instead of Yugoslavia, and when he finds that the Kanyis have been executed because of the very interest he had shown in them – then Guy's cup of bitterness is full to overflowing, and the main narrative comes to an end.

This schematic account distorts by stressing theme at the expense of local excellence: the trilogy, with its highly wrought art, clearly proposes to itself such delight from the whole as is compatible with a distinct gratification from each component part. But this gratification, however intense, must not be allowed to obscure the total pattern of meaning which the component parts serve to create. Steven Marcus, writing on *Men at Arms* and *Officers and Gentlemen* in 1956, suggested that "the qualities that make [these novels] interesting and worthy are not organic to their structure or their moral implication" – that their charm lies rather in the "buoyant and indestructible characters" and "the rich accumulation of anecdotes about the eternal mismanagement of war".[20] That view is hard to sustain with the finished work before us: Guy Crouchback's progress is so clearly and impressively the thematic core (though presented, certainly, in a dense context of admirably rendered circumstance). We do delight, of course, in the particulars that Marcus praises, but central to the pleasure the whole trilogy provides is our sense of being involved in a progressive exploration of experience. We cannot tell whether the final form of the sequence was predetermined, in the sense of its being planned in detail before Waugh began to write, or whether he made certain moral discoveries and artistic decisions in the course of composition. But we feel as we read that the author as well as the hero is achieving new self-knowledge, growing in moral insight, and we too are involved in the process: it is our own imaginative participation stage by stage in Guy's experience (including his illusions) that makes the conclusion so disturbingly effective. Paradoxically, however, this exploratory mode is combined with finished artistry. We find ourselves passing from light-hearted comedy to tragical mirth, from romantic idealism to disenchantment, from gay acceptance of life's variety to a deeper moral seriousness than we could ever have foreseen, yet these later developments are so closely connected, formally and thematically, with what has gone before that we have no sense of discontinuity, breaches in decorum, or changing conventions. The completed narrative satisfies both as aesthetic pattern and as moral vision.

To these historical accuracy is at times subordinated. The Yugoslavian episode, for example, fulfils perfectly its rhetorical function of mediating the hero's (and the author's) final disillusion with war. Yet it is demonstrably unfair as an account of the partisans' war effort. Fitzroy Maclean, who headed the British Military Mission, confirms several of Waugh's impressions, but he and his observers were convinced that the partisans were fighting the Germans and fighting them effectively. Having served with them for a year and a half, he acknowledges their considerable virtues as well as their defects, and gives a much less pessimistic account of the whole conduct of that Adriatic war. (We note, for example, that the part played by two rocket-firing Beaufighters in the reduction of Valjevo was very different from the futile show of strength which Waugh describes in the air-strike on an isolated blockhouse.)[21] Maclean was, certainly, a member of Tito's entourage: things may have looked rather different at the local level, and we shall have to wait for the official history of S.O.E. in Yugoslavia to estimate the precise degree of Waugh's distortion. It may be less than we suppose: when he portrays the Spaniards of Hookforce as disorderly, rapacious, unreliable in battle, we might attribute this to xenophobic anti-Republican bias — if we had not read accounts of the behaviour in Crete of the Spanish Company of Layforce, the Commando Brigade in which Waugh himself served. Nevertheless, an element of distortion is undoubtedly

involved in his presentation of this theatre of war: we are faced
with a conflict between the novelist's right to mould reality to
a truth at once more personal and more philosophical than
history's and his obligation to hold the mirror up to nature,
showing things as they "really" are. In literary terms Waugh's
portrayal of the partisans is convincing though one-sided: in a
hundred years it may be accepted as readily as Dickens's dis-
tortions are, as elements in a self-justifying autonomous
artistic vision. But we are close enough to the events to feel
uneasily that moral and psychological insights which compel
respect are being mediated in terms of extreme political
prejudice.

Prejudice, indeed, lies near the heart of Waugh's achievement – as of every satirist's. Through it he often confronts us
with partial truths that we would rather not acknowledge.
(Heterodoxy is always the other man's doxy, and accusations of
prejudice are usually made when our own prejudices are
offended.) Furthermore, the satirist's deliberate restriction of
sympathy, his refusal to see both sides of a question, his
unshakable confidence in his own values, give a sharp distorted
focus, a mode of perception which is the basis of Waugh's wit
(as well as Pope's). It amuses while revealing at least an aspect
of the truth – about P.T. instructors, or Highland lairds, or
Scottish Nationalists, or American war correspondents, or the
uncharted horrors of life in the R.A.F. From such comic
prejudice, indulged even to the point of fantasy, we derive an
essentially amoral delight, which can, however, be combined
with the satiric perception of error, with joy in the oddity and
variety of human nature, or even with bitter disillusion (for the
reactionary novelist may find, like Mr. Scott-King, "a peculiar
relish in contemplating the victories of barbarism"). A writer's
prejudices, like his obsessions, are indeed a reservoir of power.
Uncontrolled, they limit his achievement; carefully exploited,
they enhance it; challenged and transcended, they can convert it
into major art. Waugh's trilogy presents a uniquely successful
fusion of prejudice indulged with prejudices overcome, as the
vision that seemed by its very nature static shows itself continually capable of change and growth. That Guy's final position (or Waugh's) is not our own need not disturb us, for it is
the intensity of the process as much as the conclusions reached

that gives it its validity, wins our respect, and earns the hero his right to a wryly unconventional happy ending.

"Things have turned out very conveniently for Guy", says Box-Bender in the final sentence of the trilogy. But the Epilogue, with its changed point of view, has excluded us from the hero's consciousness and Box-Bender is himself an imperceptive unreliable observer, so that we are left to judge for ourselves the degree of irony in that conclusion. The Epilogue shows the Modern Age triumphant. Traditional values are flouted or forgotten in the dreariness of post-war London, where Waugh's social distaste still operates (not ineffectively) as moral judgement. The world of politics is rejected now with Swiftian contempt: England is ruled, we gather, by knaves like Gilpin instead of fools like Elderberry and Box-Bender, but the difference hardly seems significant. Good men may prosper, but so, more noticeably, do the wicked: the Castello Crouchback, memorial to Hermione's happy marriage with which the trilogy began, is soon to house the unholy loves of Ludovic and the Loot. From this sad world Tony has withdrawn to a monastery, Guy to the life of a country gentleman. Comparatively wealthy now, he has re-established himself at Broome – in the Lesser House, admittedly – and married the daughter of an old Catholic family like his own. She manages the home farm and bears his sons; he rarely comes to London; when we glimpse him on this last occasion he is meeting his old Commando friends (the "happy warriors") at a reunion in Bellamy's. So many fragments has he shored against his ruin that this might seem a simple case of virtue rewarded (and an unthinking reversion on the author's part to the ideals of *Officers and Gentlemen*) – except that we know Guy's heir is Trimmer's son. He has never repudiated his act of compassion or its consequences, which were not ended by Virginia's death. This is his secret sacrifice, the price he has paid and continues to pay for spiritual peace, having helped, he fears, to do so much evil. We cannot say with confidence that Guy is happy, but the modicum of worldly happiness he has is well deserved. His distinction is less military than moral, and he would hardly have qualified for the traditional Sword of Honour; but as we contemplate his progress we perceive that in an age when honour and swords seem equally archaic, when the title of this trilogy is certain therefore to be read ironically, one sword at least was not dishonoured.

NOTES

1 *The Crazy Fabric: Essays in Irony* (London, 1965), p. 187.

2 This statement appeared not in the volume itself but on the dust-jacket.

3 *A Little Learning: The First Volume of an Autobiography* (London, 1964), pp. 27-8.

4 *Sword of Honour* (London, 1965), p. 9.

5 Malcolm Bradbury, *Evelyn Waugh* (Writers and Critics Series, Edinburgh, 1964), p. 109.

6 *Sword of Honour*, p. 9.

7 Only occasionally do we applaud Waugh's second thoughts. Colonel Tickeridge's dismissive comment on Guy at the end of *Men at Arms* belied his essential kindliness; the additional effect of bleak disillusion was achieved illegitimately (we may feel) at the expense of consistent characterisation. The removal of this short passage, therefore, is a definite improvement.

8 Unpublished MS quoted by F. J. Stopp, *Evelyn Waugh: Portrait of an Artist* (London, 1958), p. 32.

9 Donat O'Donnell (Conor Cruise O'Brien), *Maria Cross* (London, 1953), pp. 125-6.

10 Bernard Bergonzi, "Evelyn Waugh's Gentleman", *The Critical Quarterly*, v (1963), 23.

11 *Sword of Honour*, p. 9.

12 F. J. Stopp, *op. cit.*, p. 168.

13 *Goodbye to All That* (London, 1931), pp. 117-22.

14 "The Man Who Was", *Life's Handicap*, Sussex ed. (London, 1937-9), iv, 108 (my italics).

15 Letter to D. M. Davin, quoted by I. M. G. Stewart, *The Struggle for Crete* (London, 1966), p. 469.

16 *Classics and Commercials* (London, 1951), p. 302.

17 Cf. Bernard Bergonzi, *op. cit.*, p. 35: "The profundity of Guy's wrongness has immensely far-reaching implications. If the quintessential gentleman is not to be trusted, then the whole scheme of values that has so far pervaded Waugh's serious fiction falls to the ground. An Ivor Claire is not necessarily better than a Hooper or a Trimmer, and the hero-worshipping of a Charles Ryder becomes altogether suspect."

18 Statement on the dust-jacket of the first edition of *Unconditional Surrender*.

19 F. J. Stopp, *op. cit.*, p. 46.

20 "Evelyn Waugh and the Art of Entertainment", *Partisan Review*, XXIII (1956), 354.

21 *Eastern Approaches* (London, 1949), p. 499.

Rayner Heppenstall and the
Nouveau Roman

[i]

A student of the English novel who has been struck by the
brilliance and originality of Rayner Heppenstall's *The Connecting
Door* and *The Woodshed* (both published in 1962) may well
wonder how it is that this writer seems to have enjoyed such
scant recognition from critics and scholars. To a French reader,
whose thinking about the novel has been influenced by the
achievement of the *nouveaux romanciers*, Rayner Heppenstall
appears to be one of the few English novelists who have done
truly experimental work, one of the very few who can – and
wish to – compete with, say, Michel Butor or Nathalie Sarraute,
on their own difficult ground. The scarcity of serious critical
attention to Rayner Heppenstall's recent fiction is all the more
surprising as both *The Connecting Door* and *The Woodshed* are
obviously "critics' (and professors') meat" (as Heppenstall
himself calls *Ulysses* in *The Fourfold Tradition*, p. 153). It is to
a substantial serving of that meat that I help myself in the
present essay, while attempting to show the connection between
Heppenstall's work and the French *nouveau roman*.

Before discussing in detail *The Connecting Door* and *The
Woodshed*, I should like to glance at the rest of Rayner Heppenstall's work. Two of his novels, *The Greater Infortune* and *The
Lesser Infortune*, are out of print at present, and with these, in
spite of a good deal of revision and compression, he has appa-

rently failed to satisfy himself. I shall therefore omit them from discussion here. The remaining work consists of three books combining criticism with biographical and/or autobiographical information, and the author's earliest novel, *The Blaze of Noon*.

Four Absentees (1960) is a history of the author's relations with Dylan Thomas, George Orwell (whom Rayner Heppenstall is reluctant to call by that name, having known him mostly as Eric Blair), Eric Gill, and John Middleton Murry. The friendships described in it were all fairly close, but often stormy, and it is only in the case of Eric Gill that Heppenstall seems to have felt something like whole-hearted admiration and affection.

The Fourfold Tradition (1961) is a more ambitious work. The title refers to the existence in both English and French literature of a second as well as a first tradition, so that the literary relationship between the two countries, the interaction of the two literatures, is at least a fourfold process. The central notion is brilliant and it is exploited with great intelligence nourished by genuine culture, although the treatment is not. Preferring always to write about what interests him at the moment, Heppenstall devotes a stimulating chapter on Marcel Proust not to showing that writer's place in the "Fourfold Tradition" – or even to determining whether he is part of the first or second French tradition – but to vindicating the character of Morel in *A la Recherche du temps perdu* against the author's alleged unfairness to him and to discussing the efficiency of Proust's English translators. For this reason, and in other ways also, *The Fourfold Tradition* provides much valuable information about Rayner Heppenstall himself.

The Intellectual Part (1963) is straightforwardly subtitled "An Autobiography". It is on the whole chronological and its main stress *is* on the political, literary, and otherwise intellectual sides of Rayner Heppenstall's life. But more private incidents – if anything can be more private than a man's intellectual evolution – also come into the picture, and the reader is treated to the author's military, professional, and medical history. *The Intellectual Part* is altogether a fascinating book. One feels after reading it and the other two works described in the foregoing paragraphs that one knows Rayner Heppenstall at least to a certain extent.

The Blaze of Noon, Heppenstall's first novel, was published in
1939. It was reissued several times after the war and even
reached the paperback stage. In 1947, it was translated into
French. The latest edition was published in 1962, apparently in
the wake of *The Connecting Door*, whose publishers, Messrs.
Barrie and Rockliff, now had in their catalogue all the works that
Rayner Heppenstall himself seemed to wish to be known by.
The Blaze of Noon is told in the first person by a blind masseur.
It is a literary feat of imaginative identification and a very good
novel, beautifully written, powerful, and original. But it is not
original in any technical sense, for the narrative is chrono-
logically ordered, with only two major flashback chapters (III
and VII), one about the narrator's past and the other about the
earlier history of the chief female character. Both are neatly
placed after the first and third fifths of the story.

From these four books, most readers, I think, will emerge
with the same conclusion: that Heppenstall *cannot* write un-
intelligently or uninterestingly about any subject whatever.

[ii]

The Connecting Door and *The Woodshed* were written (within a
few months of each other) between *The Fourfold Tradition* and
The Intellectual Part. My impression is that the writing of the
former critical work and the reflection it involved must have
stimulated the creative process which resulted in the two novels.
Possibly also, the successful writing of the novels encouraged
Rayner Heppenstall to compose his autobiography.

Some general characteristics of Rayner Heppenstall's art and
mind are apparent in the two novels under present consideration.
For one thing, he takes a serious interest in craftsmanship and
preserves *almost* to the end superb control over his material.
Critical candour compels me to admit, however, that the close
of a Heppenstall novel is normally inferior to its beginning. The
same thing has been said of most of his contemporaries, French
as well as English, and of his greatest predecessors (Dickens,
Thackeray, Charlotte Brontë). In any case, it is a fact that the
end of *The Blaze of Noon* betrays a certain hurry, that in
The Woodshed the most attractive and ingenious of the narrative devices come to be somewhat perfunctorily resorted to,

and that in *The Connecting Door*, a short book of some 160 small pages, the central Strasbourg episode is eked out by a later episode in Frankfurt, written in a style of naïve-clever journalese, whose flippancy and triviality form a disagreeable contrast with the poetical profundity in the bulk of that novel. This may well be a deliberate effect, however, since the narrator has clearly evolved towards a more superficial kind of personality by gradually relinquishing his earlier intransigence. The suggestion may be that it is possible to come to terms with oneself only at the cost of such sacrifices. Similar purposes may also account for the slighter falling-off in the tone of *The Blaze of Noon* and *The Woodshed*. But it is difficult not to connect this phenomenon at the same time with a statement in *The Fourfold Tradition*. In an interesting paragraph (pp. 149-50) about the way in which books get to be written, both by professional authors and by "subsidized amateurs", Heppenstall says: "From my own experience and from the communications of other practising novelists, I take it that a painful *accidie* normally supervenes just past the halfway mark. This has to be accepted and the book, however pointless it may have come to seem, pushed on with and completed by an effort of will." Heppenstall's seriousness as a craftsman seems to me to be confirmed rather than impaired by his perception of the difficulties of the novelist's task.

Among Heppenstall's personal characteristics are to be found a number of "pet abominations", almost Ruskin-like in their vividness, but these on the whole contribute less to his writings than the things he significantly likes: sex, places, objects, time, language. His interest in sex and his Lawrence-like frankness about its details were first brilliantly advertised in *The Blaze of Noon*, a fact which did not escape the more hostile reviewers in 1939. In the later novels, there is less insistence on sexual expertise and prowess, though the reader is made to understand that the narrator, Harold Atha, is an efficient lover of his wife (variously known as "Blod" and "Old Flowerface") and occasionally of other women as well. He even goes out of his way once in each book to put in a little piece in rather questionable taste: in *The Connecting Door* there is an elaborate paragraph about his drinking sherry out of Blod's navel (p. 115) and in *The Woodshed* a reference to the fact that the number of "intimate occasions" with her "must by now approach four figures" (p. 158). Poor Blod!

Heppenstall's interest in objects and places is evidenced by the wonderful, Robbe-Grillet-like accuracy of his descriptions. His talent in this respect can unfortunately not be illustrated by brief quotations taken out of their context. I must merely record here that the streets and houses of Strasbourg (*The Connecting Door*) and Hinderholme (*The Woodshed*), as well as the outward appearance and the very clothes of the characters assume in the reader's eyes a concrete presence.

His interest in time, like that of several major French novelists, Marcel Proust and Michel Butor among others, is intense. Much of his originality as a novelist depends on his ability to manipulate the events of his narrator's life out of their chronological arrangement while gradually and efficiently suggesting to the reader the order in which they actually happened. He has thought much and written well about the functioning of memory. In *The Blaze of Noon*, there are two especially fine pages beginning: "Memory is in one sense or another the clue to all things. It is the continuum, the ambience in which all our disjointed moments cohere into a whole" (p. 178). In a magnificent passage of *The Connecting Door*, the narrator is shown as simultaneously seeing the Strasbourg cathedral in the present (1948) during a concert and perceiving its past existence through many centuries (pp. 44-5). Time, for Heppenstall, also, assumes the specific form of tenses. At the end of *The Intellectual Part*, there is a lucid discussion of these problems (pp. 214-5) and of the way in which the novelist – either in English or in French – can best solve them by using the "continuing present".

The close attention paid to tenses is only part of his fascinated interest in language and languages. In his experience an interest in language cannot be purely literary, but has to be linguistic as well. His own close contact with French, particularly during his three years at Leeds University and his one year in Strasbourg, has obviously been a decisive influence on his literary career. *The Fourfold Tradition* is the culminating point of his reflections on French and English. In that book he complains that refusing to learn French is "an aim in which English studies at Oxford or Cambridge will give any young man every assistance. For nowadays it is strangely possible to be at once an educated person and monoglot" (p. 246), although "we cannot live without France" and "If we are men of letters or just tolerably well-read, France will mean to us in the first place French writers and the French language".(p. 247). Yet it is in *The Intellectual Part* that Heppenstall provides the most systematic account of what he thinks French has done for him: "A notion I had was that, by too much reading (and a fair amount of talking) in a foreign language, a writer might lose the mastery of his own, which was his strong rock. I was, I felt, beginning to think in French. I now find the notion absurd and am inclined to take the opposite view, *viz.*, that only through constant rubbing against a foreign language can a writer achieve mastery of his own. I am further inclined to say that the principal foreign language against which an English writer rubs must be French." (p. 120). In his novels, therefore, Heppenstall does rub against French again and again. In *The Blaze of Noon*, the blind narrator begins to rebel against his new condition and compares himself to "a man on his first solitary voyage abroad, who knows the foreign language and uses it when necessary, but who will not learn to think in the foreign language and so remains unliberated in mind, closed up in the darkness of his own thoughts and pinned to his native shore, oppressed by the bridges that he refuses to burn".(p. 59). In *The Connecting Door*, the story takes place in Strasbourg, where the narrator, an Englishman, lives amidst French people, but close to Germany, so that he can indulge in particularly complex linguistic games. In *The Woodshed* there are other linguistic games, but they are all-English and concerned mainly with the comparison between North Country and Southern pronunciation and syntax. Heppenstall's references to the French language show that his knowledge of it is astonishingly, almost unfailingly, accurate and idiomatic.

[iii]

Heppenstall's major achievement in both *The Connecting Door* and *The Woodshed* lies in his original approach to story-telling and characterization. Such technical aspects are, at any rate, the occasion of the present article. In *The Intellectual Part* and to a lesser degree in *The Fourfold Tradition* Rayner Heppenstall has written about the novelist's art and the genesis of his own work. What he has to tell is extremely interesting and in some respects illuminating. The actual writing of *The Connecting Door* took up, he tells us, only two months, but parts of it had been written some seventeen years before as an "abortive longer novel", first called *The Idiot Questioner*, then *The Alibi*. Three radio scripts, two about Strasbourg in 1948 and one about Frankfurt-am-Main in 1949 were also drawn on. The first earlier use he had made of the observer's division into three selves belonging to different periods was in the radio programme "The Return Journey" (a journey back to Strasbourg), while another of these programmes "Portrait of a City", furnished a prior exercise in interior monologue. During the writing of both *The Connecting Door* and *The Woodshed*, he found himself increasingly diverging from autobiographical fact, developing a new time-dimension and adopting a present-tense framework for a past story. Some of his statements at this point deserve being quoted in full: "In my own life and in respect of other people's lives, I have become increasingly preoccupied by the past within a present which moves forward constantly into a previous future, so that the past recedes at every moment . . . It seems natural, therefore, to me, to tell a past story within a present-tense narrative framework, which may be either interior monologue or the day-by-day notes of a man presumed writing."(*The Intellectual Part*, p. 215). Similar comments are found in *The Fourfold Tradition*: "The earliest novels were first-person *picaresque*, with, moreover, a tendency to the past indefinite, to which, it may be noted, the Latin spoken languages all tend, so that the past definite of French fiction is unnatural to begin with. It is perhaps natural in English outside London. No mean *raconteur*, the Cockney almost invariably tells his stories in the present tense . . ."(p. 158). And again: "In most kinds of writing there is some autobiographical element. In novels it is generally strong. The protagonists of young men's novels are rarely anything but young men of a background similar to the novelist's own (as he grows older, so do they), until he starts harking back nostalgically to his youth."(p. 253).

The Connecting Door is based on the central idea of a third visit paid in 1948 to Strasbourg, which, however, like the characters in Nathalie Sarraute's novels, is unnamed, by an Englishman of thirty-six who had lived there as a student in 1931 and had returned once before in 1936. The narrator, who is met at the station by Harold (aged nineteen) and Atha (aged twenty-four) remains unidentified, but in *The Woodshed* he will appear as Harold Atha all through. His two companions in Strasbourg are semi-imaginary figures and earlier selves; the real state of affairs is suggested from the very beginning, for there is no trickery in the matter; there is merely a vividly original presentation of psychological perspectives. There is even what must be termed psychological realism. The conversations of the narrator with Harold (pp. 79, 119) and his discussions of Atha's character with him (pp. 120-1 and 129-32) are such as a man might conceivably hold with his former selves on revisiting his – or their – former haunts. The narrator and Harold refer to Atha as "our middleterm" (p. 120). The dates are disclosed indirectly, but effectively, by a number of such landmarks as "It was five years since Atha had crossed the Channel. Until last year, I myself had not set foot on the European mainland for eleven years" (p. 50) or "That summer, he was going to the Olympic games in Berlin" (p. 75). At the end, which concerns the narrator's later return to Europe, a fourth self is superimposed on the picture which has by then emerged and taken shape in the reader's mind. This creates a useful distance from which to take final stock of the Harold-Atha-narrator group.

There are in *The Connecting Door* a number of interesting gimmicks – I am using that word because it is employed by Heppenstall himself when discussing Michel Butor's *La Modification* (in *The Fourfold Tradition*, p. 268). Two of these, the iteration of concrete details ("four stories of red carpeted stairs", "the Hon. Bert's Union Jack") and the contamination of three distinct cross-Channel trips into one narrative (pp. 50-1) are extremely Butor-like, though the first is equally characteristic of Alain Robbe-Grillet. More importantly, the end of the novel occurs at a moment of decisive suspense, when the narrator is about to push open a door behind which he does not know whom he will find or whether some new light is not about to be cast on the past, linking it to the present.

But the main strength of the elaborate technique used in *The*

Connecting Door lies in the narrator's distinct attitudes towards his three successive or juxtaposed selves. Of his later or present self he speaks with a kind of resigned complacency; he manages to live on good terms with himself, or would do so but for his fond remembrance of what young Harold had been. Of Harold he speaks with infinite and indeed touching tenderness, a little like David Copperfield recalling his youthful foolishness. "He felt a bit of a fool, but he did not mind."(p. 18). The foolishness of the very young, and especially one's own folly in the days when the promises of the future still shone undimmed in front of us, are by no means despicable. Besides, Harold was a poet, like Rayner Heppenstall before the war. This favouring of youth is greatly enhanced by the narrator's treatment of Atha and the dislike of the latter which he shares with Harold.

Atha's name is generally accompanied by some ironical or derogatory epithet. He is "not-quite-so-young Atha", "moderately-young Atha", "fairly-young Atha" (p. 46), "ridiculous Atha", "solemn Atha", "thoughtful Atha" (p. 51), "reasonably-well-connected Atha", "impulsive Atha" (p. 58), "not-quite-unconverted Atha" (p. 59), "lugubrious Atha" (p. 60), and the game goes on, it seems, forever. There are no fewer than ten other epithets coupled with Atha's name between p. 64 and the final "wintry Atha" of p. 157. But if one is tempted to look upon this game as tedious, too long drawn out, and gratuitous, it will be found on second thought to have a precise purpose, since the reader is thereby made to *feel* the lack of any pleasant intimacy between the narrator and his Atha-stage, which happens to have been both his religious-minded and his suicidally inclined stage.

The Connecting Door does not make easy reading. There are moments when one would like to be helped by maps, time-charts, genealogical tables (the maps and genealogies would be even more useful in *The Woodshed*), and the book has to be read at least twice before it can be fully appreciated. In that respect, it is indeed what Ludovic Janvier has called the *nouveau roman* in general, *"Une parole exigeante"* (such is the title of his critical study – published in 1964 – of the new French novel). But the effort demanded of the reader is rewarded by the high quality of the revelation afforded to him. He is shown, for instance, that Atha's quest for his past can only result in the discovery of change in himself, and that this is an agonizing experience; he may even be reminded of Rossetti's *House of Life*. Only at the end (p. 157) can the narrator write: "I am ghost-free".

The theme of the book seems to be the impermanence of human personality, and it is dramatically *shown* through Rayner Heppenstall's poetical device. The two earlier stages of Harold Atha's being he knows to have been himself; that is, he knows a number of facts about them and he knows that they are facts about himself, for he can remember the things they did, saw, wrote, and even felt at such moments. But he does not clearly experience the continuity of existence between such past moments and the present. Like Heppenstall, I believe that this is quite a common experience, and even one of the factors that make life so agonizingly difficult to live. Therefrom spring a good many of our anxieties; therefrom also our passionate quest for selfhood, a quest that may be conducted more or less consciously according to individual persons and moments. We all ask ourselves the question, Who am I? Our experience of ourselves in the present yields, and can yield, only a partial, confused, hurried, fluctuating, disappointing answer. We therefore, not unnaturally, turn to our own past for enlightenment. We can get a more orderly and coherent view of our past selves, but we do so in constant fear lest the sifting and ordering process which makes for a clearer picture should also make for a less faithful over-all impression. We see our past selves more clearly than we see our present selves because we enjoy greater detachment. But the very sense of detachment is a source of anguish, since it points to the want of continuity. I am not claiming that Heppenstall ever formulated the problem to himself in exactly those terms; but *The Connecting Door* undoubtedly suggests some such philosophical approach. Many novelists, like E. M. Forster (and perhaps William Golding) are overwhelmingly preoccupied with the problem of communication, that is, of communication with other human beings. Rayner Heppenstall seems to me to be overwhelmingly preoccupied with the problem of communication with oneself, or between one's successive selves (like William Golding again, at least in *Free Fall*). The situation Heppenstall has chosen to explore in *The Connecting Door* is admirably calculated to cast light on this problem. A man who, like his Harold Atha, revisits a place he has already visited twice before, at two distinct periods of his earlier development, is bound to come up against two of his former selves. This, again, I take to be a common experience; it has been more than once casually referred to by various novelists. In *David Copperfield*, for instance, Dickens writes: "When I tread the old ground [between Southwark and Blackfriars] I do not wonder that I seem to see and pity, going on before me, an innocent, romantic boy . . ."(chapter XI). Heppenstall's distinctive merit lies in his having more systematically and more graphically presented a similar encounter, and thus contributed more significantly to our understanding of the psychological phenomena involved in it.

[iv]

The Woodshed is partly a sequel to *The Connecting Door* and tells of incidents in Harold Atha's life. Many of these are of earlier date than Harold's and Atha's visits to Strasbourg, though the present-tense substratum of the narrative belongs to the same more recent period. In *The Woodshed* Harold Atha tells about his English and Welsh experience and makes only a passing reference to his "Rhineland pilgrimages" (p. 23). Four bulky chapters followed by a brief Coda constitute the book.

In *The Woodshed*, Harold Atha is first seen on a train. He has been abruptly summoned from Gwaelod in Wales (where he was vacationing with his family) to his parents' home in Hinderholme, where his father is seriously ill. On the train Harold recalls his last visit to Hinderholme, less than a year before. When he reaches Hinderholme, he finds that his father has died. In the course of the next few days, he takes several walks through the streets of Hinderholme, especially in the district where his parents and he (as a child) had lived earlier. He sees a number of places connected with people and incidents which had had a formative influence on him. With the help of these and certain objects in the house – particularly photographs and books – he is enabled to reconstruct a somewhat fragmentary, yet tolerably coherent picture of the child and youth he had been. The cremation of his father's body is performed in Leeds, where Harold had attended the University, and this elicits a further batch of reminiscences and allows him to bring the narrative almost to the "Harold" stage of *The Connecting Door* in the psychological history of the narrator. In the Coda, Harold Atha concludes that he has now become finally detached from Hinderholme and his childhood and youth.

The historical chronology of *The Woodshed* is again established by means of a few landmarks, such as "on the first night of the black-out, nine years ago" (p. 33: 1939 + 9 = 1948) or "That was two years later, twenty-three years ago" (p. 65). Places are described in as great detail as ever, though it is perhaps somewhat difficult to visualize Radcliffe Road, with its 'passage' and back-to-back houses (pp. 46-7). Some use of brilliant narrative devices includes the railway journey already mentioned, and old photographs looked at by the narrator in the present which give rise to all sorts of memories of persons and incidents (e.g. pp. 37f. and again pp. 67f.). Most revealing of all is the long walk taken by the narrator through the streets where he had lived, played, worked, and made friends as a child. The associative process is thus enabled to work in a perfectly natural and life-like manner. Both in the Leeds and in the Hinderholme scenes the present experiences of the adult are interpolated at irregular intervals among the episodes of childhood and youth. As I said before, the present-tense connecting thread tends to become thinner at the end, and in chapter III the two years at Carlin Beck are related almost consecutively. Yet for all the complex method involved, the book is by no means a jumble of disconnected scenes and impressions. On the contrary. A passing reference (p. 51) to one Peter Holmes, for instance, will be taken up again and fully developed later (chapter III, pp. 153ff.). Every incident is made to fit neatly into the total pattern, though the various pieces of the puzzle crop up convincingly according to the easy rhythm of memory and association. The sense of over-all arrangement is sharpened by phrases like "But it is Carlin Beck I must think of, not Leeds . . ." (p. 125) or "I must go carefully now about the order in which things happened" (p. 165).

What finally emerges is a consciousness of patterned life, fully justifying the reflections indulged in by Harold Atha in his railway carriage at the beginning of the book: "If I had a secretary sitting opposite with shorthand notebook, or a dictaphone, I could just talk like this. They reckon about ten thousand words to the hour. In a journey of eight hours, you could finish a book. A man travelling somewhere for a purpose."(p. 18). Later he is writing on the train and hopes this will help isolate him from his fellow-passengers: "They might think I was doing my accounts. I am, in a way".(p. 23). The central theme of *The Woodshed*, like that of *The Connecting Door*, has to do with the encounter between a man and his past. But, whereas in *The Connecting Door* two distinct past selves belonging to clear-cut past episodes are given almost physical existence, in *The Woodshed* a longer and more remote period is brought back to life as a kaleidoscope of fragments, from which a pattern and a picture do eventually emerge. In both books intimate emotion is suggested and conviction subtly achieved.

[v]

The intrinsic interest and value of Rayner Heppenstall's novels thus appear to me to be considerable and to make him, in common with William Golding, one of the few truly and originally creative male novelists in England since the war. It remains to be seen how his achievement connects and compares with that of his French counterparts.

Of the two French novelists whom I regard as having made the most valuable contribution to the development of the *nouveau roman*, Nathalie Sarraute and Michel Butor, Heppenstall has written very intelligent criticism. Nathalie Sarraute's "suppression of personal names" and her tropisms (her "radical intuition") are adequately analysed in *The Fourfold Tradition* (pp. 258-9 and 269), though other critics regard her technique of the sous-conversation as her most striking invention. Heppenstall's comments on Michel Butor present a more curious case. He says that when he wrote *The Fourfold Tradition* he "had only looked at *La Modification* (and in consequence was to underrate him . . .)" (*The Intellectual Part*, p. 198). But in fact what he had written about Butor was extremely shrewd: "I do not think very highly of M. Butor's writing to date. He is, however, clearly a man of brilliant intuitions. In *La Modification* . . . he uses not one but two gimmicks of the first excellence. Of all the circumstances which make consciousness, in everybody, stream, a long train journey is the most typical . . . But M. Butor has further had the notion of making his protagonist not think of himself as 'I' but address himself in the second person (moreover, not as '*tu*' but as '*vous*'). I think people do this". (*The Fourfold Tradition*, p. 268). Later, he added: "In M. Butor's actual writing, I find some lack of inner tension, of Dr. Tillyard's 'intensity', of Dr. Leavis's 'significance' ". In comparison with M. Robbe-Grillet, he is a slack writer. He is clever and hard-working, but his observation is commonplace. He describes carefully, but without illumination."(p. 269).

It is rather a pity Heppenstall has not commented on *L'Emploi du temps*, in my opinion Butor's masterpiece, a book particularly likely to interest him, since it deals with a young Frenchman's contact with an English city (called Bleston in the novel, but very much like Manchester, where Butor had taught for a year). If Nathalie Sarraute is an unparalleled analyst of what goes on in people's minds during the conversations they take part in, and of what depths of feeling and anxiety lie behind the comparatively few words actually spoken, Michel Butor is a masterly explorer of the individual's anguished and hopeless quest for selfhood, which involves him in all the disconcerting vagaries of time never to be recaptured. This is neither "commonplace" nor "without illumination". Rayner Heppenstall's own contribution is different but in no way inferior. Like Sarraute and Butor, he has shown that the novel can still be used in new ways and that through new approaches and devices it can cast fresh light on the mysterious workings of the human mind. His own conclusion seems to me to be summed up in a significant passage at the end of *The Connecting Door*, where he writes: "That is all. I shall be granted no revelation about the long significance of my own life. No imaginative creation will be finished." (p. 163). This expresses the view – central, I believe, in Rayner Heppenstall's two "anti-novels" – that a man's life is his own ever unfinished imaginative creation and that he has to find out, if he can – but who can? – its significance.

What next? Inevitably one (especially the Dickens student) tends to "ask for more". As to our chances of getting it, two statements conflict. One is the final words of *The Woodshed*: "If I again let down the deep trawl of memory, I should bring up dabs and elvers by the ton. The catch would only be to throw back."(p. 189). The other is in *The Intellectual Part*; after completing *The Woodshed*, the author writes "I had started a further novel, but I put it aside, where it still is".(p. 209). Even if a further novel or novels remain "put aside", Rayner Heppenstall's ambition has been to a large extent justified and fulfilled. When he said that he would like to have been a writer of the same kind as Jouhandeau, he made his point clearer by adding "I should have liked to write, from day to day, simply about the moment and its concerns and any past matters which pressed on the memory, the prose being merely careful, transparent, exact, easy on eye and ear, varied only by the variety of the mind's approach to what it scrupulously dealt with, utterly shameless, wholly personal. That it was quite impossible is due to the rigid formality of British literary customs" (*The Intellectual Part*, p. 87). This I believe to be a fairly accurate definition of what, with the help or at least the encouragement of the French *nouveaux romanciers*, Rayner Heppenstall has indeed achieved in *The Connecting Door* and *The Woodshed*. He has broken through the "rigid formality of British literary customs". And the fact that he has been able to do so proves that these customs were not so rigid or so formal after all.

It would probably be absurd to contend that the new novelists' works (including Rayner Heppenstall's) are likely to supersede the traditional forms, to which, in common with most of the contributors to this volume, I have devoted many years of research and study. The *nouveau roman*, however, while it is undoubtedly as arbitrary and conventional as the old, provides valuable possibilities of adding to our knowledge and understanding of man. The *nouveau roman* is not, of course, entirely new. It has had many forerunners in France (André Gide, Marcel Proust, Louis Guilloux, André Malraux, Jean-Paul Sartre, and others) and in England (Laurence Sterne, James Joyce, Virginia Woolf, Aldous Huxley, and others). In Rayner Heppenstall's works, as in Michel Butor's and Nathalie Sarraute's, it appears to me the very reverse of a dead end. Immensely lively and intellectually stimulating, it shows us, to quote Heppenstall's significant phrase once more, "a man travelling somewhere for a purpose".

A LIST OF THE
PUBLISHED WRITINGS OF
John Butt

COMPILED BY G. D. CARNALL

Books mentioned were published in London, unless stated otherwise.

The Review of English Studies, edited by John Butt from 1947 to 1954, is normally abbreviated to *RES*.

I. BOOKS AND PAMPHLETS

POPE'S TASTE IN SHAKESPEARE. Shakespeare Association Papers, xx. Oxford University Press, 1936 (pp. 21).

[With H. V. D. Dyson] AUGUSTANS AND ROMANTICS, 1689-1830. Vol. III of *Introductions to English Literature,* ed. B. Dobrée. Cresset Press, 1940 (pp. 318). Revised 1950 (pp. 320) and 1961 (pp. 338).

THE AUGUSTAN AGE. Hutchinson's University Library, 1950 (pp. viii, 152). Reissued 1962, revised 1965 (pp. viii, 156).

POPE'S POETICAL MANUSCRIPTS. Warton Lecture on English Poetry. Oxford University Press, 1954 (pp. 17). In *Proceedings of the British Academy,* XL, 1954 (pp. 23-39). Reprinted in *Essential Articles for the Study of Alexander Pope,* ed. M. Mack. Hamden, Connecticut: Archon Books, 1964 (pp. 507-27).

FIELDING. Writers and their Work, LVII. Longmans, Green and Co., for the British Council and the National Book League, 1956 (pp. 35).

[With K. Tillotson] DICKENS AT WORK. Methuen, 1957 (pp. 238). Reissued 1963.

JAMES BOSWELL. Inaugural Lecture as Professor of Rhetoric and English Literature at the University of Edinburgh. [Edinburgh: at the University Press, 1960] (pp. 18).

[With J. C. Maxwell] JOHN DOVER WILSON: A LIST OF HIS PUBLISHED WRITINGS. Cambridge: at the University Press, 1961 (pp. 32). Anonymous.

BIOGRAPHY IN THE HANDS OF WALTON, JOHNSON, AND BOSWELL. Ewing Lectures, 1962. Los Angeles: privately printed by the University of California, 1966 (pp. 48).

II. WORKS EDITED OR TRANSLATED BY JOHN BUTT

[With G. Tillotson] TWO SERMONS OF THE RESURRECTION, by Lancelot Andrewes. Cambridge: at the University Press, 1932 (pp. vi, 56).

[General Editor of] THE TWICKENHAM EDITION OF THE POEMS OF ALEXANDER POPE. 6 vols. Methuen, 1939-54.

IMITATIONS OF HORACE WITH AN EPISTLE TO DR. ARBUTHNOT AND THE EPILOGUE TO THE SATIRES, by Alexander Pope. Vol. IV of the Twickenham Edition, 1939 (pp. liv, 406). Revised 1953 (pp. liv, 408).

[Translation of] CANDIDE, by Voltaire. Penguin, 1947 (pp. 144).

MINOR POEMS, by Alexander Pope. Vol. VI of the Twickenham Edition, ed. N. Ault, completed by J. B., 1954 (pp. xxii, 492).

AN EPISTLE TO DR. ARBUTHNOT, by Alexander Pope. Methuen's English Classics, 1954 (pp. vi, 56).

LETTERS OF ALEXANDER POPE, selected and with an introduction by J. B. World's Classics, DLXXIV, Oxford University Press, 1960 (pp. xxxviii, 384). Introduction based on "Alexander Pope: a New View of his Character", *Listener* 20 June 1957 (pp. 999, 1003).

THE POEMS OF ALEXANDER POPE. A one-volume edition of the Twickenham text with select annotations. Methuen, 1963 (pp. xxix, 850).

WORDSWORTH: SELECTED POETRY AND PROSE. Oxford University Press, 1964 (pp. 240).

OF BOOKS AND HUMANKIND. ESSAYS AND POEMS PRESENTED TO BONAMY DOBRÉE. Routledge and Kegan Paul, 1964 (pp. x, 232).

[Translation of] ZADIG and L'INGÉNU, by Voltaire. Penguin, 1964 (pp. 192).

THE ART OF MARVELL'S POETRY, by J. B. Leishman. Hutchinson, 1966 (pp. 328).

IMITATIONS OF HORACE, by Alexander Pope. Methuen's English Classics, 1966 (pp. 176).

III. CONTRIBUTIONS TO BOOKS AND PERIODICALS

Notes for a Bibliography of Thomas Tickell. *Bodleian Quarterly Record*, v, 1928 (pp. 299-302).

John Donne and Lincoln's Inn. *Times Literary Supplement*, 10 April 1930 (p. 318).

A Bibliography of Izaak Walton's "Lives". *Oxford Bibliographical Society Proceedings and Papers* ii, pt. 4, 1930 (pp. 329-40).

A First Edition of Tickell's "Colin and Lucy". *Bodleian Quarterly Record*, vi, 1930 (pp. 103-4).

John Donne's "Mr Tilman". *Times Literary Supplement*, 15 Dec. 1932 (p. 963); 29 Dec. (p. 989).

Walton's Copy of Donne's "Letters" (1651). *RES*, viii, 1932 (pp. 72-4).

Izaak Walton's Copy of Pembroke and Ruddier's "Poems". *Bodleian Quarterly Record*, vii, 1932 (p. 140).

"Romantic". *Times Literary Supplement*, 3 Aug. 1933 (p. 525).

Izaak Walton's Methods in Biography. *Essays and Studies*, xix, 1934 (pp. 67-84).

Izaak Walton's Collections for Fulman's "Life of John Hales". *Modern Language Review*, xxix, 1934 (pp. 267-73).

The Facilities for Antiquarian Study in the Seventeenth Century. *Essays and Studies*, xxiv, 1939 (pp. 64-79).

Izaak Walton. In *The Cambridge Bibliography of English Literature*, ed. F. W. Bateson. Cambridge: at the University Press, 1940 (vol. I, pp. 830-1).

Charles Cotton. *Ibid.* (vol. II, pp. 261-2).

"The Way of the World". *Listener*, 1 Jan. 1942 (pp. 22-3).

The Inspiration of Pope's Poetry. In *Essays on the Eighteenth Century Presented to David Nichol Smith*. Oxford: Clarendon Press, 1945 (pp. 65-79).

Science and Man in Eighteenth-Century Poetry. *Durham University Journal*, XXXIX, 1947 (pp. 79-88).

Dickens at Work. *Durham University Journal*, IX, 1948 (pp. 65-77).

"A Master Key to Popery". In *Pope and his Contemporaries. Essays Presented to George Sherburn*, ed. J. L. Clifford and L. A. Landa. Oxford: Clarendon Press, 1949 (pp. 41-57).

Dickens's Plan for the Conclusion of "Great Expectations". *Dickensian*, XLV, 1949 (pp. 78-80). Included in *Dickens at Work*, 1957.

Dickens's Notes for his Serial Parts. *Ibid.* (pp. 129-38). Included in *Dickens at Work*, 1957.

The Composition of "David Copperfield". *Ibid.*, XLVI, 1950 (pp. 90-4, 128-35, 176-80); XLVII, 1951 (pp. 33-8). Included in *Dickens at Work*, 1957.

"David Copperfield": from Manuscript to Print. *RES.*, n.s. 1, 1950 (pp. 247-51). Included in *Dickens at Work*, 1957.

The Stephen Family. A Tradition of Scholarly Journalism. *Listener*, 28 Dec. 1950 (pp. 841-3).

[With K. Tillotson] Dickens at Work on "Dombey and Son". *Essays and Studies*, n.s. IV, 1951 (pp. 70-93).

A Plea for More English Dictionaries. *Durham University Journal*, XLIII, 1951 (pp. 96-102).

English at the University. *Journal of the Institute of Education of Durham University*, March 1951 (pp. 11-12).

English at the Universities, 1901-1951. *Universities Quarterly*, V, 1951, (pp. 218-24).

New Light on Charles Dickens. *Listener*, 28 Feb. 1952 (pp. 341-2).

"A Christmas Carol": its Origin and Design. *Dickensian*, LI, 1954 (pp. 15-8).

Editorial Problems in Eighteenth-Century Poetry. In *Editing Donne and Pope*, by G. R. Potter and J. B. Los Angeles: University of California Press, [1954] (pp. 11-22).

A Prose Fragment Wrongly Attributed to Gay and Pope. *Notes and Queries*, cc, 1956 (pp. 23-5).

Humphry House. *New Statesman*, 5 March 1955 (p. 325).

"Bleak House" in the Context of 1851. *Nineteenth Century Fiction*, x, 1955 (pp. 1-21). Revised and enlarged in *Dickens at Work*, 1957.

"The Review of English Studies". *Essays in Criticism*, vi, 1956 (pp. 475-8).

The Early Eighteenth-Century Poets. In *The Cambridge Bibliography of English Literature* (Supplement), ed. G. Watson. Cambridge: at the University Press, 1957 (pp. 409-14).

Alexander Pope: a New View of his Character. *Listener*, 20 June 1957 (pp. 999, 1003). Reprinted as "Pope Seen through his Letters", in *Eighteenth-Century English Literature: Modern Essays in Criticism*, ed. J. L. Clifford. New York: Oxford University Press, 1959 (pp. 62-7). Forms the basis (much revised) of the introduction to *Letters of Alexander Pope*, Oxford University Press, 1960 (pp. vii-xv).

Pope's Letters: some Notes and Corrections. *Notes and Queries*, ccii, 1957 (pp. 463-6).

The Topicality of "Little Dorrit". *University of Toronto Quarterly*, xxix, 1959 (pp. 1-10).

"Bleak House" Once More. *Critical Quarterly*, i, 1959 (pp. 302-7).

Pope and Johnson in their Handling of the Imitation. *The New Rambler*, ser. B, v, 1959 (pp. 3-14). Reprinted as "Johnson's Practice in the Poetical Imitation", in *New Light on Dr. Johnson: Essays on the Occasion of his 250th Birthday*, ed. F. W. Hilles. New Haven: Yale University Press, 1959 (pp. 19-34).

A University Course in English. *Scottish Secondary Teachers' Association Magazine*, xv, 1960 (pp. 11-15).

Editorial; and, Dickens's Instructions for "Martin Chuzzlewit", Plate XVIII. *Review of English Literature*, ii, 1961 (pp. 7-8, 49-50).

Editing a Nineteenth-Century Novelist. *English Studies Today*, second series, ed. G. Bonnard. Berne: Francke Verlag, 1961 (pp. 187-95).

The G.C.E. as University Entrance Qualification. In *The General Certificate of Education*. Newcastle upon Tyne: King's College, Department of Education, 1961 (pp. 37-42).

Dickens's Manuscripts. *Yale Library Gazette*, xxxvi, 1962 (pp. 149-61).

Introduction to *Clarissa*, by Samuel Richardson. Everyman's Library, 882-5. Dent, 1962 (vol. 1, pp. v-xi).

The Idea of an English School: Comment on the New Universities. *Critical Survey*, i, 1963 (pp. 115-6).

Pope: "The Rape of the Lock"; "An Essay on Man". *Notes on Literature* (British Council), xxi, 1963 (pp. 1-12).

Jane Austen: "Pride and Prejudice". *Ibid.*, xxv, 1963 (pp. 1-4).

Pope: the Man and the Poet. In *Of Books and Humankind. Essays and Poems Presented to Bonamy Dobrée*, ed. J. B. Routledge and Kegan Paul, 1964 (pp. 69-79).

Oldest School of English. *The Times*, 6 May 1964 (supplement p. v).

James Blair Leishman, 1902-1963. *Proceedings of the British Academy*, xlix, 1964 (pp. 459-65).

The Revival of Vernacular Scottish Poetry in the Eighteenth Century. In *From Sensibility to Romanticism: Essays Presented to Frederick A. Pottle*, ed. F. W. Hilles and H. Bloom. New York: Columbia University Press, 1965 (pp. 219-38).

IV. REVIEWS
(excluding some short notices)

A Garland for John Donne, 1631-1931 (ed. T. Spencer). *RES.*, ix, 1933 (pp. 228-9).

Comenius in England (R. F. Young). *RES.*, xii, 1936 (pp. 212-4).

Correspondence of Thomas Gray (ed. P. Toynbee and L. Whibley). *Modern Language Review*, xxxii, 1937 (pp. 101-3).

Seventeenth-Century Studies Presented to Sir Herbert Grierson. *RES.*, xiv, 1938 (pp. 471-3).

The Trial and Flagellation, with Other Studies in the Chester Cycle (ed. F. M. Salter and W. W. Greg). *RES.*, xv, 1939 (pp. 91-2).

Mr. Cibber of Drury Lane (R. H. Barker). *RES.*, xvi, 1940 (pp. 229-30).

The Poems of Thomas Pestell (ed. H. Buchan). *RES.*, xvi, 1940 (pp. 340-2).

John Gay: Favourite of the Wits (W. H. Irving). *RES.*, xvii, 1941 (pp. 226-7).

Hester Lynch Piozzi (J. L. Clifford). *RES.*, xvii, 1941 (pp. 359-61).

The Art of Biography in Eighteenth-Century England (D. A. Stauffer). *Oxford Magazine*, 29 Jan. 1942 (pp. 157-8).

Henry Lawes, Musician and Friend of Poets (W. M. Evans). *Modern Language Review*, xxxviii, 1943 (pp. 51-2).

Thraliana. The Diary of Mrs. Hester Lynch Thrale (later Piozzi) 1776-1809 (ed. K. C. Balderston). *RES.*, xix, 1943 (pp. 93-5).

Words for Music (V. C. Clinton-Baddeley). *RES.*, xix, 1943 (pp. 315-7).

The Dickens World (H. House). *RES.*, xx, 1944 (pp. 88-90).

Horace Walpole: Gardenist (I. W. U. Chase). *RES.*, xxi, 1945 (pp. 69-70).

Literary Study and the Scholarly Profession (H. Craig). *RES*, xxii, 1946 (pp. 150-1).

Two Centuries of Johnsonian Scholarship (R. W. Chapman). *RES.*, xxii, 1946 (pp. 241-2).

Studies in English, 1944.

Alexander Pope. A List of Critical Studies Published from 1895 to 1944 (J. E. Tobin). *RES.*, xxiii, 1947 (pp. 177-9).

Henry Vaughan: A Life and Interpretation (F. E. Hutchinson). *Durham University Journal*, xxxix, 1947 (pp. 121-2). Unsigned.

On the Knowledge which maketh a Wise Man. By Sir Thomas Elyot (ed. E. J. Howard). *RES.*, xxiii, 1947 (pp. 273-5).

James Beattie's London Diary 1773 (ed. R. S. Walker). *RES.*, xxiii, 1947 (p. 280).

Gerard Manley Hopkins (W. A. M. Peters). *Durham University Journal*, l, 1948 (pp. 98-9). Unsigned.

Elizabethan Poetry in the Eighteenth Century (E. R. Wasserman). *English Studies*, xxx, 1949 (pp. 57-8).

The Poet Wordsworth (H. Darbishire). *Durham University Journal,* XLII, 1950 (p. 123). Unsigned.

The Language of Natural Description in Eighteenth-Century Poetry (J. Arthos). *RES.,* n.s. II, 1951 (pp. 87-9).

The Age of Johnson. Essays Presented to Chauncey Brewster Tinker. (ed. F. W. Hilles) *RES.,* n.s. II, 1951 (pp. 186-7).

English Studies Today (ed. C. L. Wrenn and G. Bullough). *Durham University Journal,* XLIV, 1952 (pp. 107-8). Unsigned.

Charles Dickens: his Tragedy and Triumph (E. Johnson). *Nineteenth Century Fiction,* VIII, 1953 (pp. 151-3).

Samuel Johnson's Literary Criticism (J. H. Hagstrum). *Durham University Journal,* XLV, 1953 (pp. 121-2). Unsigned.

Boswell's "Life of Johnson", etc. (ed. G. B. Hill and L. F. Powell). *RES.,* n.s. IV, 1953 (pp. 390-1).

Letters of William Wordsworth (ed. P. Wayne). *Durham University Journal,* XLVII, 1954 (pp. 39-40).

Novels of the Eighteen-Forties (K. Tillotson). *Durham University Journal,* XLVII, 1954 (pp. 40-2).

The Letters of Sydney Smith (ed. N. C. Smith). *RES.,* n.s. V, 1954 (pp. 314-7).

The Augustan World (A. R. Humphreys). *Adelphi,* XXXI, 1955 (pp. 273-9).

De Descriptione Temporum (C. S. Lewis). *RES.,* n.s. VII, 1956 (pp. 217-8).

Samuel Johnson's Parliamentary Reporting (B. B. Hoover). *RES.,* n.s. VII, 1956 (pp. 433-5).

William Hogarth: "The Analysis of Beauty" (ed. J. Burke). *RES.,* n.s. VIII, 1957 (pp. 319-20).

William Collins: Drafts and Fragments of Verse (ed. J. S. Cunningham). *RES.,* n.s. IX, 1958 (pp. 220-2).

Hans Andersen and Charles Dickens: a Friendship and its Dissolution (E. Bredsdorff). *RES.,* n.s. IX, 1958 (pp. 331-2).

A Note-Book of Edmund Burke (ed. H. V. F. Somerset).
The Moral Basis of Burke's Political Thought (C. Parkin). *RES.,* n.s. IX, 1958 (pp. 439-41).

Politics and the Poet (F. M. Todd). *Durham University Journal,* L, 1958 (pp. 95-6).

Pope and Human Nature (G. Tillotson), *Listener*, 9 Oct. 1958 (p. 573). Unsigned.

Jonathan Swift and the Age of Compromise (K. Williams). *Listener*, 18 June 1959 (p. 1077).

Georgina Hogarth and the Dickens Circle (A. A. Adrian). *RES.*, n.s. x, 1959 (pp. 207-9).

[With P. Ure] The Making of Walton's "Lives" (D. Novarr). *Modern Language Review*, LIV, 1959 (pp. 588-91).

William Cowper of the Inner Temple, Esq. (C. Ryskamp). *Durham University Journal*, LIII, 1960 (pp. 29-30).

A Philosophical Enquiry into the Origin of our Ideas of the Sublime and Beautiful. By Edmund Burke (ed. J. T. Boulton). *Durham University Journal*, LIII, 1960 (pp. 46-7).

Speeches of Charles Dickens (ed. K. J. Fielding). *Sunday Times*, 28 Feb. 1960.

Dickens on Education (J. Manning). *Dickensian*, LVI, 1960 (pp. 98-9).

The Poems of John Dryden (ed. J. Kinsley). *RES.*, n.s. XI, 1960 (pp. 213-5).

The Maturity of Dickens (M. Engel). *RES.*, n.s. XI, 1960 (pp. 440-3).

Burns: a Study of the Poems and Songs (T. Crawford). *Scottish Historical Review*, XL, 1961 (pp. 159-61).

Augustan Studies (G. Tillotson). *Listener*, 7 Dec. 1961 (p. 998).

The Correspondence of Thomas Percy and George Paton (ed. A. F. Falconer). *RES.*, n.s. XIII, 1962 (pp. 418-9).

A Victorian Publisher: a Study of the Bentley Papers (R. A. Gettmann). *Notes and Queries*, CCVII, 1962 (pp. 116-7).

Dryden and Pope in the Early Nineteenth Century (U. Amarasinghe). *Durham University Journal*, LV, 1963 (pp. 154-5).

The Wisdom of the Scots (M. McLaren). *Scottish Historical Review*, XLII, 1963 (pp. 161-2).

The Flint and the Flame: the Artistry of Charles Dickens (E. Davis). *Nineteenth Century Fiction*, XIX, 1964 (pp. 88-91).

W. E. Aytoun: Pioneer Professor of English at Edinburgh (E. Frykman). *Scottish Historical Review*, XLIV, 1965 (pp. 82-3).

Dickens: from Pickwick to Dombey (S. Marcus). *Dickensian*, LXI, 1965 (pp. 161-2).

The Letters of Charles Dickens, Vol. I (ed. M. House and G. Storey). *RES.*, n.s. XVII, 1966 (pp. 99-103).

Pope's "Epistle to Bathurst". A Critical Reading (E. R. Wasserman).

Pope's "Essay on Criticism" 1709. A Study of the Bodleian Manuscript (R. M. Schmitz). *English Studies*, XLVII, 1966 (pp. 235-6).